Imagining a Place for Buddhism

Imagining a Place for Buddhism

Literary Culture and Religious Community in Tamil-Speaking South India

ANNE E. MONIUS

OXFORD
UNIVERSITY PRESS

2001

OXFORD
UNIVERSITY PRESS

Oxford New York
Athens Auckland Bangkok Bogotá Buenos Aires Cape Town
Chennai Dar es Salaam Delhi Florence Hong Kong Istanbul Karachi
Kolkata Kuala Lumpur Madrid Melbourne Mexico City Mumbai Nairobi
Paris São Paulo Shanghai Singapore Taipei Tokyo Toronto Warsaw

and associated companies in
Berlin Ibadan

Published by Oxford University Press, Inc.
198 Madison Avenue, New York, New York 10016

Library of Congress Cataloging-in-Publication Data
Monius, Anne Elizabeth, 1964–
Imagining a place for Buddhism: literary culture and religious community in Tamil-speaking South India / Anne E. Monius.
p. cm.
Includes bibliographical references and index.
ISBN 0-19-513999-2
1. Buddhism–India–Tamil Nadu–History. 2. Tamil (Indic people)–India–Religion.
3. Cāttaṉār. Maṇimēkalai. 4. Puttamittiraṉār, 11th cent. Vīracōḻiyam.
5. Buddhism in literature. I. Title.
BQ349.T36 M66 2001
294.3'0954'82–dc21 00-051654

1 3 5 7 9 8 6 4 2

Printed in the United States of America
on acid-free paper

Acknowledgments

I welcome the opportunity to acknowledge the many contributions that others have made to this project. Although any errors of interpretation or translation in the pages to follow are mine and mine alone, many mentors, colleagues, and friends have helped to shape this work. Long ago, as I struggled with the decision of whether to major in history or astrophysics, Diana Eck's introductory course on Indian civilization opened up a new and endlessly fascinating world to me; since then, she has been the most enthusiastic and encouraging of supporters. Charlie Hallisey carefully read every draft of the dissertation that began this book, and without his insight and challenging comments, the final product, however inadequate, would have been of immeasurably poorer quality. John Carman also served on my dissertation committee, providing much encouragement and many useful suggestions.

To George and Kausalya Hart, I owe a special debt of gratitude for introducing me to the beauty of Tamil literature during that summer of record-breaking heat nearly twelve years ago. George's insights into the relationship of Tamil and Sanskrit, discussed with unfailing enthusiasm while we struggled to read simple sentences, have hopefully come to some fruition in the following pages. George and Kausalya also welcomed me graciously for a semester of study at Berkeley, where I began my first foray into Tamil Buddhist literature with Kausalya.

A Fulbright Doctoral Dissertation Research Abroad grant, an American Institute of Indian Studies fellowship, and a Harvard University Sheldon Traveling Fellowship generously provided me with two years of study in India and a brief trip to Sri Lanka to experience a living Buddhist culture. In India, R. Vijayalakshmy of the International Institute of Tamil Studies in Taramani (Chennai) painstakingly read through the text of the *Maṇimēkalai* with me, poring over every word and leading me through the subtle beauties and complexity of the text. The staffs at the International Institute of Tamil Studies library, the Adyar Library of the Theosophical Society, the Maraimalai Adigal Library, the Dr. U. V. Swaminathaiyer Library, and the Government Oriental Manuscripts Library (all of Chennai) were unfailingly patient and kind in helping me locate relevant research materials. Iravatham Mahadevan, during the course of several friendly encounters in both Chennai and Tañcāvūr, set me straight about the nature of the early Tamil-Brāhmī inscriptions and helped me sort through the Jain and the Buddhist in early Tamil history. Many of the central ideas in the first three chapters were formulated during friendly debates over many cups of coffee or while wandering around the Madras Book Fair with Dennis Hudson during his several visits to Chennai in 1994 and 1995.

Thanks are also due to Peter Schalk of the University of Uppsala for ongoing email discussions about evidence for the presence of Buddhism in the Tamil region and for organizing a conference on the *Maṇimēkalai* in May 1995. The conference provided me with an opportunity to present a paper, and discussions with a number of participants there, especially David Shulman, Paula Richman, Alexander Dubianski, and Dennis Hudson, have found their way into the following pages.

Phyllis Granoff and Koichi Shinohara kindly invited me to present my work as part of the Numata lecture series at McMaster University; Koichi also generously allowed me to cite his important article on Chinese narratives of the Buddha's begging bowl, forthcoming from the University of Toronto Press, in chapter 3. Gary Tubb and Mary McGee provided me with an opportunity to discuss my analysis of the *Maṇimēkalai*'s ethical orientation through an invitation to speak at Columbia University's Dharam Hinduja Indic Studies Center. Many colleagues and fellow panel participants at the annual meetings of the American Academy of Religion provided guidance and insightful comments, especially John Cort, Steven Hopkins, Ginni Ishimatsu, Padma Kaimal, Leslie Orr, and James Ryan.

I thank my colleagues in the Department of Religious Studies and the Center for South Asian Studies at the University of Virginia for welcoming me so warmly and for creating an atmosphere of intellectual engagement that nurtures productive research and writing. The participants in the Religious Studies department's junior faculty colloquium in particular—Cindy Hoehler-Fatton, Judith Kovacs, Chuck Mathewes, Esther Menn, and Vanessa Ochs—have been a continual source of friendship and support as we all struggle to balance the demands of professional academic life.

The staffs of two academic libraries—Widener at Harvard and Alderman at Virginia—deserve thanks for rapidly securing the old and obscure, whether through interlibrary loan or from behind some locked door in the basement.

I also wish to thank the anonymous scholarly reviewers for Oxford University Press for their contributions, as well as Cynthia Read for first expressing interest in this work. Stephen Teiser's comments have also proven immensely useful.

Special thanks are due to my family and friends for patiently offering encouragement, advice, much-needed distraction, and all manner of assistance, especially Felix, Eleanor, and Peter Monius; Melissa Robbins; Janet Ikeda; Rebecca Manring; and Rachel McDermott.

Last, but certainly not least, I owe the greatest debt to my husband, Wilson Manoharan. The *Maṇimēkalai* and the *Vīracōḻiyam* quite unexpectedly introduced us to each other, and through him I am now welcomed as family in southern India. We often joke that we should erect a domestic altar to the Buddha and Senator Fulbright, those two men who unwittingly brought us together. In all seriousness, though, it is only through Wilson's endless patience and support that this work has taken shape at all.

The following publishers have granted permission to reprint portions of previously published articles, and I thank them for their generosity. Parts of chapter 1 have appeared as "*Ētunikaḻcci* in the *Maṇimēkalai*: The Manifestation of Beneficial Root 'Causes' and Renunciation" (coauthored with R. Vijayalakshmy, in *A Buddhist Woman's Path to Enlightenment: Proceedings of a Workshop on the Tamiḻ Narrative* Maṇimēkalai, *Uppsala University, May 25–29, 1995*, edited by Peter Schalk, 261–275, Acta Universitatis Upsaliensis: Historica Religionum, vol. 13, 1997), reprinted with permission from Uppsala University, and "Literary Theory and Moral Vision in Tamil Buddhist Literature" (*Journal of Indian Philosophy* 28/2 [2000]):195–223), reprinted with permission from Kluwer Academic Publishers. Portions of chapter 4 have previously appeared as "The Many Lives of Daṇḍin: The *Kāvyādarśa* in Sanskrit and Tamil" (*International Journal of Hindu Studies* 4/2 [2000]:1–37), reprinted with permission from World Heritage Press.

Contents

Note on Transliteration and Translation

Tamil terms are transliterated according to the system employed by the *Tamil Lexicon* published by the University of Madras (1982). Sanskrit and Pāli terms follow the conventional system of transliteration. In cases where the Sanskrit term is more commonly known than either the Tamil or the Pāli, I have used the Sanskrit word (Śiva rather than the Tamil Civa<u>n</u>, *karma* rather than the Pāli *kamma* or Tamil *karumam/karmam*, *dharma* rather than the Pāli *dhamma* or Tamil *tarumam/tarmam*).

In order not to overburden the text with italics, I have chosen only to italicize Tamil, Sanskrit, and Pāli words the first time they appear.

All translations are mine unless otherwise indicated.

Imagining a Place for Buddhism

Introduction

Buddhism in South India?

The soaring towers of the great temples dedicated to the Hindu gods Siva and Viṣṇu today dominate the religious landscape in the Tamil-speaking corner of southeastern India. Impressive shrines built by a succession of powerful medieval dynasties cover the region, from Kāñcīpuram in the north to Śrīraṅkam, Citamparam, Tañcāvūr, and Maturai. The temples of Śiva's son, Murukaṉ, mark the boundaries of the Tamil country; in 1971, the most prominent Tamil political party (the Tirāviṭa Muṉṉēṟṟak Kaḻakam, or DMK) declared Murukaṉ to be its official patron deity.[1] Tamil-speaking Hindus today enjoy the reputation throughout India of being the most traditional and the most orthodox, with their practices and institutions representing a seemingly unbroken chain of religious development that stretches back nearly two millennia. Although minority populations of Muslims, Christians, and Jains do exist, the overwhelming majority of the Tamil-speaking population in modern India practices some form of devotion to Śiva, Viṣṇu, or the goddess.

Yet the literary and historical record of religions in this region of southernmost India tells a far more complex story. Although the monarchs of the medieval Pallava, Pāṇṭiya, and Cōḻa dynasties constructed large edifices in honor of the Hindu pantheon, they patronized other sectarian communities as well, including Jains, Ājīvikas,[2] and Buddhists. Indeed, non-Hindu communities played such an important role in South Indian literary and religious culture and in the administration of the state between the fourth and seventh centuries that later Śaiva tradition labeled this period the *Kalabhra Interregnum*, the interruption of the "wicked ones" (*kaḻappaḷār*).[3] The earliest written records in Tamil, the Brāhmī inscriptions, are Jain.[4] Between the composition of the classical, or "Caṅkam," literature (roughly, the second through fourth centuries)[5] and the emergence of the Hindu devotional (*bhakti*) poet-saints in the seventh through ninth centuries, the majority of the poetic works produced in Tamil were written by either Buddhists or Jains.

Despite the presence of Buddhists, Jains, and Ājīvikas in the Tamil inscriptional, archaeological, and literary record, the significance of non-Hindu contributions to the history of religions in Tamil-speaking South India has only recently become the topic of serious academic study. In what Richard Davis calls the "standard historical narrative concerning South Indian Jainism and Śaivism," for example, scholarship has long tended to pit Hindu against non-Hindu, telling "a story of heterodox challenge and Hindu revival and triumph."[6] In this historical narrative, which has dominated the study of religion in South India for more than a century, Buddhists and Jains appear only intermittently as the "other," as foreigners to be spurned, ridiculed, and ultimately dismissed as "anti-Tamil," unable to corrupt or suppress with their emphasis on ascetic practice the natural joie de vivre of the Tamils.[7]

Several recent and important studies have begun to reverse this scholarly trend, however, particularly in regard to the long presence of Tamil-speaking Jains in South India. Leslie C. Orr's work, for example, examines the lives of both Hindu and Jain "religious women" in the inscriptional record of the eighth through thirteenth centuries, noting that Jain women were both significant temple donors and religious teachers.[8] James Ryan's study of the ninth-century poetic narrative, the *Cīvakacintāmaṇi*, demonstrates the power of literary parody in this sophisticated work by a Jain monk that overturns the classical conventions of literary love to prove "the poisonousness of lust in epic fashion."[9] Paula Richman's study of the sixth-century Buddhist narrative, the *Maṇimēkalai*, loosely follows a similar approach, demonstrating the ways in which the author inverts classical literary ideals with great rhetorical finesse to inculcate Buddhist values in his audience.[10] Examining the anti-Jain invective in the earliest devotional poetry to Śiva, Indira Peterson asserts that "we cannot assume that the Jains suddenly stopped participating in Tamil culture even as the Śaiva *bhakti* cult *began* to assert itself. It is much more likely that the Nāyaṉārs [the Śaiva saints, literally "leaders"] found it advantageous to exclude their most powerful rivals from their reformulation of Tamil culture."[11] In a thought-provoking essay that ponders the origins of the seeming similarities between Jain thought and the medieval Śaiva philosophy in Tamil known as Śaiva Siddhānta, Richard Davis suggests a model of "productive encounter" among sectarian communities, a flow of ideas back and forth despite the Śaiva rhetoric of challenge and defeat.[12] Indeed, each of the essays in the edited volume, suggestively titled *Open Boundaries: Jain Communities and Cultures in Indian History*, in which the Orr, Ryan, Peterson, and Davis articles cited previously appear, fruitfully attempts to understand the Jain tradition, from models of kingship to Jain contributions to Sanskrit literary theory, in the broader context of South Asian history and religiosity, taking into account the "challenging, borrowing, contradicting, polemicizing, appropriating, and modifying that goes on across religious boundaries."[13]

Among the many religious communities that once wielded influence in various realms of cultural life in the Tamil-speaking South, relatively little study has been made of the Buddhists. With the Buddhist strongholds of Amarāvatī and Nāgārjunakoṇḍa immediately to the north and the great monastic establishments of Sri Lanka to the east, it is certainly not surprising to find traces of a Buddhist presence in the kingdoms of the Pallavas, the Pāṇṭiyas, and the Cōḻas in the fourth through twelfth centuries. Yet while the scattered artifacts of Buddhism in the region have been examined individually over the past century or so, the significance of any one is often far from clear; the character of the Tamil-speaking Buddhist community or communities has remained largely obscure. Who were the Tamil-speaking Buddhists of southern India? What did being "Buddhist" mean in the complex religious world of the medieval South, a diverse landscape of competing sectarian communities in which Buddhists were perhaps always a minority? What can the disparate remnants of Buddhism in this region reveal to the historian of religions?

A Fragmentary Record

The sources for the study of Buddhism in the Tamil-speaking region of southern India are, at best, fragmentary, a disparate lot of bits and pieces. Even the most basic of questions—when did Buddhism first become established in the Tamil region—has been the source of much debate. In a series of recent articles, for example, Peter Schalk argues that there is no evidence for "institutionalized" or monastic Buddhism in southernmost India before the fourth century CE.[14] The earliest such evidence consists largely of the archaeological remains of a series of monastic buildings at Kāvirippūmpaṭṭiṉam (Pukār or Poompuhar) on the east coast of the modern state of Tamilnadu; the oldest archaeological layers of the site, as well as the iconographic representation of the footprints of the Buddha (*buddhapāda*), as described by Schalk, have been dated to the fourth century CE.[15] In addition to this early monastic site at Kāvirippūmpaṭṭiṉam, a variety of Buddhist artifacts have been recovered from Kāñcīpuram farther to the north.[16] One of the most striking is a life-size statue of the Buddha discovered at the turn of the last century in the heart of the Kāñcīpuram temple dedicated to the goddess Kāmākṣīyammaṉ and dated to between the fourth and sixth centuries.[17] More recently, a Tamil fisherman plying his trade three kilometers to the south of Kāvirippūmpaṭṭiṉam discovered a Buddha image fifty-three centimeters high standing in the ocean waters that has been tentatively dated to the third or fourth century.[18] Yet what can one make of such isolated artifacts? Although the image of the Buddha's feet found in the midst of monastic ruins bespeaks use as a ritual or meditational object, does the discovery of an isolated Buddha image in the midst of a Hindu goddess temple imply that the temple was once Buddhist, or that Buddhists and Hindus once worshipped at the same spot? It is simply impossible to tell.

Evidence of a different sort for an early monastic Buddhist presence in the Tamil region—evidence that is similarly incomplete and difficult to interpret—can be found in the oldest commentarial literature of the Theravāda tradition composed in Pāli. The three celebrated Pāli commentators—Buddhaghosa, Buddhadatta, and Dhammapāla, all belonging to the late fourth or early fifth centuries—have some explicit connection with monastic institutions in the Tamil-speaking region. Buddhadatta, for example, more than once states that he composed his commentarial treatises while residing at Kāvīrapaṭṭana,[19] the same Kāvirippūmpaṭṭiṉam where the oldest monastic artifacts have been unearthed in the Tamil region. At the end of each of his commentaries, collectively known as the *Paramatthadīpanī*, Dhammapāla writes that he composed the work at a monastery known as Badaratitthavihāra[20] located, according to K. R. Norman, "in South India."[21] In his commentary on the *Nettippakaraṇa*, Dhammapāla writes that he composed the work at a monastery known as the Dhammāsoka-mahārāja-vihāra, located, according to Gunawardana, in "Nāgapaṭṭana"[22] (Tamil Nākapaṭṭiṉam, another port city located roughly twenty miles south of Kāvirippūmpaṭṭiṉam). A number of Buddhaghosa's works, including the *Manorathapūraṇī*, are said to have been written at the request of Buddhist monks living in Kāñcīpuram.[23] Yet what can one make of such references? Clearly, there must have existed flourishing Buddhist monasteries looking toward Sri Lanka and the Mahāvihāra for authoritative guidance, yet were these monks and monasteries all Tamil-speaking? Were commentaries in Tamil produced there alongside the Pāli? Was there anything unique about the teachings or practices at Nākapaṭṭiṉam or Kāvirippūmpaṭṭiṉam? Did such monastic establishments enjoy royal patronage? Does the existence of such monasteries in the era of the three great Pāli commentators imply a Buddhist monastic presence in the Tamil region earlier than the fourth century? The historical record is maddeningly incomplete.

Following this earliest set of evidence for the presence of some form of Buddhism in the Tamil-speaking region in the fourth and fifth centuries, the record grows slightly larger, but its individual elements are no less disparate. Theravāda monks writing in Pāli, particularly Buddhappiya and Kassapa, continue to mention South Indian monastic institutions through at least the twelfth century.[24] In addition to these brief references, the seventh-century Chinese Buddhist pilgrim to India, Xuanzang (Hsuan-tsang), describes a pilgrimage "tour"—real or imagined—through southern India.[25] There, he often finds Buddhism waging a losing battle against the Jain "heretics" (*nirgrantha*) and Hindu "god" (*deva*) worshippers, but in Kāñcīpuram, he claims to have seen "some hundred of *saṅghārāmas* [monasteries] and 10,000 [Buddhist] priests."[26] The art-historical record, relative to the paucity of early evidence, seems to expand exponentially during the medieval period of political dominance by the Cōḻa dynasty (roughly, the ninth through thirteenth centuries). A wide variety of Buddhist images in stone and bronze have been recovered from across the Tamil region, from Kāñcīpuram to Tañcāvūr; such finds are continually being made, as witnessed by the recent announcement of a hitherto unknown twelfth-century pillar inscribed in Tamil with "sacred symbols relating to Buddhism . . . found on all the four sides of the rectangular pillar."[27] The true treasure-trove of later Buddhism in the Tamil region, however, is Nākapaṭṭiṉam, mentioned previously as the site where Dhammapāla is said to have composed his commentaries: more than three hundred Buddhist bronzes have been recovered through archaeological excavation.[28] Numerous sources from outside India itself attest to a long-flourishing Buddhist community in Nākapaṭṭiṉam.[29]

Yet again, the question must be asked: how is one to interpret the isolated Buddha image recovered from a paddy field or within the confines of a Hindu temple or even the relatively large collection of images found at Nākapaṭṭiṉam? Does a single Buddha image indicate that a temple was once Buddhist and has only gradually over time become Hindu? Or had Buddhist images simply been incorporated into more Hindu-oriented worship, as the late Pallava (eighth-century) inscription from Māmallapuram (Mahābalipuram) that lists the Buddha as the ninth incarnation (*avatāra*) of the Hindu god Viṣṇu seemingly attests?[30] Indeed, was the complex at Nākapaṭṭiṉam, although on Tamil soil, a Tamil-speaking community, given the large number of references to the location in sources other than Tamil? Does the production of Buddhist images for the laity in any way indicate a lay Buddhist presence in the Tamil-speaking region, or again, were Buddha images simply worshipped as part of a larger pantheon that included Hindu deities as well? As with the older body of evidence, it is extremely difficult to know how to "read" this material, how to place a Buddhist image—or even a Buddhist monastic complex such as the one at Nākapaṭṭiṉam—in proper historical context. The archaeological and art-historical records are fragmentary, raising perhaps more questions than the evidence itself will ever be able to answer.

Yet in addition to this fragmentary and ultimately inconclusive material and textual record, a record that certainly suggests the presence of Buddhism as one among many religions in medieval South India, there also exist remnants of a Buddhist literary culture composed in Tamil, two fully extant texts that provide a far richer means of historical contextualization. It is to these texts—the sixth-century poetic narrative, *Maṇimēkalai*, and the eleventh-century treatise on grammar and poetics, the *Vīracōḻiyam*, along with its commentary—that the discussion now turns, for the *Maṇimēkalai* and the *Vīracōḻiyam* stand at the center of this exploration of the nature of Buddhism in the Tamil-speaking region of southern India.

The Literary Remnants

The earlier of the extant Buddhist texts composed in Tamil, the *Maṇimēkalai*, roughly datable to the sixth century C.E., is a beautiful, lengthy, and sophisticated poetic narrative of a young girl, Maṇimēkalai, who is born the daughter of a courtesan yet gradually draws away from that life to become, in the final lines of the text, a renunciant in search of liberation. En route to that final vow, the would-be courtesan struggles with her sexual attraction to a prince of the city, makes virtuous use of a wondrous begging bowl that never empties if used to feed the poor, and gradually gains knowledge of the Buddha's teachings. Intricately interwoven through this primary story are numerous subplots: the story of that miraculous begging bowl, the past lives of all the principal characters, the story of a king now ruling over a Southeast Asian island kingdom, the conversion to Buddhism of a wild band of barbarians, and the tale of a virtuous woman wronged by a lust-driven royal prince. The complex and elegantly told narrative sequences are followed by two dense philosophical chapters, both placed in the mouth of the heroine's Buddhist teacher: the first dealing with inferential logic and the second with the Buddhist doctrine of causation.

The sole other remaining Buddhist text composed in Tamil is the eleventh-century *Vīracōḻiyam*, along with a commentary traditionally believed to have been composed by the author's student or disciple. The *Vīracōḻiyam* presents a formidable counterpart to the earlier *Maṇimēkalai*; neither narrative nor poetry, the text is a theoretical work that seeks to relate the grammatical and literary analysis of Tamil to that of the pan-Indian language of erudition, Sanskrit. As such, it presents a densely packed discussion of both grammatical and poetic theory and assumes knowledge of both topics in two classical languages. Yet this project of standardizing the relationship between a transregional language (Sanskrit) and a local literary language (Tamil) is explicitly claimed for Buddhism by the text, and the text, together with its commentary, provides a glimpse of what must have once been a considerable Buddhist literary corpus composed in Tamil and is now lost. In illustration of the text's theoretical points, the commentary cites hundreds of poetic stanzas that praise the Buddha, his compassionate deeds in former lives, and his teachings that lead to enlightenment.

Just as the *Vīracōḻiyam* commentary attests to how little of Buddhist literary production in Tamil has been preserved, numerous references in non-Buddhist works also hint at a substantial body of work no longer extant. References exist, for example, to a text known as the *Pimpicārakatai*,[31] "The Story of Pimpicāra," suggesting a Tamil retelling of the story of the famed king of Magadha and patron of the Buddha, Bimbisāra. Another long narrative cited numerous times in the Tamil literary record is the *Kuṇṭalakēci*,[32] again suggestive of a Tamil rendering of a well-known Pāli narrative, the story of Bhaddā Kuṇḍalakesā found in the commentaries on the *Dhammapada* and *Therīgāthā*.[33] The *Cittāntattokai*, "Collection of Doctrines," was apparently a philosophical text of some sort,[34] whereas the *Tiruppatikam*, based on the single verse preserved in a medieval Śaiva commentary, seems to have been a hymn of praise to the Buddha.[35] A medieval Sinhala text refers to a Tamil glossary of the Buddha's birth stories, or Jātakas.[36]

These glimpses of a considerable corpus of Tamil Buddhist poetry and narrative, alongside both the extant *Maṇimēkalai* and *Vīracōḻiyam* and the relative dearth of evidence for long-standing Buddhist institutions in the Tamil region, suggest that literature and literary culture were an important arena for the local Buddhist articulation of religious ideals and values. Yet despite the fact that the extant texts provide the richest basis for considering the nature of Buddhism in South India as expressed in the local language, relatively little study has been made of either. Richman's excellent discussion of the *Maṇimēkalai*, cited previously, is an exception; although she persuasively grounds the text in classical Tamil literary culture, demonstrating the many ways in which its author creatively reworks classical Tamil literary themes to Buddhist ends, little is offered by way of contextualizing the narrative as explicitly and maturely Buddhist, as participating in wider currents in the Buddhist world of the early medieval period in several languages. What scant scholarly attention has been paid to the *Vīracōḻiyam* or its commentary has placed little emphasis on the specifically Buddhist qualities of the work, focusing instead on its linguistic and theoretical merits. In the multireligious world of Tamil-speaking South India, in a region bounded by strong monastic communities to the north and to the east, and in a literary culture in which not only Tamil but also Sanskrit and Pāli served as literary language options, one might reasonably expect each of these Buddhist texts to participate in wider patterns of Buddhist and South Asian literary practice, to reveal something of Tamil-speaking Buddhism not only in relation to Tamil religious culture and classical literary themes but also in relation to other parts of the Buddhist world. Yet how is one to use an imaginative story and a theoretical treatise on grammar and poetics, their composition separated by as many as five centuries, to do history, and history of religions in particular?

Literary Culture and Religious Community

This study examines in detail each of the literary remnants of Buddhism in the Tamil-speaking region—the *Maṇimēkalai* and the *Vīracōḻiyam* along with its commentary—to see what sort of light each might shed on this relatively unillumined aspect of Buddhist and South Indian religious history. Simple questions, such as what is the main purpose or intent of each text, have never been answered fully[37] and have rarely even been posed for the *Vīracōḻiyam*. Given the disparate nature of the historical record for Buddhism in the Tamil region cited previously, each of these texts in fact provides, in very different ways, the most compelling evidence for the existence of communities of Tamil-speaking Buddhists in the region. In contrast to Steven Collins' ambitious study of the "Pāli imaginaire"—the consistent, stable mental universe of premodern Theravāda literature—in conjunction with documentable sociohistorical processes,[38] virtually no extratextual evidence exists to support such an analysis of literary versus real-world events in the Tamil case. The texts themselves are all that remain to tell us of their intended audience, of the Tamil-speaking Buddhist milieu into which they were born.

As is discussed in detail in the following pages, literary culture provided a sophisticated arena for the articulation, defense, and contestation of religious identities, ideals, and values in medieval South India in the eras of both the *Maṇimēkalai* and the *Vīracōḻiyam*. Both texts, when examined in the light of the cultural work that each performs, reveal two distinct moments in the way Tamil-speaking Buddhist communities represented and imagined themselves in a complex religious and linguistic landscape. This cultural work must be understood not only in relation to cultural and literary standards expressed in the Tamil language but also in the wider context of multiple literary language options and contested sectarian space that characterized South Indian literary culture throughout the premodern period. As works of erudite and sophisticated literature—the *Maṇimēkalai* an ornate poetic narrative and the *Vīracōḻiyam* a theoretical discourse about the nature of literary language—both concern themselves with envisioning a place for Buddhism in the context of a competitive sectarian milieu. As literature, both speak eloquently to the nature of Buddhist identity, to the imagining of Buddhist communities, in ways both coherent and complex.

What is meant by *literature* and *literary culture* requires, of course, some clarification. As José Cabezón and Roger Jackson remark in their introduction to a collection of essays on Tibetan literature, "'literature' is a theoretical construct of Euro-American intellectual culture, and as such it cannot be applied uncritically to other times and places."[39] In the case of Indological studies over the past two centuries, Vinay Dharwadker notes the ways in which the term *literature* has either been applied so broadly as to include nearly everything textual[40] or has otherwise been narrowly defined, exclusively in terms of ornate Sanskrit court poetry in the manner of the great fifth-century poet, Kālidāsa.[41] For the purposes of this study, *literary culture* is broadly defined as the production and use of literature as sophisticated and elite belles lettres, such as the *Maṇimēkalai*, including not only poetic composition itself but also theoretical discourse about the nature of poetry and language more generally, as exemplified by the *Vīracōḻiyam* and found in the South Asian context in a wide variety of languages. As suggested previously, this variety of languages must be taken seriously, for in Tamil-speaking literary culture, Tamil has always represented only one of several literary language options. As the following chapters demonstrate, the project of interpreting both the *Maṇimēkalai* and the *Vīracōḻiyam* as Tamil Buddhist works immediately requires consideration of texts not composed in Tamil, of various narratives, grammars, and theoretical works in several linguistic media, including and especially Pāli and Sanskrit. *Literary culture* is thus a term encompassing the cultivation and use of belles lettres in a variety of competing literary languages.

The understanding of community in relation to literary culture assumed here is largely informed by recent work on both textual or reading communities and the "imagined community" of the state or nation. Brian Stock, for example, in his study of the rise of literate text-based cultures in eleventh-century Europe, develops the notion of "textual communities" to describe groups of people whose lives are centered around texts and more specifically around a literate interpreter of such texts.[42] In this sense, "communities" of Tamil-speaking Buddhists might be defined as those groups of readers and listeners for whom the *Maṇimēkalai* or the *Vīracōḻiyam* (along with other texts now lost) constituted a meaningful and coherent set of ideas, images, and values. In the absence of any hard epigraphical or archaeological evidence for such a reading community, the nature of the *Maṇimēkalai*'s and the *Vīracōḻiyam*'s audiences must necessarily be inferred from the assumptions and expectations embedded in the texts themselves. Benedict Anderson's now perhaps overused notion of imagined community, the community, such as the modern nation-state, that never gathers physically around a single text or interpreter but that nonetheless envisions itself as a coherent unit bound by language, common conviction, or national identity,[43] suggests yet another level at which literature may constitute community: through creating an imaginary world—an imaginary landscape of particular characters, concepts, and values—that allows the reader or listener to envision himself as part of a larger, if not directly seen or encountered, collective. A "mutually constitutive relationship [exists between] literature and community," notes Sheldon Pollock in his study of the rise of vernacular literary cultures in India, for "sociotextual communities . . . define themselves in significant if variable ways on the basis of the literature they share, and they create new literatures in service of new self-definitions."[44] Literary culture and community are tightly bound together, in other words, at the levels of both textual reception and human imagination.

In the case of the Buddhist literature examined here, it is argued that the communities envisioned are of a particularly religious nature, defined by commitments to the Buddha, his teachings, and the moral sensibilities that such teachings demand. The examination of each text begins with a close reading meant to engage the work with eyes historically focused on the literary culture that produced it. In the absence of clear-cut evidence for the community of Buddhists anticipated by each text, literary theory—classical South Asian with a dose of modern western—is employed in the attempt to build historical context from the texts themselves, to infer from the structure and content of each something of the communities envisioned and enacted by the *Maṇimēkalai*, the *Vīracōḻiyam*, and the *Vīracōḻiyam* commentary.

Chapters 1 through 3 address the earlier of the extant Tamil Buddhist texts, the *Maṇimēkalai*. Chapter 1 builds on the work of Richman, reading the text as a consummately literary whole that resonates not only with the earlier themes of the classical Caṅkam corpus, as Richman discusses so eloquently, but also with Sanskrit-influenced poetic theory and a variety of themes found in other Buddhist literatures. Pinpointing as a central motif in the main narrative the arising of those conditions conducive to Maṇimēkalai's enlightenment (signaled by the technical term *ētunikaḻcci*), the narrative and doctrinal portions of the text are shown to be intimately connected through concern with the interdependently arising nature of the world and human relationships. Focusing on the overall structure of the narrative, as well as its thematic content, chapter 1 suggests that the labyrinthine character of the text, filled with subplots and stories within stories, is meant to evoke subtly the particularly Buddhist theory of causation, which is given formal structure only at the very end of the text. Careful attention is also paid to the *Maṇimēkalai*'s obvious concern with the moral human life, focusing on the

Sanskrit and Tamil literary theories of emotional evocation. The emotional experience the text seeks to elicit from its audience is that of pity or compassion, a central organizing principle in the *Maṇimēkalai*'s moral vision of concern and compassion for the suffering of all living beings.

Chapter 2 considers the nature of the *Maṇimēkalai*'s textual or reading community—a community about which nothing can be known directly apart from the existence of the text itself—through examination of the narrative as a literary work produced in the context of a diverse and multilingual South Indian literary culture. Through careful reading of the intertextual allusions in the *Maṇimēkalai*, particularly in relation to the principal themes of an earlier Tamil narrative from which the Buddhist text borrows its central characters and settings, a picture begins to emerge of a textual community of literary connoisseurs who are multilingual, well versed in the worldviews and literatures of various religious communities, and thoroughly engaged in the project of articulating religious identity in a literary and religious landscape of extreme diversity through the medium of ornately sophisticated poetry. The *Maṇimēkalai*'s free appropriation and translation into Tamil of Buddhist narratives and philosophical concepts found in earlier Pāli and Sanskrit transregional sources provides a glimpse of the processes of transmission of a tradition for which no other record exists. In a literary-cultural context that includes the vehemently anti-Buddhist invective of the earliest Hindu poet-saints, such easy switching from transliterated Sanskrit to translated Pāli in the *Maṇimēkalai* bespeaks a moment in Tamil literary history when language choice did not entail the same cultural, political, or religious allegiance that it would assume by the time of the eleventh-century *Vīracōḻiyam*.

Chapter 3 considers the community of Buddhists imagined within the narrative world of the *Maṇimēkalai* itself, a community whose locus is not the geographical region of Tamil-speaking southern India in the narrative present, as one might expect, but rather all of India and the far-flung reaches of Southeast Asia in the glorious era of the future Buddha's earthly birth. Focusing on the central role played by the wondrous begging bowl that never empties if used in service to the poor, this chapter argues that the bowl itself signals the coming of the future Buddha and embodies those moral values that will enable the *Maṇimēkalai*'s audience to participate in that glorious community to come. Attention to the central locations of the narrative similarly reveals the text's expansive vision of Buddhist community that involves not only the subcontinent but also an island kingdom somewhere in Southeast Asia. Through reference to other Buddhist literatures of this early medieval period, this chapter argues that the *Maṇimēkalai* participates in larger Asian patterns of redrawing the Buddhist world, relocating its centers away from the cities of northern India associated with Gautama Buddha and toward new foci of Buddhist activity in South India, Sri Lanka, China, and Southeast Asia.

Chapters 4 and 5 turn to the eleventh-century *Vīracōḻiyam* and its commentary, both of which construct a technology or theoretical vision of a multilingual literary culture that is claimed for Buddhism. Chapter 4 argues that the *Vīracōḻiyam* self-consciously combines Tamil and Sanskrit grammar and poetic theory in unprecedented ways, for the first time formalizing a relationship between two literary languages that had existed side by side for many centuries. In raising Tamil to the level of a translocal prestige language of learning, the *Vīracōḻiyam* traces the origin of this Tamil-Sanskrit literary language to the teachings of a great Buddha-to-be, Avalokiteśvara, thereby carving out a place for Buddhism in the Tamil religious and literary landscape of competing sectarian communities. Named for its heroic royal Cōḻa patron, the *Vīracōḻiyam*, like the *Maṇimēkalai* before it, also participates in wider currents within the Buddhist literary world, as South Indian Theravāda monks writing in Pāli in the tenth through twelfth centuries increasingly identify themselves and the monasteries in which they write as tied to a "Coḷiya" order.

The commentary on the *Vīracōḻiyam*, discussed in chapter 5, brings together fragments of a considerable corpus of Buddhist narrative and devotional poetry composed in Tamil, of which nothing else remains. Expanding on the *Vīracōḻiyam*'s project by substantiating the language of the Buddha-to-be with Tamil literary examples, the commentary envisions a community of readers who share a profound devotion to the Buddha and a moral vision of human kindness and self-sacrificing compassion for the welfare of others. In drawing from texts that are not explicitly Buddhist for many of his moral illustrations, the commentator clearly envisions Buddhism as one among many sectarian communities in Tamil-speaking literary culture; in quoting so broadly, he both locates and subtly reworks common intersectarian concerns and claims a part of the literary corpus in Tamil for Buddhism. In its failure to cite even once the *Maṇimēkalai*, the commentary further suggests that despite their common language and common geographical origin, the *Maṇimēkalai* and the *Vīracōḻiyam* did not belong to a single community of Tamil-speaking Buddhists. Rather, each envisions and enacts a textual community unique to its own cultural and historical location. Each text reveals a distinct moment in the way Tamil-speaking Buddhist communities represented and imagined themselves in diverse religious and linguistic landscapes.

1

Reading *Maṇimēkalai* as Buddhist Literature

> Again and again I came back to reading the *Maṇimēkalai*. Many passages that puzzled and confused me became cleared little by little. The tenets and views of Buddhism appeared clad in words of exquisite simplicity. I read them with enormous pleasure. [My friend] Raṅkācāriyar listened and could not contain his enthusiasm. "Oh! Ah! How beautiful! How apt are the words that convey the[ese] [Buddhist] ideas translated into Tamil!" he would say again and again in rapt attention and high praise.
>
> U. V. Cāminātaiyar, *The Story of My Life*

U. V. Cāminātaiyar (1855–1942), one of the scholars responsible for the preservation of and modern renaissance of interest in the oldest literary works composed in Tamil,[1] thus records his initial response to the moving beauty of a poetic narrative, a narrative whose Buddhist idiom he often found frustrating.[2] This reaction of Cāminātaiyar and his friend to the *Maṇimēkalai*, their "enormous pleasure" and "rapt attention" that overshadowed any difficulties of precise comprehension, hints at both the intricacies and literary elegance of the text, its multiple layers of meaning and many possible levels of interpretation. As a literary work, the *Maṇimēkalai* is a complex and imaginative creation meant to entertain, instruct, engage, provoke, and provide "enormous pleasure." This chapter explores some of the many layers of the *Maṇimēkalai* and offers a way of reading this Tamil text that makes sense of the work as both Buddhist doctrine and poetic creation, as both religious or philosophical teaching and sophisticated literary art.

The Text

The older of the two extant Buddhist texts composed in Tamil, the *Maṇimēkalai*,[3] or *Maṇimēkalai tuṟavu* (literally, "the renunciation of Maṇimēkalai"),[4] is a long poetic narrative of 4,758 lines arranged in thirty chapters.[5] As the story of a young girl, Maṇimēkalai, the daughter of a courtesan, who gradually turns away from her hereditary occupation to become a Buddhist renunciant, even a superficial reading of an English translation of the text[6] highlights several striking characteristics: the intricate interweaving of sixteen "branch stories" (*kiḷaik katai*) into the main narrative;[7] the seemingly abrupt shift from poetic narrative to philosophical discourse in the twenty-seventh, twenty-ninth, and thirtieth chapters; the persistent emphasis placed on the power of karma in determining every aspect of one's life; the recurring theme of the importance of womanly virtue (*kaṟpu*) to the maintenance of social and cosmic order; and the expressions of profound devotion to the Buddha that pervade the entire text.

About the real author of the *Maṇimēkalai* (the historical writer who actually sat down with pen and paper, called the "empirical" author by modern reader-response literary critics such as Umberto Eco[8]), virtually nothing is known. The preface (*patikam*) to the text simply identifies the author as "Cāttaṉ, the wealthy grain merchant" (*vaḷaṅkeḻu kula vāṇikaṉ cāttaṉ*, line 96) and adds that Cāttaṉ, or Cāttaṉār as he is usually referred to by Tamil scholars (*-ār* being an honorific ending in Tamil), first told the story of Maṇimēkalai's renunciation "with the aid of eloquent Tamil" at the request of the king, Iḷaṅkō (lines 95–98). The identity of this Cāttaṉār, and the nature of his relationship to Iḷaṅkō, the king to whom the composition of the *Maṇimēkalai*'s "sister" narrative, the *Cilappatikāram*, "The Lay of the Anklet," is attributed, have long been the subjects of much debate among scholars, particularly Tamil scholars working in South India.[9] Whether or not this Cāttaṉār bears any relationship to the Cīttalai Cāttaṉār to whom a number of classical Caṅkam poems on the love or "interior" (*akam*) theme are attributed will perhaps never be known; even if it were to be so determined, such an identification would contribute little to modern-day understanding of this Buddhist text. As Zvelebil aptly sums up the available data regarding the author of the *Maṇimēkalai*: "The only certain thing we know of C[āttaṉār] is that he was a convinced and well-educated Buddhist and a great poet."[10]

Equally problematic is the dating of the *Maṇimēkalai*; Cāttaṉār and his text have been assigned dates ranging from the second century CE[11] to the tenth.[12] Although Vēluppiḷḷai summarizes all the arguments for various dates, he concludes by finding "it difficult to decide on the date of the epic *Mēkalai*, as it stands today."[13] Indeed, the difficulties inherent in establishing even a relative chronology of early Tamil literary texts are many, and most attempts at dating the *Maṇimēkalai* have thus far been based either on problematic readings of the penultimate chapter (dealing with Buddhist logic) as a Tamil translation of Dignāga's *Nyāyapraveśa*, "The Penetration of Logic,"[14] or on the presence or absence of certain images, characters, and themes associated with a particular historical era.[15] Certainly, the *Maṇimēkalai* is later than the *Tirukkuṟaḷ*, "The Sacred Teachings in *Kuṟaḷ* Meter," the enduringly popular Tamil work dealing with the themes of virtue (Tamil *aṟam*, Sanskrit *dharma*), wealth and power (Tamil *poruḷ*, Sanskrit *artha*), and desire (Tamil *kāmam*, Sanskrit *kāma*); the Buddhist text quotes verses 54 and 55 of the *Kuṟaḷ* at xxii.59–61 and refers to its author as "the poet without falsehood" (*poyyil pulavaṉ*).[16] Beyond this, nothing can be said for certain. Based on the linguistic and stylistic analysis presented by Kandaswamy,[17] a fifth- or sixth-century date for the text, placing it somewhat earlier than, or roughly contemporaneous with, the earliest of the Śaiva devotional (bhakti) poets,[18] seems a reasonable enough working assumption.

A relatively early dating of the *Maṇimēkalai* text can perhaps also be inferred from its use of the meter known as *akaval* (later *āciriyam*),[19] "the most ancient and least complicated"[20] of the Tamil poetic meters; it is *viruttam*, the "grand meter of classical narrative poetry,"[21] that is most commonly employed by the medieval poets, from Māṇikkavācakar to Kampaṉ. Nearly all of the Caṅkam literary anthologies—each of the poems of the *Pattupāṭṭu*, "Ten Songs," and six of the collections found in *Eṭṭuttokai*, "Eight Collections"—

are composed exclusively in akaval meter, and this, along with the many themes, styles, vocabulary, and literary conventions shared by both the Caṅkam works and the *Maṇimēkalai*, would appear to place the latter text closer, at least in spirit, to the age of the Caṅkam corpus than to the later medieval period dominated by the meters and themes of Hindu devotionalism.

Assigning the *Maṇimēkalai* to a specific genre of Tamil or Buddhist literature proves no easier than naming its author or pinpointing a probable date of composition. Yet the question of genre must be raised, for, as Sheldon Pollock notes, genre is a critical factor in determining how South Asian texts were read and understood, serving as a guide to reader/audience expectations in social and historical contexts other than our own. "Genre identification," he writes, "is a map for reading a textual maze where form has its own meaning."[22] Mayilainātar's fourteenth-century commentary on the grammatical work, *Naṉṉūl*, "The Good Book," is the first to apply the term "five great poetic works" (Tamil *aimperuṅkāppiyam*, Sanskrit *pañcamahākāvya*[23]) to Tamil literature.[24] Not until the late eighteenth or early nineteenth century, however, in Kantappaiyar's *Tiruttaṇikai ulā*, are five Tamil ornate poems (Tamil *kāppiyam*, Sanskrit *kāvya*) mentioned by name: *Cilappatikāram*, *Maṇimēkalai*, *Cīvakacintāmaṇi*, *Vaḷaiyāpati*, and *Kuṇṭalakēci*.[25] Indeed, the enterprise of classifying poetic works into various genres (Tamil *pirapantam*, Sanskrit *prabandha*) appears relatively late in Tamil; the first text to deal explicitly with such classification of Tamil poetry is the eleventh-century *Paṉṉirupāṭṭiyal*, "The Twelve Essences of Poetry."[26] Certainly, the standard features of the "great poetic work" (Sanskrit *mahākāvya*) set out by the seventh-century Sanskrit literary theoretician, Daṇḍin, in his *Kāvyādarśa*, "The Mirror of Poetry," and by the twelfth-century Tamil interpretation of that work, the *Taṇṭiyalaṅkāram*, "The Poetic Ornaments of Daṇḍin"[27]—that such a poem include a peerless hero, a discussion of the four human aims (*puruṣārtha*) of wealth, love, virtue, and liberation, vivid descriptions of landscapes, weddings, coronations, and battles, for example[28]—are not all found in the *Maṇimēkalai*, a text concerned primarily with virtue (dharma) and the preparations necessary for undertaking the ascetic life that leads ultimately to liberation. As Richman notes, "generic analysis through . . . Sanskrit prescriptions does not really get at the heart of the *Maṇimēkalai*."[29] As her overall analysis of the text persuasively shows, the *Maṇimēkalai* relies primarily on classical Tamil literary conventions, using the poetic themes of inner love (akam) and outer heroism (*puṟam*), as well as landscape (*tiṇai*),[30] in new and interesting ways. Drawing on Aṭiyārkkunallār's thirteenth-century commentary on the preface to the *Cilappatikāram*,[31] Zvelebil suggests classifying both the *Cilappatikāram* and the *Maṇimēkalai* in the manner of the great medieval commentator: as narrative stanzas connected by content (*toṭarnilaicceyyuḷ*).[32]

Whatever the appropriate literary genre of the *Maṇimēkalai* might be, whether ornate poetic work (kāppiyam) or some earlier classification now lost between the Caṅkam-era theoretical work on grammar and poetics, the *Tolkāppiyam*, and the medieval genre (pirapantam) traditions, it is clear that the text, in the spirit of great court poetry, is an ornate poetic piece following strict rules of composition. Certainly, the checkered history of the *Maṇimēkalai*'s transmission indicates that it was preserved long after the last Buddhists disappeared from the Tamil region[33] as a brilliant specimen of Tamil narrative poetry. In an indirect way, for example, the active suppression of Tamil poetic works such as the *Cilappatikāram* and the *Maṇimēkalai* by the Śaiva Sanskrit enthusiasts of the late seventeenth and early eighteenth centuries, Cāminātа Tēcikar and Civañāṉa Cuvāmikaḷ,[34] points to a perception of these texts as artistic pieces dangerously unconcerned with inculcating either proper Hindu religious ideology or sufficient respect for Sanskrit literary forms. The man who first introduced Cāminātaiyar to the *Cīvakacintāmaṇi* reported that he had secured his palm leaf manuscript from "a descendant of a line of poets belonging to a place near Śrī Vaikuṇṭam . . . [whose] ancestors had composed a number of poems."[35] Cāminātaiyar's oldest and most complete manuscript of the *Maṇimēkalai* was recovered from the home of one Aḻakiya Ciṟṟampalak Kavirāyar of Mitilaippaṭṭi; the village itself had been donated to this family of "royal poets" (Kavirāyar) by a Nāyakkar ruler generations before, and Aḻakiya Ciṟṟampalak Kavirāyar presented manuscripts not only of the *Maṇimēkalai* but of the *Cilappatikāram* and various Caṅkam anthologies as well.[36] Whatever the name of its particular genre, the *Maṇimēkalai* has long been perceived and classified by Tamil poets and literary scholars alike as an example par excellence of ornate Tamil poetic composition.

The Audience

If little can be said with certainty concerning the dating, genre, or empirical author of the *Maṇimēkalai*, so, too, does the nature of the text's historical audience remain shrouded in mystery. Was this poetic narrative composed for a royal court, perhaps a sixth-century Pallava court in Kāñcīpuram? The preface, framed as a dialogue between king and poet-merchant, might suggest so, as might the fact that the narrative draws to a close as the principal characters gather near a shrine in Kāñcī. What sort of people would have constituted such a court? Again, one can only guess. In short, there is virtually no historical data at hand to shed light on the actual circumstances of the composition of the text, its author, or that author's immediate audience.

Yet, as much reader-response criticism has argued over the past two decades, the real author and historical reader of any given text are only part of the story of composition and reception.[37] As Eco indicates in his analysis of a nineteenth-century French novel, "we must deal with three entities":[38] the historical author who put pen to paper, the first-person narrator of the story, and the anonymous voice or "model" author who shapes the entire text.[39] As discussed previously, in the case of the *Maṇimēkalai* little or nothing is known of the first entity, the real Cāttaṉār. Of the anonymous voice, however, of the model author and the model reader who necessarily arises simultaneously in the act of reading,[40] quite a number of things can be suggested. Given the traditional classification of the text as a sophisticated work of poetry (kāppiyam)—or if such a classification proves an artificial medieval attempt to demonstrate the basic compatibility of Tamil literature with Sanskrit genres, its obvious characteristics of narrative complexity and poetic ornateness—the *Maṇimēkalai* itself clearly expects a certain model reader, to borrow once again from Eco's terminology,[41] or, perhaps more appropriately in the Indian context, a model audience.[42] What can be said about this implied audience? Who does the model author, the anonymous voice shaping the text through various narrative strategies, anticipate will read or listen to his text?

First, as Richman's work demonstrates, the *Maṇimēkalai* assumes an audience thoroughly versed in classical Tamil poetics as explicated in the oldest extant grammar of

Tamil, the *Tolkāppiyam*, and embodied in the Caṅkam literary corpus. Her analysis of the rhetorical strategies employed by the author, using those classical themes to his own Buddhist ends, requires an audience so familiar with the classical literary heritage as to be sensitive to the most subtle shifts and nuances in image and style. Her analysis of the five longest subplots, or branch stories, in the text shows particularly the many ways in which the author manipulates the classical landscape motifs, the techniques of suggestion (*uḷḷurai*), and the distinction of heroic and love themes characteristic of the Caṅkam poetic anthologies. The content of the narrative itself would also seem to anticipate an audience equally sophisticated in its appreciation of dance and dramatic forms. The lengthy list of the many traditional arts of the courtesan, from the different styles of dancing to the art of playing various musical instruments (ii.18–32), and the technical terminology used for the various curtains of the theatrical stage (v.3), for example, might indicate an implied audience intimately familiar with traditions of public performance and stagecraft (perhaps analogous to today's image of the sophisticated New York or London theater patron).

From various signs embedded in the text itself, it is also possible to discern an expectation, on the part of the model author, of a model audience equally well versed in the literature and poetic theories of languages other than Tamil as they might have existed in the fifth or sixth century CE. The relevance of the Sanskrit theory of aesthetic flavor, or heightened emotional response (*rasa*), to the text of the *Maṇimēkalai* is taken up later; other elements of the text also point to an author and an audience familiar with narratives, language, and imagery not found in the classical Tamil literary corpus. There are numerous allusions in the Tamil text, for example, to stories found only in the extant Sanskrit or Pāli sources of the early medieval period: a brief reference to Arjuna's masquerade as a eunuch in the *Mahābhārata* (iii.146–147);[43] several suggestions of tales of Indra, his heavenly city, and his host of consorts (e.g., xxiv.7–18 and xxv.201–204); and a condensed rendering of the battle between two Nāgas and the Buddha over possession of the Buddha's lotus seat (viii.54–60).[44] Phrases such as "[like] the sun, with its full rays, swallowed in cool mist" (*taṇ paṉi viḻuṅkiya ceṅkatir maṇṭilam*; xii.63) are not indigenous to the classical Tamil stock of poetic images. In similar fashion, the technical philosophical vocabulary found in chapters 27 (non-Buddhist teachings) and 29 (Buddhist logic), including many direct Tamil transliterations of Sanskrit words—*pakkataṉmavacaṉam* (xxix.71) for Sanskrit *pakṣadharmavācana*, "statement of the attribute of the proposition," for example—attests to an anticipated audience familiar with philosophical and narrative literature beyond the Tamil.

Again, from signs embedded within the text itself, the *Maṇimēkalai* seems to anticipate an audience sophisticated in its understanding of Buddhist teachings, values, and ideas. Given the wealth of Buddhist technical terminology, images, and allusions found throughout the *Maṇimēkalai*, an audience unfamiliar with or unimpressed by the story of the Buddha and his teachings would miss several of the central themes and most compelling images of the text. To cite but a few examples, a term indicating the five Buddhist precepts (Tamil *aivakaic cīlam*, Sanskrit *pañcaśīla*) that call for abstention from killing, stealing, sexual misconduct, lying, and intoxication, is cited at ii.68 without any definition or elaboration. In a similar vein, the central character of the narrative, Maṇimēkalai, is introduced at iii.4 with a compound referring to the arising of the conditions necessary to undertake a life of renunciation leading to liberation (ētunikaḻcci, discussed later) without any explanation. At xxiv.105–109 and again throughout the final chapter, Tamil equivalents are given for the twelve elements (*nidāna*) in the cycle of interdependent origination (Sanskrit *pratītyasamutpāda*, Pāli *paṭiccasamuppāda*) without further elaboration. As in the discussion of Buddhist inference in chapter 29, the text assumes an audience already fluent in the language of Buddhist logic and causal theory and knowledgeable about the concepts that such language implies. In addition to the Buddhist philosophical terminology found throughout the text, the *Maṇimēkalai* also makes numerous references to various Buddhist characters and narratives, from the sages Caṅkataruma<u>n</u> (Saṅghadharma; v.58–76) and Cātucakkara<u>n</u> (Sādhucakra; x.24–41)[45] to the Jātaka stories of the Buddha's former lives (xi.61–72) and the tale of his descent from Tuṣita heaven (xii.70–74).

If virtually nothing can be said of the historical audience for whom the historical author, Cātta<u>n</u>ār, first composed his poetic narrative (if, indeed, such a wealthy grain merchant ever existed), numerous elements in the *Maṇimēkalai* itself, from the Tamil "rhetorical strategies" discussed at length by Richman to the technical phrases used to describe Buddhist theories of inferential logic and causation, point to a specific audience implied or anticipated by the text: an audience sophisticated at many levels, cosmopolitan in terms of literary exposure and taste, thoroughly familiar with Tamil and perhaps Sanskrit poetics, and well acquainted with Buddhist thought and literature.

The Plot

If the *Maṇimēkalai* can thus be said to invite an audience sophisticated in its literary tastes, one additional measure of the sophistication demanded by the text is its sheer complexity, its interweaving of stories within stories, its many intertextual references and allusions, its subtle maneuvering among time frames past, present, and future. Although the *Maṇimēkalai* is the story of its central character's gradual journey toward her final act of renunciation, it is also the elaborate and intricately arranged tale of the many events that allow for the renunciatory vow to take place. The web of stories, images, characters, and events that make up the *Maṇimēkalai* lay within "the horizon of expectations"[46] only of an audience well-versed in Tamil and Sanskrit literature. Although the story of Maṇimēkalai's renunciation is unique to this Tamil text,[47] many of the elements of the narrative have close counterparts in other literary works, both Buddhist and non-Buddhist. To pave the way for the discussion that follows—an effort to make sense of the complexity of the text as a whole both literary and Buddhist—a detailed summation of the contents or plot of the *Maṇimēkalai* is first necessary.

The first chapter, "The Story of the Proclamation of the Festival," places the story of Maṇimēkalai in the city of Pukār as preparations for the festival of Indra are about to begin, a gala occasion of twenty-eight days during which "gods and human beings stroll together" (i.66) in joyous celebration.[48] Like the Indra festival (*indrotsava*) or spring festival (*vasantotsava*)[49] of Sanskrit literary tradition, the festival of Indra (Tamil *intiraviḻā*) provides an occasion for the composition and performance of sophisticated and ornate poetic works such as the *Maṇimēkalai*. Bharata, for example, is said to have first delivered his *Nāṭyaśāstra*, his foundational treatise on the performance and aesthetics of dance drama, before the gods during the festival of Indra,[50] whereas Kālidāsa's *Mālavikāgnimitra*[51] and *Abhijñānaśākuntalam*,[52] as well as Harṣa's *Ratnāvalī*,[53] *Priyadarśikā*,[54] and *Nāgānanda*,[55] to cite but a few examples, are all staged during a spring or Indra festival. The Indra festival, in South Asian literary tradition, is a season closely associated with cultural events and literary performance. This first chapter thus places the *Maṇimēkalai* in an extraordinary time and place, creating an atmosphere of heightened audience expectation, setting the stage for the recitation and enjoyment of a great poetic work.

In the second chapter, however, one learns that preparations for the festival are not proceeding altogether smoothly. Mātavi, the daughter of the doyenne of the courtesans, Cittirāpati, will not fulfill her traditional obligation to dance at the festival. On hearing of the tragic end of her exlover, Kōvalan̲,[56] Mātavi reports that she found solace at the feet of the Buddhist teacher, Ar̲avaṇan̲;[57] she vows that her daughter by Kōvalan̲, Maṇimēkalai, will "not be allowed, even for an instant, to engage in the vile occupation" of a courtesan (ii.56–57). In the following chapter, Maṇimēkalai herself is introduced, as she hears for the first time the story of her father's violent end; in her grief, she sheds tears on the flower garland she is weaving. Because the purity of the garland is defiled by the tears, Mātavi instructs her daughter to gather fresh blossoms. Cutamati, Maṇimēkalai's young friend, points to the dangers of sending such a beautiful young girl out alone (she recounts her own sad tale of being captured by a "bearer of knowledge," or semidivine being [Tamil *viñcaiyan̲*, Sanskrit *vidyādhara*], while picking flowers) and offers to accompany Maṇimēkalai to the Uvavan̲am, the flower park of the Buddha.[58] Cutamati tells of a magnificent chamber made of crystal that stands in the park, containing a lotus seat "emitting brilliant rays" and "encrusted with pristine jewels" (iii.65). Like the perfumed chamber (*gandhakuṭī*) of the Buddha discussed by John Strong that serves to create a space, perfumed by petals, to which the Buddha might return,[59] this wondrous pedestal is said to have been created by Mayan̲, the celestial builder, to demonstrate the necessity of proper intention when making offerings to the Buddha (iii.70–78). En route to the Uvavan̲am, Maṇimēkalai and Cutamati encounter a number of non-Buddhist characters, most of whom suffer the narrator's sarcasm: a dirty Jain ascetic who lumbers along "like an elephant in distress" (iii.86–91), a drunkard who taunts the Jain monk to try the discipline (*yoga*) of drinking (iii.92–102), and a Śaiva ascetic who speaks "in a senseless babble" and "fights with his shadow" (iii.103–115). The two young women also encounter a dancing eunuch (iii.116–125), a crowd of visitors (iii.126–131), and a festival dedicated to Lord Murukan̲ (iii.132–145).

In the fourth chapter, while Cutamati shows Maṇimēkalai the beauties of the Uvavan̲am, Utayakumaran̲, the son of Pukār's king, subdues a rutting elephant who is terrorizing the city.[60] The prince at that point notices a young man playing a lute, his finger plucking the string that sounds a note of tragedy; the prince questions the young man and learns that the lovely Maṇimēkalai has just walked by, "her natural beauty wilted like a flower placed in a well-constructed casket" (iii.65–68) because of her grief at learning of Kōvalan̲'s cruel death. Utayakumaran̲ is immediately overcome by an intense desire to possess the alluring Maṇimēkalai, and he rushes off to the park. Cutamati quickly shuts her friend inside the crystal chamber and tries to put off the prince with a short lecture on the impermanence of the flesh. In the following chapter, as Utayakumaran̲ spies the object of his desire through the crystal walls of the chamber, Cutamati tells in greater detail the story of how she first came to the city of Pukār, enslaved and then abandoned by the amorous semidivine being, Mārutavēkaṉ. The prince is frustrated for the moment; he leaves the park, vowing to "possess Maṇimēkalai whose waist is as slender as a *vañci* creeper" (v.81–82). Maṇimēkalai then emerges from the chamber shaken, clearly feeling a strong attraction to the lustful prince. The goddess, Maṇimēkalā,[61] suddenly appears, ready to witness the celebration of the Indra festival, and she begins to praise the Buddha.

In the sixth chapter, one which Richman rightly contends "best demonstrates Cāttaṉār's rhetorical skills,"[62] the goddess, Maṇimēkalā, describes in great detail the temple of the cosmic place (Sanskrit *cakravāla*, Tamil *cakkaravāḷak kōṭṭam*), a site deemed by most people simply a burning ground (vi.27–32). The goddess depicts the place in terms of both grandeur and horror, surrounded by magnificent walls and gates and containing all manner of corpses, scavengers, and grisly scenes. The text dwells at length on the desecration of a once-lovely courtesan (vi.107–119), a passage persuasively analyzed by Richman as an inversion of classical Tamil notions of love and female beauty.[63] Here, the goddess also tells the tale known in Pāli works as "The Story of the Mustard Seed," the narrative of a grieving mother who entreats superhuman beings (in the Pāli case, the Buddha; here the goddess, Campāpati) to revive her son. Finally, one learns that the entire site has been constructed by Mayaṉ to commemorate Campāpati's gathering together of all the deities of the cosmos to prove to the grief-stricken mother that no being has the power to revive the dead. Maṇimēkalā then, in the middle of the night, takes Maṇimēkalai to the island of Maṇipallavam[64] and leaves her there.

The goddess appears before Utayakumaraṉ in chapter 7, entreating him to leave Maṇimēkalai alone. Next, she visits Cutamati and informs her of what has befallen her friend. Cutamati then approaches a wondrous painting on a pillar in the temple of the cosmic place that tells her of her former life as Vīrai, elder sister to Maṇimēkalai, who was in that birth named Ilakkumi (the Tamil equivalent of Lakṣmī). In the next chapter, Maṇimēkalai awakens in distress on Maṇipallavam and wanders about until she stumbles upon a magnificently bejeweled pedestal, a seat belonging to the Buddha but once claimed by two warring Nāga kings.[65] Chapter 9 opens with Maṇimēkalai falling before the pedestal in adoration of the Buddha; because of the power of that structure, she has just realized the nature of her past births as the wife of Irākulaṉ (the Tamil equivalent of Rāhula), now reborn as Prince Utayakumaraṉ. In the tenth chapter, Maṇimēkalā, the goddess, reappears, worships the Buddha's jeweled seat, provides Maṇimēkalai with more information about her previous life as Ilakkumi, and bestows on the young girl three *mantras* that grant her the ability to fly through the air, change physical forms at will, and appease her own hunger.

In the eleventh chapter, Maṇimēkalai meets the goddess who protects the Buddha's seat, one Tīvatilakai, and receives from Kōmuki Lake a wondrous begging bowl known as Amutacurapi (literally, "that which secretes *amṛta*, the 'nectar of immortality'"); the bowl appears every year on the anniversary of the Buddha's birth and enlightenment and never empties if used to feed the poor and hungry.[66] Maṇimēkalai praises the Buddha and notes that she is qualified to receive such a potent gift because of her act of kindness to a sage in a previous life (xi.99–106). Here the bowl is described as "medicine" or "medicine for life which is precious" (*ār uyir maruntāy*), a theme consistently reiterated throughout the remainder of the text to describe both the bowl and the young woman who wields it as healers, as remedies for the very tangible and physical ills of the world.[67] Maṇimēkalai then returns to Pukār and her mother, informing Mātavi and Cutamati that they were once her sisters, Tārai and Vīrai, in a previous life. The three then meet the sage, Aṟavaṇaṉ, in the following chapter; he supplies yet more details concerning Maṇimēkalai's former life. Aṟavaṇaṉ also describes at length the miraculous events that will accompany the Buddha's return to earth once again in the year 1616.[68]

In chapters 13 and 14 and the opening half of 15, Aṟavaṇaṉ narrates to Maṇimēkalai and her companions the story of Āputtiraṉ (literally, "son of a cow"), the brahmin outcast who last possessed Amutacurapi in his previous life.[69] Born to a fallen brahmin woman, saved by a cow, and reared by adoptive brahmin parents, Āputtiraṉ is eventually banished from the brahmin community for his efforts to save a cow from sacrificial slaughter. He receives the wondrous begging bowl from the goddess Cintātēvi of Maturai and is eventually reborn as the king of an island kingdom known as Cāvakam.[70] Kāyacaṇṭikai, a semidivine woman suffering an insatiable hunger due to an ascetic's powerful curse, is introduced at the end of chapter 15 and, in the following chapter, tells the story of Cātuvaṉ, a shipwreck survivor who teaches an uncivilized band of Nāgas the most basic Buddhist values. Maṇimēkalai then enters the house of Ātirai, Cātuvaṉ's long-suffering wife, and receives the first morsels of food into her almsbowl, thus activating the vessel's generative powers.

The seventeenth chapter opens as Kāyacaṇṭikai finally finds relief from her twelve long years of hunger with the bounty produced by Amutacurapi; she then tells the story of how she came to be stricken by an angry ascetic's curse. Maṇimēkalai then proceeds to the public rest house near the temple of Pukār's guardian deity, Campāpati, and begins to feed the hungry masses. Cittirāpati, in the following chapter, still fuming over her daughter's refusal to carry on the courtesan tradition, persuades Utayakumaraṉ to persist in his amorous pursuit of Maṇimēkalai. The prince finds the young girl in the public rest house, where she tries in vain to persuade him of the ultimate impermanence of the flesh. Utayakumaraṉ simply renews his passionate promise to possess her. In chapter 19, Maṇimēkalai (using her newly acquired mantra) assumes the form of Kāyacaṇṭikai to avoid a confrontation with the prince and is then taken to the palace, where she successfully entreats the king to convert the royal prison into a residence for ascetics.

Chapter 20 produces a narrative climax of sorts. Kāñcaṉaṉ, the husband of the semidivine woman, Kāyacaṇṭikai, comes upon Utayakumaraṉ speaking to the disguised Maṇimēkalai (whom Kāñcaṉaṉ understandably mistakes for his own wife) and kills the prince in a jealous rage. In the following chapter, a distraught Maṇimēkalai learns of events to come from that mysterious pillar painting in Campāpati's temple: she will be reborn again and again as a man in the northern land of Makatam (Magadha) until she becomes "the chief disciple of the one who graciously teaches the dharma to others" (xxi.178–179). A group of ascetics gain an audience with the king in chapter 22 and tell him, in long and roundabout fashion,[71] of the death of his son at the hand of Kāñcaṉaṉ. The king has Maṇimēkalai placed under guard. The grieving queen, in the following chapter, attempts in turn to drive the young girl mad, have her raped, and starve her to death, but each time, Maṇimēkalai's mantraic powers save her from harm. Maṇimēkalai manages to convince the queen of the error of her ways, and the queen "becomes possessed of a mind free from enmity" (xxiii.142–143).

Cittirāpati appears again in chapter 24 to entreat the queen to return Maṇimēkalai to the community of courtesans; she also predicts the destruction of Pukār due to the wrath of the goddess Maṇimēkalā because the Indra festival will not be properly celebrated. The queen refuses to turn Maṇimēkalai over to her grandmother, and Aṟavaṇaṉ soon arrives and begins to teach. The brief exposition he provides concerning the twelve elements (Pāli nidāna, Tamil *cārpu*) of the chain of interdependent origination (paṭiccasamuppāda; xxiv.105–140), as well as the definitions he provides for the first two of these twelve elements, foreshadow the more complete explanation given in chapter 30.[72] After the Buddhist sage's instruction in the teachings of the Buddha, Maṇimēkalai travels to Cāvakam, the land of Āputtiraṉ, who is now reborn as King Puṇṇiyarācaṉ (Puṇya- or Puñña-rājan, "meritorious king").

After entreating the king to accompany her to Maṇipallavam, in chapter 25 Maṇimēkalai meets Āputtiraṉ on that isle of wondrous happenings, and both circumambulate the Buddha's jeweled seat. Āputtiraṉ then realizes the nature of his previous birth as the bearer of Amutacurapi. Tīvatilakai, the guardian of Kōmuki Lake, informs Āputtiraṉ that that former life ended there on Maṇipallavam, and she tells Maṇimēkalai that Pukār has been destroyed due to the king's sudden neglect of the Indra festival, just as Cittirāpati had foretold. Maṇimēkalai and the Cāvakam king then uncover the bones of Āputtiraṉ's former body in the sand. The two then part, the king returning to his kingdom and Maṇimēkalai proceeding to the city of Vañci.[73]

Maṇimēkalai there enters the temple erected in honor of her father, Kōvalaṉ, and his virtuous wife, Kaṇṇaki, and hears from the deified Kaṇṇaki the tragic story of the burning of Maturai (as told in the *Cilappatikāram*, with several significant differences, which are discussed in chapter 2). Kaṇṇaki also foretells of the rebirth of the couple on earth: Kōvalaṉ and Kaṇṇaki will be reborn again and again until the Buddha returns to "spread the rays of dharma everywhere in the countless cosmic realms" (xxvi.52–53). Maṇimēkalai then assumes the guise of a male ascetic and approaches the various learned religious teachers of Vañci.

Throughout chapter 27, Maṇimēkalai listens to the doctrines of ten different non-Buddhist teachers, classified as the "five-fold" system of religious doctrines (xxvii.288–289): those who believe in and worship some form of deity (the logician, or *pramāṇavādin*; the Śaivite; the *brahmavādin*; the Vaiṣṇava; and the Vedic ritualist), those who are primarily defined by their asceticism (the Ājīvaka and the Jain), the Sāṅkhya teacher, the Vaiśeṣika expert, and the *bhūtavādin*, or materialist.[74] Although this compendium of philosophical doctrines might seem, at first glance, to provide a window into the state of philosophical reflection in sixth-century South India,[75] the ornate and highly stylized quality of the text suggests a more literary or rhetorical aim, a question that is taken up for further discussion in chapter 2.

In the twenty-eighth chapter, Maṇimēkalai enters the city of Vañci proper and encounters her grandfather, the father of Kōvalaṉ, who has become a Buddhist renunciant after learning of the tragic end of his son. Mācāttuvāṉ then bids his granddaughter to go to Kāñcī, where she orders the king to construct a park and replica of Kōmuki Lake, as well as temples to the goddesses Maṇimēkalā and Tīvatilakai, next to the Buddhist shrine (*caitya*) in the southwestern corner of the city. Maṇimēkalai places Amutacurapi upon the replica of the Maṇipallavam pedestal of jewels and proceeds to feed the hungry masses of drought-stricken Kāñcī.

Chapter 29 opens with Aṟavaṇaṉ's explanation of the destruction of the city of Pukār at the hands of the goddess Maṇimēkalā because the king forgot to celebrate Indra's festival. Here, one also learns that the goddess once saved Maṇimēkalai's ancestor as he floundered in the sea; this ancestor is no doubt the Buddha in a previous incarnation, as he is called "the lord at the foot of the *bodhi* tree, the first being" (xxix.23–25).[76] Maṇimēkalā's role in helping others along the path toward liberation ("ripening the perfections [Tamil *pāramitai*, Sanskrit *pāramitā*] that they might appear" [xxix.26]) is also noted. What follows is a lengthy discussion of inferential logic (Tamil *karuttaḷavu*, Sanskrit *anumāna*), first in terms of faulty modes of reasoning, followed by examples of correct and incorrect members of a five-part syllogism: the proposition (Tamil *pakkam*, Sanskrit *pakṣa*), the reason (Tamil *ētu*, Sanskrit *hetu*), the example (Tamil *tiṭṭāntam*, Sanskrit *dṛṣṭānta*), the application (Tamil *upanayam*, Sanskrit *upanaya*), and the conclusion (Tamil *nikamaṉam*, Sanskrit *nigamana*). This chapter has attracted more scholarly attention than any other single portion of the *Maṇimēkalai* text, primarily for its seemingly close resemblance to the system of logic described by Dignāga in his *Nyāyapraveśa*.[77] As Hikosaka[78] notes, the text makes use of an interesting and rather confusing mix of technical terms, some directly transliterated from the Sanskrit (*pirattiyakkam* for Sanskrit *pratyakṣa*, "direct perception"); others more "Tamilized," to borrow Hikosaka's term (*pirattiyam* for Sanskrit pratyakṣa); and still others full Tamil translations of the Sanskrit terms (*cuṭṭu uṇarvu*, "direct realization," for Sanskrit pratyakṣa). Although logic discussed in meter might seem a bit strange to a western audience, the existence of texts such as the *Aḷavainūl*,[79] a handbook of logic (now lost) composed in metrical stanzas,[80] perhaps suggests a Tamil tradition of rendering dense philosophical discussions into verse; such a tradition might also explain the necessity of employing multiple word forms and synonyms to fit various meters.

Having explained the correct modes of inferential reasoning to Maṇimēkalai, Aṟavaṇaṉ, in the final chapter of the text, delivers an extremely terse and compact summation of the Buddhist doctrine of interdependent origination, described in Tamil as "the appearance of the dependent [things]" (*cārpiṉ tōṉṟi*; xxx.17). Although this discussion bears more in common with the Pāli tradition of interdependent origination as outlined by Buddhaghosa in his *Visuddhimagga*, "The Path of Purification,"[81] than with any Mahāyāna interpretations of dependent arising,[82] the Tamil text still contains many details and definitions not found elsewhere. Perhaps the word-for-word repetition of xxiv.105–140 at xxx.48–81 noted previously suggests that the author is quoting something akin to a (Tamil) vernacular commentarial text (*aṭṭhakathā*) of the sort that Buddhaghosa and his Tamil-born contemporary, Buddhadatta, are remembered in the Theravādin tradition for having rendered into Māgadhī, the language of the Buddha.[83] Perhaps Buddhadatta's reputation as a "great versifier" suggests a Tamil tradition of doctrinal expositions rendered in poetic form.[84] Whatever the precise model for the composition of the final chapter of the *Maṇimēkalai* might have been, this portion of the text presents an extremely terse rendering of the doctrine of interdependent origination whose details thus far have been little studied.[85] After this explication delivered by Aṟavaṇaṉ, Maṇimēkalai vows to renounce the world to "eradicate [the karmic effects of] her births" (xxx.263–264).

Although much of the secondary literature on the *Maṇimēkalai* is devoted to searching for the source of Cāttaṉār's philosophical formulations, attempting to trace discrete influences on the Tamil text, such a documentary or empirical approach to this work of poetry, it is argued later, ignores the obviously literary qualities of these chapters. Chapters 27, 29, and 30, far from simply representing philosophy "as it was" in Cāttaṉār's day, comprise a literary presentation with certain rhetorical aims. Although the Buddhist message of the final two chapters can, indeed, be said to resonate with discussions of logic in the *Nyāyapraveśa* and causal theory in the *Visuddhimagga*, the Tamil text is not simply a translation from the Sanskrit or Pāli. Indeed, Geoffrey Samuel's assessment of the Buddhist *Gesar* narrative from Tibet might well be considered equally true of the *Maṇimēkalai*: "If the Buddhism of the epic is not, by and large, that of the literary and philosophical traditions of the great monasteries, it is not fundamentally incompatible with it."[86] The *Maṇimēkalai* is, above all, an ornate poetic composition and thus has aims not wholly identical to or even compatible with those of doctrinal compilers and expositors such as Dignāga and Buddhaghosa. Even the densely packed philosophical chapters must somehow be read as literature, as poetry integral to the narrative text as a whole.

Manifesting the Precursors to Renunciation: A Central Theme

How, then, is one to make sense of the complex text of plots within plots, of dramatic narrative mixed with technical and terse philosophical exposition? Amid the intricacies of narrative detail, a careful examination of the Tamil text reveals an explicit focus: the gradual arising and manifestation of the circumstances necessary for liberation (signaled by the Tamil term *ētu*, "cause") in the life of the main character. Like so many narratives concerning the lives of the Buddha and his followers, from the tale of Aṅgulimāla, the homicidal thief converted to the dharma by the Buddha himself,[87] to the story of Maṭṭhakuṇḍali, whose "abundant beneficial root conditions" (*ussannakusalamūla*) render him "ready to receive the teaching" (*veneyyabandhava*),[88] the *Maṇimēkalai* tells the story of its central character's karmic ripening, of Maṇimēkalai's growing readiness to hear and truly understand the teachings of the Buddha. This persistent motif of the maturation of beneficial conditions (Tamil *nallētu*) not only structures the main narrative but also serves to tie together in a thematically significant way both the narrative and philosophical portions of the text.

The Tamil word for condition or cause (ētu), in combination with the verbs "to mature" (*murtital*), "to blossom" (*etirtal*), or "to manifest" (*nikaḻtal*), occurs nine times in the narrative portion of the *Maṇimēkalai* text, always in connection with the Buddha's teachings, with Maṇimēkalai's ability to hear and to comprehend those teachings, and, it seems, with the inclination to undertake a life of asceticism. Although ētu is obviously a Tamil form of the Sanskrit or Pāli hetu, generally meaning "cause," the precise manner in which the term is used throughout the narrative is not immediately apparent. However, given the various contexts in which the word appears, it must refer here to hetu in the sense of those beneficial root causes or conditions (Pāli *kusalamūla*) that give rise to karmically beneficial states, defined in Theravāda literature as nonattachment (*alobha*), lack of enmity (*adosa*), and lack of delusion (*amoha*).[89] A full discussion of the complex philosophical contexts in which this term is used in Pāli, to indicate the arising of wholesome or beneficial roots or conditions[90] that determine the quality of volitional states (Pāli *cetanā*, Tamil *ceykai*), that is, the quality of karma, lies beyond the scope of this work.[91] One might summarize the effect of the beneficial conditions, however, by noting that absence of greed is said to manifest itself in the act of renunciation and through meditational practice, lack of enmity is said to appear as ethical conduct, and absence of ignorance is said to become apparent in the acquisition of both philosophical and intuitive understanding of the nature of reality.[92] In other contexts, usually narratives or commentaries on narratives, the beneficial conditions, equated in at least one Pāli source with the term *upanissaya*, literally "basis" or "ground,"[93] are further said to be necessary preconditions for becoming a "worthy one" (*arahant*), for attaining liberation. The arising of these good conditions or beneficial roots of liberation is that which distinguishes man from beast, human birth representing the first of eight prerequisite conditions for Buddhahood.[94]

This understanding of the Tamil term ētu as the three beneficial root conditions that lead to karmically and mentally beneficial states and thus ultimately to liberation and perhaps even to Buddhahood is well supported by the nine contexts in which the word occurs in the *Maṇimēkalai*. Perhaps the most straightforward use of the term in this manner occurs at xxvi.92–94, where the conditions are specifically described as "good" (*nalla*):

> Because (*ātaliṉ*) the good conditions (nallētu) had matured (*mutirntuḷatu*) [for her],
> [Maṇimēkalai] went to the outskirts of the golden city
> that bore the name of the golden creeper [Vañci] and stayed there,
> in order to become enlightened about [the nature of] the four truths.

As in most of the occurrences to follow, ētu here is imbued with a powerful efficaciousness, not only through the general meaning of the word itself as "cause" or "condition" but through the syntax of the passage as well: here, and in six other instances to follow, ētu is connected with the words "because of" or "due to" (ātaliṉ) or with "except for" or "without" (*allatu*). Here, one learns that it is due to the maturation of these beneficial conditions that Maṇimēkalai is qualified to enter the city of Vañci, where she will listen to the false doctrines of other religious sects and thus realize the wisdom of the Buddha's Four Noble Truths. Maṇimēkalai's ability to act, that is, her decision to travel to Vañci, is due to the manifestation of beneficial conditions that serve as a genuine agent, the true catalyst for seminal narrative events.

Ētu is connected with the verb "to mature" at one additional place in the text, again in a context suggesting that matured or ripened conditions create the proper setting for advancement along the path toward liberation. At vii.19–22, the goddess Maṇimēkalā explains to a frightened Cutamati what has befallen Maṇimēkalai:

> Because (ātaliṉ) the conditions (ētu) that lead to the path of dharma (*aṟavaḻi*),
> [the path of dharma] that is the First Sage,
> have matured (*mutirntatu*) for this young creeper,
> with [my] powers I have uprooted your lady who wears shining jewels
> and have deposited her on Maṇipallavam, [a place that is] without deception.

On the island of Maṇipallavam, Maṇimēkalai gains knowledge of her past lives and receives the wondrous begging bowl, Amutacurapi. In this passage, one learns that she is transported to this place of transition and knowledge because the appropriate conditions or circumstances have matured. Maṇimēkalai herself does not decide to visit the magical island, and even the goddess is said to act in accordance with the ripening of these conditions, the implication being that supernatural beings must somehow acknowledge and conform to this process of karmic maturation, imparting dharmic knowledge only to those who are karmically prepared to receive it.

The one occurrence of the term ētu with the verb "to blossom" or "to come to pass in the [near] future" (etirtal)[95] hints at the significance of the maturation and manifestation of those conditions that lead to enlightenment. In fact, the text introduces its central character at iii.1–10 through this theme of the impending "blossoming" of karmically wholesome conditions (ētunikal̲cci). It is because of the manifestation of proper conditions to come that Maṇimēkalai sheds the defiling tears that propel her to the Buddha's flower park and the sight of the prince, thus setting in motion the principal sequence of narrative events:

> Because (ātalin̲) there would blossom (*etirntuḷatu*) for Maṇimēkalai
> a manifestation of conditions (ētunikal̲cci), like the fragrance [emanating from]
>   a flower,
> [she experienced] tremendous sorrow [on hearing]
>   that which Mātavi narrated to Vayantamālai.
> The scorchingly painful news of the great suffering that had befallen
>   [her] parents blistered [Maṇimēkalai's] inner ears.
> She became greatly distressed,
>   due to the love [she felt for them] in her heart.
> Tears of grief rolled down [her face],
>   erasing the beauty of the lady's bright, streaked eyes,
>   and bathed the garland of bright, sweet-smelling petals
>   [that she had been weaving].

Maṇimēkalai fully experiences the sorrow of her parents' tragedy because the conditions conducive to liberation will soon become manifest. "Condition" in this sense thus seems to be tied to one's ability to know and understand the nature of suffering, the primary characteristic of human existence according to the first of the Buddha's Four Noble Truths. The sequential chain of events signaled by this passage is also significant; because a manifestation of beneficial circumstances will occur for Maṇimēkalai, she is heartbroken at the story of her parents, weeps, ruins the purity of the garland she is making, and is sent out to the Uvavan̲am to gather more flowers. There, she will meet and be pursued by Utayakumaran̲, be spirited off by Maṇimēkalā to the island of Maṇipallavam, and thus begin to learn of her own past births and the teachings of the Buddha. The very first quality highlighted in the main character is the impending manifestation of the good or beneficial qualities leading to enlightenment. Like the blossoming of a fragrant flower, the flowering of the ētu lies beyond immediate human control, a natural process that will unfold fully in due time. Such a manifestation literally sets in motion the entire narrative that follows.

Ētu is also used in conjunction with the verb "to occur" or "to manifest" (nikal̲tal), and the tense of the verb switches significantly to the future. Although the proper conditions conducive to liberation have matured or ripened throughout the narrative, they are not yet fully discernible, not yet fully made manifest. This full manifestation, the text suggests, will occur at some point in the proximate future—the statement is repeatedly made that it will take place in the city of Kāñcī—presumably in the final moment of the text when Maṇimēkalai makes a renunciatory vow to free herself from the endless round of rebirths.[96] Before the main character reaches Kāñcī, however, a number of references are made to the manifestation of beneficial conditions in Maṇimēkalai's native city of Pukār as well. At vii.23–29, for example, the goddess Maṇimēkalā indicates to Cutamati that her friend's spiritual progress will be made apparent in many forms when Maṇimēkalai returns to the city of Pukār after her first sojourn to Maṇipallavam. As Maṇimēkalā reassures Cutamati:

> Having realized in detail [her] previous births,
> the virtuous lady who is like a creeper will appear in this city in seven days' time.
> Even though [Maṇimēkalai] will have assumed a disguise
> in this great, well-fortified, and wealthy city,
> on that day when she enters this city you will recognize her.
> There are many conditions (*ētup pala uḷa*)
> that will become manifest here (*nikaḻvaṉa*) here.

Here, the context suggests that Maṇimēkalai's various experiences on the island of Maṇipallavam—her vision of the Buddha's bejeweled seat and subsequent knowledge of former births and her acquisition of the inexhaustible almsbowl from Kōmuki Lake—prepare her for her activities in Pukār: the appeasing of Kāyacaṇṭikai's hunger, the distribution of food to the needy, and the conversion of both the king and queen to the Buddha's way of compassion toward all living beings. If ētu can be taken to refer to the manifestation of the karmically wholesome states of lack of attachment, lack of enmity, and lack of ignorance, line 29 ("There are many conditions that will become manifest here," nikaḻvaṉa ētup pala uḷa) must refer to the plurality of good or beneficial conditions apparent in Maṇimēkalai's impending deeds of nonattachment and nonenmity in the city of Pukār. Maṇimēkalai's appeasing of the cursed Kāyacaṇṭikai's hunger (xvii.17–20) might be interpreted as an act of compassion (adosa), as might her persuading of the king to turn the royal prison into an ascetic's residence (xvii.155–162) and her act of forgiving the queen for acts of treachery (xvii.92–147). Her selfless giving to the poor (e.g., xvii.91–98) and her final release from attraction to the prince through Utayakumaraṉ's sudden death (xx.104–107) might similarly be read as manifestations of Maṇimēkalai's lack of attachment (alobha).

If the manifestation of ētu in the city of Pukār is thus represented principally through good works of charity, selflessness, and compassion closely associated with the states generated by the beneficial root conditions of nonattachment and nonenmity, the ētu encompassing knowledge (amoha) is spatially tied to the city of Kāñcīpuram, to the place where Maṇimēkalai will comprehend fully the doctrinal teachings of the Buddha and undertake a life of complete renunciation. In connection with the future manifestations of ētu in Kāñcīpuram, the text often includes the word "whole" or "all" (*yāvum*), thus implying that the karmically beneficial states will occur in their fullest sense only in the city of Kāñcī at the feet of the Buddhist teacher, Aṟavaṇaṉ. At xii.104–107, for example, Aṟavaṇaṉ tells Maṇimēkalai directly that the complete emergence of ētu will come about for her only in that particular city. He adds that only through this full manifestation will she be able to comprehend the dharma, that is, gain true freedom from delusion:

All the manifestations of the conditions (ētunikaḻcci yāvum) will occur for you in this city;
they [the manifestations] are many (pala uḷa).
Oh lady like a flower-bearing creeper,
unless those [conditions] have become manifest there (*nikaḻnta* . . . allatu),
you will not be able to hear the doctrines of the Buddha.

The same wording is repeated at xxi.159–160, where Tuvatikaṉ, the painting on the temple pillar, foretells the future. After indicating that Maṇimēkalai will go to the city of Kāñcīpuram, discard her disguise, and distribute food from her bowl to the hungry masses (xxi.155–158), Tuvatikaṉ adds:

All the manifestations of the conditions (ētunikaḻcci yāvum) will appear, along with dharma, in that city for the lady wearing beautiful bangles;
they [the manifestations] are many (pala uḷa).

Here, the precise meaning of "along with dharma" (*aṟaṉoṭu*) is not clear. The dharma or teachings of the Buddha are omnipresent and do not suddenly become "manifest." Perhaps, as at vii.19–20, dharma refers more specifically to the path of dharma that is identified with the Buddha himself (*āticāṉ muṉivaṉ* aṟavaḻip *paṭūum*). In other words, the manifestation of karmically beneficial states enables Maṇimēkalai to embark upon the path (*vaḻi*) to true knowledge and liberation.

The term ētu also occurs once in a negative context that makes explicit the connection between the manifestation of such healthy karmic states and the cessation of the continual processes of rebirth. At ix.51–53, Maṇimēkalai recalls the words of the great Buddhist sage, Piramatarumaṉ (Brahmadharma), who, in her past life, foretold of her death and current rebirth in the city of Pukār:

Because there is no manifestation of the [beneficial] conditions here
[in this birth] (ētunikaḻcci *īṅku iṉṟu* ātaliṉ),
you will take [another] birth in the ancient city of unceasing joy that bears the name of Kavēra's daughter [Pukār or Kāvirippūmpaṭṭiṉam].

Here, the text makes clear the necessity of the good conditions made manifest to ending the cyclic processes of death and rebirth. Because of the previous lack of such manifestations, Maṇimēkalai was compelled to take her present birth, a birth in which her matured ētus will eventually appear in their fullest form in Kāñcīpuram.

A number of themes thus emerge from the *Maṇimēkalai*'s narrative use of the term ētu, themes that suggest the beneficial root conditions as the source for the text's understanding of the word. First, the ētus that "mature" and become "manifest" are efficacious, initiating events crucial to both the overall narrative sequence and the central character's spiritual progress: Maṇimēkalai's first knowledge of human suffering and subsequent shedding of tears; Maṇimēkalā's transporting of her namesake to Maṇipallavam, where Maṇimēkalai gains insight into her past lives and thus begins her journey toward eventual renunciation; the dawning of Maṇimēkalai's ability to comprehend Buddhist teachings; and the coming of the great sage, Aṟavaṇaṉ, to Kāñcīpuram.[97] Second, the maturation and manifestation of ētu are closely associated with the path of Buddhist dharma, with the capacity to understand the Buddha's teachings and undertake the life of renunciation and reflection that leads ultimately to liberation. Finally, the manifestation of ētu is absolutely necessary to achieving that final goal of liberation; as the last example indicates, the text uses the phrase "manifestation of beneficial conditions" (ētunikaḻcci) to indicate a turning point in Maṇimēkalai's long sequence of human existences, past, present, and future. The maturation and manifestation of ētu signals the awakening of right knowledge and right action that leads inevitably to the final scene of Maṇimēkalai's renunciation, and eventually, as one learns at xxi.175–179, to her (male) rebirth as the future Buddha's chief disciple.

Although few Buddhist stories in any language can be said to develop this concept of the manifestation of beneficial conditions or its Pāli equivalents in such detail, certainly the *Maṇimēkalai* reflects a common Buddhist narrative concern with readiness to hear and comprehend the dharma of the Buddha, with the development of the capacity to achieve liberation (*nibbāna*) from rebirth. In a world in which the "passageway to the great path that leads to salvation without end is blocked with *kuśa* grass and cow's thorn" (*Maṇimēkalai*, xii.59–60), who is capable of comprehending the teachings? Who is destined to become a worthy one (arahant), to renounce the world of ordinary human existence and follow the Buddha? How do such individuals become ready to receive the Buddha's instruction? From the story of Gautama's awakening to the awakenings of the many Buddhas who preceded him, the first, and, indeed, formulaic question for the Buddha newly enlightened under the bodhi tree is: "To whom should I teach the dharma?"[98]

In the host of stories concerning the Buddha and the lives of his contemporaries found in the *Jātaka*, the *Theragāthā* and the *Therīgāthā*, the *Vimānavatthu*, and their respective commentaries, as well as in the *Dhammapada-aṭṭhakathā*, for example, the Buddha is often said to survey the world at dawn, searching for the individual who is ready for his assistance, seeking out the one who is fit to approach enlightenment. In the case of Maṭṭhakuṇḍali, for example, the dying son mercilessly pushed outside the house by a miserly father, the Buddha rises from his meditation on the great compassion (*mahākaruṇāsamāpatti*) to look about the world, searching for those whose good root conditions (kusalamūla) render them ready to receive his assistance:

> On that day, very early in the morning, the Bhagavā arose from his meditation of the great compassion and, for the purpose of seeing those who had made a resolve under previous Buddhas, those whose beneficial roots were abundant, those who were ready to receive the teaching, he surveyed the world with his Buddha-eye and extended his net of knowledge (*ñāṇajāla*) over the ten thousand worlds.[99]

Like Maṇimēkalai, whose beneficial causes or conditions become "abundant" (ētunikaḻcci . . . pala uḷa) in Kāñcīpuram as she listens to Aṟavaṇaṉ's teachings, Maṭṭhakuṇḍali will attain "realization of the dharma" (*dharmādhisamaya*) and become "one who has entered the stream" (*sotāpanna*)[100] on hearing the Buddha recite a single verse from the *Dhammapada*. He is ready, like Maṇimēkalai, to hear and comprehend fully the Buddha's teachings.

In similar fashion, the story of the conversion of Aṅgulimāla, often portrayed as "a most compassionate and wonderful act of the Buddha,"[101] centers upon the robber's capacity for attaining enlightenment (upanissaya) despite his present course of violence and cruelty. Like Maṭṭhakuṇḍali, so potent is this potential for enlightenment that the hearing of a single stanza of teaching will suffice to transform Aṅgulimāla's wretched life completely: "At this time Budha was residing in Jētāwana wihāra, and he saw that

Aṅgulimāla, from the merit he had received in former births, had virtue sufficient to enter the priesthood, and become a rahat, on the hearing of a single stanza of bana."[102] The Buddha intervenes in this cruelly violent life, and Aṅgulimāla is transformed into a trusted monk, eventually achieving liberation.

This image of the compassionate Buddha converting those who are karmically ready is repeated again and again in stories of the Buddha and his followers. As in the Tamil *Maṇimēkalai*, the arising of the good conditions conducive to enlightenment (upanissaya) entails entry into the life of a Buddhist renunciant and eventual attainment of enlightenment. Only when knowledge has ripened and virtue matured, the capacity to become a worthy one firmly established over many lifetimes, does the Buddha help his followers toward their own enlightenment. One particularly poignant story in the *Dhammapada* commentary, that of Erakapatta,[103] who was once a young monk and is now reborn as a Nāga king because of the seemingly small crime of having broken off the leaf of an *eraka* tree, illustrates the importance of the beneficial conditions as definitive of human existence, embodying the first prerequisite for Buddhahood. Throughout the tale, the one-time monk laments bitterly his "causeless birth" (*ahetukajoni*), for such a birth renders him incapable of hearing the dharma and seeing a Buddha.[104] When the Buddha does appear and expound the teachings, it is said that Erakapatta, the king of the Nāgas, would have attained the "fruit of entering the stream" (*sotāpattiphala*) had he not possessed an animal nature.[105] It is Erakapatta's current "causeless" (*ahetuka*) state that does not allow for the arising of the three karmically beneficial states of nonattachment, nonenmity, and knowledge.

Although it might be noted that at least one significant difference between these Pāli narratives and the Tamil *Maṇimēkalai* is the absence in the latter of a living Buddha who is present to teach the dharma to the young girl who is, by narrative's end, ready to hear it, a number of Pāli stories make clear the fact that other beings are capable of aiding those whose wisdom and virtue mature in the absence of the Buddha. In the *Dhammapada* commentary, for example, the story of the female lay disciple,[106] who perceives that a certain group of monks are capable of achieving the status of worthy ones, even while they are all mired in the bonds of greed (here termed *rāga*), enmity, and delusion,[107] illustrates the critical role that material sustenance—food, shelter, and clothing—and proper companions play in assisting those whose are karmically ready to travel the path toward enlightenment. In Dhammapāla's commentary on the *Vimānavatthu*,[108] to cite another collection of relevant stories, it is often Sāriputta, Mahāmoggallāna, or Anuruddha who surveys the world and wonders whom he might assist.[109] In the *Maṇimēkalai*, two characters in particular play the role of help mate or instructor in the dharma: the goddess, Maṇimēkalā,[110] who brings her charge to Maṇipallavam so that she might behold the seat of the Buddha and remember her former lives,[111] and the teacher, Aṟavaṇaṉ, who instructs her in the philosophical elements of the dharma.

To return to the ētu theme in the *Maṇimēkalai*, the maturation and manifestation of those conditions that render the title character karmically ready to hear the dharma provide an overarching and consistent structure to the main narrative. As mentioned previously, the manifestation of the absence of greed or lust (alobha) is apparent in Maṇimēkalai's benevolent use of Amutacurapi to appease Kāyacaṇṭikai's hunger and feed the hungry masses, as well as in her eventual severing of emotional ties to her former husband and current suitor. In Maṇimēkalai's compassionate conversion of the queen (a woman who three times attempts to kill Maṇimēkalai or drive her mad) and through her insistence that the king turn the royal prison into a residence hall for ascetics, the emergence of pity, compassion, and lack of enmity (adosa) becomes clear. In the final two chapters of the text, with Aṟavaṇaṉ's instruction in Buddhist logic and causal theory through philosophical analysis, one witnesses the dawning of knowledge (amoha), the starting point for a life of renunciation, meditation, and eventual liberation.[112]

In fact, Aṟavaṇaṉ's final instruction to Maṇimēkalai before she makes her vow addresses directly the elimination of the three unwholesome (*akusala*) conditions, namely attachment or greed (*lobha*), ill will (*dosa*), and ignorance (*moha*). Aṟavaṇaṉ first explains that greed, anger, and mental delusion are the conditions that perpetuate the cycle of interdependent origination (xxx.252–253), and he then exhorts Maṇimēkalai (xxx.254–260) to:

> Analyze separately impermanence, suffering, absence of soul, and impurity,
> and eradicate attachment.[113]
> Knowing love, compassion, and bliss, eradicate enmity[114]
> through refined, good consciousness [meditation].
> By contemplating and experiencing the teachings, meditation, mental
> effort and true vision, eradicate mental delusion.[115]
> Through these four categories [of practice],
> dispel darkness of mind!

Now that all three of the beneficial conditions conducive to liberation have become manifest for Maṇimēkalai, Aṟavaṇaṉ instructs her that she is prepared to undertake those practices required to eradicate forever the three unwholesome or detrimental conditions. Immediately after this command of Aṟavaṇaṉ, Maṇimēkalai makes her final vow of renunciation.

These consistent references to the manifestation of beneficial conditions conducive to enlightenment also provide a thematically significant backdrop for the *Maṇimēkalai*'s continual emphasis upon karma (Tamil *viṉai*) or, in the context of interdependent origination, "volition" (ceykai). The good conditions (Pāli kusalamūla, Tamil nallētu), as those factors that determine the qualitative nature of karma—the bad leading to endless rebirths and the good to ultimate liberation—serve to explain the transformation of Maṇimēkalai's karmic state as witnessed in the narrative. Although a variety of deeds from past lives have led directly to Maṇimēkalai's situation in the present-tense narrative, her present actions culminate in the "full" (yāvum) manifestation of the good conditions (nallētu) and subsequent renunciation. In the future-tense narrative supplied by the pillar painting, Tuvatikaṉ (xxi.173–179), all mention of karmic cause and effect, karmic retribution and reward, is noticeably absent (although karma continues to be discussed in the narrative present after Tuvatikaṉ's revelation). The implication is that Maṇimēkalai, after the vow taken at the close of the narrative, will simply live out her karma accumulated from past births, being born again and again as a man until that store of karma is exhausted and she attains birth at the feet of the future Buddha:

> After performing many proper, virtuous deeds,
> your life will end in Kacci [Kāñcī].
> All [your future] births will take place in the north, in Makatam,
> and, [being born as a] man, you will not stray from the good dharma.
> Nobly born and destroying all illusions,
> you will become the chief disciple of the one who graciously teaches the
> dharma to others.

The final and full manifestation of these conditions (ētunikal̲cci) thus signals the end of the accumulation of karma for Maṇimēkalai. The narrative implies here that future deeds are of little karmic consequence. Maṇimēkalai will simply follow the dharma of the Buddha and gradually deplete her store of unwholesome karma until she is reborn as the chief disciple of the coming Buddha.

The manifestation of conditions conducive to liberation also serves to provide a framework for the narrative's complex structure, its many plots, subplots, and stories of events from past lives that have all led, in one way or another, to this transformation of Maṇimēkalai's karmic state. The multitude of circumstances necessary to change Maṇimēkalai from an ordinary, karma-accumulating being into a renunciant on the path to liberation serves as an example, in narrative form, of the intricate mesh of conditions necessary to the arising of the beneficial states.[116] Through the intricately intertwined web of events described in the narrative, the text vividly demonstrates that taking up the path of Buddhist dharma and the life of renunciation with the goal of enlightenment is not simply the result of a single intention or act of will but rather the culmination of many conditions, prerequisite events, and phenomena interwoven across many lifetimes.

The *Maṇimēkalai*'s use of ētu and ētunikal̲cci ties the text together not only in a narrative and thematic sense but also in an even more basic structural way. As discussed previously, the analytic and doctrinal knowledge expressed in chapters 29 and 30 represents a critical manifestation of knowledge (amoha), the third of the beneficial root conditions leading to enlightenment. Comprehension of inferential modes of reasoning and interdependent origination constitutes the culmination of ētunikal̲cci as the *Maṇimēkalai* presents it; Ar̲avaṇan̲ implies as much in the narrative when he states that all (yāvum) the manifestations will appear for Maṇimēkalai in Kāñcīpuram, site of the final teachings. Without the final two chapters of the text, the *Maṇimēkalai*'s presentation of ētu would be incomplete, lacking the final and crucial arising of true knowledge.

The manifestation of beneficial conditions conducive to renunciation and eventual liberation thus ties the text of the *Maṇimēkalai* together in several ways, providing a consistent thematic and narrative structure and the key to understanding the transformation of the main character from a beautiful, young courtesan-in-the-making to the determined ascetic who vows to renounce the world in the final lines of the text. Maṇimēkalai herself is borne along by the maturation and blossoming of the conditions necessary for her enlightenment; in the narrative prose of the text, ētunikal̲cci plays the role of a principal—if seldom foregrounded—character, at work behind the scenes to move the heroine toward her final act of renunciation. Yet the *Maṇimēkalai* does not simply lay out an uncomplicated narrative of a young girl's karmic metamorphosis. Indeed, as Richman's work so aptly demonstrates, the main narrative that culminates in the act of renunciation is interwoven with sixteen subplots, or branch stories, intertwined with tales of kings and princes, courtesans and merchants, and unchaste women and slovenly barbarians. Although the ētunikal̲cci theme ties together both the narrative and philosophical portions of the text and provides a framework in which to read the many subplots, certainly the ētu theme alone cannot illuminate fully the rich complexity and poetic art of the *Maṇimēkalai* text and its elegance of language and detail. It is to the art of the text, to the manner in which the story is told and the ways in which an audience might receive it, that the discussion now turns, in an attempt to examine how one might actually read the text as both poetry and philosophy, as both imaginative narrative and Buddhist doctrine.

The Literary Art of the Text

The *Maṇimēkalai* is a complex text rich in detail, imagery, and allusion; as such, there are no doubt several ways in which to interpret the text as a whole. Ētu and ētunikalcci serve to draw various parts of the text together with a relatively straightforward, consistent theme, but what of all the details, the many narratives within that narrative, the plots and subplots that envelop this principal narrative theme? Is the overtly doctrinal closing of the text best understood simply as an illustration of the content of Maṇimēkalai's dawning knowledge (amoha)? If one is to attend to the nature of the text as ornate poetry and its traditional classification as such, interpretation must push beyond consideration of directly stated theme to appreciate the manner in which the poetic text unfolds. In short, interpreting *Maṇimēkalai* becomes a question of how to read the text as literary art, of how to make sense of its intricacies of plot, its dramatic language and aesthetic appeal.

First, one must return briefly to consider the question of reader or audience. As noted previously, virtually nothing can be said about the historical reception of the text, about the real audience that first read or heard the work of that empirical author, Cāttaṉār. Despite the dearth of reliable names and dates, however, the *Maṇimēkalai* itself appears to anticipate a certain audience, one that is well-versed in both Tamil and Sanskrit literature and poetic theory, and sophisticated in its understanding and appreciation of Buddhist doctrine. Regarding such a model or implied reader/audience, it must also be noted that the audience envisioned by modern Anglo-American literary criticism—the solitary reader gazing at the printed page—is perhaps the least likely to be assumed by any classical South Asian text, including the *Maṇimēkalai*. The preface to the *Maṇimēkalai*, for example, portrays the text as originating in a public recitation before the king.[117] Line 98 of the preface, as well as one of the oldest surviving manuscripts of the text,[118] refers to the individual chapters of the narrative as song (*pāṭṭu*)[119] rather than story (katai, from the Sanskrit kathā) as in the later manuscripts and printed editions, thus perhaps suggesting a tradition of musical performance of the text. The preface (line 87) of the *Cilappatikāram*, the Tamil narrative closest to the *Maṇimēkalai* in style and genre, describes the text as verse interspersed with prose passages meant for recitation (*urai iṭai iṭṭa pāṭṭuṭaic ceyyuḷ*).[120] Indeed, the introduction of readily available printed texts is a wholly modern phenomenon in India, and it can quite easily be surmised that a premodern text such as the *Maṇimēkalai* was originally intended to be recited, sung, or performed before its audience.[121]

To envision an audience of listeners rather than individual readers need not contradict the previous assertion that the text anticipates a reception by the thoroughly sophisticated. As several recent studies of language and the ethnography of reading have demonstrated, literacy, as the ability to interpret the written word on the page, is not necessarily the best measure of literary sophistication in settings where writing is used sparingly and texts are transmitted orally. Sudipta Kaviraj, for example, in his discussion of language and identity formation in India, notes that in traditional South Asian contexts, "the distinction between literate and oral is not homologous to the one between educated and illiterate."[122] In a similar vein, Nancy Florida notes that in precolonial Javanese society, a setting in which access to the written word was reserved for the "professional literati,"[123] traditions of oral performance allowed for a "*literate* audience . . . [that] included persons who were 'illiterate' in the narrower sense of the word, and yet, through practiced and sensitive listening, had become highly conversant with literature."[124] James Baker's work in Indonesia demonstrates the highly complex ways in which meaning can be derived from oral performance, even when the audience neither speaks nor comprehends the language of the text (in this case, the Arabic of the Qu'ran).[125] Such studies suggest a potentially wider audience for a text such as the *Maṇimēkalai* than might initially be imagined. If one assumes an "illiterate" audience well-versed in poetic styles and conventions through oral performance, one need not assume that the *Maṇimēkalai* was intended only for the literary elite or professional literati of the courts.

Cāminātaiyar's autobiography offers some interesting historical glimpses of the manner in which Tamil texts were recited and performed in South India during the late nineteenth century. In his efforts to understand the manuscripts of the ninth-century Jain work, *Cīvakacintāmaṇi*, for example, Cāminātaiyar recounts how he stumbled upon the final day of a sixth-month recitation and explication of the full text in a local Jain community. He notes that "as we [Hindus] hold readings of epics like the *Rāmāyaṇam* and celebrate Rāma's coronation, so do the Jains regard *Cīvakacintāmaṇi* and celebrate the completion of the reading of that book with joyous festivities."[126] His most telling accounts, however, deal with his beloved father's public recitations of primarily Śaiva texts and the reactions of his audiences. To cite but one example, Cāminātaiyar remembers his father's performance of a contemporary devotional work known as *Nantaṉār Carittiram* when Cāminātaiyar himself was a boy of twelve or thirteen:

> When my father was giving his performance of *Nantaṉār Carittiram* at Kaḷattūr, Citampara Uṭaiyār was one among the audience who listened to it. . . . Because the rich gentleman was such a devotee of Śiva he was so eager to listen to the series on Nantaṉār's history and did not miss even a single day's discourse. His heart melted at the story of Nantaṉ. . . . As the narration of the story went on, he could not keep back his tears: he would listen, enraptured, transformed with emotion, hair standing on end. He identified with the hero, Nantaṉār . . . and he would weep.[127]

The issue of the audience's experience of any given text, the problem of how a text is received and the manner in which such experience is generated, constitutes a central concern of Indian poetic theory in both the Tamil and Sanskrit literary traditions. What is it in Cāminātaiyar's father's recitation of the *Nantaṉār Carittiram* that compels his listeners to weep, to identify with the hero, to be "transformed with emotion"? In a manner similar to modern Anglo-American reader-response criticism,[128] Indian poetic theory may be characterized as thoroughly concerned with the effect of the text on the reader and with the elements within the text that produce such an effect. The poem, narrative, or song is not an objective statement to be mined for meaning but the source of a human experience on the part of the reader or audience. As Tompkins summarizes the most basic assumption of all reader-response criticism, "a poem cannot be understood apart from its results."[129]

Those "results," in the Sanskrit tradition of literary criticism, are discussed in terms of raw emotion (*bhāva*) and heightened mood (rasa), and, in Tamil literary theory, as the psychophysical manifestations of emotion (*meyppāṭu*, literally "appearing in the body").[130] Like the two levels of narrative reader described by Eco, the first wanting simply to appreciate the narrative and see how the story ends and the second concerning himself with the interpretive signs imbedded in the text that serve "as a guide for the reader,"[131] raw emotion and heightened mood can be conceived as representing distinct levels of appreciating a poetic text or drama: raw emotion (bhāva) as a "first level apprehension of the concrete elements of the play"[132] and heightened mood (rasa) as the second level "medium of experience" or heightened "emotional awareness."[133] As Abhinavagupta, the great Sanskrit literary theoretician of the tenth century, defines the sensitive reader (*sahṛdaya*, literally "he who has his heart with it"), the full experience of heightened mood is available only to the genuine connoisseur of literature: "The word *sahṛdaya* . . . denotes persons who are capable of identifying with the subject matter, as the mirror of their hearts has been polished by the constant study and practice of poetry, and who respond to it sympathetically in their own hearts."[134] Although predating Abhinavagupta's commentary on the *Dhvanyāloka* of Ānandavardhana by at least five centuries, the Tamil *Tolkāppiyam* similarly reserves its psychophysical experience of emotion generated by literature (meyppāṭu) for the educated few. As the final stanza of the *Tolkāppiyam*'s discussion of mood or emotional awareness clearly indicates, the experience of the refined state of emotional intuition is reserved only for those sophisticated in the second-level order of reading:

> The meyppāṭu of good quality cannot be comprehended
> except by those who possess proper perspective
> [and] through proper observation and hearing.[135]

Although a full discussion of the development of Sanskrit theories of heightened mood, from its earliest attestation in Bharata's second-century *Nāṭyaśāstra* through the conflation of dramatic and poetic art forms in Ānandavardhana's ninth-century *Dhvanyāloka* and Abhinavagupta's *Locana*,[136] as well as the elaboration of its Tamil counterpart,[137] lies far beyond the scope of this project, it is useful to note here that George Hart's work convincingly argues that Tamil and Sanskrit poetics developed hand-in-hand, each influencing the other over the course of many centuries.[138] Certainly, it requires no great stretch of the historical imagination to assume that the real or empirical author of a sixth-century text such as the *Maṇimēkalai* would have been thoroughly versed in both the Sanskrit and Tamil theories of textual reception as they then existed, thoroughly concerned with producing in his audience certain emotional moods, certain effects or experiences.

If one can assume, then, in a historically responsible way that an ornate poetic text such as the *Maṇimēkalai* that combines narrative and doctrinal exposition seeks to elicit a response from its audience, an "experience,"[139] what might the nature of that experience be?[140] Perhaps a clue to the character of the response that the text seeks to evoke can be found in the placement of its overtly doctrinal chapters, particularly the final chapter that expounds the Buddhist causal theory of interdependent origination. The place of that discussion, at the very end of the narrative, exemplifying the fullest manifestation of the beneficial or wholesome qualities that compel Maṇimēkalai to make her renunciatory vow, suggests the interdependent origination discussion to be in some way the culmination of Maṇimēkalai's story, the climax of the text as a whole. Yet the thirtieth chapter concerning the twelve elements in the chain of causation (Tamil cārpu) is so extremely terse, so densely packed with technical terminology, that it is difficult to imagine any audience immediately making sense of it. How could such an opaque doctrinal discussion lend itself in any way to an experience other than complete frustration?

The answer to the problem posed by the doctrinal end to such an elegant poetic narrative may well lie in the relationship between the narrative and philosophical portions of the *Maṇimēkalai* text. The final discussion of interdependent origination takes place not in a vacuum, not as a mere addendum to an original plotline, but at the close of twenty-seven chapters of narrative that have, in several different ways, prepared their audience to comprehend, not merely at an intellectual level but in a profoundly experiential or intuitive way, the transience and interconnectedness that lie at the heart of human existence as explained by the doctrine of interdependent origination. The narrative, in short, paves the way for its audience to comprehend fully the causal processes outlined in the closing chapter. The text is carefully crafted to provide the audience that receives it with a common experience of the momentary, transient quality of existence, the profound interdependence of all moments and phenomena, and the moral values implied by such interdependence. It is this experience, developed through the narrative itself and the emotional/experiential awareness it evokes, that is then organized and defined in terms of karma, impermanence, and the elements in the causal chain of interdependent origination at the close of the text. The narrative is carefully constructed to compel its readers to appreciate, to know intuitively the truth of the life processes underlying this final doctrinal exposition.

Among the model author's techniques in this regard, the signs that he imbeds within the text to allow his reader to reflect on the conditioned arising of events and phenomena, is the characterization of Maṇimēkalai herself. As the story's heroine, Maṇimēkalai seems to have little to do with the central events that shape the narrative drama and the course of her own life. Buffeted about by circumstances that seem beyond her control and compelled throughout by others to act in certain ways, Maṇimēkalai, the beautiful young girl about to embark on a life of renunciation, never seems to decide anything for herself. She hesitates at crucial junctures in the plot; she is torn between her general interest in Buddhist teachings and her specific attraction to the strapping young prince.

It is Mātavi, Maṇimēkalai's mother, for example, and not Maṇimēkalai herself, who decides that the young girl will forego her hereditary occupation in favor of following the Buddha (ii.55–57):

> Maṇimēkalai will perform austerities.
> She will not be allowed, even for an instant,
> to engage in such a vile occupation [as that of the courtesan].

When Maṇimēkalai sheds tears and ruins the flower garland she is weaving, it is again Mātavi who sends the girl off to gather fresh blossoms (iii.14–15), thus setting in motion the chain of events whereby her daughter will be pursued relentlessly by the young prince. When Maṇimēkalai first sets eyes upon Utayakumaraṉ in the Uvavaṉam, her friend, Cutamati, must push her into hiding in the crystal chamber; Cutamati actually forces her to stay there by locking the door (iv.87–88).

Even after Maṇimēkalai is set firmly upon the Buddhist path by her namesake goddess, various catalysts emerge to prod her to her final renunciation. Transported to the island of Maṇipallavam by the goddess (who is herself compelled to act by the impending maturation of beneficial conditions, as discussed previously), Maṇimēkalai receives the wondrous bowl Amutacurapi almost by accident, as it emerges annually from Kōmuki Lake on the anniversary of the birth and enlightenment of the Buddha (xi.43–47). Tīvatilakai must instruct the young girl to seek out a virtuous person to place the first alms in the bowl (xi.119–122). It is Aṟavaṇaṉ who commands Maṇimēkalai to put the bowl to good use, warning her that "it is not proper . . . to conceal the dharmic vessel that can alleviate the great distress of this wide world [that now suffers in] poverty" (xv.53–54); Ātirai, the virtuous woman who activates the generative powers of the bowl, repeats the command at xvi.132–135. Maṇimēkalai's perhaps most publicly beneficent act, encouraging the king of Pukār to replace the royal prison with a hospice for the poor, occurs only after she has been brought before the king under armed guard (xix.141). At every turn, the text clearly points to other characters, to the maturation and manifestation of ētu, to general circumstances and conditions seemingly beyond Maṇimēkalai's control as the agents propelling the principal character through the narrative. Her entry into Vañci in the guise of a male ascetic is done at Maṇimēkalā's suggestion (xxvi.68–71), for example. Even Maṇimēkalai's final public act of compassion and benevolence, the feeding of the starving residents of Kāñcī and the erection of a glorious shrine replicating Maṇipallavam, is done at someone else's command, in this case, Mācāttuvāṉ, who instructs his young granddaughter: "It is your duty to appear in that city, like a raincloud, and protect [and feed the starving]!" (xxviii.160–161). Indeed, one of the very few times in which Maṇimēkalai appears to act decisively on her own, by assuming the form of the haggard Kāyacaṇṭikai to avoid Utayakumaraṉ (xix.31–34), ultimately ends in the prince's violent death.

The early sense of intrigue surrounding Maṇimēkalai and Utayakumaraṉ indicates a larger pattern of tension—between predilection for the ascetic life and awakening sexuality—present in the protagonist's character throughout the narrative. Although Cutamati, for example, confidently announces that her friend will remain unmoved by the prince's masculine charms (v.13–15), Maṇimēkalai is, in fact, immediately drawn to Utayakumaraṉ (v.86–89):

> [He] has slighted me.
> He wanted to have me [by suggesting that] I have no virtue,
> that I am unaware of true penance,
> that I follow no code of conduct,
> and that I am a prostitute.
> In spite of all [these dreadful] things [that he said],
> my heart went out to this stranger.

The troubled young girl is delivered from the scene of her distress only when Maṇimēkalā whisks her off to Maṇipallavam (vii.210–214). After learning there of previous lifetimes spent in Utayakumaraṉ's company (e.g., in their incarnations as Ilakkumi and Irākulaṉ), Maṇimēkalai's only question is: "Where is my husband now?" (x.19). As late as the eighteenth chapter, after Maṇimēkalai has received Amutacurapi, donned the guise of a Buddhist female ascetic (Pāli *bhikkhunī*, Tamil *pikkuṇi*), and distributed food to the hungry masses of Pukār, the prince is still capable of throwing the young girl into turmoil. When he approaches to ask why she has taken up the ascetic life, she is nervous and confused,[141] hurriedly says a few words about the nature of the human body and suffering, and then flees into a nearby temple (xviii.126–145). Indeed, the only resolution to

Maṇimēkalai's inner conflict between renunciation and sexual attraction comes about with the death of the prince through a case of mistaken identity (xx.102–107). When Utayakumaraṉ is killed, Maṇimēkalai mourns him as "My beloved!" (xxi.22).

The text thus presents its audience with a main character whose own actions and motives in the present-tense narrative contribute little to the development of the plot or to the growth of the character herself as she moves toward her final act of renunciation. Critical events occur regardless of the heroine's own volition: Maṇimēkalai's turning away from the courtesan life, her entry into the Buddha's flower park, her remembrance of past lives, her public service with Amutacurapi, or even the resolution of her conflict with the prince. As Aṟavaṇaṉ teaches in the final chapter, the elements in the causal processes of interdependent origination (cārpu), beginning with ignorance and volition and leading to craving and clinging, arise in a continuous "circle without end" (xxx.118), regardless of human intention: "there is no relationship between the agent and the thing done" (xxx.231). Maṇimēkalai, as central agent of the narrative, remains largely passive, whereas other circumstances, actions, events, and people shape the course of her story.

The passivity of Maṇimēkalai's character, in combination with the prediction made by Tuvatikaṉ that the young girl is destined to be reborn as the Buddha's chief disciple (xxi.175–179), raises a challenging question about the role of individual effort or personal moral striving in Buddhist conceptions of the process of spiritual liberation. This process of prediction inevitably fulfilled constitutes a common theme in narratives about Buddhas past, present, and future. In the *Buddhavaṁsa* and its commentary, for example, a great deal of attention is paid to the story of Sumedha, the Gautama Buddha-to-be, and his future as the Buddha is foretold in some detail.[142] In a similar way, the stories of the Buddha and his followers that frame the Jātaka tales might be said to lend an air of inevitability to each of the stories of the past; the audience realizes from the outset that all the virtuous protagonists, from Apaṇṇaka to Vessantara, are destined eventually to become the Buddha, and such characters, therefore, must act in accordance with that future. In the *Maṇimēkalai*, the young girl's future as a great ascetic is foretold at the very moment of her birth (vii.36–37), and it is Tuvatikaṉ's account of future events that is said to "relieve" Maṇimēkalai of "her delusions of mind" (xxi.189).

In addition to this general passivity that attaches to Maṇimēkalai, to this lack of decisive participation in the very events that propel the narrative along, the concrete descriptions of Maṇimēkalai also contribute to an audience experience of transience, of the interdependence among all moments and phenomena. Who, in fact, is the docile Maṇimēkalai? The answer appears to change, depending on the narrative context, on the circumstances or conditions. Her identity is, in fact, often hard to pin down.

The text continually describes Maṇimēkalai as beautiful and sexually alluring, even as she wanders the streets of Pukār distributing food to the needy. She is perhaps most often described as "she who wears choice ornaments" (*āyiḻai*); often she is referred to as "young creeper" (*iḷaṅkoṭi*), calling to mind the beautiful suppleness of her young body. Her beauty disarms even Kāmaṉ, the god of desire (iii.20–23); her long tresses are consistently described as adorned with fragrant flowers.[143] Several references are made, the last very late in the narrative, just as Maṇimēkalai is about to receive doctrinal instruction from Aṟavaṇaṉ, to the beauty of her genitalia (xxviii.220). Maṇimēkalai, ultimately bound for an ascetic life, does virtually nothing one might expect to prepare herself physically for her future as a renunciant: her head remains unshaven, she continues to adorn herself with flowers, she bedecks herself with jewels, and she wanders about the streets of the city.

Her identity is further confused by the power she gains from the mantra given to her by the goddess, Maṇimēkalā: the power to assume any form or disguise at will (x.80–82). When the young girl makes her debut as a beggar on the city streets, it is in the guise of a Buddhist ascetic (pikkuṉik *kōlam*; xv.55–58). As noted previously, her assumption of the form of Kāyacaṇṭikai (xviii.149–150) directly precipitates the confusion that leads to the prince's violent death at the hands of Kāyacaṇṭikai's husband. In the aftermath of that tragic event, Maṇimēkalai assumes the form of a man to thwart the grieving queen's attempts to discredit her (xxiii.43–57). Later, she arrives in Vañci to learn of non-Buddhist doctrines in the guise of a male sage (xxvi.68–71). The mantra of the goddess allows Maṇimēkalai to appear in various guises, although often she must be prompted by others to assume a different form; in at least one instance, the assumption of another form leads directly to a violent death.

Not only does Maṇimēkalai assume various forms or guises in the present tense, but throughout the narrative one learns only gradually of her past lives or forms. Indeed, at one point Maṇimēkalai herself seems a bit confused as to her true identity. When Tīvatilakai, the guardian of Kōmuki Lake and Amutacurapi, first asks, "Who are you?" Maṇimēkalai is uncertain how to respond. She replies, "In which birth do you mean?" and proceeds to identify herself in terms of both past and present existences (xi.9–14). As David Shulman notes in his comments on Āputtiraṉ, dawning knowledge of past lives revealed in fits and starts creates an often frightening atmosphere of disorientation in the *Maṇimēkalai*: "the Tamil Buddhist exploration of the cognitive experience of reincarnation finds the resulting awareness to be baffling, even terrifying."[144] Who is this Maṇimēkalai? Is she the unadorned female ascetic or a beautifully adorned courtesan-in-the-making? Is she the sexually awakened young woman or the firmly committed Buddhist ascetic?

Early in the narrative, the text provides one brief but critical hint as to how its audience must come to understand and appreciate its central character as complicated and multidimensional, as impossible to comprehend from a single point of view or in any static way. The text pointedly suggests that Maṇimēkalai, with all her inner contradictions and complexities, cannot be understood fully in the present tense alone or from any one interpretive or analytic angle. When Cutamati first encounters Prince Utayakumaraṉ in the Buddha's flower park, she describes Maṇimēkalai as follows (v.15–16):

> This lady who wears golden bangles
> has achieved mature powers (Sanskrit *tapas*, Tamil *ūḻtarutavattaḷ*).
> She wields arrows made of curses (*cāpacaratti*).[145]

Nothing in the narrative thus far justifies Cutamati's assessment of her friend. The audience must assume, from this point onward, that there are significant dimensions to both the story and its heroine that have not yet been revealed. Maṇimēkalai's motivations and actions can be understood, the text suggests, only in relation to other stories, other events and deeds, that will come into focus as the narrative progresses. The young girl trembling in fear inside the crystal chamber as the prince advances is certainly no arrow-wielding ascetic of "mature powers"; her existence is determined by and must be understood as the result of previous conditions and circumstances that are presently hidden from view.

As Aṟavaṇaṉ describes interdependent origination, the arising of the twelve links in the causal chain extends over the course of several tenses or lifetimes: past, present, and future (xxx.159–168). The full complexity of that chain of causes and conditions, he continues, can be fully comprehended only through examining it from many angles, from many points of view: the six designations (*vaḻakku*), the four methods (*nayam*), and the four questions and answers (*viṉāviṭai*; xxx.191–249). No phenomenon, event, or character can be fully described with a single phrase or from a single vantage point. "Nothing exists apart from the twelve links [in the chain of interdependent origination] in [their] totality" (xxx.229), Aṟavaṇaṉ instructs Maṇimēkalai, and that totality implies the neverending arising, convergence, and falling away of an infinite number of factors, conditions, and causes. The text of the *Maṇimēkalai* presents its audience with an elusive character whose story can be grasped only within such a framework. Maṇimēkalai's distance from the actions that shape her own story, her continually shifting identities and forms, make sense only within the context of interdependent origination described in the final chapter. There is no one entity "Maṇimēkalai," no straightforward causal sequence easily identified. The text's heroine operates within the context of transient phenomena and events, arising interdependently yet reducible to no single component.

The recurring image of the assumption of different forms or identities, both in the present and throughout those past lives or stories to which the present-tense narrative continually alludes, does not pertain to the character of Maṇimēkalai alone. Here the complex structure of the text, its many subplots or branch stories, serves to build the *Maṇimēkalai*'s theme of interdependent origination into an even more intricate narrative rendering of the interplay of circumstances and conditions.

As noted previously, the opening chapter, for example, frames the entire story with the twenty-eight-day festival of the god Indra, a celebration during which the gods assume mortal form, and deities and human beings stroll together in harmony (i.64–67). In this context, the goddess Maṇimēkalā appears as a pious woman of the city (v.94–96) in order to provide Maṇimēkalai with her first Buddhist instruction. In addition to providing what Eco might call a moment of narrative "lingering," slowing down the reading (or performance) pace both to increase the enjoyment of the text and to create a space for the events to follow,[146] this first chapter constructs a setting in which the audience expects to witness a changing of appearances, an assumption of new forms and guises, on the part of characters both human and divine.

Although it is Maṇimēkalai and her namesake mentor, the goddess Maṇimēkalā, who are said explicitly to assume various forms in the present tense, the text indicates in several ways that the present narrative illustrates but one small piece of a much larger pattern of continually changing, interdependently arising phenomena. After revealing the past lives of Maṇimēkalai's mother and friend, Mātavi and Cutamati, for example, Maṇimēkalai's teacher, Aṟavaṇaṉ, comments that the two women now appear before him "like actresses who have changed costumes" (xii.51–52). Not only do characters assume different forms and identities in their present lives, but experiences over past lifetimes can also be likened to the changing of costumes or forms, to the coming and going of actors on a stage. Just as no single turn of phrase can completely encompass Maṇimēkalai's character—the sexually alluring young girl, the once-devoted wife, the determined follower of the Buddha whose manifestation of wholesome conditions brings her to the threshold of total renunciation—so, too, are other characters to be comprehended only from many different viewpoints, across many lifetimes, through many different forms.

In telling the stories of intertwining lives and deeds, the text is also careful to make the audience realize that even the "stage" upon which these "actors" continually change "costumes" is no more permanent or fixed than any single character's form, appearance, or identity. The city of Pukār, where the story begins and where much of the central action takes place, is described throughout the narrative (and in the *Cilappatikāram* as well) as an ancient and enduring metropolis of tremendous wealth and virtue. The text depicts a prosperous city lavishly decorated for the celebration of the Indra festival (i.43–67); Pukār is later likened to an elegant lady, with the sun and moon for her earrings (v.109–122). The city is described in beautiful detail as dawn breaks (vii.111–126) and is praised by Kāyacaṇṭikai's husband, Kāñcaṉaṉ, as a place of wealth, virtue, and compassion (xvii.62–65). Yet suddenly the audience learns that the city has been utterly destroyed. The celebration of Indra's festival has been inadvertently forgotten, and Maṇimēkalā herself has cursed Pukār, calling on the mighty ocean to devour the city in a tidal wave (xxvi.198–200). All things, the text reminds its audience, are transient, subject to circumstances and conditions created by other actions and events often beyond anyone's particular knowledge, even a seemingly ageless and formidable city of chaste wives, wealthy merchants, Buddhist gardens, and royal palaces.

Nor is the *Maṇimēkalai*'s audience allowed to feel, even for an instant, that any of these forms, guises, or appearances assumed in past, present, or future lives are random. Each of the characters who appears in the main narrative and its various subplots is intimately tied to every other. The complex structure of the text, in other words, attests in narrative form to the processes underlying the final teaching that no event occurs without its necessary antecedents, that no one phenomenon can be fully understood without reference to its prerequisite conditions: "volition arises dependent upon ignorance; consciousness arises dependent upon volition; name-and-form arises dependent upon consciousness," and so on (xxx.104–133).

To cite but a few possible examples from the text, in chapter 4 Utayakumaraṉ learns of Maṇimēkalai's existence only through a series of events whose ultimate origin lies in the tragedy that befell Kōvalaṉ and Kaṇṇaki. After subduing a rampaging elephant, the prince notices a young man playing a lute; the youth's hand has come to rest upon the string that sounds the note of tragedy (iv.56). When the prince inquires as to the source of such sorrow, the young man replies that he has just seen the beautiful Maṇimēkalai walk by, overcome by her grief at the fate of her parents, and that sighting has recalled to his own mind the tragic tale of Kōvalaṉ (iv.65–71). Maṇimēkalai receives the inexhaustible almsbowl, Amutacurapi, in chapter 11; the story of how the bowl came to be there on Maṇipallavam for her to receive (e.g., the story of Āputtiraṉ) requires more than two chapters to tell (xiii, xiv, xv.1–54). Maṇimēkalai acquires the bowl only because, in her previous birth, she remembered an act of kindness to a Buddhist sage as she burned on her husband's funeral pyre (xi.99–106). That act of kindness itself, the audience has already learned, has determined the nature of her present birth (x.36–41). Ātirai's generous deed of placing the first morsel of food into Maṇimēkalai's bowl must be preceded by the lengthy story of Ātirai's husband, Cātuvaṉ, and his conversion of a wild band of Nāgas to the basic precepts of Buddhism (xvi.1–127); the story serves to explain how Ātirai has come to be the woman most uniquely qualified to deliver the first food into Amutacurapi, thus activating the vessel's life-saving capacities.

The text of the *Maṇimēkalai* does not, however, mechanically lay out its series of plots to show the audience a clear sequence of direct causes and effects. Rather, in the manner of the processes of interdependent origination in which every arising phenomenon must be examined from many angles as the result of multiple causes or conditions, the text artfully weaves together stories within stories to reveal only gradually, and always only partially, the fact that all of the characters have passed through many lives together. Each individual's story can be understood only in relation to all the others. The audience catches glimpses of various characters' personal tales, learning in bits and pieces the impact of past deeds on the present narrative. For example, the audience first learns of Cutamati's past in the third chapter of the text (iii.27–41); only in chapter 5, however, does one learn more fully of her illicit relationship with a semidivine being, her father's subsequent search for his missing daughter, her run-in with a band of hypocritical Jain monks, and her ultimate conversion to Buddhism by a compassionate sage (v.28–79). Similarly, the semidivine "bearer of knowledge" (vidyādhara) woman, Kāyacaṇṭikai, reveals a bit of her story in chapter 15 (xv.81–86); only two chapters later does the audience come to realize in some detail the deed that caused her to be cursed with an insatiable hunger and the circumstances that first brought her to Pukār (xvii.1–82). Of Maṇimēkalai's past and that of her companions, Mātavi and Cutamati, the text reveals bits and pieces throughout the entire narrative (e.g., vii.98–108 and ix. 9–71); when Maṇimēkalai revisits the island of Maṇipallavam in the company of Āputtiraṉ, the course of her past deeds and their present karmic results is reviewed (xxv.37–67). The *Maṇimēkalai* thus slowly reveals an intricate and complex pattern of interlocking lives, deeds, and events.

In this context of interdependent stories, it is also interesting to note the manner in which the text retells certain tales to emphasize its specific message of interdependent origination as a complex causal process. In the story of Cārṅkalaṉ and his mother, Kōtamai, told in the sixth chapter, regarding the temple of the "cosmic place" (cakravāla), the Tamil text appears to rework a narrative known in Pāli as "The Story of the Mustard Seed."[147] Moving from the Pāli renderings to the Tamil, however, one can detect certain shifts in emphasis.[148] Although the story of Gotamī and the mustard seed stresses the universality of impermanence and death, the Tamil story of Kōtamai takes the point a step further, emphasizing the role of karma and the individual elements in the cycle of interdependent origination, particularly ignorance (pētaimai) and volition (ceykai) in determining that universal principle. The goddess, Campāpati, for example, does not simply tell the grieving mother that all beings must die;[149] she insists that both Cārṅkalaṉ's birth and death are rooted in the ignorance and volition or karma that set in motion the cycle of interdependent origination and give rise to the phenomenal world (vi.150–152):

> Ghosts do not take precious lives.
> Ignorance (*pētu*) was the cause of [the life of your son]
> who wore the sacred thread upon his chest,
> and it is matured karma (*ūḻviṉai*) that has come and taken his life.

Campāpati further informs Kōtamai that no being, human or divine, can intervene in this cycle of birth, death, and rebirth. "When life departs [the body]," she teaches, "it proceeds along with its [accumulated] karma and enters another birth" (vi.158–159). The *Maṇimēkalai* thus expands the message of "The Story of the Mustard Seed," a story with which the sophisticated audience of the Tamil text might well be familiar in its Pāli forms, to address not only the fact of impermanence or transience but also its ultimate origin: the cycle of interdependent origination that begins with ignorance and karma.

The *Maṇimēkalai* also reworks the story of Kōvalaṉ and Kaṇṇaki as told in the *Cilappatikāram* in a similarly pointed way. More specifically, the Buddhist text expands the time frame of the story to illustrate the teaching (xxx.159–168) that the full cycle of interdependent origination must be understood to take place across several lifetimes, to extend through past, present, and future. When Maṇimēkalai visits the temple of Kaṇṇaki in Vañci, for example (xxvi.1–67), we learn that the virtuous Kōvalaṉ and Kaṇṇaki are presently in heaven, worshipped as deities as a result of good deeds performed in mortal life; this is where the *Cilappatikāram* leaves the couple, after they ascend to heaven at the close of the *Maturaikkāṇṭam*. Their accumulated karma, however, will play itself out in future lives, and the pair will be reborn on earth to suffer again as human beings until they eventually attain birth in the land of the Buddha. Only then, at the feet of the Buddha, will they free themselves from the endless round of rebirths (xxvi.52–61). Even deities cannot escape the inevitable workings of karma and the arising of the twelve-fold causal chain; they enjoy only briefly in heaven the rewards of virtuous deeds.[150]

Even the overall arrangement of the main events in the narrative underscores its central emphasis on complex conditions and necessary circumstances, of people, things, and events dependent on that which comes before and that which occurs all around. The subject of the narrative, for example, as stated in the preface to the text and noted previously, is the renunciation of Maṇimēkalai (maṇimēkalai tuṟavu, line 97). Her actual renunciatory vow, however, as also noted previously, does not actually take place until the very last two lines of the text (xxx.263–264). The principal event of the story thus occurs only after a detailed exploration, in narrative and then in discursive philosophical form, of the many causes and conditions that have led up to it, of the interdependent stories and events that have necessarily preceded it. One cannot comprehend the beautiful young girl's determined withdrawal from the world, implies the *Maṇimēkalai*, without first understanding the nature of her former, present, and future lives, as well as the present and past lives of all those who touch her life in some way.

The *Maṇimēkalai* thus spins a narrative web filled with characters, events, and imagery that compels its audience to confront, to reflect on, and to experience through literature both the ultimate transience and profound interconnectedness among all things that it describes theoretically only in the final chapter on interdependent origination. Although the sophisticated model audience anticipated by the *Maṇimēkalai* would certainly be intellectually familiar with the basic Buddhist doctrines of impermanence and interdependent origination, the narrative rendering detailed previously leads the audience to a direct encounter with these facts of human life. As Abhinavagupta describes the experience of attending a dramatic production in his commentary on Bharata's *Nāṭyaśāstra*: "When we go to the theatre . . . we feel: 'I will listen to and see something beyond my everyday experience (*lokottara*), something worthy (of my attention). . . . [A]ll of one's normal preoccupations (*sāṁsārikabhāva*) have been completely forgotten.'"[151]

Yet, should anyone in the *Maṇimēkalai*'s audience fail to grasp the greater significance of both narrative form and characterization, the text offers several direct clues as to the nature of its final discourse throughout the story, rather sparingly at first, but then in greater and greater detail. The first such passage occurs quite early in the narrative, as Mātavi explains the initial teachings she received at the feet of Aṟavaṇaṉ (ii.64–67):

> Those who are reborn experience increasing sorrow;
> those who are not reborn experience supreme bliss.
> The first is the result of desire;
> the next is experienced by those who have eradicated their desires.

Such comments on the nature of desire, ignorance, and karma, referring indirectly perhaps to the full cycle of interdependent origination, occur throughout the text with increasing frequency and complexity. Cutamati, for example, two chapters later, instructs Utayakumaraṉ on the basic impermanence and repulsiveness of the human body and defines the body as both the result of karma and the cause of future karma (iv.113–121). Maṇimēkalai, all alone and in great distress on the island of Maṇipallavam, cries out to her wrongly executed father that the same bad karma that drove him to his tragic end has propelled her to this lonely and frightening (yet ultimately illuminating) place (viii.40–43). Comments such as "propelled by karma" or "driven by past deeds" occur at places too numerous to list. In chapter 24, Aṟavaṇaṉ actually gives a brief preview of the doctrine of interdependent origination (xxiv.101–147) that he later explains in full to Maṇimēkalai; this short section, dealing exclusively with the first of the elements in the causal chain, namely ignorance (pētaimai) and volition, here defined as good and bad karma (ceykai), perhaps serves to highlight both ignorance and karma as foundational to the causal cycle as a whole, as the first and thus most ubiquitous and powerful of the twelve links in the chain.

The text thus gradually builds a more direct argument, not only through narrative structure and content but also through the brief philosophical reflections of its characters, for the final exposition of karmic cause and consequence in the Buddhist context of interdependent origination that formalizes and gives shape to the narrative experience of the audience. No direct link is made between narrative events and the doctrinal points made in the closing chapter; the text provides no immediate or easily discernible means of connecting its complex narrative episodes and the detailed discussion of interdependent origination. As the *Tolkāppiyam* passage cited previously indicates, genuine literary experience is to be had only "by those who possess proper perspective,"[152] by those who can draw the connections between the aesthetic "relishing" of a narrative sequence and its more overtly doctrinal formulation. Speaking for much of Indic literary tradition in both Sanskrit and Tamil, Abhinavagupta similarly explains that true aesthetic enjoyment and comprehension of the text come only from what is conveyed indirectly:

> [Aesthetic enjoyment] is something that one cannot dream of expressing in a literal sense. It does not fall within workaday expression. It is, rather, a form that must be tasted by an act of blissful relishing on the part of a delicate mind through the stimulation . . . of

previously deposited memory elements which are . . . beautiful because of their appeal to the heart.[153]

The text at several points (e.g., xi.30–35) reminds its audience that Maṇimēkalai's growing knowledge of past and future lives is a rare gift. Ordinary human beings are not so fortunate; the audience can never be so certain of its true relationship to other characters in the present narratives of their own lives. Although an individual listening to the text of the *Maṇimēkalai* cannot see at any given moment the complex unfolding of his or her own life over time, the narrative compels him to realize, think about, acknowledge, and feel the intimate connections and ultimate transience of all moments, scenes, actions, characters, and phenomena. Through careful characterization, use of imagery, and structure of plot and subplot, the text, illustrating Martha Nussbaum's principle that "in good deliberation and judgment, the particular is in some sense prior to general rules and principles,"[154] creates a literary experience that compels its audiences to recognize as real the processes of interdependent arising that are defined more abstractly in the final chapter. The narrative both illustrates and elaborates on the complex processes of arising conditions and phenomena that underlie the general formulation of interdependent origination. The story of the renunciation of Maṇimēkalai is not just one story, not simply her story, but a narrative requiring an elaborate exploration of each character and event that has created the conditions, the circumstances—in short, the unfolding of ētunikal̲cci—that enable that act of renunciation to take place. The *Maṇimēkalai*'s combined use of structure and content creates an impression, an experience, of complex relations, of lives profoundly dependent on one another, of both ultimate impermanence and interconnectedness that both substantiates and enlarges the text's doctrinal core.

The *Maṇimēkalai* does more than simply provide a particular narrative illustration of the general principle of interdependent origination or create in its audience an experiential awareness of human transience and interdependence. As the burgeoning field of narrative studies continues to explore,[155] narrative serves to expand and to elaborate, to push doctrine far beyond the relatively narrow confines of direct philosophical discourse. As Robert Alter, in his study of the Bible as literature, suggests, "the literary medium stretches ideology beyond any merely programmatic or doctrinal frame."[156] The *Maṇimēkalai*, on the one hand, presents the doctrine of interdependent origination in the context of a narrative that compels its audience to experience the reality of that doctrine's underlying complex causal processes; on the other, it also elicits from its audience a heightened emotional experience (rasa) of compassion or pathos[157] (Tamil *al̲ukai*, Sanskrit *karuṇa*), the second in the *Tolkāppiyam*'s list of eight possible emotional states,[158] an emotional experience that is also suffused with an atmosphere of profound devotion to the Buddha. Human life, defined by suffering, is conditioned by the complex interplay of ignorance, karma, craving, and the rest, insists the *Maṇimēkalai*. In the context of that ever-changing scene of transience and misery, one must feel pity for one's fellow beings and empathize with their constant and profound suffering. The text accomplishes this enlargement of the doctrine of interdependent origination in a number of ways.

That the *Maṇimēkalai* seeks to evoke a heightened mood or emotional experience of pathos or compassion in its sophisticated audience of literary connoisseurs is evident in the basic language of the text, the precision of word choice, and the many terms used to describe psychophysical states of grief and despair. Vayantamālai, for example, is described as listless and weary of body, physically overwhelmed with grief, by the sad news of Mātavi's renunciation (*ayarntu mey vāṭiya aḻivinaḷ*; ii.11). Maṇimēkalai, waking to find herself alone on the island of Maṇipallavam, is said to be drenched in sorrow, and cries out in words born of grief (*vīḻ tuyar eytiya viḻumak kiḷaviyil tāḻ tuyar uṟuvōḷ*; viii.38–39). The text's use of simile (Tamil *uvamai*, Sanskrit *upamā*) in this regard is particularly telling. To return to Vayantamālai again, Mātavi's friend and former fellow courtesan, who has just learned that Mātavi is determined to become a Buddhist renunciant, at ii.72–75 she is gravely distressed to see her friend commit herself to such a life; she must "wrench" herself away (*kaiyaṟṟup peyarntaṉaḷ*) from that spot, distraught and grieving "like one who has lost a precious gem in a sea of high swells" (*arum peṟal mā maṇi ōṅku tiraip peruṅ kaṭal vīḻttōr pōṉṟu*). At iv.65–68, Maṇimēkalai's distress at learning of her father's cruel end is likened, by the young man who watches her pass by, to the suffocating confines of a coffin: "Maṇimēkalai's . . . natural beauty had wilted, like a flower placed inside a well-built casket" (*vakai varic ceppiṉuḷ vaikiya malar pōl*). At vii.127–134, to cite another example, a number of similes combine to convey the intense suffering and anxiety experienced by both Cutamati and Mātavi as Cutamati reports on the disappearance of Maṇimēkalai (she has been taken by her namesake goddess to Maṇipallavam). Cutamati, "in agony" (*iṉaintu*), "like a peacock pierced by an arrow" (*ē uṟu maññaiyiṉ*) and "like a body that has forfeited its life" (*iṉ uyir iḻanta yākkaiyiṉ*), tells her story, which leaves Mātavi "suffering great anguish" (*taṉit tuyar uḻappa*) "like a cobra that has lost its jewel" (*nal maṇi iḻanta nākam pōṉṟu*). Nor are such emotive similes reserved for the principal characters; even the setting for the story is described in terms that evoke grief, pity, and compassion. At v.137–140, for example, the coming of twilight to Pukār is likened to a grieving widow:

> Twilight, her body pallid[159] and her grief increasing
> at the setting of the sun,
> like a woman [who returns] to her own people
> after losing her husband on the battlefield,
> covered the great city.

Moving beyond the level of individual words and phrases, many of the images and subplots of the *Maṇimēkalai* also serve to create a mood or heightened experience of grief, pity, and compassion. Indeed, of the sixteen branch stories highlighted by Richman,[160] from the tale of Cutamati's abduction by a lecherous semidivine being to that of the curse placed on the city of Pukār, most might be said to evoke an audience experience of profound pathos. Certainly, the story of Kōvalaṉ and Kaṇṇaki that underlies the entire *Maṇimēkalai* narrative, first mentioned at ii.54 as Mātavi relates to Vayantamālai the manner in which Kaṇṇaki "wrenched off her large and beautiful young breast bathed in tears" and flung it at the city of Maturai, engulfing the city in flames, is one evoking great pity. In contrast to the story told in the *Cilappatikāram*, where Kaṇṇaki's triumphal transformation into a goddess could be said to evoke the sentiment of the heroic (Tamil *perumitam*, Sanskrit *vīra*), this story, as mentioned previously, causes Maṇimēkalai herself to shed bitter tears (iii.1–10). Cutamati's pathetic story of abduction and abandonment, in which her father is gravely injured and his pleas for assistance rejected by heartless Jain monks, culminates in the appearance of the compassionate Buddhist sage, Caṅkataruma<u>n</u> (Saṅghadharma), whose "gracious words, mixed with love, filled [Cutamati's and her father's] ears and cooled [their minds]" (v.63–64). A<u>r</u>avaṇa<u>n</u> narrates to Maṇimēkalai the story of Mātavi and Cutamati in their former lives, as her sisters Tārai and Vīrai, and again, it is a story full of pathos, evoking both pity and compassion (xii.41–49):

> With a broken heart the king wept aloud,
> and narrated with great sorrow that which had occurred to the ladies who wore shining ornaments.
>
> "Vīrai, in a drunken state, stepped in front of a newly captured elephant without taking care, and she perished.
> Tārai heard that [news of her sister's death], climbed onto a terrace, and, unable to bear [her sorrow], fell [down] and died."

So full of such scenes of grief and despair, giving rise to feelings of pity and compassion in the audience, is the *Maṇimēkalai* that is simply impossible to mention them all. Kōtamai pitifully bewails the death of her son, asking who will now tend to her family's sacred fires (vi.132–141). Ātirai, the virtuous wife of the shipwrecked Cātuva<u>n</u>, cries out in despair from her funeral pyre: "What shall I do? I am a person of bad deeds, and [even] fire does not kill me!" (xvi.35–36). The story of Āputtira<u>n</u>, from the scene of his abandonment in the middle of the night by an unchaste and uncaring mother (xiii.8–14) to his expulsion from his adopted brahmin community because he sheds tears at the sight of a cow about to be sacrificed (xiii.27–103), his utter despair at finding no one to feed with his miraculous almsbowl (xiv.55–69), and his eventual uncovering of the remains of his own body from a former life, evokes, across more than two chapters of the text, a persistent sense of pity due specifically to the four sources of pathos cited in the *Tolkāppiyam*: disgrace, deprivation, suffering caused by loss of position, and poverty.[161]

The Doomed Couple

Among the many stories of despair and woe found in the *Maṇimēkalai*, among the most poignant is that of the two bearers of knowledge or semidivine beings (Sanskrit vidyādhara, Tamil viñcaiya<u>n</u>), Kāyacaṇṭikai and her husband, Kāñca<u>n</u>a<u>n</u>, the two characters so central to the climactic dramatic event of the narrative: the death of Utayakumara<u>n</u>.[162] Kāyacaṇṭikai has been cursed to suffer an insatiable hunger for twelve long years because she once inadvertently stepped on an ascetic's piece of fruit (xvii.21–46). Kāñca<u>n</u>a<u>n</u> offers her the choicest foods to appease her hunger, but to no avail (xvii.58–59). He sends her to Pukār to live on the charity of the good citizens there and visits her each year during the celebration of the Indra festival. Unbeknownst to her husband, Kāyacaṇṭikai's hunger is alleviated by the almsbowl, Amutacurapi, and she leaves to return home to her husband (xvii.73–74). Kāñca<u>n</u>a<u>n</u> returns to Pukār for the Indra festival, searches everywhere for his wife, and flies into a jealous rage when he witnesses Maṇimēkalai, now disguised as Kāyacaṇṭikai to avoid the amorous advances of the prince, speaking intimately with Utayakumara<u>n</u> (xx.71–78). Utterly distraught, he stalks Utayakumara<u>n</u> and cuts the prince down with his sword. Attempting to seize Maṇimēkalai (who is still disguised as Kāyacaṇṭikai), Kāñcaṉaṉ is stopped by the painting on the temple pillar and told that the woman in his arms is, in fact, Maṇimēkalai. He then learns what has become of his true wife (xx.114–121):

> Hear what happened to Kāyacaṇṭikai, her great hunger appeased,
> as she was traveling through the sky!
> Those who travel through the sky do not go above the great Vinta hills
> where an *antari*[163] lives.
> If anyone goes there, the *vintākaṭikai*[164] who guards the Vinta [hill] becomes enraged;
> she draws them in with her shadow, and [then] her stomach engulfs them.
> Going over that hill, [your wife] was [thus] engulfed by her stomach.

Kāñcaṉaṉ at this point simply departs to suffer the agony of his wife's demise.

The entire subplot concerning the couple, from Kāyacaṇṭikai's innocent misstep that results in twelve years of suffering to the ironic scene of her untimely end—the woman so recently relieved of an insatiable hunger is swallowed up into the stomach of a hungry goddess—creates a mood of unjust and grievous suffering, a feeling that such pain should be alleviated. This mood of pathos (aḻukai or karuṇa) is evoked in several ways in this poignant subnarrative of Kāyacaṇṭikai and Kāñcaṉaṉ, first and most obviously, as in the larger narrative discussed previously, at the level of language, of individual words and phrases that in Tamil are able to express a profound range of psychophysical states of grief and despair. Kāyacaṇṭikai's name itself, no less than her pitiful story, immediately brings to mind one of the most pointed images of physical pain and suffering to be found in the *Maṇimēkalai*: she is "Caṇṭikai" or Candikā in "body" (*kāyam*), like the fearful goddess Candikā/Durgā, with the word kāyam (from the Sanskrit *kāya*) also signifying in the Tamil a wound, bruise, or scar. Immediately the audience learns that she suffers "incomparable pain" (*taṉit tuyar uṟūum*; xv.84) because of bad karma (*valviṉai*) and that she "wanders about [afflicted with] the want of a great, unappeasable hunger " (*vīvu il vem paci vēṭkaiyoṭu tiritarum*; xv.85). As Kāyacaṇṭikai explains her predicament to Maṇimēkalai, she describes the pathetic inability of her husband, the "splendid vidyādhara" (*ilaku oḷi viñcaiyaṉ*; xvii.52), to cope with her suffering (xvii.50–54):

> In distress (*viḻumamōṭu*) he approached [me and said],
>
> "You are suffering without reason because of that divine ascetic of
> extraordinary austerities.
> Rise into the sky!"

Kāyacaṇṭikai has, of course, lost her ability to fly; she tells him only of her "stomach-withering hunger so powerful it may take my life" (*ūṉ uyir nīṅkum uruppoṭu tōṉṟi vayiṟu kāy perum paci varuttum*; xvii.56–57). Kāñcaṉaṉ, feeling great sorrow (*neṭum tuyar*), offers her the choicest foods to appease her hunger, but to no avail (xvii.58–60). He sends his wife of Pukār, "a city of virtue," and faithfully visits her there each year during the Indra festival (xvii.60–70), but, as Kāyacaṇṭikai explains, "he witnesses my great hunger, feels pity (*iraṅki*), and departs [again], thinking of the [many] years yet to come" (xvii.71–72). Later, Kāñcaṉaṉ's heartache is clear as he searches the city for his wife, saying (xx.22–25):

> Twelve years have passed [since] the curse was placed upon [my] wife
> by the great ascetic, as a result of her karma,
> on [the banks of] the wild river of bamboo thickets on Mount Potiyil,

whose summit is engulfed in clouds.
[Still] Kāyacaṇṭikai has not come.

Almost palpable is the tragic turn of Kāñcaṉaṉ's mind from sympathy and sadness to rage as he later witnesses Maṇimēkalai, disguised as Kāyacaṇṭikai, speaking intimately with Utayakumaraṉ (xx.71–78):

She does not take into account my words that have praised her.
She regards me as a stranger and follows after someone else.
Having given a mature discourse full of knowledge to the son of the king
who wears a garland of fragrant flowers,
her smile of shining white pearls between two pieces of red coral
and her red[-streaked] eyes that are like lilies have given [the prince]
a look that expresses love.
Because this [prince] here is her lover, [my wife], a woman who wears
beautiful ornaments, has remained here.

In the end, Kāñcaṉaṉ's greatest source of suffering or pain (Tamil tuyar, a word that occurs repeatedly throughout this subnarrative) is his own mistaken anger, his own pitiable inability to grasp the true nature of the scene before him.

The mood of pathos is further evoked in the manner outlined explicitly in the *Tolkāppiyam*, through scenes of disgrace (*iḻivu*), deprivation (*iḻavu*), loss of position (*acaivu*), and poverty (*vaṟumai*).[165] Most significant for the Buddhist context of the *Maṇimēkalai*, the cause of each of these results lies in bad karma (*tīviṉai*). Time and time again, Kāyacaṇṭikai explains her disgrace and deprivation as the inevitable result of bad karma. It is due to the arising of bad or relentless karma (*vevviṉai uruppa*) that Kāyacaṇṭikai and her husband first come south to Mount Potiyil (xvii.23); because of bad karma, she trods on the sage's wondrous fruit (tīviṉai *uruttaliṉ*; xvii.33). Kāyacaṇṭikai suffers disgrace (iḻivu) before the sage who learns that the fruit he eats but once every dozen years has been crushed; her husband suffers the same in sending his ailing wife off to Pukār to rely on the charity of others.[166] The woman's hunger is the embodiment of deprivation (iḻavu), and that same hunger keeps her banished from the wealth (acaivu) and status (vaṟumai) she enjoys in her husband's great northern city. Like the hunter reduced to begging in the following poem, quoted from the Caṅkam anthology *Puṟanāṉūṟu* by the thirteenth-century commentator on the *Tolkāppiyam*, Pērāciriyār, as an example of loss of position, Kāñcaṉaṉ, the mighty ruler of a great city to the north, is transformed into a nursemaid for his wife, bringing her "sweet fruits, yams, and well-cultivated produce . . . without leaving that place" (xvii.58–61):

Bathing in the roaring white waterfall
has changed his color.
His matted locks are brown leaves
on a blinding tree,
and he is now plucking for food
a bunch of thick leaves
from a bindweed.

He was a hunter once.[167]

The once-splendid couple, reduced to hunger and futile attempts to alleviate that hunger, suffer all four of the *Tolkāppiyam*'s situations evocative of pity.

The story of Kāyacaṇṭikai and Kāñcaṉaṉ evokes pathos in yet another way, one that inverts nearly all Caṅkam literary depictions of the suffering of male and female characters in love. The loss of position (acaivu) is made all the more poignant in this subnarrative by the fact that it is Kāñcaṉaṉ, the glorious male figure, who suffers at the demise of his wife, turning upside down the images of grieving widow that dominate earlier poems of the heroic genre. The widow in the following selection (also from *Puṟanāṉūṟu*), for example, is utterly distraught, her normal eating patterns disrupted, at the loss of her husband:

The little white lilies,
poor things,

gave me tender leaf
to wear, when I was young.

Now, my great husband is dead,
I eat at untimely hours

and the lilies give me lily seed,
a widow's rice.[168]

Instead, in the *Maṇimēkalai*, it is Kāñcaṉaṉ who grieves for his starving wife, just as it is he, and not Kāyacaṇṭikai, who worries what his lover is up to off in the great city of Pukār. Kāñcaṉaṉ's fretting over the his wife's supposed attachment to Utayakumaraṉ echoes the following image drawn from the earlier anthology of poems on love known as *Kuṟuntokai*:

As for me,
I am here.

My virtue lies
with boundless grief
in a salt marsh.

He is in his town
and our secret
has become gossip
in common places.[169]

Iḷampūraṇar, the eleventh-century commentator on *Tolkāppiyam*, quotes as an example of a Caṅkam scene evoking pathos the following poem from *Puṟanāṉūṟu*, which similarly underscores the gender inversion that makes Kāñcaṉaṉ an even more tragic sight. Here, the grieving, soon-to-be widow implores her wounded warrior husband to try to stand up, "to walk a little," in the manner of Kāñcaṉaṉ, the mighty scion of the north, imploring his wife to eat just a little, to get up and fly with him back to their native city:

I cannot cry out.
I'm afraid of tigers.
I cannot hold you,
your chest is too wide
for my lifting.

Death
has no codes
and has dealt you wrong,
may he
shiver as I do!

Hold my wrist
of bangles.
let's go to the shade
of that hill.
Just try and walk a little.[170]

The pitiable nature of this subplot is, in short, made all the more poignant by the reduction of the mighty male character to the classical role played by a woman, one filled with sorrow and, in other circumstances, jealousy. Kāñcaṉaṉ's mistaken realization, that his wife (Maṇimēkalai in disguise) has remained in Pukār as Utayakumaraṉ's lover, echoes such love themes mentioned previously, making the events that follow all the more tragic.

One final way in which the author of the *Maṇimēkalai* elicits a heightened emotional experience of pity or compassion in the story of Kāyacaṇṭikai and Kāñcaṉaṉ, a technique not wholly unrelated to the gender inversion noted previously, is through the poignant juxtaposition of two closely paired themes in the classical love and heroic genres of Tamil poetic composition: transience (*kāñci*) and improper love (*peruntiṇai*). For the heroic theme of transience, discussed at length by Richman in her treatment of the sixth chapter of the *Maṇimēkalai*,[171] the *Tolkāppiyam* enumerates two sets of situations (*tuṟai*) that evoke a sense of the transitory or impermanent, each touching in some way on death and the grief of the surviving spouse.[172] Improper love, held explicitly by classical Tamil literary tradition to be the love or the inner counterpart of the heroic or outer transience theme, depicts inappropriate or nonmutual love relationships.[173] What is striking about the story of Kāyacaṇṭikai and Kāñcaṉaṉ in this regard is that although the theme of transience is readily apparent–Kāyacaṇṭikai is suddenly stricken by a curse, her body withered, and she is ultimately consumed by the goddess of the Vinta hills–Kāyacaṇṭikai and her husband constitute the only couple in the entire *Maṇimēkalai* narrative who are not representative of improper love. Their genuine concern for each other is truly touching; Kāñcaṉaṉ, literally "the golden one," tenderly cares for his wife and sends her off to the distant city of Pukār for her own welfare, visiting her faithfully each year. In contrast, the tragic story of the ill-suited Mātavi and Kōvalaṉ provides the backdrop for the *Maṇimēkalai* story; Maṇimēkalai herself is pursued by the amorous Utayakumaraṉ, whose advances leave her confused and sometimes frightened. Kāyacaṇṭikai and Kāñcaṉaṉ are the only characters whose wedded happiness and tender love for each other we are allowed to witness, yet even their relationship is doomed. That they, too, suffer the pain of the classical widow grieving the loss of her husband on the battlefield greatly sharpens the evocation of pathos in their story. Those who should enjoy wedded bliss and contentment instead suffer the vagaries of an ascetic's curse and a guardian goddess's hunger.

From the Emotional Experience of Pathos to an Ethic of Compassion

In creating such an atmosphere or mood of profound and senseless suffering caused by unknown or unrealized karmic circumstances, the story of Kāyacaṇṭikai and Kāñcaṉaṉ and the heightened emotional experience of pathos that it evokes, in the wider context of the *Maṇimēkalai* as a whole, suggest something more at stake in the play of emotion than simply the aesthetic enjoyment of the text. Given the *Maṇimēkalai*'s overall concern with karma (viṉai) and the manner in which human beings can and should live most responsibly in a world ruled by forces beyond their control, the audience's heightened emotional awareness of pathos or pity would seem to imply not merely a mode of experiencing the *Maṇimēkalai* as a literary work but a mode of inquiry into how one should respond to human suffering, how one should act and live in a world in the constant presence of human pain. If literature, to borrow Paul Ricoeur's metaphor, can be envisioned as a "vast laboratory . . . through which narrativity serves as a propaedeutic to ethics,"[174] then a Buddhist narrative such as the *Maṇimēkalai* might be considered an inquiry, an experiment in thinking through the value of human life and the possibilities for human action in a world comprised of interdependently arising phenomena (paṭiccasamuppāda), driven by karma (viṉai) and defined by human suffering (tuyar).[175] Fostering in the reader or audience an experience of heightened emotional awareness inherently demands that one think about others, about human situations beyond one's own immediate knowledge.[176] That experience, in the context of Indian poetic theory in general and the *Maṇimēkalai* in particular, is defined in terms of human feeling, of emotional awareness; such emotion, however, is not the immediate, crude, gut response of raw feeling (bhāva) but highly refined and sophisticated aesthetic appreciation (Sanskrit rasa, Tamil meyppāṭu). Such heightened emotional awareness and experience carries with it a certain cognitive or moral value, for the experience of pathos consistently arises in tandem with the most persistent and basic of ethical questions raised by the *Maṇimēkalai* text: in a world ruled by the powerful forces of karma, how should one live?[177]

As Hart notes in his introduction to the work of the seventeenth-century Sanskrit literary theoretician, Jagannātha, "there is . . . a tendency in India to see literature in moral terms—if a work has no possibility for the moral upliftment of people, its value is questioned."[178] Indeed, Indic literary theory has long equated the heightened emotional experience of the literary connoisseur with ethical or moral realization. Acute emotional awareness constitutes not merely entertainment but an intuitive experience of truth. Abhinavagupta, in his commentary on Ānandavardhana's *Dhvanyāloka*, for example, asserts that it is only such heightened emotional awareness (rasa) that can enter into the hearts of "princes, who are not educated in scripture," and instruct them in "the four goals of man."[179] Although the principal aim of great poetry is, according to Sanskrit literary theoreticians, enjoyment, Abhinavagupta persistently emphasizes the moral, instructional value of the genuine work of literature, that "educative effect (*vyutpādana*) . . . is different from that which comes from scripture through its mandates and from history through its narrations."[180] The two Hindu epics dealing in great narrative detail with the ideal or moral life, for example, the *Rāmāyaṇa* and the *Mahābhārata*, instruct their audiences on the nature of dharma not only through direct injunction but by evoking specific emotional states that grant each "meaning specially acquired and superior beauty" (*arthaviśeṣalābhaṁ chāyātiśayaṁ ca*).[181] The *Rāmāyaṇa*, for Ānandavardhana, instructs through the experience of pathos, whereas the *Mahābhārata* evokes both equanimity or peace (*śānta*)[182]—a ninth category of aesthetic experience added to the standard list of eight moods or states perhaps by Buddhist and Jain authors[183]—and liberation from worldly life (*mokṣa*). To experience literature from the classical Indian critic's point of view is to be transported beyond oneself, to think and feel the experience of others, to be forever transformed by that experience. Literary experience and ethics (rasa and dharma), poetry and liberation, go hand in hand.

To return to the story of the doomed husband and wife, Kāñcaṉaṉ, "fearful" and "in distress" (xvii.50–52) that his wife has been cursed, at first refuses to acknowledge the terms of her suffering; although the ascetic has clearly stated that Kāyacaṇṭikai will no longer possess the mantra that allows her to fly, Kāñcaṉaṉ commands his wife: "Rise into the sky!" (xvii.55). Now fully aware that his wife is earthbound and ravenously hungry, Kāñcaṉaṉ seems unsure what to do to alleviate her pain; he begins by tempting her with the choicest foods and refuses to leave her. In desperation, he sends his wife off to Pukār, where the good citizens "help those who are helpless" (xvii.64), and faithfully visits her each year to check on her progress. The characters' repeated acknowledgment of the karmic causes of their suffering does not in any way diminish their love for one another. In fact, their continuing devotion and mutual concern as the two are buffeted about by forces beyond their control contributes significantly, as discussed previously, to the poignancy of their story. In the face of his wife's acute pain, Kāñcaṉaṉ transforms himself into servant and nurse, tenderly caring for his wife and eventually sending her away in great anguish. Kāyacaṇṭikai's suffering is, in a very real sense, her husband's suffering as well, and for twelve long years, Kāñcaṉaṉ devotes himself to attending to his wife.

It is his sudden and desperate feeling that all his sacrifice has been for nothing, that his wife has betrayed his trust with Utayakumaraṉ, that results in the one tragic instance in which Kāñcaṉaṉ acts not from a feeling of compassion but from selfish jealousy. At xx.123–126, Kāñcaṉaṉ is explicitly informed by Tuvatikaṉ, the painting on the temple pillar, that even though the prince's death can, in one sense, be attributed to Utayakumaraṉ's own bad karma, the jealous husband is guilty of acting "without due consideration" (*aṟiyāy*; xx.124). The bad karma arising for Kāñcaṉaṉ as a result will follow him through many lifetimes (*avviṉai niṉṉaiyum akalātu āṅku uṟum*; xx.126). Kāñcaṉaṉ has, in fact, been a bad reader of the text of his own life situation. Where circumstances called for empathy and understanding, Kāñcaṉaṉ acted out of anger and haste, "like a ferocious snake bearing its venomous fangs, rising up in great wrath and opening its hood" (xx.104–105), committing a heinous crime for which he will suffer through many lifetimes.[184]

Although both are said to be semidivine beings (vidyādharas), Kāñcaṉaṉ and Kāyacaṇṭikai are consummately human characters—in many ways the most human and humane in the text—facing situations of love, pain, and resentment that would be familiar to any audience. In using the dramatic and emotionally evocative language and imagery discussed previously, the story of Kāñcaṉaṉ's confusion, his compassionate concern for his wife, and his ultimate submission to jealousy and rage serve to draw the audience into the experience of the couple and to consider the same questions that confront them: how does one respond to the suffering of a loved one? How should one act in the face of seeming betrayal and ingratitude? The question of how to live with, and for, others in a world governed by the seemingly cruel and impersonal forces of karma is raised not only by the story of Kāñcaṉaṉ and Kāyacaṇṭikai but throughout the text of the *Maṇimēkalai*. In consistently eliciting an experience of pathos, the text invites its audience to reflect on the needs and desires of others, to relate to other human beings with compassion and care. Pathos represents here not simply an aesthetic experience (meyppāṭu or rasa), not simply a heightened mood of the piteous, but a call to act compassionately in the world.

Like the mighty male character who redefines himself as caregiver, Maṇimēkalai, too, as discussed previously, is constantly transformed by the various human situations in which she finds herself. Borne along by past karma and the force of her impending renunciatory vow, Maṇimēkalai displays no one identity or self, but seems always to act in accordance with the particular context. Although the *Maṇimēkalai* espouses no firm moral principles beyond the five traditional Buddhist prohibitions against killing, stealing, lying, illicit sexual behavior, and drinking,[185] the character of Maṇimēkalai herself exudes an ethic of concern and caring, of selfless acting in the interest of other human beings.

In the company of Prince Utayakumaraṉ, for example, Maṇimēkalai is a beautiful and sexually awakened young woman, obviously drawn to the man who was once her husband but conflicted by her equally obvious predilection for the ascetic life. Even though she is troubled by the prince's presence (e.g., xvii.130–133), Maṇimēkalai attempts to instruct Utayakumaraṉ on the nature of suffering and transience at a level he is capable of understanding: the fleeting pleasure of the human body (xx.40–69). Having thrown herself on Utayakumaraṉ's/Irākulaṉ's funeral pyre in her former birth, Maṇimēkalai painfully reflects, after the death of her beloved in this life, that she took the form of Kāyacaṇṭikai (thus precipitating the tragic murder) so that Utayakumaraṉ might actually listen to what she was telling him about the sorrows of the flesh (xxi.11–24). In a similar fashion, Maṇimēkalai assumes an equally sympathetic role in the company of the grieving queen, enduring attempts at poisoning, rape, and starvation to transform the queen's sorrow into a source for moral growth. Acknowledging that with the power of her mantras she might easily have flown away from the palace at any time, Maṇimēkalai tells that queen that she stayed "in order to dispel the bad karma and eradicate the great distress of the mother of my lover in lives gone by" (xxiii.98–101). Maṇimēkalai's character, her personality, dissolve into the background as she serves as a vehicle, a medium, for the growth and maturation of others.

It is when she wanders the streets of Pukār and Kāñcīpuram in the guise of a female ascetic (pikkuṇik kōlam; e.g., xv.58), holding Amutacurapi in her hand and feeding the hungry, however, that Maṇimēkalai exhibits her strongest character, and the *Maṇimēkalai* makes its most consistent argument for an ethic of care and concern for the public good. With the miraculous almsbowl in her hands, the timid young girl hiding from the prince in the crystal pavilion is transformed into a confident protector of the poor, able to withstand the assaults of a disapproving grandmother and citizenry. Although the theme of hunger and its alleviation is a persistent one throughout the text,[186] with Amutacurapi the *Maṇimēkalai*'s appeals to attend to the ills of the world that are very real, tangible, and physical, come to the fore. Like the Buddha himself,[187] Maṇimēkalai with Amutacurapi is referred to numerous times as a healer, a doctor, a "physician for life that is precious" (ār uyir *maruttuvi*; e.g., xvii.15). Hunger is cited as the cause of all human ills (xi.76–80), and "the life of virtue is found only among those who eradicate the hunger of the helpless" (xi.93–94). Maṇimēkalai likens her life with Amutacurapi to that of a mother nurturing her children (xi.114–118), and it is, indeed, through the acquisition of the power to help others that Tīvatilakai informs the young girl, "you have become strong" (*uravōy āki*; xi.97). Maṇimēkalai's withdrawal from the world at the end of the text does not negate the ethical concern represented by Amutacurapi; Maṇimēkalai, on the eve of her renunciation, leaves the bowl atop the Maṇipallavam replica outside Kāñcīpuram where it continues to generate food to feed "the blind, the deaf, the lame . . . [and] many hundreds of thousands of flocks of animals" (xxviii.217–233).

Beyond the subtleties of aesthetic evocation and the concern for the public good represented by Amutacurapi, the *Maṇimēkalai* continually exhorts its characters and, by extension, its audience to care about the welfare of others, to concern themselves with well-being beyond their own. As King Puṇṇiyarācaṉ is about to embark on his journey to Maṇipallavam, for example, his minister chides him for thinking of himself before the lives of his subjects, who "will cry out" when their king departs "like children bereft of their mothers" (xxv.110–111). "Is it not the duty of the chief among living beings," the minister asks, "to protect the lives of others and not care for one's own life?" (xxv.116–117).[188] The goddess Maṇimēkalā commands Prince Utayakumaraṉ to give up his selfish interest in Maṇimēkalai and remember that "all living beings [constitute] the life of the king who rules the world" (vii.11–12), inverting the classical Caṅkam literary ideal in which the king's duty is "to know he's the life of the wide, blossoming kingdom."[189] Kaṇṇaki and Kōvalaṉ, though destined to achieve liberation at the feet of the coming Buddha, will nonetheless remain on earth through many lives, exercising their powers to the good of human beings everywhere (xxvi.60–61).

The call to act compassionately is stated even more boldly in what constitutes perhaps the most significant of the text's direct ethical statements, far-reaching in its implications for an audience of ordinary human beings: Maṇimēkalai's instructions to the queen, who grieves over the loss of her son, Utayakumaraṉ—the direct narrative result of Kāñcaṉaṉ's misplaced rage—and who blames Maṇimēkalai for his sudden and bloody demise. Although Maṇimēkalai herself has already become that rare recipient of knowledge of her former births and her place in the greater karmic scheme of human relationships, her exhortation to the queen to care for others is predicated not on special knowledge or powers but on the ordinary state of human ignorance (xxiii.67–79):

> On that day when [I] burned away my life,
> unable to bear living after the snake of poisonous eyes took the precious life of Irākulaṉ . . .[190]
> where were you weeping for your son,
> you who are a good flowering creeper, [now] doing things that are not proper?
> Do you weep for his body?
> [Or] do you weep for his essence?[191]
> If you weep for [his] body, who raised up your son and placed him on the cremation ground?
> If you weep for [his] essence, it is difficult to know which life it will enter [next] through the workings of karma.
> If your love is for that life-essence, lady of beautiful bangles, then your weeping (*iraṅkal*)[192] must be for all lives.

The ethic of compassion assumes not the copious knowledge of past lives gained by Maṇimēkalai in the course of her spiritual maturation, a knowledge to which few are entitled,[193] but ignorance of such things. It is precisely because the queen cannot be sure of her son's whereabouts in his next incarnation that she must transfer her love and concern for him to all living beings. Here, Maṇimēkalai might well be speaking directly to the text's audience of karmically unaware beings, to Kāyacaṇṭikai and Kāñcaṉaṉ, who most poignantly represent that situation, as well as to the queen. The dramatic passages of the text, Maṇimēkalai seems here to be implying, should create not simply an aesthetic experience of pity and compassion for the characters of the *Maṇimēkalai* but for all characters, for all living beings. "Those who [never] cease loving all human beings," she continues (xxiii.136–137), "are those who realize the final truth that eradicates suffering."

In the world of the *Maṇimēkalai* marked by human suffering, only transient joys, and complex and interdependent causal processes, it is the heightened emotional experience evoked by the text, that of pathos, that underlies the moral vision, the ethical stance of the narrative. As Geoffrey Harpham notes, true ethical inquiry "does not solve problems, it structures them."[194] Compassionate concern for the well-being of others guides Maṇimēkalai, Kaṇṇaki, Kāñcaṉaṉ, and Āputtiraṉ as they seek to live with and for others. In evoking the emotional experience of the piteous, the text also inherently demands that its audience ponder the same problems, think about characters and situations at some distance from one's own life, enter into a "communal inquiry"[195] about the quality of human interaction and the public good. Indeed, as early as the second century, the Sanskrit dramatic theoretician, Bharata, notes the inextricable interconnections among literature, emotional experience, and morality: "The highest type of character (*uttama*) has control over his senses, is wise, knowledgeable about many practical arts, generous and having noble ideals, a comforter of those who are afraid, knows the meaning of many sciences, is profound (or dignified, *gāmbhīrya*), noble (*audārya*), and has qualities of generosity and firmness."[196]

The need for compassionate care of all living beings, the empathy with the suffering of all forms of life, is further framed by the text's many direct testimonies of love for and devotion to the Buddha. The Buddha of the *Maṇimēkalai*, although not a character present in a physical sense in the narrative, is praised and worshipped throughout as the paradigmatic healer, as the great alleviator of suffering, as the consummately compassionate being "who possesses an incomparable resolve to protect all life" (iii.59–60). The goddess Maṇimēkalā praises the Buddha before the magical pedestal on Maṇipallavam (x.7–15):

> When all living beings had lost their consciences,
>   when ears were blocked to the bestowal of truth,
>   when knowledge was lost,
>   when the world was impoverished,
> you appeared,
>   like the splendid morning sun,
> in order to perpetuate the dharma at a time when the world
>   groped in darkness.
> I worship your feet. . . .
> I praise you!
> My head touches your feet!
> I keep you in my heart!
> May sorrow cease!

The Buddha appeared to aid an impoverished world; Maṇimēkalā, keeping the Buddha "in her heart," also helps those in distress, those who are ready to hear the dharma. The Buddha himself provides the model for compassionate behavior, a model followed by all the principal characters of the text according to their abilities, from Maṇimēkalai, who feeds the hungry masses with Amutacurapi, to the king of Pukār, who converts his prison into a dwelling place for virtuous ascetics. The Buddha took pity on the world and came to its aid; through the stories of Maṇimēkalai and Āputtiraṉ, Kāyacaṇṭikai and Cutamati, and Kāñcaṉaṉ and Ātirai, the audience is encouraged to do the same.

The *Maṇimēkalai* is a rich and complex literary text, one that can be read in many different yet complementary ways: as simply a good story, full of vivid descriptions and plenty of dramatic action; as an initiation of sorts into the Buddhist life through the arising of the proper karmic factors; as a narrative illustration of the doctrine of interdependent origination; as a series of scenes eliciting an audience experience of profound pity and compassion for the suffering that characterizes all human life; and as an ethical inquiry into the nature and value of human relations in a world ruled by karma. The aesthetic enjoyment or pleasure of reading or listening to the text lies perhaps in this appeal to both mind and heart, in its elegant narrative and philosophical rendering of a fundamental doctrine through stories of intense human suffering and equally intense empathy with that suffering. In short, the *Maṇimēkalai* evokes an experience in its audience that might be described as thoroughly Buddhist, rooted in transience and interconnectedness, suffused with love for the Buddha and compassionate pathos for the plight of human beings. The several ways in which the text anticipates and imagines a community of Buddhists to share in this experience and system of values are the subject of the following two chapters.

2

The *Maṇimēkalai*'s Community of Readers and Listeners

The previous chapter offered a reading of the *Maṇimēkalai* as a consummately literary work, as a complex poetic narrative that employs and evokes not only the literary themes, images, and sentiments of classical Tamil poetry but also Buddhist ideas and values, among them the manifestation of those conditions leading to renunciation and enlightenment, interdependent origination, transience, and compassion. Attributing to the *Maṇimēkalai* a high level of literary sophistication, such a reading attempted to demonstrate the several ways in which the text's literary qualities, in the manner of the aesthetic experience such qualities evoke, engage the reader, leading the audience to reflect on the value of human life, the profound interrelationships among all people and phenomena, and the proper way to live one's life in such an intricately interrelated world. The text, in all its narrative and philosophical richness, is multidimensional, complex, and engaging.

Yet what of the community, the audience, for whom the *Maṇimēkalai* was first intended? For whom might such a text have been composed? Given that very complexity and richness, how can one relate a modern reading of the text to the *Maṇimēkalai*'s sixth-century audience in a historically responsible way? Or, to raise the broader underlying question, how can a literary reading of the text prove useful for historical work? As discussed in the previous chapter, the historical particulars surrounding the production of the *Maṇimēkalai* text—the date and place of composition, the authorial intent, and the actual audience—may never fully be known. No commentarial tradition exists to hint of the text's reception at an elite or scholastic level. On the basis of the content of the text itself, as well as the number of disparate literary and archaeological sources that attest to a Buddhist presence in the sixth-century Tamil-speaking South, one can merely say with some certainty that the *Maṇimēkalai* anticipated a Tamil-speaking audience knowledgeable about a variety of Buddhist ideals, concepts, and images. Equally certain is that such a Tamil-speaking audience inhabited a cultural landscape that was exceedingly diverse, both religiously and linguistically. There exists, in short, no direct historical evidence for the reading or textual community of the *Maṇimēkalai*, for the group of individuals for whom this text represented a meaningful and significant articulation of ideas, images, and values.[1]

Yet if history can be said to include those processes by which individuals form a sense of themselves, their identity, and their community, works of the imagination such as literature and art, as Jacques Le Goff argues, play an important role in historical scholarship. "The imagination nourishes man and causes him to act," notes Le Goff. "It is a collective, social, and historical phenomenon."[2] The *Maṇimēkalai*'s mere existence supplies the most significant piece of evidence for the presence of Buddhism in the Tamil-speaking region of early medieval southern India; as a Tamil Buddhist work of sophisticated and ornate poetic composition, it provides access to the history of the Buddhist imagination in a particular time and place. Access to the empirical or historical community of Tamil-speaking Buddhists who read or listened to the *Maṇimēkalai* is only inferential. The context in which to understand the text and, by extension, the nature of the community for whom the text was intended must be drawn from the content of the *Maṇimēkalai* itself. In inferring the existence of such a textual community, a literary reading of the text—if done with historically informed eyes conscious of the complex, multilingual literary culture in which the *Maṇimēkalai* participated—serves as part of the historical evidence for the text's reception, a circumstantial point of entry into the textual or reading community of this Tamil Buddhist poetic work.[3]

This chapter considers the reading community of the *Maṇimēkalai* that can be inferred both from the text itself and from the literary culture that surrounds it, discussing the several ways in which the text imagines a place for Buddhist values in a religiously competitive milieu. It begins by examining the literary culture of early medieval South India to which the *Maṇimēkalai* contributed a specifically Buddhist voice. The reading of the text suggested in the previous chapter clearly precludes interpreting the *Maṇimēkalai* as a historical documentary of actual events. Although the text may not be able to supply historically verifiable names, dates, and faces, as a literary work the *Maṇimēkalai* contains much evidence concerning the milieu in which it was first written and received, concerning the culture of text, transmission, and aesthetic appreciation of which it was a part. The text itself, in short, can be used to build context, to establish the contours of the literary culture and the discourse of the "present" in which it participated. As Dominick LaCapra notes, any text, literary or otherwise, is a "'place' where long tradition and specific time intersect," always "situated in a fully relational network."[4] Recovering that "relational network," the web of intertextual references, allusions, and polemics to which the *Maṇimēkalai* contributes a Buddhist voice, is critical to understanding its articulation and vision of both "long tradition" and "specific time," its role in the historical processes of shaping identity and community.

In attending to the complex literary culture of debate and religious polemic to which the *Maṇimēkalai* lends a Buddhist voice, the community of readers and listeners, those engaged by and in the ideological, aesthetic, and ethical debates played out in the literary text, emerges more clearly. In the very existence of a Tamil Buddhist work of poetry such as the *Maṇimēkalai*, one can begin to discern the place of Buddhism in South Indian literary culture. One can also glimpse the historical processes of transmission and localization of Buddhist tradition in the Tamil-speaking region of the early medieval period for which no other records exist. It is possible to infer, in short, from the complex literary milieu in which the *Maṇimēkalai* engages itself, that the literary culture of poetic narrative played an important role in the articulation and sustenance of religious community in Pallava-era southern India.

For the sophisticated literary connoisseurs who comprised the *Maṇimēkalai*'s audience, the text imagines a place for Buddhism in the linguistically and religiously diverse

Tamil cultural landscape. In South India's multilingual culture of dialogue and competition among literary texts of different religious and philosophical persuasions, the modern notion that great art or literature should always remain above the fray of religious or political debate[5] simply cannot apply. In the religiously diverse Tamil world of the sixth century, religious identity[6] and tradition are defined and defended in the realm of literary culture. A literary work such as the *Maṇimēkalai* does not mirror or reflect social or religious "facts" so much as it attempts to create, shape, and envision them. The experience of connectedness and compassion elicited by the *Maṇimēkalai* is embedded in and identified with participation in a community of Buddhists imagined[7] across space and time, far into the future and far beyond the reaches of what might be called the Tamil-speaking region of southern India. This chapter discusses the literary culture and reading community of the *Maṇimēkalai*, focusing on the text's polemic techniques and use of language in mapping out a Buddhist claim to a portion of the Tamil landscape, a landscape defined by the text in religious terms. The following chapter then moves on to discuss the ways in which the text imagines a Buddhist community by recasting that local landscape through space and time, envisioning a gloriously liberated community of the future and a Buddhist world with the poetic narrative's characters and landmarks at its center.

A Literary Culture of Poetic Debate

Even a cursory glance through the early medieval textual corpus in Tamil reveals several striking depictions of the connection between literature, specifically poetic literary expression, and religion or religious experience. One such obvious link is that portrayed between individual experience of an extraordinary or religious nature and poetic narrative as that which authenticates or legitimates such experience. In such a context, ornate poetic expression serves not simply as entertainment or aesthetically pleasing diversion but as a purveyor of religious truths, as the authentic embodiment of transformative human experience.

In the preface to the *Cilappatikāram*, for example, Cāttaṉ narrates to the king, Iḷaṅkō,[8] what amounts to a plot summary of the text to follow, ending with the story of how he, Cāttaṉ, in the middle of the night saw the guardian deity of Maturai appear before Kaṇṇaki in the temple of Śiva and predict the transformation of both Kaṇṇaki and her murdered husband into divine beings (lines 10–54). Iḷaṅkō responds by saying that the two must compose the story in poetic form (*nāṭṭutum yām ōr pāṭṭuṭaic ceyyuḷ*; line 60), yet Cāttaṉ contends that Iḷaṅkō himself is best qualified to fashion such a text (lines 61–62).[9] The final lines (87–89) of the preface indicate that Cāttaṉ, the wealthy grain merchant of Maturai, listened to (*kēṭṭaṉaṉ*) the poetic composition of the king, thus reiterating what has already been suggested: that Cāttaṉ's initial rendition of Kaṇṇaki's story and his own experience in the Maturai temple are somehow inadequate, not comprehensible, not fully legitimate, until they are retold in sophisticated and artful verse. A similar notion of the power of the poetic to authenticate religious experience is inherent in the new forms of expression championed by the early medieval Hindu devotional poets. "They will attain release," sings Campantar, one of the earliest of the Śaiva saints, "who know these ten fine verses . . . in praise of the Lord who dwells . . . among the fragrant groves."[10] Kāraikkālammaiyār, the celebrated female devotee of Śiva, claims that only when she gained the power of speech as a child did she feel the love of the lord: "When I was born and learned to speak I was overcome with love."[11]

The appearance of the two characters, Iḷaṅkō and Cāttaṉ, in the prefaces of both the *Maṇimēkalai* and the *Cilappatikāram*, which suggests that the two texts are somehow connected or in dialogue with one another, points to yet another obvious aspect of sixth-century Tamil literary culture: rivalry, or, more specifically, competition among various philosophical or religious worldviews to present themselves as more accurate, as authenticating a more powerful experience. All the long poetic narratives of this period, like the *Maṇimēkalai* and the *Cilappatikāram*, are paired in some way according to Tamil literary tradition: the ninth-century Jain work, *Nīlakēci*, for example, is said to be a response to or refutation of the earlier Buddhist work (now lost), the *Kuṇṭalakēci*;[12] the twelfth-century hagiographic treatise of Cēkkiḻār, the *Periyapurāṇam*, is said to have been written to lure its author's royal patron away from his interest in an older Jain poetic narrative, the *Cīvakacintāmaṇi*.[13] It is in the realm of literature, of long poetic narrative in particular, that Tamil Buddhists and Jains debate both philosophical and lifestyle issues (e.g., in the *Nīlakēci*).[14] In similar fashion, the Śaivas and Jains offer competing visions of the place of love (*aṉpu*), both divine and human, in the course of the *Cīvakacintāmaṇi* and the *Periyapurāṇam*. The early Śaiva devotional poets vehemently condemn the presence of Buddhist and Jain "heterodoxies" in the Tamil-speaking region, not through philosophical prose or ideological debate, but through poetic appeals to the glory of Lord Śiva, "who is beyond the deluded doctrines of the base Buddhist monks."[15]

Nor is the literary culture of debate restricted to texts composed in the Tamil language. Tamil literary culture by the sixth century was, as noted previously, multilingual. The first known Sanskrit satirical dramas (*prahasana*), for example, "The Farce of the Saint-Courtesan" (*Bhagavadajjukam-prahasana*) and "The Farce of Drunken Sport" (*Mattavilāsa-prahasana*), attributed to the seventh-century Pallava monarch, Mahendravarman I,[16] were composed in this milieu of literary-religious competition and debate, suggesting the presence of a shared regional literary culture that crossed linguistic lines. In these two pioneering farces, Mahendravarman I, a multitalented artist and patron of the arts,[17] would appear to satirize in Sanskrit not only the perceived shortcomings and hypocrisies of various religious groups[18] but also the style of presentation found in Tamil literary works such as the *Maṇimēkalai*. Mahendravarman as the model author, in other words, assumes a multilingual model audience well-versed in Sanskrit and Tamil (as well as in Pāli and other Prākrit?) literature of his day. Only if one reads the *Mattavilāsa* and the *Bhagavadajjukam* with such a cosmopolitan literary culture in mind do the full subtleties and complexities of each drama's satirical elements become readily apparent.

The *Bhagavadajjukam*, the earliest extant example of the satirical dramatic genre, tells of the "exchange" of souls between an ascetic (*parivrājaka* or *bhagavan*) and a courtesan (*gaṇikā*, addressed with the respectful term *ajjukā*) who has just been bitten by a snake. The ascetic, horrified by his disciple's wish to have known the courtesan sexually while she was alive, decides that, "out of respect for him," he will "make the seed of conviction sprout in him by showing him the real power of yoga, [by] inject[ing] [him]self into the body of th[e] [deceased] courtesan."[19] For the sophisticated reader or listener well-versed in both Sanskrit and Tamil poetic literature, not only are the images of "sprouting" and "injecting" in the mouth of a supposedly celibate ascetic slyly humorous, but such a plot might also be read as a lengthy parody on the notion of one's "life" (Tamil uyir) traveling intact from one body to another at the moment of death that is so soberly depicted in both the *Maṇimēkalai* and the *Cilappatikāram*.[20] In the *Maṇimēkalai*, at vi.158–159, for example, Campāpati asks the grieving Kōtamai:

Is there any doubt that,
  when precious life (ār uyir) departs,
it [the precious life] travels along with [its] karma
  and enters another birth?

At xvi.95–105, Cātuvaṉ explains to an incredulous Nāga chieftain:

Hear this without becoming angry!
While life (uyir) lives, it is conscious of what occurs.
If life leaves a particular body,
  [the body] does not feel anything, even if it is put into the [funerary] fire.
[Thus] you realize that there is something that leaves the body,
  [and] there is an abode for that [life] which has left.
Not just I, but all [people] realize [this].
[When] the body perishes, life travels a distance of many *kāvatam*,[21]
  as you see [when] dreaming.
You realize that life, departing in this way, enters [another] body adorned with karma.

The opening scene of the Sanskrit drama, in which the ascetic considers the human body as a receptacle for disease and a source of delusion, similarly appears to put a comic twist on the Buddhist text's (e.g., the *Maṇimēkalai's*) insistence on the repulsiveness of the human body, its role as both the result and cause of karma, and the overwhelming need to shoulder moral responsibility even in this deluded, embodied state. As the ascetic in the Sanskrit farce reflects while searching in vain for his missing disciple:

He's not to be seen. Quite fitting for one who is surrounded by the darkness of ignorance. For:

The body, a mine of diseases, subject to old age,
  poised on the brink of hidden Death
 Is like a tree on a river bank,
  about to be uprooted by the ever-battering wave.
And though such human embodiment is earned
  through numerous good deeds, yet,
 Deluded by materialism, intoxicated with his strength,
  good looks, and youth, man is blind to those defects grave.

Therefore, really, this poor fellow can't be blamed.[22]

This flippant attitude toward blame stands in sharp and even comic contrast to the teaching delivered by Cutamati to the lusty prince to save her friend from his amorous advances. Speaking specifically for Utayakumaraṉ's benefit (iv.122–123), so that he might see the error of his passionate ways, Cutamati exhorts the prince at iv.113–121:

This body is the result of karma and is the cause of further karma.
When all adornments are thrown aside, the flesh [alone] is exposed.
[The body] grows old and dies.
It is the dwelling place of dangerous diseases.
[The body] is the place onto which desires graft themselves;
it is the receptacle for all faults. . . .
Turn it inside out, and see [how repulsive it is]!

For the literary connoisseur of sixth- or seventh-century Kāñcīpuram, both the *Bhagavadajjukam* and the *Mattavilāsa* poke persistent fun at Buddhist monks for their fixation with food and creature comforts—both turn the fifth of the Buddhist precepts, abstention from drinking, into "abstention from not eating regularly"[23]—transforming the *Maṇimēkalai*'s compassionate concern with feeding, nurturing, and caring into obsessive self-concern. On the one hand, the Sanskrit plays might well be ridiculing a real-life situation in seventh-century South India, in which Buddhist monastic institutions might have been relatively wealthy and their monks well-fed. On the other hand, the *Maṇimēkalai* might easily be perceived by an unsympathetic audience as more than a bit hypocritical on the subject of Buddhists feeding and nurturing others. Although Maṇimēkalai poetically likens the powers granted her by the wondrous begging bowl to "the breast of a mother that secretes sweet milk" (xi.114–115), she actually feeds the masses through Amutacurapi with little or no exertion on her part. She is herself forever shielded from hunger pangs by the mantra given to her by the goddess Maṇimēkalā (x.90–91), a mantra that she puts to good use when imprisoned by the queen (xxiii.61–62).

Although such elements might be said to speak to general Buddhist ideas or images that simply happen to appear in the *Maṇimēkalai*, Mahendravarman perhaps moves more specifically toward a critique of the *Maṇimēkalai* text in particular when the ascetic's disciple, Śāṇḍilya, claims the deceased courtesan as "one of our own" because she, "like *sannyāsins* [renunciants] . . . hadn't the least sense of loving attachment."[24] This turns the repeated assertions of a character such as Cittirāpati—that she and her protégés are "like bees who, after eating the sweet pollen, abandon the flower when it is without nectar" (xviii.19–20)—upside down, equating the virtues of the courtesan whom Cittirāpati champions with the asceticism she so despises. In a similar fashion, if one approaches the text through the eyes of the early medieval Tamil-speaking reader familiar with the Tamil tradition of ornate poetic narrative, Śāṇḍilya's perfunctory recitation of the kinds of flora and fauna he sees in a local garden—the list of trees alone comprises a compound of thirty-one members—along with a pavilion and "young maidens whose hearts are filled with sorrow due to separation from their lovers,"[25] would seem to parody in quite hilarious fashion the careful and lengthy attention paid to descriptions of gardens and parks in the *Maṇimēkalai*. *Maṇimēkalai* iii.160–169 and iv.1–24, for example, each describe at length and in beautiful and reverent detail the flowering trees and wildlife of the Buddha's Uvavaṉam. In contrast, vi.80–89 describes the barren and flowerless trees and shrubs of the cremation ground. Although lengthy descriptions of various landscapes can be found in the *Cilappatikāram*, it is the *Maṇimēkalai* in particular that dwells on the precise names and attributes of various trees and flowers.

The *Mattavilāsa*, the story of a drunken Śaiva ascetic, or Kāpālika, who loses his skull-bowl and accuses a Buddhist monk, Nāgasena, of stealing it, continues the scathing attack on a perceived Buddhist monastic interest in wine, women, and song. Nāgasena is said to yearn for the "unexpurgated, original texts" of the Buddha that permit drinking and the enjoyment of women,[26] and those "original texts" themselves are further maligned for being plagiarized versions of the *Mahābhārata* and various Vedānta philosophical treatises.[27] The Śaiva's description of his equally inebriated wife, who he says has assumed her new form through her severe ascetic practice (tapas), would seem to parody, almost line for line, the Tamil descriptions of Maṇimēkalai's beauty, even as she is described as being of "mature spiritual powers" (tapas; v.16) and as she changes forms through the power of her mantra. As the appreciative Śaiva husband describes the changes in his wife's appearance:

> Your face spangled with beads of perspiration,
> eyebrow-creepers in graceful agitation,
> Wanton movements, causeless smiles,
> speech with slurring syllables.
> A pair of rolling eyes with languid side-long glances,
> and with reddish tinge suffused,
> Hair falling over your shoulders,
> its garland all unloosed![28]

The face "spangled with beads of perspiration" contrasts to Maṇimēkalai's face likened to the pale, cool moon (iii.12). The "wanton movements" and "slurred syllables" turn upside down Maṇimēkalai's peacock-like gait and sweet, bird-like speech (iii.151–157). The "rolling . . . reddish tinge[d]" eyes offer a sharp contrast to Maṇimēkalai's eyes beautifully streaked with red, like the veins of a lotus flower (iii.7–10). The unkempt hair with flowers in disarray seems to parody the many consistent descriptions of Maṇimēkalai's hair bedecked with the sweetest-smelling flowers (e.g., iii.16–17). The descriptions of these two women of mature spiritual powers (tapas)—one drunk, the other sober—seem to play off one another, the satirical Sanskrit drama using specific phrases of female beauty in a ludicrous context of drunken revelry.

Even the descriptions of a specific, named city in the Sanskrit drama appear to parody the lengthy descriptions of locations in the Tamil Buddhist text. Like the description of the garden in the *Bhagavadajjukam*, the sarcastic description of Kāñcīpuram in the *Mattavilāsa*, where "flower-garland shops look . . . like the very source of creation of the spring season" and the "tavern resembles a sacrificial hall,"[29] might be read as a parody of the grand descriptions of Pukār (e.g., i, vii.42–82) and Vañci (xxviii.3–67) found in the *Maṇimēkalai* or the pathetic description of Kāñcī as a city where "because the rain has withheld its prosperity, human lives have ended and the beauty of gold-walled Kacci has faded" (xxviii.156–157). The silly allegorical rendering of a Kāñcīpuram tavern as Vedic sacrificial altar, where "the signpost . . . is the sacrificial post; liquor, the Soma juice; [and] those who are drinking are the priests,"[30] can perhaps also be interpreted as a comic transformation of the more majestic likening of the city of Pukār at *Maṇimēkalai* v.109–122 to a beautifully bejeweled woman, where "the lady's full, rounded shoulders are the pillars at each side of the gate."

Did Mahendravarman have the *Maṇimēkalai*, or similar Tamil works of narrative poetry, in mind as he composed the *Bhagavadajjukam* and the *Mattavilāsa*? That will never be known for certain. Yet that such scathing attacks on various religious ideas and practices, in dramatic literary form, should first appear in Sanskrit in the Tamil region at a time when interreligious debate through literature in the local language was already fully under way attests to a strong literary culture of competition, debate, and rebuttal that was not in any way restricted to works composed in Tamil. That the satirical drama is clearly a South Indian tradition,[31] as well as the fact that the performance of such plays has survived primarily in Kerala,[32] a region culturally tied to and linguistically indistinguishable from the Tamil until the thirteenth or fourteenth century, further suggests the existence of a strong, regional, multilingual literary culture concerned with defining and defending religious values and ideas through narrative, dramatic, and poetic works. In fact, doctrinal debate following the Sanskritic format of philosophical presentation—challenge (*pūrvapakṣa*) rebutted by final philosophical conclusion (*siddhānta*) in a straightforward, expository manner without any framing narrative—makes its debut relatively late in Tamil, with the thirteenth-century Śaiva work, "Philosophical Conclusions on the Knowledge of Śiva" (*Civañāṉacittiyār*). In southern India in the early medieval period, religious doctrine, philosophical ideas, and visions of the world are defined and defended in the realm of the literary. The literary landscape imagined in ornate poetic narrative and drama assumes a multilingual audience fully capable of seeing ideas, arguments, and even humor across literary genres and languages.

In Response to the *Cilappatikāram*

The *Maṇimēkalai* itself is one of the primary resources for the study of this debate through poetry in early medieval South India. Even a quick reading of a summary-style translation of the *Maṇimēkalai* reveals the polemic nature of the text; the ornate poetic creation concerned with eliciting a profound aesthetic experience of pathos or compassion is also thoroughly and quite obviously engaged in debate, in vigorously defending certain of its doctrines, ideas, and sentiments. This argument for a particular vision of the world is carried on in several layers of the *Maṇimēkalai* text, ranging from overt disputes embedded in the narrative itself to the more subtle undermining of other texts and worldviews.

A certain amount of the *Maṇimēkalai*'s polemic content is obvious as part of the narrative, particularly in the story of Cittirāpati's efforts to control both her daughter, Mātavi, and her granddaughter, Maṇimēkalai. As Cittirāpati warns Vayantamālai, Mātavi's friend and one-time fellow courtesan, a "rumor has spread among the people of this great and benevolent city" (ii.9) that Mātavi will not dance at the Indra festival, and such a rumor indicates that Mātavi's renunciation is a controversial event. "In the [length and] breadth of this ancient city," Vayantamālai reports to her friend, "the talk is not flattering. [Your renunciation] is a shameful act" (ii.33–36). Throughout the text, Cittirāpati battles public opinion, trying to make her daughter realize that she "has become the laughing stock of this great, large city" (xviii.9). At iii.149–150, the townspeople surround Maṇimēkalai and contend that "a mother who would cause [a daughter] of such beautiful appearance to undertake austerities is a cruel woman and an unfit mother!" If the accusing townsfolk may be taken as an audience within the audience, as representative of some portion of the *Maṇimēkalai*'s anticipated readers or listeners, perhaps the power of Maṇimēkalai to feed the poor and hungry and eventually to stand as the Buddha's chief disciple is intended to persuade both audiences of the ultimate value of Maṇimēkalai's transformation into a Buddhist renunciant. As Richman notes throughout her work on the *Maṇimēkalai*, relying on the image of Amutacurapi as symbolic of female nurturance, the text, at least on the narrative surface level, appears to be arguing for the validity and worth of female renunciation.

Although Maṇimēkalai and her mother suffer ridicule at the hands of the good citizens of Pukār, such derision is nothing compared to the contempt shown by the text for characters of other religious communities. The pattern of sarcasm begins early, as

Maṇimēkalai and Cutamati walk to the Buddha's Uvavaṉam. En route they encounter a Jain monk, described as dirty, shameless, and neurotically concerned with microscopic life forms (iii.86–91); a drunkard who attempts to lure the Jain monk into his "discipline" of drinking (iii.92–102); and a Śaiva ascetic described as a "madman" who "fights with his shadow" (iii.103–115). The perceived hypocrisy of Jain monks, so careful not to harm the tiniest of microbes, is depicted in the story of Cutamati's arrival in Pukār: Cutamati's father, cruelly gored by the horns of a cow and "holding his bloodied intestines in his hands" (v.47–49), is refused entry into a Jain monastery (v.53–55). The young Āputtiraṉ is cast out from his adopted brahmin community, even as he reminds those who ridicule him for being "born of a cow" that many of their most revered sages were the sons of cows, tigers, and jackals (xiii.63–69). The Nāgas "converted" by Cātuvaṉ are depicted as uncouth barbarians, surrounded by "dried white bones, the stench of flesh, and vats of boiling toddy" (xvi.66–67) and utterly incapable of giving up their toddy-drinking, flesh-eating ways (xvi.108–111). Even the most dignified teachers of the Vaidika, Sāṅkhya, and Vaiśeṣika doctrines, whom Maṇimēkalai visits in Vañci, receive no more respect; Maṇimēkalai simply "laughs" (xxvii.280) in response to their teachings and reports to Aṟavaṇaṉ that she "did not keep the five religions in [her] mind, as they were [all] without truth" (xxix.43–44).

The twenty-seventh chapter, in which Maṇimēkalai travels to Vañci to learn the so-called truths of the non-Buddhist schools of thought, contains not only an explicit level of polemic (i.e., Maṇimēkalai simply laughs, a blanket dismissal of all the teachings) but also a more subtle one. The overall presentation of the ten various schools—amounting to discussions of logic, the role of divine intervention in human life, and the constituent elements of the universe—carefully paves the way for the "correct" Buddhist version of these doctrines as explained by Aṟavaṇaṉ in the final two chapters of the text. The summation by the logician of the various means of right knowledge (*pramāṇa*) held by various schools (xxvii.5–85), for example, supplies the straw-man challenge to be thoroughly refuted in the final doctrinal conclusions expounded by Aṟavaṇaṉ in the twenty-ninth chapter on Buddhist inferential reasoning. The doctrines of the Śaivite ("his appearance removes the sorrows [of his creation]"; xxvii.93) and the Vaiṣṇavite ("Nāraṇaṉ is [our] protection"; xxvii.98–99) provide the starting point for the final chapter's discussion of the twelve elements in the causal chain of interdependent origination as the cause of rebirth and redeath (*saṁsāra*), in which "there is no one who assigns bondage and liberation" (xxx.250–251). Finally, the explanations of the Ājīvika (xxvii.110–165), Jain (xxvii.171–201), Sāṅkhya (xxvii.201–239), Vaiśeṣika (xxvii.242–262), and materialist (xxvii.264–283) systems of thought dwell at length on the respective theories of substance (*poruḷ*), the constituent material of the universe,[33] thus paving the way for the redefinition of substance as "dependent entity" (cārpu) in chapter 30, transforming the static stuff of life in the non-Buddhist teachings into the interdependently arising elements in the chain of causation.

Yet the point most consistently argued throughout the text of the *Maṇimēkalai*—from Cutamati's first instruction to the ignorant Utayakumaraṉ that "the body is the result of karma and the cause of further karma" (iv.113) to the prediction that Kōvalaṉ's bad karma will eventually be overcome to ensure his spiritual liberation (xxviii.138–144)—is that concerning karma (viṉai) and its persistent force in shaping human lives in the context of interdependent origination and the arising of the good or beneficial root conditions (ētunikaḻcci). Karma is invoked time and time again as the most potent catalyst to the arising of human suffering, as the primary power behind the pain and anguish experienced by each of the characters. To cite but a few of the more poignant examples, Maṇimēkalai attributes her fear and loneliness at finding herself all alone on the unfamiliar island of Maṇipallavam to the same bad karma (vevviṉai) that led to her father's tragic end (viii.40–43); Utayakumaraṉ's similarly violent death is explained to the king as the result of the prince's bad karma (tīviṉai), with that karma acting as the agent in each of the sequential actions leading up to the actual stabbing (xxii.193–203).[34] The sad tale of the loving couple, Kāyacaṇṭikai and Kāñcaṉaṉ, repeatedly appeals to the law of karma to explain pain, both physical and emotional.

Indeed, so repetitive are these appeals to karma, particularly to bad karma (tīviṉai), that the *Maṇimēkalai* appears to be engaged in debate with someone or something, pointedly making a case for the power and efficacy of karma, defending the doctrine of karmic cause and effect against those who would question its force in human lives. In fact, were it not for the text's framing of karmic law with the specifically Buddhist concepts of interdependent origination and the arising of conditions conducive to liberation, the *Maṇimēkalai* might be accused of coming dangerously close to the first of the "three positions of the heretics" (*tīṇi titthāyatanāni*) outlined by the Buddha himself:[35] that all experience is due solely to previous actions (*pubbekatahetu*).[36] Karma would thus seem to be a concept in need of some defense, explanation, definition, and elaboration, at least in its proper Buddhist context. Was the doctrine of karma under attack in some way in fifth- or sixth-century South India?

Given the literary milieu of intertextual engagement and debate, outlined previously, with which the multilingual sixth-century reader of the *Maṇimēkalai* would be thoroughly familiar, the challenge lies in identifying both the text(s) to which the *Maṇimēkalai* might be responding and the character or nature of that response. As with the *Kuṇṭalakēci/Nīlakēci* and *Cīvakacintāmaṇi/Periyapurāṇam* pairings discussed previously, the *Maṇimēkalai* has long been closely associated, in Tamil literary tradition, with the text that supplies the full narrative of the Kaṇṇaki and Kōvalaṉ tragedy, the *Cilappatikāram*. The *Cilappatikāram*, a narrative of thirty chapters in poetry, prose, and song dating perhaps from the fifth century C.E., begins with the marriage of young Kōvalaṉ and Kaṇṇaki. Kōvalaṉ, however, soon leaves his wife to live with the courtesan, Mātavi. Eventually, he returns, penniless, to his wife, and the two set out for Maturai to begin life anew. They are accompanied by a female ascetic, Kavunti, who offers them instruction on topics such as karma and virtue. In Maturai, Kōvalaṉ attempts to sell the last item of value the couple possesses, Kaṇṇaki's anklet, and is falsely accused by an unscrupulous goldsmith of having stolen the anklet of the queen. Kōvalaṉ is killed by the king's guards for his supposed crime. Kaṇṇaki, in a rage, tears off her breast and hurls it at Maturai, engulfing the city in flames. Kaṇṇaki and her wronged husband then ascend to the heavens, and the final book of the text concerns the establishment of a royal shrine to Kaṇṇaki the goddess outside the Tamil city of Vañci. The basic story itself is no doubt drawn from older narrative sources; references to a woman who tears off her breast are found in the Caṅkam poetic works *Naṟṟiṇai*[37] and *Puṟanāṉūṟu*.[38] Although the narrative obviously concerns itself with the value of womanly virtue (kaṟpu), it is also the story of a young girl gathering up her powers (*siddhi*) that culminates in her emergence as Kaṇṇaki-Pattiṉi the goddess.[39]

Although the *Cilappatikāram* and the *Maṇimēkalai* are often called twin texts or epics, the precise nature of the relationship between the two has remained unclear and much debated. The *Maṇimēkalai*, as noted previously, clearly assumes audience familiarity with the story told in the *Cilappatikāram*: the tale of Maṇimēkalai begins without any real introduction to the characters involved, and the tragedy of Kōvalaṉ and Kaṇṇaki is alluded to several times throughout the *Maṇimēkalai* as a paradigmatic instance of human suffering that propels various characters, from Maṇimēkalai herself to Mācāttuvāṉ, toward a life of asceticism and renunciation. The introductory chapters of the two texts, even if added centuries later, obviously convey a tradition of appreciating these two narratives as somehow related: Cāttaṉār asks Iḷaṅkō to render into poetic form the marvelous events he has witnessed and heard about[40] and then graciously tells the story of the renunciation of Maṇimēkalai when King Iḷaṅkō so requests.[41] In addition to various narrative elements, the two texts are also closely related in terms of language and style.[42]

Aṭiyārkkunallār's thirteenth-century commentary on the *Cilappatikāram*, removed some seven or eight hundred years from the composition of the narrative itself, is the first to suggest that the *Cilappatikāram* and the *Maṇimēkalai* are related through their joint exposition of the four human aims (puruṣārtha). According to the classical Sanskrit definition of the ornate narrative poem supplied by Daṇḍin in the seventh century and interpolated into Tamil in the twelfth-century *Taṇṭiyalaṅkāram*, such a work of poetry should address each of the four goals of an ideal human life: virtue (dharma), wealth and power (artha), love (kāma), and ultimate liberation of the soul (mokṣa). Following such a formula, Aṭiyārkkunallār contends that the *Cilappatikāram* and the *Maṇimēkalai* together form a complete poetic creation, with the *Cilappatikāram* addressing the first three aims of virtue (Tamil aṟam), wealth and power (Tamil poruḷ), and love (Tamil *iṉpam*) and the *Maṇimēkalai* encompassing the final aim of liberation (Tamil *vīṭu*).[43] Such a conception of the two texts is also echoed in the epilogue (*nūl kaṭṭurai*) of the *Cilappatikāram*, a postscript that could easily have been added after Aṭiyārkkunallār's commentary.[44] It is, however, difficult to see such a neatly divided treatment of the four human aims in the texts themselves. As Richman notes in her analysis of the *Maṇimēkalai*, the *Cilappatikāram* addresses the issues of renunciation and liberation through the characters Kavunti and (briefly) Maṇimēkalai, while the *Maṇimēkalai* can easily be shown to concern itself with virtue, wealth, and even love.[45] Although the medieval commentator might well have been eager to prove the compatibility of great works of Tamil literature with Sanskritic norms, the analysis according to human goals seems overly simplistic. Each text deals with all four of the aims but frames these goals with very different overall objectives: the *Cilappatikāram* with the emergence of Kaṇṇaki-Pattiṉi as a powerful goddess and the *Maṇimēkalai* with the taking of a renunciatory vow.

Moving beyond the obvious shortcomings of the medieval human aims analysis, it is, indeed, difficult to read the *Maṇimēkalai* and the *Cilappatikāram* as continuous or as twins at all. Far too many discrepancies between the two can be found, bits of narrative discord involving central characters and events, to allow for the reading of one as fulfilling or completing the other. The violent murder of Kōvalaṉ and Kaṇṇaki's enraged and awesome response in the *Cilappatikāram*, for example, are said to lead Kavunti to starve herself to death, Kōvalaṉ's father to give away his wealth and become a Buddhist monk, Kaṇṇaki's father to become an Ājīvika ascetic, and Mātavi to retreat with

Maṇimēkalai to a Buddhist nunnery (xxvii.70–108); the brahmin, Māṭalaṉ, likens this withdrawal from the world to death ("they died," *iṟantōr*; xxvii.109). The *Maṇimēkalai*, however, as mentioned previously, portrays the Kōvalaṉ-Kaṇṇaki tragedy not as a source of death or despair but as a spiritual turning point, the beginning of a new Buddhist life for Mātavi, Maṇimēkalai, and Mācāttuvāṉ that will culminate one day in liberation.[46] To cite another example of narrative discrepancy, the goddess of Maturai, Maturāpati, appears to Kaṇṇaki in the *Cilappatikāram* (xxiii) after the burning of the city to put the event into proper karmic perspective; in the *Maṇimēkalai* (xxvi.11–34), the goddess arrives before the conflagration in a futile effort to dissuade Kaṇṇaki from taking action. Another such difference in detail occurs when Mātavi shaves her young daughter's head in preparation for entering the nunnery in the *Cilappatikāram* (xxx.24–28); in the *Maṇimēkalai*, the young girl is pointedly and consistently described as sexually alluring and wearing sweet-smelling flowers in her hair. The rescue of Kōvalaṉ's ancestor from the sea by the goddess, Maṇimēkalā, is attributed in the *Cilappatikāram* to the fact that the ancestor had previously performed meritorious acts of giving (*puṇṇiya tāṉam purintōṉ*; xv.30); in the *Maṇimēkalai*, Kōvalaṉ's ancestor is clearly depicted at xxix.23–25 as the future Buddha.[47] One of the most strikingly significant narrative discrepancies between the *Cilappatikāram* and the *Maṇimēkalai*, if not an outright rejection of the former by the latter, is the portrayal of the Cēraṉ king, Ceṅkuṭṭuvaṉ. Throughout the final book of the *Cilappatikāram*, he is the champion of the deified Kaṇṇaki-Pattiṉi, subduing the armies of the north to bring back a Himalayan stone to carve into an image of the goddess. In the *Maṇimēkalai* (xxviii.103–119), however, the Cēraṉ ruler is said to have experienced his own manifestation of the conditions necessary to liberation (ētunikaḻcci)—he is the only character other than Maṇimēkalai to whom this term is applied—and to have heard the teachings of the Buddha from the lord of dharma himself. In the Buddhist text, he will certainly construct no shrine to the deified Kaṇṇaki.

With these differences of narrative detail, not surprising are the divergent themes that emerge from these two twin texts. Maṇimēkalai, as discussed in detail in the preceding chapter, is swept along to her final vow of renunciation by the manifestation of causes and conditions built over many lifetimes; Kaṇṇaki certainly plays a more active role in the unfolding of her own narrative. Her virtuous fidelity to her husband (kaṟpu) and her rage at the injustice of his death both culminate in her emergence as a great goddess, as a bestower of rain and fertility. In keeping with the fate of Kaṇṇaki and Ceṅkuṭṭuvaṉ in the Buddhist version of the story, as described previously, relatively little attention is paid to the events of the final book of the *Cilappatikāram* in the *Maṇimēkalai*; there are no royal battles in the latter, no triumphant march through the northern regions of India, no grand celebration to mark the installation of Kaṇṇaki's divine image. Indeed, if the *Maṇimēkalai* can be said to evoke an aesthetic experience of pity or compassion (Tamil aḻukai, Sanskrit karuṇa), the heightened emotional experience more obviously elicited by the tale of the *Cilappatikāram* is that of the heroic (Tamil perumitam, Sanskrit vīra), the glorious transformation of the young, chaste wife into a powerful goddess.

If the two texts cannot, then, be read as seamlessly continuous, certainly they are still related in some way. Even if the prefaces were added long after the narratives were originally written, the literary tradition to which they attest, that the *Cilappatikāram* and the *Maṇimēkalai* were composed in relation to each other in some way, cannot be lightly dismissed. If the *Maṇimēkalai* does not self-consciously seek to complete the story begun in the *Cilappatikāram*, certainly it alludes to that text, makes use of its narrative content, images, and language, and recasts the story to fit its own view of the world. In fact, the *Maṇimēkalai*, like the other Tamil literary pairings discussed previously, responds to the *Cilappatikāram* in a number of ways, challenging various philosophical, ideological, and ethical points of the earlier narrative. The *Maṇimēkalai*'s emphasis in particular on the power of karma in the context of interdependent origination offers a subtle reworking, an expansion, of the notion of karma found in its sister text. The *Maṇimēkalai* transforms the *Cilappatikāram*'s rather simplistic and fatalistic notion of karmic cause and effect into a more sophisticated and complex force operating across multiple and diverse conditions. Whereas the *Cilappatikāram*'s most commonly used term for karma (ūḻviṉai) suggests an element of the Ājīvika notion of fate (Sanskrit niyati, Tamil ūḻ),[48] the *Maṇimēkalai* presents karma (viṉai)[49] as a power at work in the ever-changing complex of interdependently arising phenomena.[50] In short, the *Maṇimēkalai* responds to the *Cilappatikāram* by redefining karma and its accompanying processes in a specifically Buddhist context.[51] In developing its vision of karma as a powerful force at work in the complex web of conditions generated by the processes underlying interdependent origination, the *Maṇimēkalai* envisions a new literary and religious landscape in which Buddhist ideas and values rise to the fore.

The *Maṇimēkalai* argues for its complex Buddhist view of karma (as viṉai) over and against the *Cilappatikāram*'s presentation of karma (as ūḻviṉai) in a number of interesting and imaginative ways, beginning with its retelling or elaboration in new directions of stories found in the *Cilappatikāram* text. Most obvious is the central story of Kōvalaṉ and Kaṇṇaki, transformed in the *Maṇimēkalai* into a meditation on the powerful and far-reaching effects of karma projected into a distant future. The great goddess of the *Cilappatikāram*, as discussed in the previous chapter, is reduced in the *Maṇimēkalai* at xxvi.40–41 to simply another karma-accumulating individual who "will return to the ocean of births and be caught in [the cycle of] birth and death" once again after enjoying the fruits of her good karma in heaven. This statement, in keeping with the general Buddhist understanding of divine beings as subject to karma and rebirth in the same manner as human beings,[52] does nothing less than negate the powerful images of the final book of the *Cilappatikāram*; the deification of Kaṇṇaki-Pattiṉi, "giver of abundant rain" (*vāṉ taru ciṟappiṉ*),[53] becomes but a temporary and ultimately unsatisfactory state, for it is only in human birth that one can achieve final liberation. Whereas Maturāpati explicitly informs Kaṇṇaki after the burning of Maturai that she will see her husband again only in his heavenly, not earthly, form in the *Cilappatikāram* at xxiii.173–176, the *Maṇimēkalai* at xxvi.54–61 projects an image of a compassionate and caring couple returned to earth to live out their remaining karma[54] until the Buddha comes again, performing deeds of kindness "for all people for a long time" (lines 60–61). Although the *Maṇimēkalai* and the *Cilappatikāram* both attribute Kōvalaṉ's bloody end to bad karma accumulated during his previous birth as Parataṉ,[55] the Buddhist version of the tale expends far more time and energy explaining the working out of that karma into the future, culminating ultimately in liberation at the feet of the coming Buddha. Kaṇṇaki's current status as goddess is presented as little more than a brief stage in the Buddhist text, the transitory reward for past good deeds, and Kōvalaṉ's previous bad karma, as well as the goddess's past act of anger, have far-reaching and complex consequences leading to pain and suffering, compassionate service, and ultimate release.

The *Maṇimēkalai*, in similar fashion, continues the story of the semidivine being (vidyādhara) and his lady friend told in the *Cilappatikāram* at vi.1–71 in the tale of Cutamati's abandonment by the beautiful and illustrious Mārutavēkaṉ (iii.33–41, v.32–79).[56] Like the male figure in the *Cilappatikāram*, Mārutavēkaṉ comes to earth to witness the festival of Indra celebrated in Pukār (*Maṇimēkalai*, ii.33–35), but unlike the solicitous tour guide of the *Cilappatikāram*, Mārutavēkaṉ abandons Cutamati because of her past karma (v.35–36). As with the story of Kōvalaṉ and Kaṇṇaki, that past karma is the source of a complex variety of events extending far into the future: Cutamati meets the sage Caṅkataruman̲, becomes a follower of the Buddha, remains in Pukār, thus comes to know Mātavi and Maṇimēkalai, learns (first at vii.98–108) that in a previous life she was Maṇimēkalai's sister, and because of a virtuous deed performed in that previous existence, she will eventually obtain liberation (xii.108–113). Here again, karma is seen to act in complex ways across time, setting in motion a number of events at once, a chain of narrative sequences.

The pitiful tale of Kōtamai, imploring the goddess, Campāpati, to revive her deceased son, told in Maṇimēkalā's recitation concerning the temple of the cosmic place (*Maṇimēkalai*, vi), would seem to provide a reworking of the story of the brahmin woman, Mālati, first told in the opening lines of *Cilappatikāram*, ix, and retold at xxx.71–81. While Mālati, like Kōtamai, appeals to all available deities for help,[57] at the temple of one Pācaṇṭacāttaṉ[58] the deity himself enters the lifeless body of the child and causes Mālati's son to "live" once again (ix.23–25). In stark contrast, as discussed in the previous chapter, Campāpati explicitly states that ignorance and matured karma have caused both the life and death of Cāṅkalaṉ (*Maṇimēkalai*, vi.150–152). The guardian deity of Pukār also emphasizes and the temple of the cosmic place persistently reminds that the saving of life is beyond the power of any deity. Indra and Mayaṉ, the most important of the divine beings to appear in both the *Cilappatikāram* and the *Maṇimēkalai*, are similarly transformed into good Buddhists in the latter text, in direct response, one might argue, to their portrayal in the former. Whereas Mayaṉ, the divine builder, is said to have created the luxurious, bejeweled couch that graces Mācāttuvāṉ's (Kōvalaṉ's father's) mansion in the *Cilappatikāram* at ii.11–13, in the *Maṇimēkalai* at iii.78–79 he is said to have built a "couch" of a very different sort: the lotus seat (*pīṭikai*) of the Buddha that stands inside the crystal pavilion in the Uvavaṉam park. The commemoratory model of the universe on the cremation grounds (vi.201–202) and the painting on the pillar that foretells the future (xxi.131–132) are also attributed to Mayaṉ in the *Maṇimēkalai*. In similar fashion, the king of the gods, Indra, who is the first to worship Kaṇṇaki-Pattiṉi in her newly deified form in the *Cilappatikāram* at xxiii.193–197, in the *Maṇimēkalai* at xxv.60–65 builds the great pedestal on Maṇipallavam and is said to worship no being other than the Buddha.

Another technique employed by the *Maṇimēkalai* to convey a different and more complex view of karma than that presented in the *Cilappatikāram* is its structure of flashbacks, its narrative episodes that combine past, present, and future actions as discussed in the previous chapter. The *Cilappatikāram* presents the workings of karma (as ūḻviṉai) in more or less straightforward causal sequences, in which one particular action in the past has yielded a specific result in the present. In the *Cilappatikāram* at ix.54–56, for example, Kaṇṇaki's friend, Tēvanti, informs her that Kōvalaṉ has run off with Mātavi because, in a former incarnation, Kaṇṇaki failed to keep a vow on Kōvalaṉ's behalf. Kōvalaṉ's murder is similarly attributed entirely to a single past incident (xxiii.137–176). The *Maṇimēkalai*, although certainly stating repeatedly that characters are propelled by karma into certain situations and actions, surrounds the central action of its narrative, the renunciation of Maṇimēkalai, with a host of characters, events, and karma stories that are all necessary to the eventual taking of the renunciatory vow. One striking difference between the *Maṇimēkalai* and *Cilappatikāram* texts is the sheer number of characters and stories introduced in the former, from Āputtiraṉ, Kāyacaṇṭikai, and Aṟavaṇaṉ to Maṇimēkalā, Cātuvaṉ, and Utayakumaraṉ. All of their karmic narratives, not only Maṇimēkalai's karma from past births, are necessary to explain fully both her manifestation of beneficial conditions and her subsequent withdrawal from the world. What the *Cilappatikāram* presents as a straightforward "A yields B" karmic causal formula, the *Maṇimēkalai* weaves into an intricate tapestry of prerequisite conditions: A yields B, provided that C, D, E, and F are present to provide the proper environment in which both A and B can come to full fruition.

The *Maṇimēkalai* also explicitly refutes specific statements regarding the working of karma made in the *Cilappatikāram*. Whereas karma (as ūḻviṉai) and the power of wifely virtue (kaṟpu) are presented as the primary causes of the Kōvalaṉ-Kaṇṇaki tragedy in the *Cilappatikāram*, for example, karma—redefined as volition (ceykai) in the *Maṇimēkalai*'s doctrinal exposition of interdependent origination—is tied to and dependent on each of the other eleven elements in the causal sequence, acting as one force among many in this powerful process. As noted in the previous chapter, not only the elements in the chain of interdependent origination but other phenomena as well, such the arising of the beneficial root conditions necessary to liberation, are imbued with an efficaciousness, propelling Maṇimēkalai and her accumulated karma toward renunciation. The *Cilappatikāram* states directly several times that the force of karma can be eliminated, the karmic slate wiped clean, within the scope of a single lifetime. Tēvanti tells Kaṇṇaki that the effects of her broken vow in a previous life can be remedied by bathing in the temple where the river Kāviri meets the sea (ix.56–63), while Kavunti, accompanied by Kōvalaṉ and Kaṇṇaki, prays to a sage near Śrīraṅkam for her karma born of previous deeds to be eradicated (x.164). Later, Kavunti curses a couple for making fun of Kaṇṇaki and turns them into jackals but reports that the two will be relieved from their suffering within twelve months (x.241–244). In sharp contrast, the *Maṇimēkalai* presents karma as a powerful force operating across many lifetimes, extending its effects from one person to another, eradicated only through the most severe of ascetic practices. The same karma that killed Kōvalaṉ, for example, brings Maṇimēkalai to Maṇipallavam (viii.40–43), whereas it is also said that Maṇimēkalā is compelled to bring the young girl to the wondrous isle because her conditions conducive to liberation have sufficiently matured (vii.19–22), thus attributing multiple causes to a significant narrative and karmic event. The virtuous karma accumulated by Maṇimēkalai in feeding the monk, Cātucakkaraṉ, in a previous existence has generated her present, transformative birth and will eventually be the vehicle of her liberation (x.40–41). Utayakumaraṉ's murder, in a previous life, of the bumbling cook who botched Cātucakkaraṉ's breakfast (xxi.47–62) destroys him in both the past- and present-tense narratives (xxiii.82–85); the text states explicitly that karma may return again and again throughout future lives (xxi.68–69).

Particularly at odds with the *Cilappatikāram* is the *Maṇimēkalai*'s moral vision, its insistence that the doctrine of karma does not relieve one of personal responsibility. In the *Maṇimēkalai*'s depiction of a world ruled by karmic forces beyond human control, human compassion and concern for others are valued above all else. Karma does not negate human intention or moral obligation. Swept into pain and suffering by karmically induced chains of events, still Kāñcaṉaṉ cares for Kāyacaṇṭikai, Āputtiraṉ serves the poor with Amutacurapi, and the grieving king and queen learn to rule more wisely. In contrast to the Buddhist text's evocation of the heightened emotional or aesthetic experience of pathos, culminating in Maṇimēkalai's statement to the queen that "your pity must be for all lives" (xxiii.78–79), karma (as ūḻviṉai) in the *Cilappatikāram* often appears to neutralize any sense of moral or ethical responsibility. Karma is repeatedly blamed for human suffering and anguish in the latter text, often to the relief of the principal characters. In the *Cilappatikāram* at xiii.94–95, for example, Kōvalaṉ, waiting with his faithful wife on the outskirts of Maturai, receives a note from Mātavi asking what she has done to deserve such suffering; realizing that Mātavi is without fault, Kōvalaṉ exclaims, "It is my bad karma (*eṉ tītu*)!" and his burden of guilt or depression over abandoning his lover is thus lifted (*taḷarcci nīṅki*). At xvi.156, the unscrupulous goldsmith of the Pāṇṭiyaṉ king approaches Kōvalaṉ, who is "trapped in the net of [his] bad karma" (tīviṉai *mutir valaic ceṉṟupaṭṭiruṇṭa*). Before the queen of Maturai and immediately following her confrontation with the unjust Pāṇṭiyaṉ king (xxi.1), Kaṇṇaki declares, "I am a slave to bad karma!" (*koṭuviṉai āṭṭiyēṉ*). Karma leaves the principal characters of the *Cilappatikāram* seemingly without choice and without much directly articulated sense of personal responsibility. Events are dictated by karma, which "traps" and "enslaves." Indeed, the only principal character who appears motivated by a powerful force in addition to karma is Kaṇṇaki, whose wifely virtue (kaṟpu) enables her to confront the Pāṇṭiyaṉ king and is ultimately cited as the course of her transformation into a goddess. Female virtue, tested by karma, emerges triumphant. Once that transformation is complete, however, due to both karma and womanly virtue, little is said about karma in the final book of the text; karma (indicated by viṉai in compound) appears only six times, either in reference to the story told in the earlier two books or in the context of direct instruction to the Cēraṉ king about the nature of rebirth.

In the *Maṇimēkalai*, however, the murder of Utayakumaraṉ, an event attributed entirely to the prince's bad karma as noted previously (xxii.193–203), leaves a trail of personal guilt, blame, and retribution, even though all of the characters are said to be driven to their various roles in the dramatic scene by Utayakumaraṉ's bad karma. As Tuvatikaṉ informs Kāñcaṉaṉ after the killing (xx.122–129):

> "Hear this!
> Even though matured karma has come
>   and taken the precious life of Utayakumaraṉ,
> without due consideration you have committed a bad deed,
>   oh Kāñcaṉaṉ the semi-divine being!
> That karma will persist without leaving you. . . ."
>
> The semi-divine being arose,
>   with bad karma coming into force [and causing] suffering in his heart,
> and traveled through the sky.

Whereas Kaṇṇaki's burning of Maturai and subsequent deification are presented in the *Maṇimēkalai* as simply one stage on a long journey toward compassionate service and eventual liberation (xxvi.33–61), in the *Cilappatikāram* the conflagration itself, the power it represents, and the deity created by that power[59] constitute the narrative climax of the text. Karma, both good and bad, in the *Cilappatikāram* is a driving force of great significance that ultimately generates, in conjunction with the central character's unwavering wifely fidelity, the emergence of the goddess, Pattiṉi. In the *Maṇimēkalai*, karma is a vehicle of suffering against which human values of love and care must continually be tested.

In contrast to the straightforward, almost fatalistic version of karma presented in the *Cilappatikāram*, the *Maṇimēkalai* thus takes a longer and more complex view of karma as one of several powerful agents at work in shaping the course of human lives. If the *Cilappatikāram* can be said to tell the story of the beginnings of a Pattiṉi cult in South India, as Zvelebil and others have suggested,[60] of the virtuous Kaṇṇaki traveling through the Tamil countryside gathering up and strengthening the power of her chastity, the *Maṇimēkalai* can perhaps be read as a response in subverting those powers, in subordinating deification to renunciation, devotion to the Buddha, service to others, and concern for ultimate liberation. Maṇimēkalai, consistently identified throughout the Buddhist text with Kaṇṇaki rather than with Mātavi, her biological mother,[61] is not a goddess but a Buddha-like figure, feeding the poor and hungry until her eventual liberation as the chief disciple of the coming Buddha. Although both the *Maṇimēkalai* and the *Cilappatikāram* perhaps draw on older narratives circulating in South India at the time, each text sets the story in its own religious and philosophical context.[62]

The *Maṇimēkalai* reworks the *Cilappatikāram*'s presentation of karma in particular to articulate a specifically Buddhist vision of karma at work in the world, karma that is redefined in terms of the complex causal processes that underlie interdependent origination. The suffering that befalls Kōvalaṉ and Kaṇṇaki and that culminates in the deification of the couple in the *Cilappatikāram* serves simply as a catalyst for spiritual and moral transformation in the Buddhist narrative, as a story that causes Maṇimēkalai to shed tears of grief, as the tale told by a goddess of Vañci who realizes herself to be midway through her journey to the Buddha. The karma at work in the first text still functions in the second yet propels characters and events in entirely new directions. In both texts, karma is at work in the world, shaping human lives, but the way in which it works, the complexity with which it functions, the fruit that it bears, and the moral responsibility it entails are very different in each. The *Maṇimēkalai*, in short, responds directly to the text of the *Cilappatikāram*, molding the same basic narrative material into a new vision of the world and the workings of karma, marking out a place for Buddhist thought, for a Buddhist moral vision, in the Tamil-speaking religious milieu. The *Maṇimēkalai*, in responding to the *Cilappatikāram*, claims a place of honor for Buddhism in the diverse Tamil literary landscape, the landscape that serves as the setting for debate over religious doctrine and values.

In the Tamil literary culture of the sixth century, the *Maṇimēkalai* suggests that one important technique employed to establish the legitimacy of this newly imagined literary-religious landscape lies in claiming the allegiance of other texts. As noted briefly in chapter 1, for example, the *Maṇimēkalai* (xxii.59–61) quotes the *Tirukkuṟaḷ* on the subject of a virtuous wife's ability to command the rains and pointedly cites the author of the earlier text as "the poet who is without falsehood" (poyyil pulavaṉ).[63] Although the *Tirukkuṟaḷ* has long been received in the west as a nonsectarian ethical work of universal import[64] and has, at one time or another, been claimed by every religious group in the Tamil-speaking region, the proper historical and religious context in which to read the *Kuṟaḷ* remains largely a mystery. The text is often assigned Jain authorship,[65] based largely on certain vaguely Jain elements in the text and on Camayativākaravāmaṉar's fourteenth-century commentary on the more obviously Jain *Nīlakēci* that claims the *Tirukkuṟaḷ* as "our text."[66] Yet the *Maṇimēkalai* is significantly the first in a long line of texts to claim affiliation with the *Kuṟaḷ*, no doubt already a well-known work by the time of the *Maṇimēkalai*'s composition. Although the *Kuṟaḷ* text might not have existed in the sixth century in precisely the same form in which it now does, the reference to "the poet without falsehood" suggests a well-known, authored text rather than a random verse or stray bit of oral literature. What, precisely, might this self-conscious affiliation with the author of the *Kuṟaḷ* suggest?

Perhaps it indicates that the "poet without falsehood" is a fellow Buddhist to whom the *Maṇimēkalai* can appeal for confirmation and legitimation of its own vision of the world. There is nothing in the *Kuṟaḷ* to suggest that it is not a Buddhist work,[67] and certainly the emphasis on virtue (Tamil aṟam) throughout the text—even in those sections ostensibly devoted to wealth and power (Tamil poruḷ) and love (Tamil kāmam)—is thoroughly in keeping with the spirit of the *Maṇimēkalai*. More positively, a number of the early verses describing the supreme being (*kaṭavuḷ*) envisioned by the *Kuṟaḷ* might easily be read as descriptions of the Buddha. The first verse, for example, names this being the "first lord" (*ātipakavaṉ*), whereas the *Maṇimēkalai* addresses or refers to the Buddha three times as "lord" (*pakavaṉ*, at iii.61; xxvi.54; and xxviii.174), once as "first sage" (*āticāṉ muṉivaṉ*, at vii.19), and three times as "first being" (*ātimutalvaṉ*, at xii.37; xii.108; and xxix.23). Such observations, however, are at best inconclusive in assigning the *Kuṟaḷ* to any specific sectarian context. Perhaps, in quoting the "poet without falsehood," the *Maṇimēkalai* simply seeks to align itself with Tamil literary tradition more generally, particularly on the issue of the value of female virtue.[68] As Richman notes, in the narrative context in which the guardian deity of the city quotes the verse, by "structur[ing] his speech as a gloss upon a verse from a venerated text, he makes his argument in a traditional and accepted manner."[69] Whatever the specific intention behind such a quotation and whether or not the *Tirukkuṟaḷ* can be called Buddhist, the *Maṇimēkalai* clearly seeks to present itself as thoroughly compatible with other important Tamil literary works, as a full and legitimate member of the literary culture in which it participates.

In citing a text and claiming the allegiance of a fellow poet who may well not be Buddhist at all, the *Maṇimēkalai* also begins to make an argument for the uniqueness of its vision of the literary/religious landscape: that it is far more inclusive, open to all, amenable to many points of view and types of teachings, than the landscapes imagined by the Jain monks, who turn their backs on Cutamati's ailing father, or the brahmins, who oust Āputtiraṉ because of the circumstances of his birth. As in other Buddhist narrative traditions, the *Maṇimēkalai* envisions a Buddhist landscape, a community, that is accessible to all beings, from the chief of the cannibalistic Nāgas converted by Cātuvaṉ to the king of the island of Cāvakam. Here, Maṇimēkalai's asceticism, the impending renunciation of a would-be courtesan, provides a powerful vehicle for constructing this revisionist landscape. As Richard Valantasis argues, the ascetic "rejects precisely to embrace another existence . . . construct[ing] an alternative to the cultural givens."[70] In literary terms, it might be said that the *Maṇimēkalai*, featuring the female child-ascetic, is "subversive,"[71] withdrawing from, to overturn, the conventions of the Caṅkam-era Tamil literary tradition,[72] imagining a new landscape of openness and limitless possibilities (with such limitless possibilities including the future rebirth of the title character as the chief disciple of the Buddha). Particularly if the *Maṇimēkalai* is read as a response of sorts to the *Cilappatikāram*, Maṇimēkalai, an ascetic in the making, serves as the perfect figure to reject the world envisioned by the latter and construct the new: she is identified with Kaṇṇaki as one of mature spiritual powers (tapas) and great womanly virtue (kaṟpu) yet relegates deification to something less than renunciation. Her travels from Pukār to Vañci and Kāñcīpuram realign and re-establish the landscape described in the *Cilappatikāram* as distinctly Buddhist. Her eventual rejection of the courtesan life in favor of compassionate service through Amutacurapi carries with it an implicit rejection of the *Cilappatikāram*'s moral sense of karmic relief and Kaṇṇaki's rage in the face of karma (as ūḻviṉai). In short, Maṇimēkalai's impending ascetic renunciation implies liberation to withdraw from one view of the Tamil-speaking landscape to construct another, more open one. The ascetic figure of mature spiritual powers who "wields arrows made of curses" (v.16) contains within herself the power of change. The narrative of the daughter of a courtesan who renounces the world is ripe with possibility.

Yet however sweeping, however far-reaching those possibilities might be, in the present-tense *Maṇimēkalai* narrative Buddhism remains part of a diverse and, at times, hostile landscape, simply one of many religious communities existing side by side. Its aims in the present-tense narrative are primarily ethical or moral: to convince the Nāga chieftain, at the very least, to refrain from killing living beings (xvi.112–117); to persuade the Bhāgavata king[73] to convert the royal prison into a dwelling place for ascetics (xix.157–162); and to compel Āputtiraṉ, as King Puṇṇiyarācaṉ, to return to his kingdom and "provide food, shelter, and clothing to all human beings" (xxv.229–231). Neither the Bhāgavata king of Pukār nor King Puṇṇiyarācaṉ of Cāvakam builds a Buddhist shrine in the manner of the *Cilappatikāram*'s emphasis, in its third and final book, on the construction of a temple to Pattiṉi. A primary goal of the *Maṇimēkalai* would appear to amount to inculcating proper moral concerns; the king can remain a Bhāgavata so long as he rules compassionately, wisely, and generously, whereas the Nāgas can continue to live their Nāga lifestyle as long as they refrain from killing. The doctrinal expositions of chapter 27 aside, the non-Buddhist characters of the narrative—Jains, brahmins, and Nāgas—are criticized not for any doctrinal position but for being uncaring, hypocritical, and hurtful.[74] The *Maṇimēkalai*, at least in its present-tense narrative, would seem to articulate an expansive vision of Buddhist community that is ultimately based on an ethic of caring and compassion for others.

In its emphasis on the power of karma in the context of interdependent origination and the aesthetic evocation of compassion, the *Maṇimēkalai* transforms the worldview of the *Cilappatikāram*, the landscape envisioned by the text, and reimagines the Tamil landscape to include a powerful community of devoted and caring Buddhists. For an audience of connoisseurs familiar with the literary culture that also produced the Caṅkam poetic anthologies, the *Cilappatikāram*, and the *Tirukkuṟaḷ*, the figure of Maṇimēkalai, the pubescent girl about to renounce ordinary human existence and undertake severe austerities, provides a powerful character through which to imagine a new world, a new community. Yet the *Maṇimēkalai* is also careful, at every turn, to make that newly envisioned Buddhist landscape a distinctly local one, tied to regional traditions, stories, images, and vocabulary. It is to the issue of language, to the fact that the *Maṇimēkalai* is written in a regional language rather than in the Pāli of Buddhadatta or the Sanskrit of Mahendravarman I, that the discussion now turns.

Localization and the Transmission of Tradition

The *Maṇimēkalai*, self-consciously responding to its sister narrative, the *Cilappatikāram*, imagines a place for Buddhism in the religiously diverse and competitive world of early medieval South India; the text is equally concerned with making that Buddhism thoroughly local or Tamil. If one considers the reading community of the *Maṇimēkalai*, a community of literary connoisseurs for whom the intertextual allusions and references discussed previously were both obvious and significant, this Buddhist poetic narrative composed in Tamil provides the only historical evidence available for the transmission of Buddhist tradition (images, doctrines, values) throughout the Tamil-speaking region of southern India in the early medieval period. Given the array of literary languages actively in use in sixth-century South India (at the very least, Tamil, Sanskrit, and Pāli), that the *Maṇimēkalai* is composed in Tamil represents a conscious choice on the part of the author, both real and model, to render a transregional, multilingual religious tradition into the local or regional language.[75] Literary language choice, "in a multilingual space," notes Pollock, "is [itself] part of a larger cultural strategy for establishing or discontinuing associations, addressing more important, or larger, or different audiences, and creating new identities."[76] By translating or rendering into Tamil various narratives, terms, and concepts associated with a translocal Buddhist tradition, the *Maṇimēkalai* transforms Anderson's "immense community" of a world religion made possible through transregional languages such as Sanskrit and Pāli[77] into a local, regional one. Buddhist tradition becomes part of Tamil literary tradition, part of the imagined community "in the good world [where] Tamil is spoken, between northern Vēṅkaṭam and southern Kumari."[78]

Although the *Maṇimēkalai* is the earliest extant Tamil text to make obvious and substantial use of material from non-Tamil sources, similar texts soon follow. The *Maṇimēkalai*, in fact, marks the beginning of an era of considerable literary output in Tamil, much of it Buddhist and Jain, and much of it drawing on material found in Sanskrit, Pāli, and Prākrit sources. The lost *Kuṇṭalakēci* was almost certainly a Tamil retelling of the story of Bhaddā Kuṇḍalakesā found in the commentaries on the *Dhammapada* and *Therīgāthā*, for example,[79] whereas the (also no longer extant) *Pimpicārakatai*[80] likely "translated" or retold the story of the famed king of Magadha and patron of the Buddha, Bimbisāra.[81] The ninth-century Jain poetic narrative mentioned previously, the *Cīvakacintāmaṇi*, tells the story of Jīvaka or Jīvandhara found in a number of Sanskrit and Prākrit works, including Guṇabhadra's *Uttarapurāṇa* and Puṣpadanta's *Mahāpurāṇa*, but was perhaps based on a Prākrit original now unknown.[82] The early medieval *Peruṅkatai* retells the story of Udayana (Tamil Utayaṉaṉ) found in various Sanskrit and Prākrit versions of the *Bṛhatkathā*,[83] and a portion of the Jain *Mahāpurāṇa* is retold in the tenth-century *Cūḷāmaṇi*.[84] Even the early Śaiva devotional poets, celebrated in South Indian religious tradition and secondary scholarship alike for their "Tamilness" (a theme to be discussed later), arguably translate into Tamil a number of Śaiva myths and images found in the *Mahābhārata* and the Sanskrit mythological narratives (*purāṇa*).[85]

Although the story of Kōvalan̲ and Kaṇṇaki and the basic plot concerning Maṇimēkalai, the would-be courtesan, are unique to the *Cilappatikāram* and the *Maṇimēkalai* and would appear to be indigenous to South India, the *Maṇimēkalai*, quite in contrast to its earlier counterpart, contains numerous examples of phrases, images, characters, and stories obviously drawn from other languages and literary cultures and translated into Tamil. Translation here implies a process of cultural transmission that extends beyond the simple exchange of a word or phrase in one language for another. As Pollock notes, the practice of translation from one language to another has long been a ubiquitous one in South Asia, yet there exists "no Sanskrit or other Indian discourse on translation; in fact, there exist [*sic*] no common word for translation in any premodern Indic language."[86] Although the *Maṇimēkalai* quite obviously does, in fact, substitute Tamil words, or simply Tamil transliterations, for a host of technical philosophical terms in Sanskrit and Prākrit (see later), it also reworks and reinterprets the images and stories found in the "sacred language[s]" of the Buddhist world's "great sacral culture."[87] As recent translation theorists have noted, translation creates new possibilities and "should, where appropriate, reveal and accentuate difference."[88] The rendering of the foreign into the local or the familiar has the power to form and shape identity,[89] to "domesticate" the foreign or remote.[90] As Rita Copeland argues in her study of medieval European strategies of translation from Latin into regional vernaculars, translation offers a means of challenging, undermining, and eventually appropriating the ideologies and values of the dominant, transregional discourse (in her case, Latin); translation, in other words, is "a vehicle for expressing or playing out large questions of cultural difference."[91] Pollock's discussion of six "regimes" of translation is helpful here, particularly that of "incorporation" (surreptitiously adapting the ideas, images, and values of another text or textual language) and "retelling," wherein a transregional literary paradigm is creatively adapted to the local literary culture.[92] In the late medieval translations of the *Mahābhārata* discussed by Velcheru Narayana Rao, for example, the Sanskrit epic is not simply retold in the regional language; the text "is transformed into a regional story of medieval south India," freely reinterpreting the Sanskrit narrative and "creat[ing] an elevated and regional discourse and values."[93] Whether or not specific sources for the *Maṇimēkalai*'s various stories and ideas can be pinpointed—whether or not searching for particular sources for the text's notions of compassion or interdependent origination, for example, is even relevant—through the writing and reading of the *Maṇimēkalai* as a Tamil Buddhist narrative poem, the immense community and tradition of transregional Buddhism are gathered in, refocused through the local language and literary culture. Buddhist tradition becomes local tradition, a part of the local literary culture.

Among the most readily apparent direct translations (or often simply transliterations) are the numerous philosophical terms employed throughout the text but particularly in the twenty-ninth and thirtieth chapters dealing with inferential reasoning and interdependent origination: for "agreement," Tamil *annuvayam* for Sanskrit *anvayam*; for "difference," Tamil *vetirēkam* for Sanskrit *vyatireka*; the names of the individual elements in the cycle of interdependent origination; and, of course, ētu and ētunikaḻcci, used throughout the narrative to refer to the arising of the beneficial root conditions that lead to renunciation and ultimate liberation.[94] *Taṉmam* (from Pāli or Prākrit *dhamma*) is used for the first time in Tamil in the *Maṇimēkalai* as a synonym for the Tamil word for virtue (aṟam),[95] and *kaṉmam* (from Pāli or Prākrit *kamma*) is similarly used for the first time in Tamil as an equivalent term for karma (viṉai).[96]

Yet for all of the technical phrases translated or transliterated into Tamil in the chapters on logic and interdependent origination, the *Maṇimēkalai* surprisingly lacks translations of those Pāli and Sanskrit terms specifically used to describe enlightenment, salvation, renunciation, and the various Buddhist paths leading to liberation. Although the principal characters of the text are clearly anything but ordinary human beings, nowhere in the text do the words for "stream-winner" (sotāpanna), "worthy one" (arahant), "Buddha-to-be" (bodhisatta), or any Tamil equivalents thereof appear. Maṇimēkalai exhibits several of the eight characteristics of a Buddha-in-the-making—human birth (signaled by, among other things, her ētunikaḻcci), birth as a male (in the future), seeing a teacher (again, to be accomplished in a future birth)—yet consistently she is referred to only as a "young creeper" (*iḷaṅkoṭi*) or, at most, as "she who has realized her past births" (*pōṉa piṟappiṉ pukuntatai uṇartōḷ*; xxx.2). The many references to the coming of the future Buddha—in many ways a central focus of the text, discussed further in chapter 3—never once mention him by name (Pāli Metteyya, Sanskrit Maitreya). The *Maṇimēkalai* dwells at length on the power of karma and its lasting effects both good and bad, yet the text never once employs the expected term "merit" (*puñña*) to describe the virtue cultivated by Maṇimēkalai's offerings to Cātucakkaraṉ (x.40–41) or by her feeding of the poor through the power of Amutacurapi. Although the ultimate goal of liberation is variously described as "the greatest bliss" (*perum pēr iṉpam*; ii.65) or "the great boon" (perum *pēṟu*; xxiv.109, xxx.49), a clearly transliterated or translated Tamil term for enlightenment (Pāli nibbāna) is never used. The reasons for this curious gap are not entirely clear. Perhaps this aspect of the *Maṇimēkalai* suggests that terms such as merit (puñña) or enlightenment (nibbāna) were actually quite narrowly defined, used only in particular contexts and circumstances, whereas the ways to liberation and the goal itself were more broadly conceived. The possible paths to liberation, at least from the *Maṇimēkalai*'s point of view, are multiple, amorphous, extending far beyond the possibilities reflected in one or two specific terms of scholastic or monastic origin. A text such as the *Maṇimēkalai* is simply far more concerned with human situations and appropriate models of human response—in short, with moral or ethical inquiry—than with establishing the specifics of a salvific vocabulary.

To return to the *Maṇimēkalai* as a translated text, also quite obvious as borrowings from other, non-Tamil sources in the *Maṇimēkalai* are images such as "the sun, with its full rays, swallowed in cool mist" (xii.63) cited previously and the many descriptions of and epithets directed toward the Buddha. The great sage, Caṅkataruman, for example, refers directly to the previous lives of the Buddha (v.72–73), and Maṇimēkalai, after receiving Amutacurapi from Kōmuki Lake, addresses the Buddha with a succession of phrases that refer directly to specific episodes in the Buddha's life or past lives (xi.61–72): "you of steadfast mind who conquered Māra";[97] "you who donated your eyes to another";[98] and "you who annihilated the suffering of the Nāgas."[99] In similar fashion,

Aṟavaṇaṉ's list of the wondrous happenings that will accompany the birth of the future Buddha (xii.83–98), from plentiful rains to the disappearance of all human suffering, closely parallels the catalogue of miracles found in the *Nidānakathā* in conjunction with the Buddha's conception and birth.[100]

In addition to such words, phrases, and images that would appear to originate in non-Tamil literary sources, the *Maṇimēkalai*, whenever it leaves behind the core *Cilappatikāram* story of Kōvalaṉ, Kaṇṇaki, Mātavi, and Maṇimēkalai, often incorporates narratives that are also found in Buddhist literature composed in Sanskrit or Pāli.[101] Yet nowhere does the *Maṇimēkalai* simply translate verbatim from the Pāli or Sanskrit per se; rather, the text offers a Tamil version of stories found in non-Tamil sources, many of them composed much earlier than the *Maṇimēkalai*. The story of Kōtamai and her son, Cārṅkalaṉ, for example, as discussed in chapter 1, offers a new version of the Pāli story of Kīsagotamī and the mustard seed that pays particular attention not only to the facts of death and impermanence but also to ignorance (pētaimai) and karma or volition (ceykai) as their ultimate cause. The tale of the warring Nāgas who covet the Buddha's pedestal, told first at viii.54–61 and referred to briefly at ix.58–60, presents a condensed version of a similar story found in the *Mahāvaṁsa* (as discussed in the previous chapter). To cite but a few more examples, the narrative of the virtuous woman, Vicākai, who is wronged by the son of King Kakantaṉ (xxii.82–158), explicitly emphasizes the importance of giving (Sanskrit *dāna*, Tamil *tāṉam*),[102] closely following the Visākhā of Pāli narratives, who is portrayed as a pious Buddhist householder, foremost among laywomen who support the Buddhist community of monks and nuns (*saṅgha*).[103] The story of Kōvalaṉ's shipwrecked ancestor rescued from the sea by the goddess Maṇimēkalā (vii.33–38, xxix.14–33) closely parallels Maṇimekhalā's deliverance of the Buddha-to-be found in the Jātakas.[104]

Perhaps the most obvious shift from the translocal to the local can be seen in the stories concerning Maṇimēkalai's past and future lives. In these stories, the names and places clearly emerge as Tamil forms of North Indian locales and Indo-Āryan words: Kāntāram for Gandhāra (ix.12), Ilakkumi for Lakṣmī (ix.41), Irākulaṉ for Rāhula (ix.46), Tārai for Tārā and Vīrai for Vīrā (x.50–51), and Kaṅkai for Gaṅgā (x.56). Maṇimēkalai's future, as well as that of her parents, Kōvalaṉ and Kaṇṇaki, is also clearly tied to nonlocal places associated with the Buddha: the land of Makatam (Magadha; xxi.175) and the city of Kapilaiyam (Kapilavastu; xxvi.44). Whether or not the *Maṇimēkalai* simply invents the entire story of its central characters is unclear. Perhaps the possible connection between the narratives of Maṇimēkalai/Maṇimēkalā and the female ascetic Uppalavaṇṇā noted in the previous chapter[105] suggests a Pāli source for the *Maṇimēkalai* text, particularly for the stories regarding the past lives of the protagonists (as Ilakkumi and Irākulaṉ) who have been together through many lifetimes. As Tuvatikaṉ informs Maṇimēkalai (xxi.29–32):

> He was born as husband to you,
> and you were born as wife to the one who warms your heart,
>   many times in many births,
> not just in [those] births that you have seen [revealed to you on Maṇipallavam].

The *Apadāna* explicitly ties Rāhula (the son of the Buddha) to Uppalavaṇṇā, stating that both were born of the same parents[106] and have similar inclinations or tendencies (*samānacchandamānasa*).[107] This perhaps suggests a (now lost) series of narratives concerning the two characters from which the Tamil text draws its inspiration.

Whatever the sources for the stories found in the *Maṇimēkalai*, the overall effects of such translation as the vehicle for the transmission or localization of Buddhist tradition are several. The *Maṇimēkalai* might be said to domesticate its vision of Buddhism and Buddhist tradition in a number of ways. In quoting the *Tirukkuṟaḷ*, for example, a text that, as suggested previously, may or may not be Buddhist, the *Maṇimēkalai* seeks to align itself with Tamil literary tradition and values, to claim as its own and reinterpret in a Buddhist context the *Kuṟaḷ*'s teachings concerning the virtue (kaṟpu) of chaste women and its power to command the rains. In domesticating its vision of Buddhism, the *Maṇimēkalai* transforms rather than simply copies the images, ideas, and stories it borrows. Making Buddhism part of the regional cultural landscape is to envision a new set of stories and ideas, a new sort of community and tradition.

At the level of individual words and phrases, for example, the Tamil translations of Buddhist philosophical terms found throughout the *Maṇimēkalai* serve to charge those terms with new etymological significance not necessarily found in the Pāli, Prākrit, or Sanskrit source word. The *Maṇimēkalai*, for example, is the first Tamil text to render the cosmological term "cakravāḷa" into Tamil (as *cakkiravāḷam* at vi.24); the text also offers a full translation of the term, however, as *āḻittāḻi* (vi.173), translated into English by Richman as "the urn of the sphere."[108] As Richman further explains, this term captures the Buddhist view of cosmological form to an even greater degree than the Sanskrit "wheel" (*cakra*), for "the urn (*tāḻi*), shaped like a half-sphere, replicates the shape of the upper half of the cosmic sphere as seen by a viewer on earth," and "the sphere (*āḻi*) of the cosmos is visualized here as consisting of two such jars placed mouth to mouth."'[109] In similar fashion, the *Maṇimēkalai* translates the individual elements in the causal cycle of interdependent origination as cārpu (xxx.17); this Tamil term, from the verbal root "to depend upon, take shelter in" (*cārtal*),[110] thus carries with it a conceptually significant connotation of interdependence. Various elements in the causal chain are also given etymologically significant names. Ceykai (Pāli *saṅkhāra*), for example, derived from the verbal root "to do" (*ceytal*), thus connoting the active nature of karma, is also called *puṉai* at xxx.171, a word derived from "to make, form" (*puṉaital*),[111] suggesting the formation of action or volition. Translation, in instances such as these, implies great specificity of meaning; in the process of localization of tradition, technical terms themselves point with new clarity to the concepts they signify.

The terms ētu and ētunikaḻcci, discussed at length in chapter 1, provide a more complex occasion for considering the effect and function of direct translation of Buddhist technical terms in the *Maṇimēkalai*. Although Maṭṭhakuṇḍali's "abundant beneficial root conditions" (ussannakusalamūla) and Aṅgulimāla's "sufficient virtue" are mentioned only briefly in the Pāli and Sinhala narratives cited previously, Maṇimēkalai's impending ētunikaḻcci provides the central structural framework for the entire Tamil text. The *Maṇimēkalai*'s intricate interweaving of subplots and characters offers a narrative illustration of the processes by which such beneficial conditions arise that is more elaborate and far more detailed than that found in any of the non-Tamil sources. In the *Maṇimēkalai*, for example, one sees the gradual unfolding of each of the beneficial conditions as the central character turns away from her attachment to the prince, converts the queen, and eventually learns formal Buddhist doctrine from Aṟavaṇaṉ. Where hetu is said to mark the human birth that is the first of eight prerequisites for Buddhahood in the story of Erakapatta and in Buddhadatta's *Buddhavaṁsa* commentary, ētu in the *Maṇimēkalai* marks not simply human birth but human birth at a crucial and transformative stage, birth on the threshold of renunciation leading to liberation.

Like the translation from the arising of the beneficial roots in Pāli (kusalamūla) to ētunikalcci in Tamil, the *Maṇimēkalai*'s rendering of various stories found in non-Tamil sources expands and enlarges on those stories in a number of interesting ways. Among the more obvious effects of translation or interpolation into Tamil—particularly into a literary form meant to evoke the aesthetic experience of pity or compassion—is the immediate expansion of the psychological and emotional register and the amplification, more specifically, of scenes involving human grief, anguish, and despair.[112] As George Hart and Hank Heifetz characterize the particular qualities of literary Tamil, "very characteristic of Tamil literature is the rapid alternation of emotions . . . a quality of intense, rapidly rising and sometimes rapidly quenched emotion, sliding and shifting very rapidly."[113] The Tamil stories seem more psychologically charged than their Pāli or Sanskrit counterparts, more loaded with imagery and language meant to evoke a powerful emotional response on the part of the audience.[114] To return once again to the story of Kōtamai and her dead son, Cāṅkalaṉ, for example, the differences between the Tamil and the Pāli versions of the Kisāgotamī tale extend far beyond the disparities of narrative content taken up in chapter 1. Where the Pāli rendering[115] simply notes, in rather blunt fashion, the death of Kisāgotamī's unnamed child as soon as he is able to walk (*so padasā gamanakāle kālam akāsi*),[116] the *Maṇimēkalai* (vi.105–131) dwells at length on the macabre sights of the cremation ground witnessed by the young boy immediately prior to his demise: the scavengers feeding upon the once-beautiful body of a dead courtesan and the ghoulish dance of a female demon as she plucks and eats the eyes of the corpse. Whereas the Pāli version attributes Kisāgotamī's futile search for medicine to cure her son to her general ignorance of the nature of death,[117] it is the great anguish of losing a son that propels Kōtamai in the Tamil narrative to implore the goddess, Campāpati, for help. "Clasping her son's body to her bosom," Kōtamai cries out to Campāpati in "extreme pain" (*koṭuntuyar*; vi.139–141). Kōtamai goes on to explain what has happened in the most pitiful of terms (vi.146–149):

> I do not have anyone.
> My innocent son entered this cremation ground. . . .
> Look at him lying there, as though he were [merely] sleeping.

The grieving mother offers to exchange her life for that of her son, so that Cāṅkalaṉ might "aid and protect [her] blind husband" (vi.154–155). In sharp contrast to the anger and pain suffered by Kōtamai, to her desperate pleas to the goddess to restore her son to life, Kisāgotamī's exchange with the Buddha is a rather straightforward and emotionless one. The mother is sent by the Buddha to collect a pinch of mustard seed from any house in which no one has died; finding that she is not alone in facing death, Kisāgotamī's heart, once tender with affection for her son, becomes hardened,[118] and she becomes a stream-winner on hearing the word of the Buddha. The shock and fear experienced by the son and the profound grief of the mother, so apparent in the Tamil rendition of the Kisāgotamī story found in the *Maṇimēkalai*, are virtually absent from the Pāli narrative.[119] The language and imagery of the Tamil version pointedly evoke the aesthetic experience of pathos, the heightened sense of human compassion, described in the previous chapter.

In similar fashion, if the Uppalavaṇṇā/Rāhula connection alluded to in the *Apadāna* (discussed previously) can, indeed, be taken as a source of sorts for the narratives of Maṇimēkalai/Ilakkumi and Utayakumaraṉ/Irākulaṉ, the *Maṇimēkalai* might well have been understood by its reading community fluent in both Tamil and Pāli as a long and complex consideration of those "similar tendencies" (samānacchandamānasa), as an emotionally charged exploration of the powerful bond between two human beings across many lifetimes. The persistent tension felt by Maṇimēkalai between sexual attraction to Utayakumaraṉ and predilection for renunciation signaled by her ētunikaḻcci provides a complicated and nuanced view of the road to liberation, one that is full of conflicting emotions and powerful human bonds. Although Maṇimēkalai's "heart goes out" to the prince (v.89), her matured ētu propels Maṇimēkalā to bring the young girl to Maṇipallavam (vii.19–20); although Maṇimēkalai employs Amutacurapi in compassionate service to the poor, she mourns the murdered Utayakumaraṉ as her "beloved" (xxi.22). The Tamil rendition of the Rāhula/Uppalavaṇṇā connection specifically addresses the force and value of human connections, the nature of the powerful emotions that tie one human being to another.

The *Maṇimēkalai*'s transmission of a number of stories, images, and terms from non-Tamil sources functions in a number of ways to domesticate Buddhism, to make Buddhist ideas and values local, to bring Buddhism into the linguistic and aesthetic community of the text, to engage the audience in the human situations of its characters. The story of the Buddha and his future rebirth on earth, the narratives concerning Maṇimēkalai, Utayakumaraṉ, and their past births, and the terminology of logic and interdependent origination are self-consciously connected in the *Maṇimēkalai* to things Tamil, to regional, familiar sites and characters, to the story of Kōvalaṉ and his virtuous wife, Kaṇṇaki, a story that would appear to be indigenous to Tamil-speaking South India. By rendering into Tamil the story of the Buddha, by tying its Tamil characters to the Buddha's future appearance on earth, by translating into Tamil key Buddhist cosmological and philosophical concepts, the *Maṇimēkalai* brings the "great community" of Buddhists into the Tamil literary/religious landscape.

This section began by pointing out that the fact that the *Maṇimēkalai* was composed in Tamil represents an obvious choice on the part of the author. The emergence of the Sanskrit farcical drama in seventh-century Kāñcīpuram certainly suggests the existence of a multilingual literary culture in which a text such as the *Maṇimēkalai*, with all of its biting sarcasm aimed at non-Buddhist groups, might just have easily been written in Sanskrit. The preceding pages suggest why the story of Maṇimēkalai was composed in Tamil, as a means of claiming a place for Buddhism in a religiously diverse landscape and literary culture and making that immense community envisioned also local, familiar, close at hand. Even the text of the *Maṇimēkalai* itself at one point appears to acknowledge the place of regional or local languages in the transmission of Buddhist tradition. When language is introduced as a topic in the tale of Cātuvaṉ and the Nāgas, it is said that Cātuvaṉ converts the Nāgas and creates on that wild island a Buddhist lay community of sorts because he can speak their language eloquently. "Because he had learned thoroughly the language of the others" (*maṟṟavar pāṭai mayakkaṟu marapil kaṟṟaṉaṉ ātaliṉ*; xvi.60–61), he "became one of them by binding them with language" (*pāṭaiyil piṇittu avaṉ pāṉmaiyaṉ āki*; xvi.70).[120] The Nāgas need not learn the Tamil Cātuvaṉ speaks to become more "civilized"; rather, they must simply abandon their customs of cannibalism and killing live animals for food. Language, albeit language used in sophisticated and eloquent fashion, is merely a practical point, a pragmatic concern, a powerful medium for teaching and transmission.

Yet in the literary culture of early medieval South India, at a time roughly contemporaneous to the composition of the *Maṇimēkalai*, language choice, particularly in relation to religious identity, became an issue of tremendous and self-conscious concern to a variety of sectarian communities. With the appearance of the devotional poetry of the Śaiva saints in the seventh through ninth centuries, the choice to compose in the Tamil language emerges as a critical factor in defining religious and cultural identity. These Śaiva poets attempt to write Buddhists and Jains out of the Tamil religious and literary landscape by assailing, among other things, the linguistic and literary quality of their Tamil. Language and language choice, in short, cease to be neutral issues of pragmatic or domesticating concern. Tamil language emerges as a basic means of articulating religious, cultural, and political orientation,[121] as a highly valued indicator of cultural and religious identity, arguably remaining so into the modern era.[122] That the *Maṇimēkalai*, indeed, makes no claim regarding the superiority of its language or the fact that it is written in Tamil rather than in Sanskrit or Prākrit underlies a potentially strong argument for an early dating of the text. Few Tamil texts, after the poetry of the Śaiva and Vaiṣṇava poet-saints is formally anthologized in the late tenth and early eleventh centuries, exhibit such neutrality on the issue of language.

That the devotional poets, particularly the first of the Śaiva saints, Tirunāvukkaracar (Appar) and Tiruñāṉacampantar (Campantar), vehemently and persistently condemn both the Buddhists and Jains on a number of grounds, ranging from their style of dress and manner of eating to their lack of proper respect for Vedic sacrificial ritual, has been well noted in several recent studies of religion in South India.[123] The religious landscape of inclusion imagined by the *Maṇimēkalai*, one in which the daughter of a courtesan will serve the future Buddha as his chief disciple, is transformed by the Hindu poets into a literary "geography of exclusion,"[124] into a rabidly sectarian vision of the Tamil landscape that is determined on the basis of, among other things, linguistic capabilities.[125]

Although many devotional poets, both Śaiva and Vaiṣṇava, criticize the Buddhists and Jains, it is Campantar, the late sixth- or early seventh-century Śaiva devotee closest in time, perhaps, to the composition of the *Maṇimēkalai* text, who most consistently and vehemently criticizes these non-Śaiva communities, particularly on the issue of language. Although Campantar's sarcastic comments regarding "dirty Jain monks who walk about like rutting elephants"[126] might bear close resemblance to the anti-Jain attitudes expressed in the *Maṇimēkalai*,[127] Campantar's poetry clearly differs from the Buddhist text in its condemnation of a perceived Buddhist and Jain disregard for both the Tamil and Sanskrit languages. Where the *Maṇimēkalai* would appear to be rather neutral on the issue of language choice, Campantar is extremely self-conscious about his use of Tamil. At least one verse, often if not always the tenth, of each of Campantar's hymns devotes itself entirely to ridiculing the Buddhists and/or Jains, particularly on their perceived "foreignness" due to an inability to speak either good Tamil or good Sanskrit.

He writes:

> With Araṉ of Ālavāy by my side,
> I will easily defeat those filthy Jain monks who . . .
> mutilate the good Sanskrit of the Āgama and mantra texts,
> loudly declaiming in the corrupt Prākrit tongue.[128]

In the same hymn, he continues:

> I will easily defeat those blind fools . . .
> who . . . know neither good Tamil nor the Sanskrit language.[129]

In the eleventh and final signature verse, Campantar then proceeds to portray himself as the master of pure Tamil, the author of verses in sweet language that grant liberation at the feet of the lord. He closes the hymn quoted previously, for example, by stating:

> There is no misery
> for those who chant these ten verses
> well composed by the Tamil poet Ñāṉacampantaṉ.[130]

In nearly every closing verse, Campantar contrasts the futile and senseless babble of the Buddhists and Jains with the power and beauty of his own Tamil verse:

> The highest world is within easy reach
> for those who can sing in good Tamil modes
> these words [of] Ñāṉacampantaṉ.[131]

Campantar's Tamil is "pure" (*centamiḻ*)[132] and "rhythmic" (*cantam*),[133] to be "sweetly sung" (*iṉ nalam pāṭa*).[134] Nampi Ārūrar or Cuntaramūrti (Cuntarar), following Campantar by nearly two centuries, further develops the theme of Tamil as the language that draws the divine being near. "The Lord . . . was moved by the sweet, melodious Tamil hymns that Ñāṉacampantaṉ sang to him every day,"[135] and Lord Śiva wanders the world "with a desire to hear good Tamil songs."[136] In the lord's town of Niṉṟiyūr, even "parrots know pure, grammatical Tamil."[137] The use of the Tamil language becomes central to the religious identity articulated in the poetry of the early saints; only those who know "pure, grammatical Tamil" can claim to see the lord, can claim to be part of the lord's Tamil-speaking landscape. Language and language choice become central to the construction of identity, to the definition of oneself over and against a foreign other.

That a text such as the *Maṇimēkalai* does not participate in this self-conscious use of language as a marker of religious identity serves to underscore Peterson's point that the Śaiva saints sought to invent a new kind of Tamil culture, "devot[ing] their major energies to setting up links and equations among originally unrelated elements in the Tamil society and culture of their era, thus constructing a Śaiva *bhakti* version of Tamilness that is quite different from the Tamil identities of previous eras."[138] Certainly, the Śaivas' relentless assaults on "the deluded doctrines of the base Buddhist monks" suggest an embattled and embittered minority, struggling for recognition from the religious and cultural fringe. Not only are Buddhists considered stupid, deluded, overfed, overdressed, and linguistically challenged, but their teachings are thought to lead to misfortune and ruin; one must worship only Lord Śiva "if you do not wish the unfortunate fate of the Buddhists."[139] Language use as a sectarian challenge no doubt found easy targets among

Tamil-speaking Buddhists and Jains, for both communities, by the time of Appar and Campantar, were generating a wide variety of translations and interpolations across linguistic lines.[140] At least four centuries separate Appar and Campantar, the earliest of the Śaiva poets and the most vehemently anti-Buddhist and anti-Jain, from the legendary eleventh-century rediscovery and anthologizing of their hymns by Nampi Āṇṭār Nampi,[141] further suggesting that the early poet-saints did, indeed, denounce from the borders, as outsiders looking in.

The Śaiva poets' jettisoning of the culture of multilingualism, their equation of Tamil language with religious identity, remains a powerful force in Tamil literary and religious culture, as is seen in following chapters concerning the eleventh-century Buddhist grammar, the *Vīracōḻiyam*. Although the *Maṇimēkalai*, in comparison with the poetry of Appar, Campantar, or Cuntarar, displays no apparent self-consciousness in its use of the Tamil medium, language nonetheless plays an important role in shaping a vision of Buddhism and Buddhist community that is also local, intentionally bound to texts, narratives, and values of the regional literary landscape.[142] Far from being foreign or alien, the Buddha and Buddhist community in the *Maṇimēkalai* are made near, familiar, part of the regional literary culture. The immense community of Buddhists, for the reading community of the *Maṇimēkalai*, is also close at hand. In responding to the *Cilappatikāram*'s narrative, to its moral vision, to its presentation of karma, the *Maṇimēkalai* evokes in its audience an experience of karma, transience, and interconnectedness that is explicitly tied to Buddhist images, characters, and values, thus claiming a place for Buddhism in the local literary and religious landscape. How that local landscape and the local reading community of the text are then reimagined through space and time, recast forward and outward, redefining the immense through the local, is the subject of the following chapter.

3

The *Maṇimēkalai*'s Buddhist Community Envisioned

From the complex web of intertextual allusion and debate discussed in the previous chapter, one can infer a reading or listening community for the *Maṇimēkalai* that is sophisticated, multilingual, and well-versed in Buddhist doctrine and in a wide variety of literary texts and genres. Articulating its vision of the world in response to that expressed in the *Cilappatikāram*, the *Maṇimēkalai* claims a place for Buddhism in a literary and religious landscape of competitive diversity. Through complex and creative processes of translation and elaboration, and through marshaling other local texts to support its worldview, the *Maṇimēkalai* domesticates a great tradition and an immense community, locating the lives and values of the Buddha and his followers in the local literary culture.

Yet the textual or reading community that can be inferred from the *Maṇimēkalai* and from the literary culture in which it participates is not the only point of access to examining the historical relationship of literature to the formation and articulation of religious identity; the text of the *Maṇimēkalai* itself considers at length the nature and significance of Buddhist community. As Le Goff notes in his study of the arts and literature of medieval Europe, works of the imagination constitute "a historical reality unto themselves,"[1] direct evidence of a society's or community's collective images or "mental structures."[2] The *Maṇimēkalai*, as a sophisticated poetic work, provides access to a Buddhist imagining of religious community in a particular cultural context at a specific historical moment. Even more light may be shed on the *Maṇimēkalai*'s articulation of community and identity if one considers these Tamil poetic "mental structures" in the wider context of Buddhist literary imaginings from across Asia in the fourth through seventh centuries. Whereas the two previous chapters focused primarily on the *Maṇimēkalai* as an example of Tamil narrative literature, interpreting the text in relation to the Tamil-speaking literary culture that surrounded it, new insights can be gleaned from shifting the interpretive lens to emphasize the *Maṇimēkalai* as a Buddhist text that happens to be written in Tamil. This chapter examines the notion of community envisioned by the text—and the manner in which the text engages its reading community in that vision—paying particular attention to the *Maṇimēkalai*'s imagining of time and space in conjunction with contemporary imaginings of the same from across the Buddhist world. Time and space, Le Goff notes, are "the essential dimensions of history,"[3] whether that history be of actual historical happenings or of the imagination. Indeed, it is in focusing on the *Maṇimēkalai*'s temporal and spatial images that the text's vision of community emerges most powerfully.

Despite the attention paid to local conceptions of landscape, narratives, and images, as well as to stories of the past that bear in some measure on the narrative present, the *Maṇimēkalai* displays far more concern with the translocal and the future than with the here and now. Like the medieval European exemplum described by Le Goff as a narrative whose "ultimate aim was eschatological,"[4] the story of the renunciation of Maṇimēkalai "unfold[s] in narrative but invariably point[s] toward eternity—the eternity that [is] promised to the listener only if he [knows] how to draw the lesson contained in the [text]."[5] As a Buddhist narrative, like the Pāli chronicle (vaṁsa) literature described by Steven Collins as a combination of "linear . . . narrative . . . interw[oven] . . . with the texture of all time, past, present, and future,"[6] the *Maṇimēkalai* continually shifts back and forth from the narrative present and past to timeless glories yet to come. The *Maṇimēkalai* vividly imagines a community of devout disciples gathered around the future Buddha yet leaves open the question: who will participate in that future community? Where will such a community be located? In such a context, this chapter argues, the idea of aesthetic experience (rasa, meyppāṭu) functions not merely as an aesthetic category for the literary connoisseur but as a medium of engagement with great soteriological import for the reading community of the text. Engagement with the text, and with its ethical concerns, is presented by the *Maṇimēkalai* as the means for gaining admission to the Buddhist community to come.

In imagining such a community and the pivotal role played therein by both the principal characters of the narrative and, by extension, those members of the reading community who grasp the lessons of the text and heed its ethical call, the *Maṇimēkalai* envisions a Buddhist world with its own local landscape at the center. The localization of tradition discussed in chapter 2, in the context of the community envisioned by the text, also implies a certain centralization. As in other texts from across the Buddhist world written in the centuries surrounding the composition of the *Maṇimēkalai*, the centers of the Buddhist world are reimagined, redrawn to reflect the community of the text. The foci of the Buddhist sacred landscape lie not in North India, in the places where the Buddha was born, attained enlightenment, preached, and died, but in the cities and landscapes of the *Maṇimēkalai*: Kāñcīpuram, Irattiṉatīvam, and the "cool isle" of Cāvakam somewhere in Southeast Asia.

At the Feet of the Future Buddha

For all its emphasis on the maturation of karma and beneficial root conditions leading to enlightenment, the *Maṇimēkalai* is ultimately a forward-looking text, persistently turning its attention to events of great soteriological import yet to come. Even the stories of the past, comprising the bulk of the narrative, are in some manner always related to future events, their karmic consequences projected forward. The time of the narrative shifts continually from present to past, from past to future, with all energy and anticipation focused squarely on coming events. The *Maṇimēkalai*'s central theme of the arising of those beneficial root conditions necessary to renunciation and liberation, for example, is inevitably forward-looking. Not only is the manifestation (nikaḻcci) of such conditions always referred to in the future tense, as something that will but has not yet fully come to pass, but the ultimate result of the arising of these factors—liberation from the cycle of births and deaths—is an event that will take place long after the narrative proper ends. Although Maṇimēkalai's impending manifestation of beneficial conditions itself must be explained with constant reference to past events and actions, to her kind feeding of the sage Cātucakkaraṉ and her subsequent vision as she burns to death on her husband's funeral pyre, the liberating processes signaled by the arising of the such conditions propel the audience into a future far beyond the narrative time of the text itself. Maṇimēkalai's karmic transformation is only beginning in the present of the text; one must imagine into the future her complete awakening and liberation. The *Maṇimēkalai* focuses its attention on the coming of the future Buddha, and in real time the narrative ends not with Maṇimēkalai's renunciatory vow at xxx.263–264 but with her birth as the chief disciple of the Buddha-to-come (xxi.178–179). Although the text is not prophetic in the sense that it does not dwell at length on the details of the future Buddha's life and reign, it focuses squarely on the lives and karmic doings of those who seek to participate in the community of that future Buddha.[7]

In similar fashion, the *Maṇimēkalai*'s vision of karma and moral responsibility consistently emphasizes the ramifications of past and present actions on the future, particularly in comparison to the narrative as told in the *Cilappatikāram*. Although both texts share the core story of Kōvalaṉ, Kaṇṇaki, and Mātavi, the narrative trajectory of the *Maṇimēkalai* extends into a future far beyond that of the *Cilappatikāram*. As noted in the previous chapter, the karmic fortunes of Kōvalaṉ and Kaṇṇaki are limited in the *Cilappatikāram* to present events and their past causes. In the *Maṇimēkalai*, however, those personal karmic narratives are projected into the future, and compassionate concern for other living beings becomes the model for all future lives. Kaṇṇaki's karma comes to full fruition in the *Cilappatikāram*, for example, in her present-tense transformation into a powerful goddess. In the *Maṇimēkalai*, her good deeds, like those of Maṇimēkalai herself, will witness their final reward only at the feet of the coming Buddha after many lives spent in service to others.

In addition to these broad themes or currents in the text, the *Maṇimēkalai*'s concern with future events can also be seen in its details, its characters, images, and language. Aṟavaṇaṉ, the Buddhist sage who never forgets "in each and every birth . . . to worship the feet of the lord who is celebrated for sitting at the feet of the bodhi tree" (xii.101–103), is the first to predict the coming of another Buddha to earth at xii.57–100. Because the "good and excellent" teachings of the previous Buddha have not flourished as they should (xii.57–71), the divine beings of the world will petition the future Buddha currently residing in Tuṣita heaven (Tamil Tuṭitalōkam) to descend to earth (xii.72–74).[8] Amid many glorious and miraculous happenings (xii.80–100), the Buddha will be born among human beings "in the year 1616"[9] (xii.77). The text's anticipation and excitement at the coming of the future Buddha grows increasingly palpable throughout the narrative. At xv.23–35, for example, wondrous events that accompany Āputtiraṉ's rebirth on the island of Cāvakam throw various savants into a state of agitated confusion:

> "Even though it is not time for the earthly birth of the great ascetic
> of the bodhi tree, auspicious signs are seen!"
>
> [Thus] the great ascetics who lived in the temple of the cosmic place wondered
> with tremendous excitement.

All of the principal characters of the *Maṇimēkalai*, the audience gradually learns, will be reborn in the company of this future Buddha, as members of his immediate community or retinue. Although all remember, with great reverence and devotion, the compassionate acts of the previous Buddha (consider, e.g., Maṇimēkalai's song of praise at xi.61–72), all are karmically and soteriologically tied to the Buddha of the future. Maṇimēkalai will be reborn (as a man) as the Buddha's chief disciple (xxi.175–179). The great sage Aṟavaṇaṉ will be reborn again and again "until the sun that is the Buddha appears . . . driving away the darkness of non-virtue (Tamil *maṟa iruḷ*, Sanskrit *adharma*), in order that [all] living beings might rejoice" (xxi.165–167). Kōvalaṉ and Kaṇṇaki will descend from their current deified state to help suffering beings through their spiritual powers (Tamil *irutti*, Sanskrit *ṛddhi*) until achieving liberation "when the Buddha spreads the rays of his teachings everywhere in the countless cosmic worlds" (xxvi.54–61). At the time of Kōvalaṉ's enlightenment and release, his father, Mācāttuvāṉ, will also "hear the virtuous words" spoken by the Buddha (xxviii.141–147).[10]

Not only the main characters but the principal monuments of the text—the lotus seat found in the crystal pavilion of the Uvavaṉam park (iii.65–79), the Buddha pedestal on the island of Maṇipallavam, and by extension, its replica erected by Maṇimēkalai and King Iḷaṅkiḷḷi in the southwest corner of Kāñcīpuram (xxviii.175–214)—although revealing the nature of past lives or deeds, are nonetheless all oriented primarily toward the future. The pedestal or Buddha seat on Maṇipallavam, for example, was not constructed in commemoration of the previous Buddha's sojourn on earth but rather in anticipation of the coming of the next Buddha. Before the pedestal for a second time in the present-tense narrative at xxv.54–65, Maṇimēkalai remembers her conversation, in a previous birth, with the sage Piramataruma, in which she asked why the pedestal had been constructed "before the appearance of the Great One." Piramatarumaṉ responds by saying that the seat or pedestal (pīṭikai) creates a space for the coming Buddha, for "other than the lord who is fully realized, the highest being, that pedestal will not bear another."[11] The time shifts in this narrative sequence are complex, even somewhat difficult to follow in the Tamil, and display quite clearly the manner in which narrative linear time is persistently interwoven with references to an idealized, liberating time of the future. Maṇimēkalai, in the narrative present, remembers a conversation from a past birth that bears directly on the future arrival of the Buddha on earth. The pedestal, a vehicle for enlightening knowledge of the past, ultimately serves to reserve a space, a consecrated throne, to which the Buddha might return. The empty seat contains, in its very emptiness, the promise of the future.

Yet what, exactly, is the promise of the future? Why is the *Maṇimēkalai* so concerned with a time distant from the present of the narrative itself? The text indicates repeatedly that it is only in the presence of the future Buddha that human beings will attain ultimate release from the cycle of deaths and rebirths. "Those who hear the good teachings of the one born on that [future] day," Aṟavaṇaṉ explains to Maṇimēkalai, "will transcend the sorrowful [round of] births" (xii.99–100). "Except for those who hear his teachings on that day [of the Buddha's arrival on earth]," Maṇimēkalai recalls the words of the sage Piramatarumaṉ, "no one can escape miserable births" (xxv.47–48). For each of the principal characters—Maṇimēkalai, Kaṇṇaki and Kōvalaṉ, Mācāttuvāṉ, and Aṟavaṇaṉ—austerities, compassionate service to others, and profound devotion to the Buddha will find their ultimate reward only at the feet of the coming Buddha. Ascetic practice and moral action do not, in and of themselves, lead directly to liberation, the text suggests, but gain for one the right to participate in the liberating glories of the future, to be a part of the community that will once again gather around a living Buddha. Although absent in a literal sense from the present-tense narrative, the Buddha is nonetheless a powerful force of the future in the world of the *Maṇimēkalai*. Only those who ready themselves, karmically and morally, will see the coming Buddha.[12]

Like the traditions of the coming Buddha (Sanskrit Maitreya, Pāli Metteyya) found throughout the Buddhist world, the coming Buddha in the *Maṇimēkalai* serves as "a symbol of hope, of the human aspiration for a better life,"[13] acting as a "guarantor of the future,"[14] holding the promise of human enlightenment and liberation. To see Metteyya, the living Buddha, is a common wish voiced by narrative characters, poets, and commentators alike. The *Jātaka* commentary, for example, ends with its author's aspiration to be born in the city (i.e., heaven) of Tusita and listen to Metteyya's teaching.[15] Buddhaghosa, describing virtue (*sīla*), offers as an example the elder Mahāsaṅgharakkhita who self-consciously postpones his own enlightenment so that he might see the "Blessed One Metteyya."[16] The chance to see a living Buddha, to hear the teachings from his own lips, to serve him as disciple, and to attain liberation at his hand all provide a powerful impetus for human striving and hope in a wide variety of Buddhist texts and traditions.

Yet the *Maṇimēkalai*'s vision of the future Buddha is in several ways unique, one not found in quite the same formulation in other parts of the Buddhist world. The *Maṇimēkalai* presents not a generic view of some vaguely utopian paradise of the future but one filled with specifics, with details, that appear to have few if any parallels in other Buddhist literary traditions. Nattier's succinct categorization of Maitreya myths based on the projected time and place of the future Buddha's appearance, for example,[17] would need to be modified somewhat to accommodate the *Maṇimēkalai*'s "here and there/not too much later" vision to be discussed in detail later. The Pāli sources that address themselves directly to the reign of the coming Metteyya[18]—nearly all of them much later than the *Maṇimēkalai*—also differ significantly in detail from the future Buddha described in the Tamil text. The *Cakkavattisīhanādasutta* of the *Dīghanikāya*, containing the only canonical reference to Metteyya, for example, tells of the arising of the Buddha Metteyya in conjunction with the world ruler Saṅkha after a period of dharmic decline followed by a gradual lengthening of the human lifespan to eighty thousand years.[19] At the end of the *Buddhavaṁsa*, Metteyya is simply mentioned as the fifth and final Buddha of this cosmic era.[20] The *Anāgatavaṁsa*, attributed by the *Gandhavaṁsa* to the twelfth-century South Indian author, Kassapa,[21] relates a similar story of the gradual decline in human fortunes, followed by a return to gloriously long lifespans that culminates in the appearance of Metteyya.[22] References to Metteyya are scattered throughout the Pāli chronicle literature, beginning with the identification of the great king Duṭṭhagāmaṇi as the chief disciple of the future Buddha.[23] The differences in detail among these texts and the *Maṇimēkalai* provide several potentially interesting clues as to the nature of the Tamil text's vision of the future Buddha and the community to surround him.

Perhaps the most obvious difference between the stories of the future Buddha found in the Pāli literature and in the *Maṇimēkalai* is that the Buddha in the latter text is never named but simply referred to as "the one of mature understanding" (*pēr aṟivāḷaṉ*; xii.78) or "the great one who graciously [teaches] the dharma to others" (*piṟakku aṟam aruḷum periyōṉ*; xxi.178). Yet the lack of proper name in no way lends a vague or generic quality to the text's vision of the future. On the contrary, the *Maṇimēkalai* is quite specific regarding the identity of both the coming Buddha and those who will serve him most intimately.

The future Buddha is clearly identified, for example, with the ancestor of Maṇimēkalai's father, Kōvalaṉ, who was nine generations ago rescued from the sea by the goddess Maṇimēkalā. Indra here identifies the shipwrecked man as the Buddha-to-be, "the lord at the foot of the bodhi tree, the first being" (xxix.23–25). Elsewhere, it is said that after his dramatic rescue, this ancestral Kōvalaṉ distributed his wealth to the needy, erected a shrine in honor of the previous Buddha outside the city of Vañci, and undertook a life of austerities (xxviii.123–133).[24] Maṇimēkalai is specifically named for the goddess who saved the Buddha-in-the-making from a watery death, and her resolve to renounce the world is tied explicitly in the text to the scene of her ancestor's rescue and subsequent renunciation (xxix.30–33). The coming Buddha is, in short, intimately associated with the principal characters of the *Maṇimēkalai* narrative. In his future reign he will be attended by those who have been his close relatives in past births: Maṇimēkalai, Kōvalaṉ and Kaṇṇaki, and Mācāttuvāṉ (Kōvalaṉ's father and Maṇimēkalai's grandfather).[25] His "local" family will furthermore be transported to northern India, to the sites of the previous Buddha's birth and enlightenment (xxi.175, xxvi.42–43), thus integrating the most sacred Buddhist centers into the landscape envisioned by the *Maṇimēkalai.*

The future Buddha of the *Maṇimēkalai*, then, is thoroughly tied to local characters and stories, to the Kōvalaṉ-Kaṇṇaki and Maṇimēkalai-Mātavi story that underlies both the *Maṇimēkalai* and the *Cilappatikāram* narratives. This coming Buddha is never named, for reasons that cannot be known for certain. Yet in not tying the text's ultimate vision of the future to extant stories surrounding the future Buddha Metteyya, the *Maṇimēkalai* envisions a new and different future, one in which the daughter of a courtesan and a once wayward husband play crucial roles. The community to form around the coming Buddha will be led, the *Maṇimēkalai* suggests, by characters who have waged human struggles against lust and greed, suffering and hunger. The members of this core community envisioned by the text are also those with whom the members of the audience, through the progression of the text itself, have become thoroughly familiar and sympathetic. The Buddha of the future is made familiar by the *Maṇimēkalai*, the fortunes of his future community tied to the audience's aesthetic appreciation of the travails of the text's main characters. The coming Buddha is not some distant and unapproachable Metteyya but a relative close at hand. His most trusted confidantes will be those same characters with whom the audience has come to empathize and identify.

That Maṇimēkalai herself will become the most trusted of these confidantes, the Buddha's chief disciple, points to yet another unique feature of the text's vision of the future Buddhist community: that the illegitimate daughter of a former courtesan may serve as the future Buddha's most devoted follower and will perhaps eventually become a Buddha herself. As noted previously, Tuvatikaṉ's prediction at xxi.175–179, that Maṇimēkalai will be reborn as a man and will eventually "become the chief disciple of the great one who graciously [teaches] the dharma to others," stands outside the Buddhist literary tradition that more commonly imagines a king fulfilling such a role. Beginning with the *Mahāvaṁsa* passages cited previously, predicting that King Duṭṭhagāmaṇi will serve the future Buddha,[26] a long tradition of identifying kingship with the ideal of a Buddha-to-be can be traced through the Buddhist literatures of Sri Lanka and Southeast Asia.[27] Yet here it is Maṇimēkalai, the young girl torn between her attraction to Utayakumaraṉ and her predilection for a life of asceticism, who will lead the community of devoted disciples. The "young creeper" whose withdrawal from the world is mourned early in the narrative by the citizens of Pukār[28] is destined, after the personal anguish and compassionate service that comprise the bulk of the text, to be reborn at the center of the glorious community of the future.

Yet it would also seem that Maṇimēkalai will serve as more than simply the human center of the coming Buddha's community on earth. Several clues in the text indicate that the young girl is destined to become a Buddha herself, perhaps the Buddha to follow the one due to arrive in 1616. As noted in each of the two previous chapters, Maṇimēkalai's impending manifestation of those conditions that lead to enlightenment (ētunikaḻcci), if interpreted with reference to Pāli commentarial literature composed in roughly the same era as the Tamil text, clearly signals that she has attained the first of eight prerequisites for Buddhahood: birth as a human being (*manussattam*). Looking to the future predicted by the text beyond the point where the narrative proper ends, the second prerequisite, birth as a male (*liṅgasampatti*), will be accomplished in Maṇimēkalai's next birth (xxi.175). The third of the preconditions, possessing a cause or condition (hetu), is perhaps related most directly to Maṇimēkalai's gradual manifestation of the beneficial ētu that lead to enlightenment. The fourth of the requisite conditions, seeing a teacher (*satthāradassanam*) will certainly be achieved when Maṇimēkalai, in male form, serves the coming Buddha as his chief disciple. Going forth (*pabbajā*) to live an ascetic life Maṇimēkalai accomplishes with her final vow of renunciation (xxx.263–264). Of the final three conditions for Buddhahood—attainment of special qualities (*guṇasampatti*), act of merit (*adhikāro*), and possession of great resolve (*chandatā*)—little can be said in regard to Maṇimēkalai. Yet through both her impending ētunikaḻcci and the predictions of the mysterious painting on the temple pillar, Tuvatikaṉ, Maṇimēkalai is clearly marked as one capable of aspiring to Buddhahood, if not in the immediate present of the narrative (given her current birth as a woman), then certainly in her future (male) birth as the Buddha's most devoted disciple.

Beyond the apparent propensity for Buddhahood signaled by the manifestation of Maṇimēkalai's beneficial root conditions, various other pieces of literary evidence can be marshaled to suggest that the *Maṇimēkalai* imagines a Buddhist community of the future with its heroine at the center. The *Padīpadāna-jātaka*, for example,[29] attests to the literary fact that the notion of a female birth for a future Buddha lies not completely beyond the pale of the Buddhist imagination. Here, the Buddha narrates the story of his birth as a virtuous princess who donates a measure of sesame oil to the great elder, Tipiṭakadhara. Although the text notes several times that the girl's resolution to become a Buddha will remain unfulfilled so long as she is born in female form,[30] her aspiration will be acknowledged, and her future Buddhahood predicted, by Tipiṭakadhara when he is himself reborn as a fully enlightened Buddha.[31] Although composed several centuries later than the *Maṇimēkalai* but perhaps in the same geographical region, the *Anāgatavaṁsa* uses an interesting simile that echoes the Tamil text's image of its central character's spiritual attainments. When the future Buddha (in this case Metteyya) arrives in full splendor on earth, the Pāli text predicts, "there will be a happy fruition of meritorious deeds for that venerable one, the best of Buddhas, whose unimaginable splendor will diffuse [like the scent of?] flowers."[32] Such imagery used in reference to Metteyya calls to mind the Tamil phrase used to describe the power of Maṇimēkalai's impending ētunikaḻcci that marks her as a potential aspirant to Buddhahood: "The manifestation of beneficial root conditions would [soon] blossom for Maṇimēkalai, like the fragrance of a flower."[33] Such a simile is not found elsewhere in Tamil literature; in its connection to the critical term ētunikaḻcci, this "odor-like" mode of permeation or diffusion of virtuous and wholesome qualities perhaps also indicates Maṇimēkalai's future transformation into a fully enlightened Buddha. To cite but one additional piece of evidence that might suggest the *Maṇimēkalai* to be envisioning its central character as a future Buddha herself is the text's emphasis on interdependent origination as the final and most important teaching to be mastered by Maṇimēkalai before her renunciation. Although the doctrine of interdependent origination obviously holds a central place in all Buddhist traditions and is the critical understanding leading to the Buddha's enlightenment in canonical texts, the understanding of interdependent origination is, in at least one text, the *Śālistamba-sūtra*, tied specifically to the qualifications of Metteyya/Maitreya to become the future Buddha.[34]

Whether or not such disparate sources bear any direct relation to the language and imagery of the *Maṇimēkalai* itself, the Tamil text's consistent reference to the arising of those factors that lead to enlightenment in connection with its central character suggests that Maṇimēkalai is destined to become not only the Buddha's chief disciple but also a Buddha herself in some even more distant birth. In the context of the future community envisioned by the text, the *Maṇimēkalai* might be understood as a Jātaka story in ornate poetic form, a narrative of a future Buddha's former life as a human being meant to engage its audience in the human struggles and ethical dilemmas of the fully enlightened being-in-the-making. The aspiration to Buddhahood becomes the province of a human character with conflicting emotions and desires, not simply the virtuous act of a great and wondrous being. In placing Maṇimēkalai, the daughter of a royal courtesan, the trusted advisor of the Cōḻa king and queen, and a traveler through the Tamil capitals of Pukār, Vañci, and Kāñcīpuram, at the center of its imagined future, the *Maṇimēkalai* further domesticates or localizes its vision of the Buddha's community. The world of Maṇimēkalai becomes absolutely central to the fortunes of the future community of Buddhists.

A third unique feature of the *Maṇimēkalai*'s depiction of the coming of the future Buddha is the specific date assigned to his arrival: "in the year 1616" (xii.77). The reference point for such a date is unclear. Perhaps 1616 refers to a particular year in a long forgotten calendrical system; perhaps it refers to some future date 1,616 years from the present of the text (i.e., "in 1,616 years" or "1,616 years from now"). More likely, perhaps, given the widespread use throughout the Buddhist world of the Buddha's bodily death (*parinirvāṇa*) as the zero point in the calculation of time, is that "1616" refers to 1,616 years after the death of the previous Buddha, a date perhaps some four or five centuries in the future from the present of the *Maṇimēkalai* narrative. Whatever the particular referent for the number given, the *Maṇimēkalai* clearly pinpoints a date for the arrival of the future Buddha that is both far more specific and substantially smaller than those encountered in Pāli sources. Prophetic texts such as the *Anāgatavaṁsa*, for example, supply numbers that are extremely vague; the Buddha known as Metteyya will appear only in "a hundred thousand rainy seasons" (*vassakoṭiye*).[35] If one adds up the number of years between generations in the era of increasing human life-spans found in the *Cakkavattisīhanādasutta* ("the sons of these sons will come to live for eighty years; their sons for one hundred sixty years"),[36] Metteyya will not be due to appear on earth for many hundreds of thousands of years. Indeed, as Nattier points out, "canonical texts are unanimous in asserting that Maitreya will remain in Tuṣita Heaven for many millions (if not billions) of years"[37] before being born on earth.

Throughout the *Maṇimēkalai*, even beyond the specific mention of the year 1616, a certain atmosphere of heightened expectation prevails, suggesting that the coming of the future Buddha is, indeed, close at hand. Not only does the text fail to refer to any intervening waiting period of thousands or millions of years, but several details in the stories of each character's karmic future suggest the arrival of the coming Buddha within the foreseeable, or at least humanly conceivable, future. Kōvalaṉ's ancestor, the Buddha-to-be rescued nine generations ago, for example, has already been reborn as the king of the gods in Tuṣita heaven, awaiting the divine petition that will compel him to an earthly birth (xii.70–74). Aṟavaṇaṉ, in the passage immediately preceding, indicates that the status of the teachings given by the previous Buddha is in steady decline (xii.57–62), yet nowhere does he mention any intervening period of gradual moral uplift and increased human life-span before describing the coming of the next Buddha. The prophetic painting on the pillar informs Maṇimēkalai that the birth immediately following her present one will transport her to Makatam (Magadha) as a man (xxi.175–176). The passage suggests that male birth in the land of the Buddha is the only prerequisite for Maṇimēkalai to serve as chief disciple (xxi.177–179), and that prerequisite will be achieved in her next birth; there is no hint of thousands of rebirths across millions of years for Maṇimēkalai to see the Buddha. In similar fashion, Kaṇṇaki and Kōvalaṉ are said to perform compassionate service for the sake of others "for a long time" (*anēkakālam*; xxvi.60) until attaining liberation at the feet of the future Buddha, but the term used here (anēkakālam), literally "time which is not short or small," carries no connotation of the countless years found in the Pāli sources. Mācāttuvāṉ's prediction of his own liberation, in the company of his son, at the feet of the future Buddha might well be describing an event that could happen tomorrow or the next day (xxviii.141–147). In short, not the slightest suggestion can be found that the characters of the *Maṇimēkalai* will need to wait for billions of years for their enlightenment and liberation.

The *Maṇimēkalai*, with its portrayal of the future Buddha as an intimate member of the main characters' family and the suggestion of his imminent arrival, would thus seem to envision a Buddhist community of the future that is quite different than that found elsewhere in Buddhist literature. Yet, with the exception of the brief references to a future Buddha named Metteyya in the *Dīgha-Nikāya* and the *Buddhavaṁsa*, all of the so-called prophetic texts composed in Pāli are relatively late; the earliest, the *Anāgatavaṁsa* attributed to Kassapa Coḷa, can, if the evidence from the *Gandhavaṁsa* cited previously is taken as reliable, be dated to the late twelfth or early thirteenth century.[38] The Pāli texts that directly address the coming of a future Buddha are, in short, all substantially later than the *Maṇimēkalai*.

In fact, if one looks beyond, or more appropriately before, the Pāli literature that obviously concerns itself with the future Buddha, scattered bits of evidence can be found to suggest that the *Maṇimēkalai* was not alone in the sixth century in imagining the arrival of a living Buddha within centuries rather than billions of years. In the various renditions of the life of Buddhaghosa, for example, it is reported that the monks of the

Mahāvihāra greeted the composition of the *Visuddhimagga* by crying out to its author, "Without doubt he is Metteyya!" (*nissaṁsayaṁ sa metteyo*).[39] Although such a statement might easily be interpreted, on the one hand, as hyperbolic praise, likening only rhetorically the genius of Buddhaghosa to the wisdom of the future Buddha, on the other hand, such an identification might well depend on the expectation, like that of the ascetics confused by the miraculous events accompanying Āputtiraṉ's rebirth in the *Maṇimēkalai* (xv.23–35), that Metteyya's arrival on earth can happen at any moment. Such scattered phrases are certainly difficult to evaluate. Much more interesting and potentially useful for the consideration of the *Maṇimēkalai*'s vision of the future, given the central place of the wondrous almsbowl, Amutacurapi, in the text, is a story told by the fifth-century Chinese pilgrim to India and Sri Lanka, Faxian (Fa-hsien), concerning the begging bowl of the Buddha and the coming of Metteyya/Maitreya to earth.[40]

In the thirty-ninth chapter of his account of his travels,[41] Faxian records that while visiting the Mahāvihāra in Sri Lanka, he listened to an Indian monk describe the movement of the Buddha's begging bowl throughout the Buddhist world: originally preserved in the city of Vaiśālī, the bowl is moved from location to location every "few hundred years"[42] until it returns to "Central India" and then to Tuiṣta heaven. There, Maitreya will recognize it as the bowl of Śākyamuni Buddha, and it will return to earth to be protected under the sea by a dragon king until Maitreya takes earthly birth. When Maitreya is about to attain enlightenment, "the bowl will break up into four pieces and return to its place of origin on Mt. Vinataka."[43] Faxian then notes that "the one thousand Buddhas of the Age of the Wise will all use the same bowl."[44] The eventual disappearance of the bowl signals the decline of virtue in the world, and the usual description of the gradual return of righteousness and long lives, as found in Pāli texts from the *Cakkavattisīhanādasutta* to the *Anāgatavaṁsa*, follows. When human beings have succeeded in cultivating a lifespan of eighty thousand years, Maitreya will come to earth to turn "the first wheel of dharma," bringing salvation to those who are deserving.[45]

What is interesting about the connection of the bowl to the coming of Maitreya in Faxian's account is the suggestion of a calculated number for the date of the bowl's ascension to Tuṣita heaven and the subsequent resolve of Maitreya to come to earth. Although the details that follow in the Chinese text—concerning the decline and subsequent rise of virtue until human beings live for eighty thousand years—are not mentioned in the Tamil, Faxian provides, albeit in a second-hand manner, the only other early medieval Indian account of the coming of the future Buddha that assigns his arrival a specific date.[46] Faxian unfortunately forgets the precise number of years between each movement of the bowl (perhaps suggesting an uneven or difficult number to remember), but it is obviously not very large, one that he approximates as "a few hundred years." Given the various cities cited by the Indian monk of Faxian's account as future homes of the relic, the bowl will ascend to Tuṣita heaven in something like twelve or thirteen hundred years from the present recorded by Faxian, initiating a long series of events that will eventually culminate in Maitreya's earthly birth. Like the 1616 of the *Maṇimēkalai*, a number that would seem to be the result of some specific mathematical computation, Faxian's Indian monk suggests a date initiating dramatic transformations in human affairs that is both precise and relatively close at hand.

Faxian's story of the Buddha's almsbowl and its intimate connection to the coming of Maitreya provides a potentially enlightening parallel to the narrative of the bowl and the coming Buddha found in the *Maṇimēkalai*. Such a parallel, especially given the relative proximity to the time and place of the *Maṇimēkalai*'s composition of Faxian and the Indian monk who tells the story at the Sri Lankan Mahāvihāra, may help to illumine the Tamil text's vision of the future and the community to form around the coming Buddha. The almsbowl of the Buddha is one of the most important of the Buddha's relics, and much evidence exists to suggest that the Buddha's bowl relic was worshipped "from the Mauryan period onwards."[47] The story of the bowl's ascension to Tuṣita heaven, for example, is depicted in visual detail in a second-century CE stone relief from Amarāvatī, described as: "cross-bar with a number of gods and goddesses clustering round a bowl in a tray carried aloft and adorned with great reverence. Nagas, garudas, and other demigods dance while dwarf yakshas make soft music with conch and drum and divine damsels soar above with hands joinds [*sic*] in adoration."[48] Kuwayana Shōshin argues persuasively that a physical object known as the Buddha's begging bowl existed as an important focus of ritual worship in Gandhāra.[49] On a more literary note, royal struggles to possess the Buddha's bowl relic, in addition to the tooth relic, constitute a major theme in the Pāli chronicle literature. The connection of the bowl to the coming of Metteyya/Maitreya supplies an interesting lens through which to view the *Maṇimēkalai*'s emphasis on both the future Buddha and the almsbowl, Amutacurapi.

As indicated by the story recounted in Faxian's text, a Buddhist narrative tradition imagining the position of the bowl relic as intimately tied to the future Buddha—a tradition in which the relic, like the Buddha-pedestal of the *Maṇimēkalai* discussed previously, might be understood as anticipatory rather than commemorative or nostalgic—appears to have been in circulation in Sri Lanka by the fifth century C.E. (although Faxian is quick to point out that the monk who tells the tale is from India). Certainly, the position of the bowl relic in the Buddhist world constitutes a significant literary theme in a variety of texts dating from the same historical period as the *Maṇimēkalai* and beyond.[50] Faxian himself claims to have seen the bowl relic enshrined at "Fo-lau-sha" or "Puruṣapura";[51] some two centuries later, the Chinese pilgrim Xuanzang (Hsuan-tsang) reports that the bowl rests in the palace of the king of "Po-la-sse" or Persia.[52] A variety of Chinese monastic authors claim to have seen the bowl relic in Gandhāra, from Fotudeng in the third century to Huilan in the fifth.[53] In the Pāli chronicle literature, particularly in the *Mahāvaṁsa*, possession of the bowl relic is portrayed as an important point of contention between rival Tamil and Sri Lankan kings. Brought to Sri Lanka by Sumana,[54] along with the tooth and right collar-bone relics, for example, the bowl in the *Mahāvaṁsa* is kept by King Devānaṁpiyatissa in his palace while the other relics are ensconced in their own shrines (*thūpa*).[55] Under King Vaṭṭagāmaṇi, the bowl is captured by a Ḍamila (Tamil) invader and taken away to the "further shore."[56] Although the importance of the bowl relic seems to diminish somewhat throughout the course of the *Cūlavaṁsa*, with the bowl mentioned, in nearly every instance, in tandem with the tooth relic,[57] the medieval Italian traveler, Marco Polo, notes that in the late thirteenth century, the "Great Kaan" of China sent a company of ambassadors to procure from "Seilan" the tooth, hair, and bowl relics.[58]

Yet is the *Maṇimēkalai*'s bowl, Amutacurapi—its name meaning literally "that which generates (*curapi*) the nectar of immortality (Tamil *amuta*, Sanskrit amṛta)"—really to be understood as the bowl relic of the Buddha?[59] Several clues in the text of the *Maṇimēkalai* itself suggest that that is precisely how the model author imagines this wondrous almsbowl. Like the Buddha's bowl that appears in the Chinese travel accounts and the Pāli chronicle literature, Amutacurapi in the Tamil text is venerated very much like a relic. Maṇimēkalai, for example, places the bowl on the lotus pedestal built in Kāñcīpuram as a replica of the monument on Maṇipallavam (xxviii.216–219), just as Xuanzang depicts the "precious tower" that once held the Buddha's dish (*pātra*) in Gandhāra,[60] and Kings Parakkamabāhu II and Parakkamabāhu IV each place the caskets containing the bowl and tooth relics on ornate, bejeweled seats.[61] Just as Parakkamabāhu IV is said in the *Cūlavaṁsa* to celebrate an elaborate festival in honor of the relics,[62] so, too, does King Kiḷḷi of Kāñcīpuram proclaim a festival in honor of the bowl after temples dedicated to Maṇimēkalā and Tīvatilakai are constructed next to the pedestal (xxviii.210–215). The *Maṇimēkalai*, at least to the extent that it places great emphasis on the almsbowl Amutacurapi, reads very much like a chronicle (vaṁsa) focusing on a particular relic. Such texts, like the *Dhātuvaṁsa* or the *Chakesadhātuvaṁsa* cited previously, are said by Collins "usually [to] end with [the relic] being enshrined in a particular place"[63] and, very much like the *Maṇimēkalai*, to "recount a linear historical narrative" while simultaneously "interweaving . . . timeless nirvanized Buddhahood with the texture of all time, past, present, and future."[64] Amutacurapi both recalls the compassion of the former Buddha and points to the liberating glories of the Buddhist community yet to come.

Amutacurapi, like the bowl relic depicted in a variety of other Buddhist texts, wields extraordinary powers and requires special powers of those who seek to possess it. Reminiscent of the four great treasures (*mahānidhi*, *mahānidhāna*) said in various Sanskrit and Pāli sources to reappear when Maitreya/Metteyya comes to earth,[65] Amutacurapi emerges from the Kōmuki Lake every year on the anniversary of the Buddha's birth and enlightenment (xi.40–45). That almsbowl, "worthy of adoration since ancient times" (*toḻuntakai marapiṉ*; xi.58), enters into the world of human beings only "if there appears a protector of precious life who follows the teachings of the Buddha" (xiv.93–94), just as the bowl relic depicted by Faxian can only be possessed by someone who is karmically prepared to do so. In recounting his travels to the country of Puruṣapura where he claims to have seen the actual bowl relic, for example, Faxian tells the story of the king of "Yueh-she," who unsuccessfully tried to remove the bowl from the spot where it was enshrined. Unable to move the relic even with a battalion of powerful elephants, the king, Faxian notes, "knew that the time for an association between himself and the bowl had not yet arrived."[66] Faxian further records that although poor people can easily fill with flowers that relic at Puruṣapura, rich men "are unable to fill it up, though they offer a hundred, or a thousand, or ten thousand bushels"[67] of flowers. Maṇimēkalai's bowl also requires people of virtue both to activate and use it; the bowl's generative powers are summoned only when Ātirai, the virtuous and long-suffering wife of the seafaring Cātuvaṉ, places the first morsel of food into the bowl at xvi.132–135. The bowl itself, in other words, recognizes the virtue of Ātirai and produces bountiful food in accordance with that virtue. In a similar vein, the biography of the early fifth-century Chinese traveler, Zhimeng, indicates that devout Buddhists often lifted the bowl relic in worship: "the bowl changed its weight depending on the depth of the worshiper's faith."[68]

Like Amutacurapi's ability to generate an unending supply of food, the Buddha's bowl relic in the Pāli chronicle literature is said to possess "ten powers" (*dasabalassa*).[69] Indeed, it is the power to feed the poor and hungry in particular, Amutacurapi's most prized quality in the *Maṇimēkalai*, that is also most commonly associated with the almsbowl of the Buddha. The *Cūlavaṁsa* (xxxvii.189–198), for example, describes how King Upatissa II, in a time of great drought and famine, fashioned a golden image of the Buddha, filled the bowl relic with water, placed both upon a chariot, and paraded them around the royal city, with monks sprinkling the water and chanting to summon a great rain cloud.[70] The thirteenth-century travel narrative of Marco Polo, perhaps drawing a modest parallel to the Gospel story of the loaves and fishes, records that the "Great Kaan" desired the almsbowl of the Buddha because his ministers "find it written in their Scriptures that the virtue of that dish is such that if food for one man be put therein it shall become enough for five men."[71]

If the *Maṇimēkalai*, then, can be understood to imagine the almsbowl Amutacurapi as a relic of the Buddha, then it is a relic with two significant characteristics. First, although relics are often interpreted as symbols of nostalgia for an absent Buddha, as media for creating a sense of presence in the face of physical absence,[72] Amutacurapi, if understood in light of Faxian's story, is less a symbol or relic of the past than an emblem of hope for the future. The movement of the bowl throughout South India (from Maturai to Maṇipallavam) and its eventual enshrinement in Kāñcīpuram are intimately tied to the karmic fortunes of Maṇimēkalai, the young girl meant to be reborn as the Buddha's chief disciple at a precisely calculated future date. Second, although the *Maṇimēkalai* never directly states that Amutacurapi is the almsbowl of the Buddha, the text does explicitly establish the vessel as the embodiment of what it perceives to be the Buddha's single most compelling moral quality: his ability to cure, to heal, to alleviate human suffering. The Buddha, for example, is repeatedly portrayed as "the great physician who cures the disease of rebirths" (*piṟavip piṇi maruttuvaṉ*; ix.61); Amutacurapi is likewise described as "the medicine for precious life" (*ār uyir maruntāy*; xxviii.228), and Maṇimēkalai, feeding the hungry with Amutacurapi in her hands, is the "woman who cures the disease known as hunger" (*pacip piṇi tīrtta pāvai*; xxviii.234).

In the world imagined by the *Maṇimēkalai*, the Buddha is coming, and he is coming relatively soon. Who will participate in the glorious reign of the future Buddha, when "the virtue that is beyond measure will enter into human lives wholeheartedly" (xi.81–82) and "human beings will not know deformity" or any other form of suffering (xi.97–98)? The almsbowl Amutacurapi serves to remind the audience of both the future Buddha's imminent arrival and the ethical action—compassionate service to others—that will admit one to the future community of disciples. The aesthetic experience of pathos or compassion ceases, in this context, to serve merely as heightened emotional awareness for the literary connoisseur and becomes rather an experience of soteriological significance. The aesthetic experience of empathy or compassion provides the emotional basis for the moral action that will lead one to future liberation at the feet of the coming Buddha. As a relic of the former Buddha that also signals the coming of the next, Amutacurapi as presented in the *Maṇimēkalai* embodies the moral force of the Buddha, his compassionate care of and service to others that will win for Maṇimēkalai herself a birth as the future Buddha's chief disciple. Those who engage the text in the manner of the literary connoisseur—experiencing a heightened perception of compassion—and heed its ethical call will, by extension, also earn the right to participate in the liberating glories of the future.

The *Maṇimēkalai* thus imagines this glorious community of disciples gathered around the Buddha of the future in a number of ways: through its anticipation of events yet to come; its vision of the coming, if unnamed, Buddha; the pride of place afforded the illegitimate daughter of a courtesan in that future vision; and its use of the almsbowl Amutacurapi to signal both the coming of the future Buddha at a specific date relatively close at hand and the compassionate service to others necessary to see that coming Buddha. The enshrining of the bowl in the Maṇipallavam replica outside Kāñcīpuram marks that city as an important site in the Buddhist world. As Shinohara notes, images of Buddha relics, and the bowl relic in particular, have long been strategically used to mark sacred landscapes far from the North Indian sites associated with Śākyamuni Buddha's life.[73] The bowl, in connection with the specific date 1616 and the story told by Faxian, further marks an important regional Buddhist tradition in the early medieval period that envisioned the coming of the future Buddha as a very real possibility demanding urgent attention.[74] Although the *Maṇimēkalai* imagines a community of Buddhists who, to cite Strong, "can best be thought of as living devotionally in between two Buddhas, trying to recollect, on the one hand, the glories of Śākyamuni, and looking forward, on the other, to the coming of Maitreya,"[75] the reign of the future Buddha is not some vague and indefinite hope. Preparation for participation in the future Buddha's imminent community through compassionate understanding and care of others is crucial, in the world of the *Maṇimēkalai*, to nurture the hope of liberation at the Buddha's feet, critical to being Buddhist. Unlike Pāli prophetic texts such as the *Cakkavattisīhanādasutta* and the *Anāgatavaṁsa*, the focus of the *Maṇimēkalai* lies not in the details of the future Buddha's appearance on earth but on the eminently human struggle of its many characters to see him, to gain the right to be near him and attain final liberation. Through its engagement with questions of human suffering and its engagement with its audience through the very human emotion of pathos or compassion, the *Maṇimēkalai*'s vision of liberation, as Collins so aptly puts it in his study of narrative and Buddhist enlightenment, "form[s] part of the religious lives of ordinary thinking and feeling human beings."[76]

Recentering the Buddhist World

In both the *Maṇimēkalai* and the story told by Faxian, the Buddha's bowl relic signals the coming of the future Buddha. In the *Maṇimēkalai*, as argued previously, Amutacurapi further embodies that moral quality, compassionate concern for others, that earns one the right to participate in the glorious community to come. Yet more than simply pointing toward soteriologically significant events of the future, the bowl relic, in both the Chinese and Tamil texts, also serves to mark the boundaries of that community, to map out the central locations of the Buddhist world envisioned by each narrative. Although Faxian is careful to distance himself from the source of his story of the Buddha's bowl,[77] for example, the lands to be visited by the bowl relic mirror, perhaps not coincidentally, the Chinese monk's own travels throughout the Buddhist world: Vaiśālī; Gandhāra;[78] the "Western Yu-chi"; Khoten; Koutche; "the land of the Han";[79] "the land of the Lions";[80] and "mid India."[81] In the *Maṇimēkalai*, the bowl Amutacurapi is similarly connected, either directly or indirectly, with each of the major sites depicted in the narrative: Maturai (where Āputtiraṉ is first given the bowl), Maṇipallavam (where the bowl emerges from Kōmuki Lake), Pukār (where Maṇimēkalai first uses the bowl efficaciously), Kāñcīpuram (where the relic is eventually enshrined), and Cāvakam (where the bowl's previous owner, Āputtiraṉ, is reborn). The bowl, then, not only embodies a vision of the future and a compelling moral attitude but hints at a landscape, a geographically bounded community, as well. The *Maṇimēkalai*'s envisioning of a Buddhist community involves a particular territory, a distinct terrain. Amutacurapi serves not simply as a symbol of the propagation of Buddhism or the legitimation of dynastic rule[82] but, as Shinohara demonstrates so persuasively in his examination of the role of the begging bowl in the revelatory sermon of the seventh-century Chinese monk, Daoxuan,[83] as a medium for reimagining the contours of the Buddhist world. The *Maṇimēkalai* is not simply forward-looking but also outward-looking, imagining and defining a Buddhist community through space and time. The boundaries of that reimagined space extend not only to the borders of Tamil-speaking southern India but also to the distant shores of Southeast Asia. The nature of this ambitious project of spatial imagination becomes more distinct when one considers the *Maṇimēkalai* in the wider context of other Buddhist literary cultures engaged in similar processes of community formation and articulation in the fourth through seventh centuries.

The poetic anthologies of classical Caṅkam Tamil and the *Cilappatikāram* imagine a South Indian landscape dominated by the capitals of three powerful dynasties: Kāvirippūmpaṭṭiṉam or Pukār, the Cōḻa capital; Maturai, the seat of the Pāṇṭiyaṉ kings; and Vañci, home of the Cēraṉ royal family.[84] Although the *Maṇimēkalai* also envisions a landscape that includes this trio of royal cities, the cities themselves are transformed by the text into Buddhist sites, their general importance eclipsed in several ways by images of other, more significant lands. The *Maṇimēkalai*, in short, reimagines the classical Tamil literary world, imbuing a new landscape with powerful Buddhist images and events, turning the classical literary landscape into an eminently Buddhist one. The terrain of the Caṅkam corpus is here rendered in religious terms and extended to a Buddhist world far beyond the royal walled cities of Pukār, Maturai, and Vañci.

The *Maṇimēkalai*'s revisioning of the Buddhist world begins close to home with these literary capitals of the Caṅkam royal dynasties. Kāvirippūmpaṭṭiṉam, celebrated in the Caṅkam work known as *Paṭṭiṉappālai*[85] and known as the birthplace of the great goddess-in-the-making in the *Cilappatikāram*, for example, is depicted in the *Maṇimēkalai* as (1) the birthplace of a Buddha-to-be, Maṇimēkalai; (2) the site of both a beautiful park associated with the Buddha (the Uvavaṉam)[86] and a temple depicting the Buddhist cosmos where a mysterious deity predicts the future; (3) a place visited by the compassionate Buddhist sage, Caṅkatarumaṉ, "who possesses a face like the cool moon [even] when the sun's rays are scorching" (v.60); (4) the home of a learned Buddhist teacher, Aṟavaṇaṉ; and (5) a city of compassion where "wealthy people . . . help those who are helpless" (xvii.63–64). Although not central to the flow of events in the present of the narrative, the city of Maturai is similarly transformed by the *Maṇimēkalai*. Celebrated in the *Maturaikkāñci* as a metropolis of wealth and contentment[87] and in the *Cilappatikāram* as the site of Kaṇṇaki's terrible revenge, the *Maṇimēkalai* depicts Maturai as a refuge for the compassionate whose good intentions are scorned[88] and as a resting place for the Buddha's bowl relic.[89] The Caṅkam poetic work, *Ciṟupāṇāṟṟuppaṭai*, portrays Vañci as a fertile kingdom ruled by a chieftain who once conquered northern lands;[90] the *Cilappatikāram* elaborates at length on this theme of vanquishing northern armies, as King Ceṅkuṭṭuvaṉ defeats various enemies to secure a Himalayan stone for the image of the deified Kaṇṇaki.[91] Although Vañci in the *Maṇimēkalai* remains home to the temple of Kaṇṇaki (xxvi.1–6) and a variety of non-Buddhist teachers, Kaṇṇaki is transformed in the Buddhist text into a compassionate follower of the Buddha's teachings, and the Vaidikas, Ājīvikas, Jains, and materialists are made to look ridiculous. Not only is Vañci now home to Maṇimēkalai's grandfather, Mācāttuvāṉ, who has undertaken the life of a Buddhist ascetic in the wake of his son's tragic death (xxviii.93–100), but it is also the spot where the Buddha-to-be himself, Kōvalaṉ's ancestor of nine generations ago, resolved to give up his wealth, erect a grand shrine, and practice asceticism (xxviii.119–132). Pukār, Maturai, and Vañci, in short, become cities of Buddhist significance in the religious landscape envisioned by the *Maṇimēkalai.*

Yet as the three royal cities are being reimagined as primarily Buddhist sites, their importance is at the same time eclipsed by other, more significant, locations. Pukār, for example, succumbs to a tidal wave, Maṇimēkalai ultimately leaves her grandfather behind in Vañci, and the bowl Amutacurapi eventually makes its way from Maturai to Kāñcīpuram. It is Kāñcīpuram, in fact, that assumes central importance in the text's imagined world after the destruction of Pukār. Not only does Kāñcī figure prominently in the story of Maṇimēkalai's spiritual maturation—as the place where all the beneficial root conditions crucial to her liberation become manifest (ētunikaḻcci yāvum, as at xii.104–107 and xxi.155–158) and she learns both logic and the doctrine of interdependent origination—but the city emerges as a new center for Buddhist worship and relic veneration: the almsbowl Amutacurapi is enshrined on a replica of the wondrous pedestal on Maṇipallavam, the Kōmuki Lake is recreated, and temples to the goddesses Maṇimēkalā and Tīvatilakai are constructed (xxviii.201–219). By the close of the text, Kāñcīpuram has replaced a flooded Pukār as the central Buddhist location in the Tamil literary landscape envisioned by the *Maṇimēkalai.*[92]

The *Maṇimēkalai,* however, also imagines a landscape reaching far beyond the Caṅkam poetic tradition of the "good world [where] Tamil is spoken," between northern Vēṅkaṭam and southern Kumari.[93] Included, for example, albeit briefly and only in reference to former or future lives, are several important Buddhist sites of northern India. Mātavi and Cutamati, in their former lives as Maṇimēkalai's sisters Tārai and Vīrai, earned their present birth through circumambulating the imprint of the Buddha's foot on Mount Pātapaṅkayamalai, situated on the banks of the river Kaṅkai (Sanskrit Gaṅgā; x.61–74). Aṟavaṇaṉ also worships "the feet of the First Lord on the hill known as Pātapaṅkayamalai, [the feet] that wash away karma" (xii.35–38). Maṇimēkalai remembers the former life of the sage, Piramataruman, who saved the lives of many by accurately predicting an earthquake in the land of Kāntāram (Gandhāra; ix.9–37). Most important of the North Indian sites, however, is the city of Kapilaiyam (Kapilavastu), likened to a beauty mark (*tilakam*) on the "forehead" of the fertile land of Makatam (Sanskrit Magadha; xxvi.42–43), birthplace of the future Buddha (xxvi.46), with Maṇimēkalai as his chief disciple (xxi.175–179) and Kōvalaṉ and Kaṇṇaki as his devoted followers (xxviii.141–144).

As mentioned previously, however, the Buddhist sites of North India are named only in passing, in relation to the events of past lives or the future arrival of the Buddha. In the present-tense narrative, the South Indian locations come to the fore. Tārai, Vīrai, Ilakkumi, and Irākulaṉ are all reborn in Pukār, for example, and Aṟavaṇaṉ resides first in Pukār and then in Kāñcīpuram rather than dwelling on the side of Mount Pātapaṅkayamalai. Beyond even the sites of South India properly revisioned as central locations in the Buddhist world, however, the *Maṇimēkalai* includes in its landscape a variety of islands and island kingdoms, from the fabulous and wholly imaginative landscape of Maṇipallavam to the far-off and more "realistically" depicted kingdom of Cāvakam.

The contours of this extended Buddhist world are both terrestrial and fantastic, alternately portrayed with realism or in vividly creative strokes of imagination. Maṇipallavam, some several hundred miles (in Tamil, thirty *yōcaṉai*, Sanskrit *yojana*) to the south of Pukār (vi.211–212),[94] for example, is squarely located, for any reader with the slightest geographical sense, near no known island or tract of land and serves as home to two important and other-worldly sites: the bejeweled lotus seat of the Buddha that grants knowledge of former births (viii.43–53) and Kōmuki Lake, which harbors the Buddha's bowl relic until Maṇimēkalai appears to claim it (xi.37–50). The island of naked cannibals converted by Cātuvaṉ seems more a standard Buddhist caricature of a non-Buddhist culture[95] than any identifiable locale. Although Cātuvaṉ's efforts there can hardly be said to create a cultured center of Buddhist thought and practice, "the island of the Nāgas" perhaps represents a counterpoint to the cultured sophistication of the text's Tamil cities, a literary paradigm for the role that Buddhism might play in "uncivilized" lands.[96]

The *Maṇimēkalai* moves closer to identifiable geography in its depiction of Irattiṉatīvam (Sanskrit Ratnadvīpa), "Jewel Island," a name used in a variety of Buddhist sources to refer to Sri Lanka.[97] That the *Maṇimēkalai* should mention the island of Sri Lanka and its famous mountain is not surprising, given the numerous literary testimonies of interaction between South India and Sri Lanka in the early medieval period. In addition to the commentarial remarks of Buddhadatta and Dhammapāla, for example, that attest to allegiance to the Mahāvihāra while residing in South India, the *Mahāvaṁsa* also includes South India along with Sri Lanka in its vision of the Buddhist world. Yet references to Jewel Island are scant in the *Maṇimēkalai*, perhaps because the text anticipates a South Indian audience fully aware of the Buddhist significance of the island that lies so close to the east. Like Makatam, Kapilaiyam, and Mount Pātapaṅkayamalai, Jewel Island is briefly but significantly mentioned in the *Maṇimēkalai* as the site where the great sage, Cātucakkaraṉ, "turned the wheel of the Buddha's teachings and abandoned all mental confusion" (x.25–26) and where the footprints of the Buddha are enshrined on the mountain known as Camantam or Camaṉoḷi (now more popularly known as Adam's Peak). The footprints, like "a ship of virtue to cross the great ocean that is [our] births" (xi.24–25), are presented as what they remain to this day, an important pilgrimage site, worshipped reverently by Tīvatilakai, the guardian of the Buddha's bowl (xi.26), and by the sages who instruct the Cēraṉ king on the occasion of the manifestation of conditions leading to his enlightenment (ētunikaḻcci; xxviii.107–112).

The most interesting of the island kingdoms and the one that clearly takes center stage in the Buddhist world imagined by the *Maṇimēkalai* is that of "cool Cāvakam"[98] with its "great mountains of camphor" (xv.3).[99] The Tamil text takes significant care to establish the island as a less fantastic or imaginary place than Maṇipallavam; Cāvakam is ruled by a king (Āputtiraṉ reborn as King Puṇṇiyarācaṉ) plagued by an all-too-human ennui,[100] whose minister reminisces at xxv.12–20 about his former ambassadorial trip to Pukār to "establish good relations with [King] Kiḷḷivaḷavaṉ." Āputtiraṉ's story provides a direct link with the landscape of southern India, for he was, in a former lifetime, born and abandoned by his mother ten miles from the South Indian city of

Koṟkai (xiii.84–85) and cast out by his adopted brahmin community, only to be reborn from the womb of a virtuous cow and adopted by the childless king, Pūmicaṇṭiraṉ (Bhūmicandra), on the island of Cāvakam (xv.45). Āputtiraṉ's greatness in his birth as King Puṇṇiyarācaṉ is foretold by the sage of Cāvakam, Maṇmukaṉ (xv.9–14); the miracles that surround Āputtiraṉ's birth on Cāvakam mirror those of the Buddha's birth and confuse the sages of the temple of the cosmic place back in Pukār, who realize that "it is not the time for the earthly birth of the great ascetic of the bodhi tree" (xv.29–30). As Aṟavaṇaṉ earlier describes the auspicious events to accompany the future Buddha's arrival on earth (xii.87–98), Āputtiraṉ's reign over Cāvakam is said to usher in an era of unfailing rains and prosperity (xxv.100–109). Cāvakam is imagined in the *Maṇimēkalai* as the home of a wise and compassionate follower of the Buddha who attains enlightening knowledge of former births before the great lotus seat on Maṇipallavam (xxv.134–137).

Indeed, the more easily identifiable sites in the *Maṇimēkalai* text (leaving aside Maṇipallavam) are bound together by a series of strong, narratively derived connections. A wise Buddhist king, a great "universal conqueror" or "world-ruler" (Pāli *cakkavattin*), in other words, is born far from the North Indian cities and towns associated with the life of Śākyamuni Buddha. Pukār is thus bound to Cāvakam through two extraordinary births. Pātapaṅkaya Mountain on the banks of the Gaṅgā is tied to Sri Lanka through footprints of saving power. Kāñcīpuram, as the site of a newly constructed and important Buddhist shrine to the bowl relic, is bound to the mythical Maṇipallavam through monuments enshrining a relic and granting enlightenment. Pukār, Kāñcīpuram, Irattiṉatīvam and Cāvakam mark the boundaries of the Buddhist world, setting the stage for the religious community of the future envisioned by the *Maṇimēkalai*.

The inclusion of such distant locales in the *Maṇimēkalai*'s vision of religious landscape and community marks a significant departure from the literary landscapes envisioned in the classical Tamil poetic anthologies. Although historians have long recognized the complex maritime networks of trade, immigration, and cultural exchange that have connected the Indian subcontinent, and South India in particular, with Southeast Asia since at least the beginning of the common era,[101] the *Maṇimēkalai* is the only extant Tamil text of the medieval period to incorporate the contours of the historians' economic or political world into a literary vision of religious community. Place names not associated with the landscape of southern India, for the first time in the *Maṇimēkalai*, represent not simply the names of trading posts or important commercial ports but significant sites in a world defined by Buddhist events and values.

Both the Caṅkam work known as *Paṭṭiṉappālai* and the *Cilappatikāram*, for example, mention cities whose names have been identified by a number of historians with important trading centers of Southeast Asia. In describing the merchandise available in the city of Pukār, the *Paṭṭiṉappālai* includes *kāḻakattu ākkam*, glossed by the fourteenth-century commentator, Nacciṉārkkiṉiyar, as "goods produced in Kaṭāram";[102] the eighth-century Tamil Jain lexicon, *Tivākaram*, similarly identifies *kāḻakam* with Kaṭāram,[103] leading Nilakanta Sastri to conclude that "Kaḍāram is clearly Kedah on the west coast of the Malay peninsula."[104] In somewhat similar fashion, the *Cilappatikāram* at xiv.106–110 refers to incense, silk, sandalwood, perfume, and camphor brought in ships to Maturai as a tribute from "the people of Toṇṭi."[105] On the basis of both the nature of the products offered and the mention of the "east wind" (*koṇṭal*), Nilakanta Sastri concludes that Toṇṭi must refer to some location in Southeast Asia "as yet unidentified."[106] Whatever the precise location of Kāḻakam or Toṇṭi might be, clearly neither text fully incorporates such sources of trade and manufactured goods into its literary world. The people of Toṇṭi (*toṇṭiyōr*) are mentioned only in passing in the *Cilappatikāram*; the religious world of the text is marked by the cities of Kōvalaṉ and Kaṇṇaki and not the far-flung outposts of those paying tribute to the king. The *Maṇimēkalai*, in short, expands the landscape of classical Tamil literature in unprecedented ways. That landscape is further defined in religious terms by events, sites, and phenomena that mark the contours of a world made fundamentally Buddhist.

Even more striking, perhaps, is the extent to which the *Maṇimēkalai*'s inclusion of Pukār as the home of a Buddha-in-the-making and Cāvakam as a place where a great Buddhist world ruler can be born signals a departure from earlier literary visions of the Buddhist landscape beyond the Tamil. Although the *Milinda-pañha*,[107] for example, mentions trading voyages to the lands known as Cīna,[108] Kolapaṭṭana (perhaps a reference to Kāvirippūmpaṭṭiṉam), and Suvaṇṇabhūmi,[109] the world of the text clearly centers on those North Indian sites associated with the life of Śākyamuni Buddha.[110] Suvaṇṇabhūmi similarly figures in a number of Jātaka tales, each time simply as a far-off land of riches for which the Buddha-to-be sets sail, his quest for replenished wealth invariably thwarted by shipwreck.[111] The religious landscape of the Jātaka collection—its vision of the Buddhist world—remains thoroughly rooted, however, in "Majjhimadesa" or the "Middle Country," the area of north-central India encompassing the kingdoms, cities, monasteries, and parks associated with the birth and life of the Buddha from whose mouth the stories are said to issue forth.[112] The canonical commentary, *Mahāniddesa*, likewise mentions a number of Southeast Asian lands, including Suvaṇṇabhūmi and "Javam,"[113] yet simply lists each as a far-flung outpost to which travel is exceedingly difficult. In relating the lives of the twenty-five Buddhas in a highly stylized and repetitive fashion, the *Buddhavaṁsa* ("Chronicle of the Buddhas")[114] clearly imagines a discrete and single landscape as home to all Buddhas in all times, a landscape restricted to the ancient literary capital cities of northern India, from Rammavatī and Uttara to Khema and Kapilavatthu.[115] According to Buddhadatta's fifth-century commentary on the text, all Buddhas in particular must have a dwelling place at Jetavana, perform the "Miracle of the Double" (*yamakapāṭihāriya*)[116] at the gates of the city of Sāvatthī, and descend to earth at the city of Saṅkassa after teaching Buddhist doctrine to the heavenly beings.[117]

Although the *Maṇimēkalai* obviously does not abandon completely the literary landscape associated with the life of the Buddha in these Pāli texts, its vision of Buddhist community clearly pushes to the periphery the northern sites of Kāśī, Magadha, and the Gaṅgā and makes central the cities of Pukār, Kāñcīpuram, and Nākapuram (the capital of Cāvakam). Whether or not Maṇimēkalai's ētunikaḻcci renders her a Buddha-in-the-making and whether or not the miraculous signs that accompany Āputtiraṉ's rebirth paint him a great universal monarch or yet another Buddha-to-be, those narrative elements central to the *Maṇimēkalai*'s imagining of community—the almsbowl Amutacurapi as a relic signaling the coming Buddha and the ethos of compassion embodied by the bowl and engaged through the aesthetic experience of compassion—are at play in a world recentered in southern India and some portion of Southeast Asia. Through the enshrining of the bowl relic, the establishment of the site replicating the Buddha's lotus seat on Maṇipallavam, the final instructions and renunciatory vows of its central character, and the enlightenment of King Puṇṇiyarācaṉ before the Buddha pedestal on Maṇipallavam, the Tamil text places the South Indian city of Kāñcīpuram and the island kingdom of Cāvakam at the very center of its vision of the present Buddhist world.

In this shifting of the sacred centers of the Buddhist world southward and eastward, away from the North Indian sites associated with the earthly life of the Buddha, the *Maṇimēkalai* participates in a wider pattern of Buddhist imaginative literary development in the sixth century. A wide range of literary texts roughly contemporaneous with the *Maṇimēkalai* underscores the importance of literary geography to the imagining and articulation of religious community. Throughout the Buddhist world of the premedieval and early medieval period, in a variety of literary cultures and languages, the Buddhist landscape is reimagined through narrative literature to forge a link of continuity not only between Kapilaiyam/Kapilavastu and Kāñcīpuram but also between Magadha and Anurādhapura, between Rājagṛha and the "kingdom of the Han."[118] In such a literary context, the *Maṇimēkalai* is unique not in redrawing the Buddhist world per se but in reimagining a Buddhist landscape with southern India and maritime Southeast Asia at its center, in redefining the literary landscape of classical Tamil literature in fundamentally religious terms and extending the boundaries of that landscape far beyond the reaches of South India proper. Like contemporary narrative literature in Pāli and Chinese, the *Maṇimēkalai* reimagines a Buddhist community and Buddhist world with its own regional or local landscape at its center.

The Pāli chronicle literature, for example, suggests that by the sixth century CE,[119] Theravāda authors writing in Pāli began to reimagine a Buddhist world not focused on the South Indian Pallava capital of Kāñcīpuram but with the Mahāvihāra of Anurādhapura at its center. The *Mahāvaṁsa*, for example, compiled in an artful manner "for the emotion and equanimity of good people"[120] and possessing "many claims to be regarded as a kāvya,"[121] does nothing less than reorient the Buddhist landscape around Sri Lanka and its monastic institutions, while paying due reverence to the major Buddhist sites of North India. The visit of the Tathāgata himself serves to consecrate the island as part of the Buddha's own landscape (i), as do the visit of Aśoka's son, Mahinda (xiii), and the arrival of the Buddha's relics, including the almsbowl relic (xvii) and the great bodhi tree (xviii–xix). In the manner of the *Maṇimēkalai* envisioning a young girl of Pukār as the chief disciple of the future Buddha, as discussed previously, the *Mahāvaṁsa* imagines King Duṭṭhagāmaṇi and his family as the future servants of Metteyya. The *Mahāvaṁsa* refashions a Buddhist world that includes Magadha, as well as Suvaṇṇabhūmi, Kasmīra, and Gandhāra,[122] but places "the lovely island of Laṅkā" (*laṅkādīpa manuñña*)[123] squarely at its center. Such a narrative reimagining of the Buddhist world is also echoed in the Pāli commentarial literature of the period, as in Buddhaghosa's fifth-century commentary on the *Aṅguttāra-nikāya*, the *Manorathapūraṇī*. There Buddhaghosa extends the lands of Majjhimadesa or "Middle India," as the home of all Buddhas, to include all of Jambudvīpa (*sakalo pi hi jambudīpo majjhimadeso nāma*); he further adds that on the island of Sri Lanka or "Tambapaṇṇi," the city of Anurādhapura serves as the "middle country" (*tambapaṇṇidīpe anurādhapuraṁ majjhimadeso nāma*).[124]

Although obviously departing substantially from the forms and styles of South Asian literary cultures, Chinese narrative texts from roughly the fourth through eighth centuries CE reveal similar patterns of imagining a Buddhist landscape with ties to North India but fundamentally centered elsewhere. The Chinese pilgrims to India of this period, Faxian (fifth century), Xuanzang (seventh century), and Yijing (I-tsing; seventh century), all devote substantial portions of their narrative journeys to the sites associated with the Buddha and with stories of his former births. Certainly, these narratives of pilgrimage represent a very different kind of text than the *Maṇimēkalai*, yet each imagines a Buddhist world that extends far beyond those North Indian sites. Each pilgrim's text reveals a Buddhist landscape envisioned from northern India to Sri Lanka, from South India to Southeast Asia, with various important centers in each of these regions. Faxian's story of the bowl, for example, discussed at length previously, maps out a Buddhist world that includes not only "mid-India" but China and Sri Lanka as well. Faxian remains in the latter country for two years, collecting various texts as yet unknown in China[125] and portrays the island as a pious center of the Buddhist world, a place visited by the Buddha himself and graced by his footprints[126] and home to the very bodhi tree of the Buddha's enlightenment[127] and to his tooth relic.[128]

Some two centuries after Faxian, the pilgrim Xuanzang envisions South India, and Kāñcīpuram in particular, as a land once visited by the Buddha himself.[129] He describes a mountain, farther south, called Po-ta-la-ka and known as the abode of the Buddha-to-be, Avalokiteśvara.[130] Among the Chinese pilgrim monks, it is Yijing who, in portraying his efforts to bring to his homeland the proper observance of monastic discipline and thus "build a second Rājagriha City in the Divine Land of China,"[131] most clearly imagines a Buddhist world that includes both India and the island kingdoms of Southeast Asia. Although consistently noting the differences in the Buddhist practices of Indian and Southeast Asian monks and laypersons, for example,[132] Yijing repeatedly casts Buddhist India and the South Sea islands as united by more correct observance of the monastic rules of conduct (in contrast to China). The land of "Śrībhoja" in particular, interpreted by several scholars as referring to Java or Śrīvijaya,[133] is noted by Yijing to be a center of Buddhist scholarship; there he stays for six months to study Sanskrit grammar (*śabdavidyā*),[134] and he later cites the same region as the home of a renowned scholar, one Śākyakīrti, "who traveled all through the five countries of India in order to learn."[135] In the era of the Chinese pilgrims, the Buddhist world and the world of Buddhist literature and learning in particular reaches far beyond the monastic centers that are the principal foci of pilgrimage. By the time of Yijing, Śrībhoja, marking a territory perhaps not unrelated to the *Maṇimēkalai*'s Cāvakam, is envisioned as a center of Buddhist scholarship and practice midway between India and China.

Other medieval Chinese texts point to a world enlarged and recentered. The "Lives of the Nuns" (*Pi-ch'iu-ni chuan*), compiled by Shih Pao-ch'ang in the early sixth century CE,[136] for example, conceives of the Chinese female monastic tradition as a bastion of dharma in a world marked by the decline of the virtue brought by the Buddha's teachings.[137] Throughout the stories of the sixty-five exemplary Chinese Buddhist nuns, it soon becomes apparent that the text conceives of Sri Lanka as a similarly pure and virtuous monastic center for women.[138] The sixth-century Chinese work known as the *Scripture of the Monk Shouluo*,[139] in the manner of the early medieval Chinese apocalyptic literature that envisions the future Buddha Maitreya's impending arrival in China, imagines the birth and benevolent rule in China of the Buddha-to-be, Candraprabha.

Given the substantial number of texts in a variety of literary languages that reimagine the contours of the Buddhist world in the early medieval period, the *Maṇimēkalai*, although obviously departing significantly from the landscape envisioned by earlier Tamil poetic literature, would seem to be less unique as an instance of Buddhist narrative. In imagining a world and a Buddhist community extending from Pukār and Kāñcīpuram to Cāvakam, the *Maṇimēkalai* participates in a pattern of Buddhist literary imagining that appears at roughly the same time across the literary cultures of the Asian Buddhist world. Yet why this particular vision of the Buddhist world in the *Maṇimēkalai*, why this specific region stretching from South India to at least one corner of maritime Southeast Asia? Are these boundaries randomly drawn, the creative act of a vivid literary imagination? Beyond simply serving as a piece of evidence in the history of the Buddhist imagination in a specific literary culture bound by time and place, does the *Maṇimēkalai*'s vision of Buddhist landscape allow one to infer anything of the reading community of the text? For what sort of reading community would the imagined Buddhist world of the *Maṇimēkalai* provide meaningful mental territory, a compelling vision of religious space or landscape? Just as obviously as the *Maṇimēkalai* anticipates a model audience sophisticated in its knowledge of both classical Tamil literature and Buddhist values, as discussed in preceding chapters, so, too, does the text expect an audience for whom a literary landscape stretching from South India to Sri Lanka and Southeast Asia would suggest at least the possibility of a coherent region, of an identifiable territory or world. At what level, however, might such an envisioned region actually be coherent? What might the connection between Pukār and Cāvakam mean for the reading community of the *Maṇimēkalai*?

The World of the *Maṇimēkalai* beyond South India

As Le Goff argues in the introduction to his study of medieval European imaginings of space and time, the literary world includes "geographical as well as imaginary realities," forests, fields, and gardens both as "places [where] work was done and social practices enacted" and as "powerful symbols, objects of fear and desire and subjects of dream and legend."[140] The real and the imagined, in other words, are intertwined, often inextricably, in the literary world. Le Goff's study of the documents from the thirteenth-century Council of Lyons, for example, reveals the imagining of a new sort of Christendom, one thoroughly centered in Europe after the loss of the Holy Land in the post-Crusade era.[141] Following Le Goff, one might point, in the case of the *Maṇimēkalai*, to the substantial body of historical evidence cited previously that connects South India to Southeast Asia through the twelfth century via ties both economic and political. That a Buddhist text written in Tamil and claiming as its imagined center the cities of Kāñcīpuram and Pukār should also envision a Buddhist world that includes the islands of Southeast Asia and Cāvakam in particular is certainly not beyond the pale of historical possibility. A long-standing relationship among various monastic establishments in the Tamil port city of Nākapaṭṭiṉam, roughly twenty miles from the Buddhist ruins unearthed at present-day Kāvirippūmpaṭṭiṉam, or Pukār, and the Śailendra kings of Java and Sumatra can be traced to at least the early eleventh-century reign of the Cōḻa king, Rājarāja I. One of the so-called Larger Leiden Plates commissioned by Rājarāja I records grants to the "surpassingly beautiful Cūḷāmaṇivarma-vihāra" at "Nāgīpattana" that had been built by "the glorious Māravijayōttuṅgavarman" of the "Śailendra family" of "Śrī Vishaya."[142] More than three hundred bronze images of the Buddha and various Buddhas-to-be have been recovered from Nākapaṭṭiṉam.[143] The name of the royal dynasty, Śailendra, literally "Indra of the mountain," perhaps provides some point of reference for the rather enigmatic statement found in the *Maṇimēkalai* (xxiv.164–165) that Nākapuram, the city in Cāvakam ruled over by Āputtiraṉ-reborn-as-King-Puṇṇiyarācaṉ, is "the great city of the nephew of Indra."[144] Nākapaṭṭiṉam was also home to another Buddhist monastic establishment patronized by "foreigners": the so-called Chinese pagoda sketched by Elliot in the nineteenth century before the structure was torn down by Europeans to build a Jesuit college.[145] The fifteenth-century Kalyānī inscriptions of Burma relate the story of several monks who travel to Nāgapaṭṭana to visit a monastic institution known as Padarikārāma and to worship the image of the Buddha in a temple constructed by the king of "Cinadesa."[146] The *Maṇimēkalai* itself, as noted previously, imagines a diplomatic connection of sorts between King Puṇṇiyarācaṉ of Cāvakam and the Cōḻa king of Kāvirippūmpaṭṭiṉam (xxv.13–18), and Puṇṇiyarācaṉ, as Āputtiraṉ reborn, amounts to a Cāvanese ruler hailing originally from southern India. From the earliest inscription found at Vo-canh in present-day Cambodia[147] to the medieval flowering of Old Javanese narrative poetic works on the Sanskrit model, it is clear that Sanskrit as a literary language provided at least one basis for a transregional literary culture—described by Pollock as a "supralocal . . . symbolic network . . . mak[ing] similar kinds of claims about the nature and aesthetics of polity" and dubbed the "Sanskrit cosmopolis"[148]—that extended from India to Cambodia, the Malaysian archipelago, and Java and endured for more than a millennium.

Yet the *Maṇimēkalai*'s vision of territory is a distinctly religious one, its boundaries marked by the activities of a Buddha-in-the-making and a Buddhist monarch. The kinds of regions or landscapes imagined and/or enacted through trade, diplomatic missions, or "claims about . . . kingly virtue and learning; the dharma of rule; [and] the universality of dominion"[149] are not necessarily identical to imagined cultural or religious landscapes. Religious and political visions may but need not overlap. Any number of texts from the historical period under consideration, for example, imagine a Buddhist landscape binding Sri Lanka to South India, while implicitly acknowledging a political landscape that clearly separates the single religious world into easily distinguishable political regions. Even as Xuanzang depicts the confusion brought about by a "heretical" Cōḻa king ruling in Sri Lanka, for instance,[150] the pilgrim's biographer, Huili (Hwui Li), conceives of Kāñcīpuram as a refuge for Sri Lankan monks fleeing the turmoil in their homeland.[151] The colophon of the twelfth-century Pāli treatise attributed to Buddhappiya, *Upāsakajanālaṅkāra*, describes the monastic institutions patronized by a South Indian Pāṇḍya (Tamil Pāṇṭiyaṉ) ruler as a safe haven for monks seeking refuge from a "great Tamil conflagration" in Sri Lanka.[152] The fourteenth-century *Nikāya-saṅgrahaya*, in similar fashion, portrays "the town of Kāvira" in particular as home to a group of "Vaitulya" monks expelled from Sri Lanka by the king at the request of the rival Mahāvihāra.[153] As noted previously, the *Maṇimēkalai* makes few but significant remarks about Sri Lanka as the "Jewel Island," as if anticipating a reading audience already thoroughly familiar with that place and the importance of its Buddhist sites and communities. South Indian kingdoms and Sri Lanka, in other words, are quite consistently conceived in literary terms in at least two languages as part of a single Buddhist monastic community or world, a singularity often at odds with the political landscapes envisioned by various rulers.

Although historical evidence exists for the transmission of goods and texts in a Buddhist world stretching from India to Java and China throughout the medieval period, various literary cultures envision such a world in different and unique ways. Although southern India, for example, figures prominently in several Chinese renditions of the Buddhist landscape as the location of Mount Potalaka, the abode of the Buddha-to-be, Avalokiteśvara, as discussed previously, China (cīṉam) is mentioned only in passing in relatively few Tamil texts[154] and is certainly not included as part of the religious landscape envisioned by a Buddhist narrative such as the *Maṇimēkalai*. Although numerous scholars of South Indian history and religions have pointed to the ancient histories of Periplus and Ptolemy as indications of trading contact between the port city of Kāvirippūmpaṭṭiṉam (Ptolemy's Khaberis) and the Mediterranean world in the early centuries of the common era,[155] no evidence exists to suggest that such a trading network to the west ever captured the imagination of South Indian literary culture. Despite the "Indian influences" seen in the massive eighth-century Buddhist monument of Barabuḍur in central Java, no Indian Buddhist text imagines such a monument as part of its landscape.[156] Despite the numerous theories of the Hinduization or colonization of Southeast Asia from India argued in the literature cited previously, the inscriptions of both Southeast Asia and India, with few exceptions, are remarkably silent on the topic of direct contact between the two regions.[157]

Premodern Indic literature in general takes little notice of lands beyond India proper. In the cultural region or ecumene based on the literary practices associated with the perceived aesthetic powers of Sanskrit[158] and where Tamil may or may not have been "an everyday Southeast Asian koiné,"[159] the *Maṇimēkalai*'s imagining of a Buddhist world extending to maritime Southeast Asia and centered in the Tamil city of Kāñcīpuram offers a unique counterpoint to the Sanskrit tendency to ignore "the progressive cultural conquest of Sanskrit on [India's] eastern periphery."[160] The cultural connections between India and Southeast Asia are enacted and perceived quite differently according to the literary language chosen. Although Tamil might have been, as Pollock contends, a language of the everyday in the Sanskrit cosmopolis he describes, it also serves as a literary medium integrating South India and Southeast Asia as religious landscapes in at least one extant Buddhist text. In the case of the *Maṇimēkalai*, Tamil as a literary language unites Pollock's "mainland" (South India) and "periphery" (Cāvakam) into a single religious community, a single Buddhist world.

From the audience of literary connoisseurs anticipated by the model author of the *Maṇimēkalai*, one can infer some sort of region of established cultural/literary contact in a language other than Sanskrit. Were Tamil simply the language of the everyday, of trade or political campaign, it would, indeed, be difficult to imagine who the model readers of the *Maṇimēkalai* might be, that they envision (in Tamil) South India and Cāvakam as part of a single religious community. The evidence for such a "literary territory" connecting South India to Southeast Asia, from the Southeast Asian side, appears only several centuries after the composition of the *Maṇimēkalai* (all of it obviously influenced by Sanskritic literary forms and styles).[161] Yet, given the *Maṇimēkalai*'s inclusion of Cāvakam in its literary landscape, it is interesting to note that of all the regions of Southeast Asia, it is Java that has left behind the largest corpus of pre-Muslim literature[162] and the Javanese/Sumatran kingdom of Śrīvijaya that is noted in a variety of sources spanning several centuries to be a center of Sanskrit learning and culture.[163] The Buddhist literary connection between Kāñcīpuram and Cāvakam continues in the fourteenth-century Javanese poetic work, the *Nāgarakṛtāgama*, in which a monk known as Śrī Buddhāditya, hailing from "a place called Kāñcīpurī of the Six Monasteries . . . in India," is said to have composed "a eulogy [of] . . . countless verses" in honor of the Javanese king.[164] In the absence of any major notice of Southeast Asia in Sanskrit literature from India and some 300 or 400 hundred years before the literary evidence (beyond epigraphy) from Southeast Asia attests in any significant way to cultural contact between South India and Java, the *Maṇimēkalai* imagines such a connection and imbues it with religious significance.

Although the historical record is scanty, the *Maṇimēkalai* provides several hints that this imagined connection between Kāñcīpuram and Cāvakam does not arise from nothing, that it is not a wholly created space like the magical island of Maṇipallavam. While little or no direct evidence of South India–Southeast Asia as a distinct literary/cultural territory exists in the period of the *Maṇimēkalai*'s composition, certain recurring themes and images in the text itself, literary images and themes found in other parts of South and Southeast Asia, provide some glimpse of literary and cultural connection, of a meaningful cultural region which the *Maṇimēkalai* makes explicitly Buddhist. More than sixty years ago, for example, Sylvain Lévi first postulated a cultural or literary region of sorts, extending from Cape Comorin (Kanyākumārī) to the "merveilleux Eldorado de l'Extrême-Orient,"[165] based on the presence of the sea goddess, Maṇimekhalā, in literary works from South India, Sri Lanka, and various regions of Southeast Asia. "While the Tamil country, Ceylon, Burma, Siam, and Cambodia afford so many evidences of her long notoriety there," he writes, "nothing has come as yet to be found concerning her beyond this zone of earth and water."[166] Indeed, the evidence for Maṇimekhalā (Tamil Maṇimēkalā) as a poetic narrative figure serving as both guardian of the sea and faithful follower of the Buddha, if taken together, draws a map of a literary world whose contours overlap to some degree with those of the Buddhist world envisioned by the Tamil *Maṇimēkalai.*

The goddess appears, for example, in both the *Mahājanaka* and *Saṅkha-jātaka*s of the canonical collection,[167] saving the shipwrecked Buddha-to-be en route to Suvaṇṇabhūmi, just as she is said in the *Maṇimēkalai* to have rescued the Buddha-to-be in his birth as Kōvalaṉ's ancestor as he floundered in the sea.[168] In each of the Pāli narratives, she is commanded by the gods to guard the sea, neglects her duty for a time, and only on the seventh day rescues the Divine Being; in the latter tale, Maṇimekhalā provides the Buddha-to-be with a fabulously bejeweled ship for his return. Maṇimekhalā is mentioned in a variety of Sinhala texts of the twelfth through fourteenth centuries, including the *Butsarana* and the *Saddharmālaṅkāra*.[169] The seventeenth-century *Rājāvaliya* depicts the goddess saving a virtuous princess "destined to become the mother of the Maitrī Buddha" who has been cast adrift in the ocean by her father to appease the angry gods of the sea.[170] In the folk ballads and ritual songs collected by Barnett and Obeyesekere, Maṇimekhalā is known not only as a goddess of the sea but also as a deity with close connections to Pattiṉi (Kaṇṇaki) and Kōvalaṉ, who figure so prominently in both the *Cilappatikāram* and the *Maṇimēkalai.*[171] The *Chakesadhātuvaṁsa* from Burma, cited previously, ties Maṇimekhalā to the construction of a South Indian shrine to house a hair relic of the Buddha, and the stories of the so-called apocryphal Jātakas provide evidence of Maṇimekhalā as a literary character throughout Southeast Asia. In the Burmese recension known as the *Paññāsa-jātaka*, for example, the goddess Maṇimekhalā furnishes the Buddha-to-be with eighty-four thousand ships filled with ocean jewels;[172] guards his jewel-laden ships;[173] rescues him after seven days of swimming in the sea, having neglected her duties to attend a gathering of the gods;[174] and is identified as having been the Buddha-to-be's own mother seven births previously as she once again saves him from drowning in the ocean.[175] The scene of Maṇimekhalā's rescue of the future Buddha from the sea in the story of Mahājanaka is frequently depicted in Southeast Asian temple paintings and murals.[176]

With similar themes of festival, ocean, jewels, and neglected duty, the goddess Maṇimekhalā is also found in several Southeast Asian versions of the *Rāmāyaṇa* story, versions of the narrative which, as Frank Reynolds argues, present "Rāma as a royal hero who embodies Buddhist values."[177] The relevant story in each of the recensions runs as follows: Naṅg or Muni Mekhalā attends a celebration of the gods and displays a beautiful crystal in her hands. An evil demon known as Rāmasun or Rāmasur covets the jewel and throws his axe at the goddess to wrest the crystal from her. The god Orajun (Arjun) intervenes but is killed when thrown against Mount Meru. Śiva gathers together the gods to straighten out the sacred mountain, now tilted to one side, and Mekhalā and Rāmasur return to their respective homes.[178] This narrative lives on in the folk literature of Vietnam and Cambodia as a story explaining the origins of thunder (Rāmasur's axe) and lightning (Mekhalā's crystal)[179] and in classical Khmer dance drama performed to summon the rains.[180]

What is the significance of these scattered references to Maṇimēkalā/Maṇimekhalā for a deeper understanding of the Tamil narrative text? From the presence of Maṇimēkalā as a central character in the *Maṇimēkalai* and in a variety of literary forms and genres throughout Southeast Asia, one can infer early cultural contact between South India and Southeast Asia unrelated to or extending beyond both the "Sanskrit cosmopolis" and mere economic or political exchange, a cultural region claimed for Buddhism by the Tamil narrative text. Although several scholars have located evidence of specifically Tamil influence on the *Rāmāyaṇa* traditions of Thailand, Cambodia, and Laos,[181] Maṇimēkalā/Maṇimekhalā appears in no Indian rendition of the *Rāmāyaṇa* story, including the twelfth-century Tamil version, the *Irāmāvatāram*, attributed to Kampaṉ. Her relative popularity in literary cultures beyond India perhaps suggests that cultural influence did not flow merely in an easterly direction. Jaini, in fact, in his discussion of the *Paññāsa-jātaka*, simply assumes Maṇimekhalā to be "an indigenous Southeast Asian deity."[182] Although the details of the transmission of the story of Maṇimēkalā, whether from South to Southeast Asia or vice versa, will probably never be known, the presence of the goddess as a compassionate savior of the shipwrecked future Buddha in a variety of languages and literary forms is certainly suggestive of a discrete cultural/literary region extending from South India through mainland and maritime Southeast Asia, a transregional motif at the very center of the Tamil Buddhist *Maṇimēkalai*.

The *Maṇimēkalai*'s imagining of a coherent cultural region extending from South India to Southeast Asia can also be inferred from the shared story of the tragic marriage of an Indian prince and a serpent (*nāgī*) princess, a narrative found in both Pallava and Cambodian inscriptions and deemed important enough to be repeated three times in the *Maṇimēkalai* (xxiv.27–61, xxv.178–204, and xxix.3–12). In the *Maṇimēkalai*, it is the Cōḻa King Kiḷḷi of Pukār who falls in love with the lovely and mysterious woman known as Pīlivaḷai, the daughter of a Nāga king. The woman gives birth to a son who is lost in a shipwreck. The distraught king forgets to celebrate the annual Indra festival while frantically searching for his missing infant son, thus precipitating the destruction of Pukār by a massive flood and the moving of the Tamil capital to the city of Kāñcīpuram. A strikingly similar story is associated with the founding of the Southeast Asian kingdom generally known as Funan, a narrative referred to briefly in the third-century CE inscription of Baksei Caṁkroṅ in Champa[183] and elaborated on in various Chinese accounts of Funan dating from the third century.[184] Two ninth-century inscriptions provide a similar genealogy for the Pallava dynasty of Kāñcīpuram. The first, attributed to the Pallava monarch Skandaśiṣya, explains the birth of the founder of the royal line, also known as Skandaśiṣya, as the result of the union of Aśvatthāma and a female serpent (nāgī).[185] The second, attributed to Nandavarman III, again cites a female serpent as the mother of the first Pallava monarch, Skandaśiṣya.[186] Although it is impossible to determine historically whether or not the story in Cambodia signals direct Tamil influence in the region,[187] the presence of such similar narrative accounts of royal lineage suggests some measure of cultural contact that spans the cultural worlds of Sanskrit epigraphy (the Cambodian and Pallava inscriptions) and Tamil literary text (the *Maṇimēkalai*).

The *Maṇimēkalai*'s articulation of a geographically transregional yet coherent Buddhist community is also signaled by the presence of Akattiyaṉ (Sanskrit Agastya), mentioned in Tamil for the first time in the *Maṇimēkalai* and celebrated as both the source of the Kāviri river[188] and as "the one who practices severe penance on the very esteemed mountain."[189] Akattiyaṉ, as a Tamil literary figure associated both with a grammatical school and with the Tamil medical tradition (*siddha*),[190] is perhaps most consistently portrayed in Tamil narratives as a master of both Tamil and Sanskrit "whose greatness appears to lie in his command of *both* traditions."[191] Agastya appears in a number of Southeast Asian inscriptions,[192] but it is in Java where the story of Agastya seems to have been most popular.[193] The Javanese legends of the cultural hero, Aji Saka, "the reputed introducer of a new religion and social order . . . also of a script and a calendar,"[194] bear a sometimes striking resemblance to the Tamil and Sanskrit narratives of Agastya/Akattiyaṉ as the bearer of culture to South India.[195] The eleventh-century Old Javanese work known as the *Agastyaparva*, a "remarkable" text relating the genealogy of the great sages (*brahmarṣi*) as told by the sage Agastya whose "Indian model has hitherto not been traced," presents an interesting combination of philosophical reflection and narrative reminiscent of the structure of a Tamil narrative such as the *Maṇimēkalai*.[196] As a figure associated specifically with letters and literature—and in the case of both the *Maṇimēkalai* and the *Vīracōḻiyam* (discussed in the following two chapters) with Buddhist literary culture expressed in Tamil—Agastya the literary character provides yet another possible glimpse of the types of cultural contact that existed among various regions of South and Southeast Asia, a cultural and religious world made Buddhist by the *Maṇimēkalai*.

The literary presence of the goddess Maṇimēkalā/Maṇimekhalā, the story of the Indian king and the serpent princess, and the occurrence of the sage Akattiyaṉ/Agastya in the *Maṇimēkalai* and in the inscriptions and texts of various regions of Southeast Asia do not, of course, establish any specific economic or political ties between the two regions, nor do such shared images prove that the *Maṇimēkalai*'s anticipated audience possessed first-hand knowledge of the lands of Sri Lanka, Cambodia, or Java. What such literary parallels do suggest, however, is the possibility of a cultural region extending far beyond the borders of South India proper, a region built by shared narratives, by shared literary culture, long before the appearance of the first full-fledged Old Javanese court poetry (kakawin) in the late ninth or early tenth century.[197] Such a cultural territory or region would seem to have existed alongside, largely if not fully independent of, the Sanskrit cosmopolis discussed by Pollock. That the *Maṇimēkalai* is the first Tamil text to mention the sage Akattiyaṉ and at the same time incorporate Cāvakam into its vision of religious community and landscape, that the *Maṇimēkalai* is the only Tamil text and one of only very few Indian texts to feature the goddess Maṇimēkalā, who constitutes an important figure in Southeast Asian literary and performative cultures, further underscores the significance of these stories and literary figures as indicators of a shared cultural region extending from South India to Southeast Asia as early as the sixth century. Clearly, the *Maṇimēkalai* anticipates an audience capable of conceiving of South India and Cāvakam as part of a single religious world. The cultural connections glimpsed in the text are strong enough that the Tamil narrative can claim this transregional landscape for Buddhism, marking its boundaries with the lives and activities of the Buddha's bowl relic and various Buddhist characters, all of whom evince a compassionate concern for the well-being of those who share their world.

To return briefly to the issue of language and language choice raised in the previous chapter, the fact that the *Maṇimēkalai* is composed in a regional or local language yet envisions a transregional or translocal landscape and community, including some portion of modern-day Sumatra/Java, raises an interesting question about the status of Tamil as a literary language in the sixth century. As discussed in the final section of the previous chapter, the translation of Buddhist stories, ideas, and images into Tamil serves, among other things, to localize Buddhist tradition, to make Buddhism part of a local South Indian literary culture. In the context of the Buddhist world envisioned by the *Maṇimēkalai*, in which Kāñcīpuram is imagined as a vital center after the destruction of Pukār and the enshrining of the bowl relic, that the vision of the world is expressed in the regional literary language of the imagined center is perhaps not surprising. Yet what of the inclusion of Cāvakam in this world vision of Buddhist community? Does the *Maṇimēkalai* imply that Tamil was, at the very least, imagined to be a transregional literary language, at least in the Southeast Asian Buddhist world?[198] In the realm of ornate poetic narrative, Tamil is used for the significant business of articulating and defining religious community on a transregional scale. The *Maṇimēkalai* attests to the use of Tamil as a suitable vehicle for the imagining of a religious community that encompasses lands far beyond the local region commonly associated with the language. A local literary language, in other words, is used to expressed a supralocal religious vision of the world.

In imagining a Buddhist community through time and space, the *Maṇimēkalai* recasts the literary worlds imagined by classical Tamil poetic narrative to embrace landscapes never envisioned by the Caṅkam anthologies or the *Cilappatikāram* at a time when Buddhist literary cultures across Asia were engaging in similar processes of recentering the Buddhist world. Although Buddhism is incorporated into the local literary and religious culture of Kaṇṇaki, Kōvalaṉ, Mātavi, and Maṇimēkalai in the *Maṇimēkalai*, the local is also made immense again, to borrow Anderson's term, projected forward in time and outward in space. The almsbowl relic of the Buddha, as a crucial character in the text, serves not only to mark the boundaries of a Buddhist world newly envisioned but also to signal the coming of the future Buddha, who will glorify and liberate that world, and to embody those moral qualities of compassion and pathos that will admit one to the great community of future disciples. In marking the contours of the Buddhist world through the stories of Āputtiraṉ, Maṇimēkalai, and Amutacurapi, the *Maṇimēkalai* imagines a Buddhist community and world that includes not only the classical centers of the Tamil literary landscape but also a new Buddhist center—Kāñcīpuram—and the islands of Southeast Asia.

The most important point to take away from this discussion of the *Maṇimēkalai*, however, as a prelude to the coming examination of the one other remaining Buddhist text composed in Tamil, is to recall where this study began: with the consummately literary character of the text, its complexity of ideas, its multiple layers of meaning, and its beautiful poetic style, imagery, and language. Narrative poetry in its most ornate and intricate Tamil form[199] here serves as the vehicle or medium for the articulation of a vision of Buddhist community. For the audience anticipated by the text, the *Maṇimēkalai* imagines a place for Buddhism in a complex and multilingual literary culture, transforming the local landscape of classical poetry into a vision of an immense and glorious community of the future, extending far beyond the horizons of Tamil-speaking South India proper. The *Maṇimēkalai* reveals not only something of the literary imaginings of a particular religious community in a particular historical time and place but also something of the status of language, the nature of literary culture, and the character of the transmission of ideas and values in early medieval South Asia. The importance of language and literature, in particular the use of highly stylized language in the genre of ornate poetic narrative, to the articulation of religious community and identity is further discussed in relation to the Buddhist treatise on grammar and poetics, the *Vīracōḻiyam*, in the following two chapters.

4

The *Vīracōḻiyam*

Language, Literary Theory, and Religious Community

In turning to the second of the two remaining Buddhist texts composed in Tamil, one is immediately struck by the distance—historical, literary, and cultural—that separates the world of the *Vīracōḻiyam* from that of the *Maṇimēkalai*. Written some four or five hundred years after the composition of the *Maṇimēkalai*, the *Vīracōḻiyam* belongs to the opening centuries of what is often termed the "Golden Age of Tamil Culture,"[1] that roughly 400-year period during which the Cōḻa dynasty, centered in the Kāviri delta region, constituted a "dominant cultural, artistic, religious, and political force in south India and beyond."[2] The *Vīracōḻiyam* ushers in a historical period in which texts can be dated and placed with far greater certainty, in which Tamil authors identify themselves by name and location, often citing their royal patrons as well. The text further marks a sharp literary transition from Tamil Buddhist poetic narrative or ornate poetry in practice (of which the *Maṇimēkalai* is the sole remaining example) to a sophisticated analysis of the nature of language and literary composition itself. As a poetic grammar self-consciously engaged in discourse about the nature of language, text, and literature, the *Vīracōḻiyam* constructs a "technology" of literary culture, a theoretical framework for literary practice in a multilingual context.

Such a technology of Tamil grammar and poetics might seem at first glance to have little or nothing to do with the issues of religious identity and community raised in previous chapters. Indeed, as mentioned previously, the *Maṇimēkalai* and the *Vīracōḻiyam* inhabit different literary-historical worlds, and the poetic grammar, in its very nature as self-reflexive discourse about text and language, entails a different mode of imagining than that encountered in the narrative *Maṇimēkalai*. Yet Martin Irvine's comments on the nature of early medieval European literary culture are instructive in turning to consider the significance of a text such as the *Vīracōḻiyam*. Irvine, in defining the medieval art of *grammatica*, suggests that "the art of interpreting the poets and other writers and the principles for speaking and writing correctly"[3] perform "larger cultural work" beyond the merely literary; the discipline of grammatica in medieval Europe was, according to Irvine, "foundational . . . [with] social, intellectual, and ideological function[s]" to fulfill and a "broad . . . social and intellectual agenda."[4] Pollock's recent work on South Asian literary cultures argues in similar fashion that the creation of literary languages and their associated technologies—grammars, dictionaries, and treatises on literary theory and criticism—have important social and political causes and repercussions.[5] This chapter and the following argue that among the "intellectual and ideological functions" of the *Vīracōḻiyam* as a medieval South Asian grammatica text is a fundamentally religious project. Both the *Vīracōḻiyam* and its commentary employ the analysis of poetic language to envision a Buddhist literary culture, a Buddhist textual community of poets and readers. The literary and aesthetic vision of the text, in other words, entails an imagining of human community explicitly made Buddhist.

The Text

The *Vīracōḻiyam*,[6] as previously noted, is a treatise on Tamil grammar and poetics in 181 verses, excluding the three-verse preamble (*pāyiram*), composed in metric stanzas of either sixteen or seventeen syllables (*kaṭṭaḷaik kalitturai*),[7] a verse form favored by Tamil devotional poets from the sixth-century Śaiva poetess, Kāraikkālammaiyār,[8] to the celebrated fifteenth-century devotee of Murukaṉ, Aruṇakirinātar.[9] The text is arranged in five chapters (Tamil *atikāram*, Sanskrit *adhikāra*), each dealing with a specific grammatical or poetic topic. Each chapter is further divided into subchapters (Tamil *paṭalam*, Sanskrit *paṭala*), although only the second chapter has more than one subsection. The first chapter is devoted to phonemes, literally "letters" (*eḻuttu*), although the heading of its sole subchapter narrows the topic to the changes in initial and final letters of words in euphonic combination (Tamil *canti*, Sanskrit *sandhi*). Morphemes, literally "words" (*col*), are discussed in chapter 2 under the following six headings: (1) cases (*vēṟṟumai*), (2) the types of relationships between the noun and the action established by the verb (Tamil *upakārakam*, Sanskrit *upakāraka* or *kāraka*), (3) compounds (tokai), (4) nouns derived from other nouns (Tamil *tattitam*, Sanskrit *taddhita*), (5) verbal roots (Tamil *tātu*, Sanskrit *dhātu*), and (6) finite verbs (Tamil *kiriyāpatam*, Sanskrit *kriyāpada*). The third chapter with its one subsection is devoted to "meaning" or poetic content (poruḷ), the fourth addresses metrics (*yāppu*), and the fifth outlines the principles of poetic ornamentation or embellishment (Tamil *alaṅkāram*, Sanskrit *alaṁkāra*).

Even a cursory glance at the structure of the text reveals the extent to which the *Vīracōḻiyam* combines the framework and vocabulary of the earliest extant Tamil grammar, the fourth- or fifth-century *Tolkāppiyam*, with a variety of terms and categories from Sanskrit models of grammar and literary theory. As the text states explicitly in the third verse of the introduction, the five topics listed previously are "declared according to the ancient rules of grammar [sanctioned by] northern texts" (*vaṭanūl marapum pukaṉṟu koṇṭē*). In its structural insistence that the workings of language are inseparable from poetic application, the *Vīracōḻiyam* is clearly indebted to a distinctly Tamil literary tradition exemplified by the *Tolkāppiyam*. In other words, the *Vīracōḻiyam*, like the *Tolkāppiyam* and a host of later Tamil grammatical treatises, assumes phonology and morphology to be inseparable from the treatment of poetic theory, in contrast to the Sanskrit treatment of grammar (*vyākaraṇa*) and literary criticism as separate disciplines. The *Vīracōḻiyam* similarly follows the *Tolkāppiyam* in its broad topical divisions of phonemes, morphemes, and poetics. Although the *Vīracōḻiyam*'s 181 verses appear to constitute an exercise in brevity alongside the *Tolkāppiyam*'s more than 1,500[10] and more than half of the former's verses are devoted to the topics of poetic content, metrics, and poetic ornament,[11] the

Vīracōḻiyam fundamentally models itself on the *Tolkāppiyam* and applies Sanskrit rules and usage to that Tamil paradigm. In self-consciously aligning itself with the grammar of "northern texts" (vaṭanūl),[12] however, the *Vīracōḻiyam* obviously departs from the *Tolkāppiyam* in a number of ways, appropriating and focusing on Sanskrit terminology and concepts not found in the earlier text.

Although a full assessment of the many ways in which the *Vīracōḻiyam* works Sanskrit vocabulary and modes of analysis into its presentation of Tamil grammar and poetic theory lies beyond the scope of this project,[13] a brief look at the contents of the text provides a general sense of its integrative endeavor. Whereas the *Tolkāppiyam*'s treatment of phonemes ranges at length from the nature of individual vowels and consonants to the bodily processes involved in their production and the changes undergone in the combination of letters, for example, the *Vīracōḻiyam* greatly condenses that discussion[14] and employs the Sanskrit terms "substitution" (Tamil *ātēcam* from Sanskrit *ādeśa*), "augmentation" (Tamil *ākamam* from Sanskrit *āgama*), and "elision" (Tamil *lōpam* from Sanskrit *lopa*) for the *Tolkāppiyam*'s *meypiṟitātal*, *mikutal*, and *kuṉṟal*, respectively.[15] In the process of integrating Sanskrit rules of euphonic combination (sandhi) with the Tamil, the *Vīracōḻiyam* also applies Sanskrit concepts of vowel incrementation (Tamil *virutti* from Sanskrit *vṛddhi*, Tamil *kuṇam* from Sanskrit *guṇa*) for the first time.[16] Within such a framework, the *Vīracōḻiyam* offers several new possibilities for the combination of letters or phonemes in Tamil. To cite but a few such examples, the *Tolkāppiyam* allows *c-* as an initial consonant except when followed by the vowels *-a*, *-ai*, or *-au*;[17] the *Vīracōḻiyam* allows *c-* (along with *k-*, *t-*, *n-*, *p-*, and *m-*) as an initial consonant when followed by any of the vowels,[18] allowing for the straightforward transliteration into Tamil of a significant number of Sanskrit words that begin with *śa-*, *śai-*, and *sa-*. In similar fashion, the *Tolkāppiyam* allows initial *ñ-* only when followed by *ā*, *e*, and *o*,[19] whereas the *Vīracōḻiyam* enables the transliteration into Tamil of a number of important Sanskrit words (e.g., *ñattuvam*, "the faculty of knowledge," from Sanskrit *jñatva*) by allowing initial *ñ-* followed by *a*.[20] Indeed, whereas the *Tolkāppiyam* provides only the broadest of rubrics for transliteration from Sanskrit into Tamil (see the following discussion), the "Vīracōḻiyam describes for the first time the method of Tamilizing foreign words as summarily as possible,"[21] a technical discussion that occurs at the end of the chapter on verbal roots.[22]

The *Vīracōḻiyam*'s discussion of morphemes (col) similarly differs from that found in the *Tolkāppiyam* by virtue of its focus on Sanskrit terms and grammatical models, beginning with the very definition of *word* itself. Whereas the *Tolkāppiyam* defines a word as that which conveys sense or meaning—"all words indicate meaning" (*ellāc collum poruḷ kuṟit taṉavē*)[23]—for example, the *Vīracōḻiyam* follows Pāṇini's definition of *word* as "that which ends in [the functional marker] *sup* [for nouns] or *tiṅ* [for verbs]" (*suptiṅantam padam*)[24] in stating that the particle *-cu* is added to nouns in the nominative singular and then dropped.[25] Elsewhere in the discussion of morphemes, the *Vīracōḻiyam* takes up the *Tolkāppiyam*'s treatment of compounds (tokai)[26] exclusively in terms of Sanskrit categories.[27] The *Vīracōḻiyam* also describes the formation of the passive by the addition of *-paṭu* to the infinitive, followed by the appropriate marker of person, gender, and number;[28] whereas the passive voice is rarely used in the classical Caṅkam poetic corpus and the *Tolkāppiyam* never directly discusses its formation, Sanskrit routinely makes use of passive constructions.

In its discussion of poetics, however, the *Vīracōḻiyam* borrows most directly from the northern textual tradition, particularly in the last chapter dealing with poetic ornamentation (alaṅkāram). Whereas the *Tolkāppiyam* treats poetic content (poruḷ) as a single topic, analyzing the various poetic landscapes of love (*akattiṇai*, *kaḷavu*, and kaṟpu), heroic narrative (*puṟattiṇai*), aesthetic experience (meyppāṭu), simile (uvamai), metrics (*ceyyuḷ*), and usage (*marapu*), the *Vīracōḻiyam* treats separately, in three distinct chapters, the topics of poetic theme (poruḷ), metrics (yāppu), and ornamentation (alaṅkāram). The chapters on thematic content and prosody both offer, in essence, condensed versions of earlier discussions of Tamil poetic content and meter.[29] In turning to the principles of ornamentation, however, the author of the *Vīracōḻiyam* states explicitly that he "explains [poetic embellishment] according to the statements of Taṇṭi [Sanskrit Daṇḍin]" (*taṇṭi coṉṉa karai mali nūliṉ paṭiyē uraippaṉ*).[30] Following closely Daṇḍin's *Kāvyādarśa*,[31] the text then enumerates the ten aspects of style that constitute the "breath" (Tamil *pirāṇaṉ*, Sanskrit *prāṇa*) of sweet and noble poetry.[32] Next, the means of poetic embellishment, from describing the object as it is (Tamil *taṉmai*, Sanskrit *svabhāvokti*) and simile (Tamil uvamai, Sanskrit *upamā*) to the expression of extreme self-assurance or arrogance (Tamil *ūkkam*, Sanskrit *ūrjasvi*) and coherence of the entire poetic work (Tamil *pāvikam*, Sanskrit *bhāvika*), are listed and discussed for the remainder of the text, in close accord with the *Kāvyādarśa*.[33] Unlike Daṇḍin, however, the *Vīracōḻiyam* does not include poetic examples of each of the "ornaments" but instead leaves the task of illustration to its commentator. Not only does the *Vīracōḻiyam* incorporate the phonetic and morphological categories of Sanskrit grammatical theory, but Sanskrit literary theory as well is used to describe Tamil poetics in new and innovative ways.

In thus working out a presentation of Tamil grammar and poetic theory that borrows so heavily from the Sanskrit, the *Vīracōḻiyam* is a text of many firsts in Tamil literary tradition. The *Vīracōḻiyam* marks the beginning of a distinct trend in Tamil grammatical thought, one that Zvelebil describes as "Pāṇiniyan" in contrast to the "indigenous Tamil system" of the *Tolkāppiyam* (although the two texts in addition to the *Vīracōḻiyam* that exemplify this trend, Cuppiramaṇiya's *Pirayōkavivēkam* and Cuvāmināta Tēcikar's *Ilakkaṇaviḷakkam*, do not appear until the eighteenth century).[34] Certainly, in its treatment of poetic ornamentation, the *Vīracōḻiyam* is the first Tamil grammatical text to cite directly from Sanskrit sources, in particular those of Daṇḍin or "Taṇṭiyār,"[35] an effort that anticipates the full Tamil rendition of the *Kāvyādarśa* a century or so later in the *Taṇṭiyalaṅkāram*.[36] As mentioned previously, the *Vīracōḻiyam* is also the first Tamil text to expand the treatment of poetic content into three discrete topics of theme, metrics, and ornamentation. Given the text's attention to the application of Sanskrit grammatical categories and vocabulary to Tamil, it is perhaps not surprising that the *Vīracōḻiyam* is also the first text in Tamil to provide a definition of "rubies and coral" (Tamil *maṇippiravāḷam*, Sanskrit *maṇipravāla*), a style in which Sanskrit words and suffixes are conjoined with the Tamil.[37] When Sanskrit letters are interspersed with Tamil, the style is known as a "mixture" (*viraviyal*); when Sanskrit words are mixed with Tamil, the style is known as rubies and coral.[38] Although rubies and coral becomes a standard style for Tamil Vaiṣṇava and Jain prose commentaries in the twelfth through fifteenth centuries, it is interesting to note that the *Vīracōḻiyam* appears to assume both mixture and rubies and coral to be poetic forms rather than prose: in the same verse (180) that defines each term, the author adds that there is no need to employ initial rhyme (*etukai*) when composing in either style (etukai *naṭai ētum illā*). Finally, among the *Vīracōḻiyam*'s many claims to firsts is the fact that the text is among the earliest in Tamil to be commented on in prose.

The historical or empirical author of the text, to borrow Eco's terminology once more, is identified in the first verse of the preamble as Puttamittiraṉ (Sanskrit Buddhamitra, "friend of the Buddha"), the "lord of Poṉpaṟṟi" (*poṉpaṟṟi maṉ*). Verse 3 declares that the treatment of grammar and poetry to follow is offered "through the revered name of Vīracōḻaṉ" (*vīracōḻaṉ tiruppeyarāl*), "whose chariot bears a white umbrella," a symbol of Cōḻa royalty.[39] Although a certain amount of controversy has surrounded the historical placement of this monarch,[40] a general scholarly consensus exists that identifies Vīracōḻaṉ with Vīrācēntira (Sanskrit Vīrarājendra) Cōḻa, who ruled briefly from 1063/1065 to 1069/1070.[41] Nilakanta Sastri identifies Puttamittiraṉ's domain, Poṉpaṟṟi, with the town of Ponpetti in the Paṭṭukkōṭai subdistrict (*tāluq*) of the Tanjore district.[42] Beyond placing the text in the mid to late eleventh century, neither the name of the author nor that of his royal patron sheds much light on the nature of the *Vīracōḻiyam* itself, the circumstances in which it was composed, or the audience for which it was primarily intended.

Of the model author and audience, however, of the assumptions embedded in the text itself and the readership anticipated by those assumptions, a bit more can be said. From the treatment of phonemes and morphemes outlined previously, in which the *Vīracōḻiyam* applies Pāṇinian grammatical categories to Tamil syllables and words, the model author is clearly familiar with both Sanskrit and Tamil grammatical literature. From the application of Daṇḍin's poetic analysis to Tamil literary forms, one can safely assume a model author thoroughly well-versed in the forms of literary analysis in at least two languages. The model author obviously anticipates a model audience that is equally well-acquainted not only with the *Tolkāppiyam* but with the *Kāvyādarśa* as well. Although several scholars have speculated that the *Vīracōḻiyam* was used as a Buddhist teaching text for non-Tamil-speaking monks,[43] the text presupposes such a high degree of literacy in both Sanskrit and Tamil, such a thorough acquaintance with grammatical and poetic theory in two languages, that one wonders if simple pedagogy could have been foremost in the mind of the author, either model or historical. The *Vīracōḻiyam*, in short, anticipates an audience of multilingual literary connoisseurs who are not only well-versed in literature but have a sophisticated grasp of literary theory as well. For the first time in the extant corpus of premodern Tamil literature, the *Vīracōḻiyam* formalizes the relationship, both grammatically and poetically, between two languages that had been in use in Tamil-speaking literary culture for at least a millennium.

Despite the significance of the *Vīracōḻiyam* as the first text to integrate so self-consciously the grammatical models of Sanskrit and Tamil, as the first text in Tamil to draw explicitly on Daṇḍin's *Kāvyādarśa*, and as the first text to provide a Tamil definition of the important rubies and coral (maṇipravāla) style—in addition to the fact that the *Vīracōḻiyam* stands more or less alone in this regard for more than five centuries—Puttamittiraṉ's text has been little studied. Although the text and its commentary comprise fully half of the Buddhist literary remains in Tamil that have come down to us, few studies of Buddhism in Tamil-speaking southern India have taken any significant notice of the *Vīracōḻiyam*.[44] Most studies of the text by Tamil scholars have focused on its departures from the tradition of the *Tolkāppiyam* and have lambasted its Buddhist author for "proceed[ing] to violently dragoon Tamil language and grammar into the groove of Sanskrit."[45] Shanmugam Pillai, in the paper cited previously, argues against the "dragoon" theory but continues with a grammatical/linguistic analysis in describing the *Vīracōḻiyam* as a "contrastive-transfer grammar" that attempts to teach a second language (in this case, Tamil) through the application and transfer of categories from the student's first language (in this case, Sanskrit).[46] A completely different brand of linguistic analysis is offered by Vēluppiḷḷai, who argues for the *Vīracōḻiyam* as a "descriptive grammar . . . for the language of Tamil inscriptions."[47] Among this relatively small number of studies, only Vijayavenugopal's brief article, cited previously, considers the place of the *Vīracōḻiyam* and its commentary in a wider cultural context, particularly in relation to the Śaiva and Vaiṣṇava devotional literature of the Cōḻa era.

As so little study of the *Vīracōḻiyam* has been undertaken that looks beyond its linguistic peculiarities, before venturing to discuss the ways in which the text embodies a particular vision of Buddhist identity and community, one must consider at some length the context of this first Tamil–Sanskrit poetic grammar, the nature of the literary culture in which it participates. Although the *Maṇimēkalai*, several centuries earlier, obviously borrows Sanskrit and Prākrit terminology for its discussion of logic and interdependent origination, why in the eleventh century does a Buddhist author conceive a grammar that so directly draws on the Sanskrit rules and paradigms of Pāṇini and Daṇḍin? Where the preface of the *Maṇimēkalai* relates the composition of the text rather vaguely to a dialogue between king and grain merchant, how does the author of the *Vīracōḻiyam* come to name his work after the reigning monarch? In what ways has the South Indian literary world changed since the era of the *Maṇimēkalai*'s composition, and what significance can one attach to the *Vīracōḻiyam*'s dual-language project in a multilingual literary culture?

Coḷiya Monks and Language Choice

The era of Cōḻa dominance in the Tamil-speaking region of southern India from the mid-ninth century through the thirteenth century was one of significant and enduring innovation in all areas of Tamil cultural life, from political administration to religious thought and literary culture. While powerful Cōḻa monarchs such as Rācēntiraṉ I (Rājendra I, who reigned from 1012 to 1044) waged battle as far north as the river Gaṅgā, political relations and trade flourished with China and Southeast Asia.[48] As Burton Stein persuasively argues in his detailed examination of the medieval epigraphical record,[49] Cōḻa kings established unprecedented alliances with brahmin populations, while brahmins in turn cemented new relationships with the Tamil land-owning caste, the Veḷḷāḷas. Hindu communities, particularly those devoted to Śiva, gained royal patronage, as Cōḻa kings embarked on massive campaigns of temple-building at major pilgrimage centers. In Cōḻa literary and artistic culture, as Shulman notes, "a profound measure of reflexivity, self-awareness, and self-confidence became evident."[50] Such "reflexivity" and "self-awareness" are evident throughout the Buddhist world as well and provide an important backdrop for understanding the cultural project of the *Vīracōḻiyam*.

Pollock, in describing the eventual demise of the South and Southeast Asian Sanskrit cosmopolis, ties the rise of vernacular literatures and discursive texts about vernacular literature and grammar, such as the ninth-century Kannada *Kavirājamārgam*, to the emergence of new local polities (e.g., the Cōḻa) with new regionally specific sensibilities. Vernacular poetry, expressed in heavily Sanskritized idioms, is thoroughly tied to polity; the *Kavirājamārgam*, Pollock argues, "strives consciously to *territorialize* . . . old Kannada literature . . . [and] emerges from within the center of the Rāṣṭrakūṭa court."[51] Certainly, the *Vīracōḻiyam*, written a century or so after the Kannada text and embarking on a similar project of interpreting the local language and poetic corpus through Sanskrit rules and paradigms, displays some connection to the regional polity; not only is the text, as described previously, named after a local king, but the Tamil language under discussion is defined specifically as "the pure Tamil spoken by the Cōḻa king, Vīrarācēntiraṉ, whose white umbrella of victory rules over the entire world" (*ellā ulakum mēviya veṇ kuṭaic cempiyaṉ vīrarācēntiraṉ taṉ nāvu iyal centamiḻ*).[52] Yet, the relationship of political formation to poetry is only one among several factors to be considered in attempting to place the *Vīracōḻiyam* in some sort of wider context. In addition to appeals to the pure Tamil of the king, the *Vīracōḻiyam* also bears witness to a literary world in which the nature of language and language choice, the relationship of the local to the translocal, and the role of language and literature in the articulation of religious identity and community have been transformed in the centuries since the composition of the *Maṇimēkalai*. Although such changes in literary culture perhaps cannot be marked with distinct events or assigned specific historical causes, what can be discerned is, as Clifford Geertz notes in his introduction to the history of the Balinese state (*negara*), "historical change as a slow but pattered alteration in which . . . it is nearly always difficult, if not impossible, to put one's finger exactly on the point at which things stopped being what they were and became instead something else."[53]

Looking from the multilingual literary culture of premedieval and early medieval southern India described earlier (in chapter 2) to that of the Cōḻa period, among the most readily discernible of such "patterned alterations" is the emergence of new Tamil literary styles and genres, mature and confident in their vision of religious communities both Śaiva and Vaiṣṇava. Gone, for example, are the high-pitched and rather vague condemnations of the Buddhists as "deluded" and "base"[54] or as "demons" full of "lies and deception"[55] in the hymns of Appar, Campantar, and Cuntarar. A host of Cōḻa-era narrative texts instead turn the scene depicted in the twenty-seventh chapter of the *Maṇimēkalai* (in which the young girl rejects the doctrines of non-Buddhist teachers) on its head, portraying Śaiva and Vaiṣṇava saints as calm victors in debate over well-meaning but ignorant Buddhist monks. With confidence, Hindu devotional poets of the Cōḻa era proclaim themselves and their communities to stand at the very center of the Tamil literary and religious landscape. Cēkkiḻār's twelfth-century compendium of the lives of the sixty-three Śaiva saints, the *Periyapurāṇam*, for example, depicts Campantar as a compassionate and sophisticated debater who convinces a group of Buddhist monks residing at Pōtimaṅkai that "other than Śaiva [teachings], there is nothing else" (*caivam allātu maṟṟu oṉṟum illai*).[56] The various medieval hagiographies of the Vaiṣṇava poet-saints (Tamil *kuruparamparai*, Sanskrit *guruparamparā*) provide vivid accounts of the exploits of Tirumaṅkai Āḻvār as he travels "to Nāgapaṭṭaṇam, [steps] inside the Buddha temple at the place, carrie[s] away the gold image that [i]s enshrined within it and melting the same utilise[s] the amount in building walls and other structures at the Raṅganātha temple at Śrīraṅgam."[57] In a similar vein, Kaṭavuḷamāmuṉivar's *Tiruvātavūrarpurāṇam*, a fourteenth-century hagiography of the celebrated ninth-century Śaiva poet-saint, Māṇikkavācakar, details the victory of its hero in debate with a group of Buddhist monks from Sri Lanka in the Tamil temple town sacred to Śiva, Citamparam. By the end of the narrative, even the Sri Lankan king adorns himself with sacred ash in the name of Lord Śiva.[58] Beginning with Cēkkiḻār's twelfth-century hagiography, in other words, Śaiva and Vaiṣṇava poets give voice to distinct visions of religious identity and community through denigrating Buddhists and Buddhist institutions.

Yet in South Asian languages other than Tamil, particularly in the Pāli of Theravāda monastic tradition, South India emerges as a bastion of conservative Buddhist orthopraxy during the Cōḻa period. At the same time that Cēkkiḻār imagines in literary Tamil the humble conversion to Śaivism of the last remnants of Buddhism in the Tamil-speaking region, Buddhist monks writing in Pāli increasingly identify themselves or are identified by others as "Coḷiya" or "Ḍamila." Earlier generations of commentators with some South Indian affiliation often place themselves in particular monastic institutions or identify themselves by city or town. Buddhadatta, for example, traditionally held to be a contemporary of Buddhaghosa, notes in the closing verses of his *Abhidhammāvatāra* that he writes while residing in a monastery built by Kaṅhadāsa in Kāveripaṭṭana,[59] and the redactor of the text identifies Buddhadatta as a teacher dwelling in the Tamil city of Uragapura.[60] Although monks like the great eleventh-century commentator on the Abhidhamma, Anuruddha, traditionally held to be a native of Sri Lanka,[61] might continue to be placed by their compilers in the South Indian town or monastery where the text was composed,[62] in the era of the *Vīracōḻiyam*'s composition, with the writings of South Indian Buddhist monks such as Buddhappiya, Kassapa, and others, the terms of articulating identity, an author's place in the Buddhist world and literary culture, change dramatically. Pāli commentators and editors writing in a transregional language associate the authors of their respective texts with the Cōḷa or Tamil country or realm (*coḷaraṭṭhe, ḍamilaraṭṭhe*) or simply refer to the writer as Coḷiya or Ḍamila.

Kassapa, traditionally held to be the author of both the Abhidhamma commentary known as the *Mohavicchedanī* and the Vinaya commentary known as *Vimativinodanī* and generally assigned to the twelfth century,[63] for example, is identified in the former as "the great elder Kassapa of the Coḷa country" (coḷaraṭṭhe *mahākassapatthera*).[64] The *Sāsanavaṁsa* identifies the author of the latter text as "resident in the Ḍamila country" (*ḍamilaraṭṭhavāsi*);[65] although the *Sāsanavaṁsa* is a relatively late work composed in Burma,[66] the following discussion of the contents of the *Vimativinodanī* should make clear the author's association with South Indian literary culture. A century later, the scholar-monk Buddhappiya, also known as Dīpaṅkara, identifies himself as "a lamp in the Ḍamila country" in his Pāli grammatical treatise, the *Rūpasiddhi*.[67] To Buddhappiya is also ascribed an elaborate poem of praise to the Buddha in one hundred four stanzas, the *Pajjamadhu*, composed in a "partly Sanskritized Pāli" that is somewhat "laboured and artificial"[68] but which calls to mind the theoretical project of the *Vīracōḻiyam*: applying the poetic styles and conventions of Sanskrit to another literary language.[69] In the twelfth century, the Sri Lankan author, Buddharakkhita, declares himself to be "one who has received consecration at the hands of eminent scholars in the . . . Coḷiya [country]."[70] Epigraphical sources as well point to a common identification of monks as Coḷiya. A twelfth-century inscription from Polonnaruva, for example, praises the elder known as Ānanda for spreading religious discipline among the Cōḷas (*coḷesu*).[71]

Somewhat unclear, of course, is the precise meaning of Coḷa/Coḷiya or Ḍamila in the above contexts, all of which are expressed not in a regional language (Tamil or Sinhala) but in a translocal one (Pāli). Although *raṭṭha* clearly refers to a geographical region, a kingdom or polity, does the term Coḷiya refer to a king/dynasty, a political unit, or a cultural area? Does Ḍamila imply a linguistic region, a cultural affiliation, a political realm, or something else? Much as the historical meaning of the term Sinhala has been hotly contested in recent Sri Lankan scholarship fueled by the current ethnic conflict,[72] so, too, have many scholars of South Indian history and culture assumed Cōḻa to imply some sort of uniform Tamil ethnic identity and culture, tied to a particular language and region.[73] Gunawardana argues persuasively, however, that far from indicating an ethnic or cultural identity, Sinhala initially referred primarily to the ruling dynasty at Anurādhapura and only gradually came to encompass as a political identity other realms of society (e.g., associations of craftsmen) in the medieval period.[74] In similar fashion, the expression *coḷaraṭṭha* might easily be taken to refer to land ruled by Cōḻa monarchs and, by extension, to monastic institutions situated on such lands. The term Ḍamila, even in conjunction with raṭṭha, is perhaps more complex; is the land or kingdom defined by language generally, the language of the ruling dynasty in particular, or some more abstract and self-conscious conception of cultural identity?

Whatever the political, cultural, or linguistic implications of this new medieval vocabulary of Buddhist identification might be, it is clear from the material indicated previously that Coḷiya defines, above all else, a particular monastic community (saṅgha) at pains to distinguish itself from other such communities. To return to the twelfth-century *Vimativinodanī* of Coḷiya Kassapa, for example, the text refers to a dissenter or heretic (*bhinnaladdhika*) named Nāgasena, who inspired the composition of a work known as *Kuṇḍalakesi-vatthu* (Tamil *Kuṇṭalakēci*) written "in the form of a Tamil composition" (*ḍamiḷakabbarūpena*). According to Kassapa, among Nāgasena's heretical views included in the Tamil poem was the notion that drinking wine was unwholesome (akusala) for monks only when done unknowingly (*jānitvā'va*). The great elder Buddhappiya (perhaps the same Coḷiya Dīpaṅkara who composed the *Pajjamadhu* and the *Rūpasiddhi*) succeeded in purifying (*sodhitam*) the doctrine, yet according to the *Vimativinodanī*, the wine-drinking practice has arisen again in the Vinaya commentary known as *Sāratthadīpanī*. The author of the *Vimativinodanī*, Kassapa, thus endeavors in his own text to show that such a wrong view must be rejected outright.[75] Elsewhere in the text, Kassapa notes again that the view that only the monk who consumes liquor knowingly commits an offense is an unacceptable and heretical one.[76] Here, the Coḷiya author presents himself and his fellow Coḷiya monk, Buddhappiya, as more orthodox, more correct in discipline and practice, in relation to a number of other communities or groups represented by the monk Nāgasena; the author of the Tamil poem, *Kuṇḍalakesi-vatthu*; and the author of the Pāli commentary, *Sārātthadīpanī*. By criticizing in Pāli the views expressed in a Tamil poetic narrative, the *Kuṇṭalakēci*, classified as one of the great ornate poetic works of Tamil literary tradition and held in considerable esteem by the commentator on the *Vīracōḻiyam* (discussed in the following chapter), Kassapa seems not to understand Coḷiya as implying any cultural or linguistic allegiance tied to Tamil language use. In taking exception to the views expressed on monastic drinking by a fellow commentator on the Vinaya, Kassapa perhaps understands Coḷiya to imply orthopraxy.

That Coḷiya as a term of Buddhist monastic identification was often related to perceptions of correctness of practice on the part of a particular monastic community situated in South India is further attested to in the thirteenth-century treatise on boundary marking, the *Sīmālaṅkāra* of Vācissara. Vācissara, a Sri Lankan monk, presents the proper determination of a monastery boundary (*sīmā*) as a means of purifying the community and expresses his wish that the unorthodox views of the Coḷiya monks of South India be rejected to perpetuate the well-being of the order (*sāsana*).[77] Coḷiya here seems to refer to a monastic community geographically situated, this time accused of being less than orthodox. The *Cūlavaṁsa*, however, portrays the Coḷiya monks as far more pure in practice than those of Sri Lanka; King Parakkamabāhu II, after sending gifts to the "great Cōḻa kingdom" (*coḷamahāraṭṭha*), invites the Coḷiya monks to purify the island community and thus "establish harmony between the two orders" (*kārāpesi samaggaṁ so rājā ubhayasāsanam*).[78]

Identification as Coḷiya did not imply any profound separation from the traditions of the Mahāvihāra, nor could it have entailed any significant political identification with the Cōḻa royal dynasty. Although Kassapa, for example, might be critical of some of the practices endorsed by certain Sri Lankan monks (e.g., those of Sāriputta, author of the *Sāratthadīpanī*), still he claims to be following the tradition of the Mahāvihāra (*mahāvihāravāsīnaṁ kamābhatanayānugaṁ*).[79] As discussed previously in chapter 3, monks from South India and Sri Lanka appeared to enjoy good relations even as war raged between their respective monarchs. As Liyanagamage notes, "Cola *mahatheras* like Dipankara and Kassapa were held in the highest esteem in Ceylon, and nowhere in the record is the slightest insinuation that they hailed from an 'enemy' territory or belonged to a different racial group."[80] In the colophon of the *Upāsakajanālaṅkāra*, a South Indian monastery, Perampalli, built by a "ruler of the Pāṇḍya country, of the Vaññi tribe, known as Coḷagaṅga," is portrayed as a safe haven for Sri Lankan monks even as a Cōḻa king invades the island.[81] The *Cūlavaṁsa* further tells of King Parakkamabāhu IV's appointment of a great elder from the Coḷa country (*coḷadesīyam*), well-versed in literary and philosophical works in several languages and particularly adept at Jātaka recitation, to the office of "royal teacher" (*rājaguru*).[82] Coḷiya monks may criticize the practices of Sri Lankan monks and vice versa in the case of the proper establishment of monastic boundaries, but such self-identification and criticism take place within the context of allegiance to the Mahāvihāra tradition. Coḷiya as a mark of Buddhist monastic identity would seem to operate independently of political or ethnic associations, for Coḷiya monks often act at odds with the political activities of Coḷiya kings in the premodern literary record.

Coḷiya as a way of indicating a particular monastic order, one that feels itself to stand apart from, even to be superior to, other communities in terms of at least two areas of praxis noted previously (drinking and establishing monastery boundaries), perhaps provides an important clue to the nature of the *Vīra"cōḻiya"m*'s overall project. Although Puttamittiraṉ, the "lord of Poṉpaṟṟi," who is also a "friend of the Buddha," may or may not have been a monk, he obviously identifies himself with a particular geographic region, a particular monarch (something that the Pāli commentators discussed previously never do), and embarks on a program of linguistic and poetic analysis whose aim is quite opposite to that expressed by Buddhaghosa some five centuries earlier: to make the "commentary. . . . composed in the language of Sīharadīpa" intelligible to "the monks beyond the island."[83] In the *Vīracōḻiyam*, it is the local language that takes pride of place, articulated and analyzed through the categories of transregional Sanskrit. The regional language (Tamil) and its literary/poetic corpus are the focus, and northern textual traditions are invoked to show the translocal qualities of Tamil. Tamil thus becomes a grammatical and poetic standard, like Sanskrit. The *Vīracōḻiyam*, although maintaining an allegiance to the Sanskrit grammatical and poetic tradition, ultimately assumes, in its very nature as a Tamil poetic grammar, that Tamil language (*tamiḻmoḻi*) is the superior or best of languages. Given the fact that much of Sri Lanka was under Cōḻa rule in the era of the *Vīracōḻiyam*'s composition (roughly the mid-tenth through late-eleventh centuries) and that at least one Tamil-speaking Buddhist monastery, the Rājarājaperumpaḷḷi, is believed to have flourished in the Trincomalee District of Sri Lanka during the eleventh century,[84] perhaps the identification of Coḷiya monks and Cōḻiya grammar in this era is tied to a closer association of two different orders—the Tamil-speaking and the Sinhala-speaking—than ever before; close contact might have created a need to differentiate, to mark boundaries between monastic associations ever more clearly. However, the breakdown in international relations, particularly those between South India and Sri Lanka, near the end of the tenth century[85] perhaps also contributed to a new-found need to associate oneself and one's monastic lineage with one side of the conflict, even if such political machinations did not necessarily translate into animosity among various monastic communities. Whether or not a distinct causal relationship can be established for the emergence of a self-consciously Coḷiya/Cōḻiya order, what is readily apparent is that from the eleventh century onward, Buddhist community begins to be imagined and expressed in new and different ways.

In addition to these new ways of articulating Buddhist identity that can be seen in the Pāli literature of the eleventh through fourteenth centuries, equally important for understanding the historic milieu in which the *Vīracōḻiyam* was first composed are the changing relationships among literary languages, particularly Tamil and Sanskrit, in the multilingual literary culture of South India during this medieval era. One clear indicator of such change, in a literary culture in which Tamil and Sanskrit had both existed as viable language choices for nearly a millennium, is the introduction of Tamil as an inscriptional language option. As both Pollock[86] and Menon[87] discuss at some length, the first South Indian dynasty to inscribe its edicts in stone and on copper plates—the Pallavas who ruled from Kāñcīpuram—first wrote in a rather peculiar form of Prākrit full of "gross irregularities."[88] Sanskrit remained a sacerdotal language, its use both highly charged and, with a few important exceptions, largely restricted to Vedic exegesis and interpretation, above the mundane realm of political pronouncement or worldly administration. Only during the reign of Śivaskandavarman in the mid-fourth century did Sanskrit become a suitable epigraphical language choice, with the royal invocation (*praśasti*) composed in "textbook Sanskrit."[89] Tamil makes its debut as an inscriptional medium in the mid-sixth century, but its use is initially quite restricted. "For the entire 600-year duration of the Pallava dynasty," notes Pollock, "there exists not a single inscription in which Tamil does any work beyond recording the everyday—to record a remission of taxes, the boundaries of a land grant, [etc.]. . . . [The] local language is not permitted to *interpret* the world."[90] Not until the eleventh century, the era of the composition of the *Vīracōḻiyam* and the reign of the Cōḻa monarchs Rājarāja I and Rājādhirāja, does Tamil assume the poetic and interpretive functions of inscriptional Sanskrit.[91] Although inscriptions constitute the most public expression of literary culture and certainly cannot be said to represent fully the character of the South Indian literary world, the shift in epigraphical language preference away from Sanskrit and toward Tamil is indicative of wider patterns of linguistic and literary change in the medieval South.

Pollock further argues, in relation to Sanskrit as an inscriptional language of power and politics used throughout South and Southeast Asia for more than a millennium, that the power of Sanskrit used in this way is primarily an aesthetic one: Sanskrit embodies the "common aesthetics of political culture, a kind of poetry of politics."[92] Tamil, for the first time in the century of the *Vīracōḻiyam*'s inception, assumes those same aesthetic and interpretive powers in the realm of kingly pronouncement. Elsewhere, Pollock notes that "seizing the privilege of literary inscription"[93] is "often accompanied by intensive grammaticalization"[94] that standardizes the literary language. The *Vīracōḻiyam* in several ways touches on these two points raised by Pollock. In an age in which Tamil assumes functions previously allowed only to Sanskrit, in which Tamil takes on the poetic-declarative role of royal invocation and pronouncement, the *Vīracōḻiyam* presents Tamil as a language fully compatible with the grammatical rules of Pāṇini. As Tamil moves from epigraphical language of business transaction to a language of the "poetry of politics," the *Vīracōḻiyam* shows Tamil to be equal to the expression of Daṇḍin's aesthetic principles of poetic ornamentation. The *Vīracōḻiyam*'s principal project, in other words, the exposition of Tamil as a literary language in full accord with Sanskritic rules of grammar and aesthetic principles, closely parallels the emergence of Tamil as an inscriptional language equal to, if not surpassing, the power and aesthetic appeal of Sanskrit.

Indeed, although he does not draw the connection to the epigraphical shift toward Tamil outlined previously, Vēluppiḷḷai argues that the *Vīracōḻiyam*'s first two chapters on phonemes and morphemes constitute "the best descriptive grammar available . . . for the language of the Tamil inscriptions."[95] Although a full treatment of the linguistic peculiarities of the corpus of Tamil inscriptions in relation to the *Vīracōḻiyam* lies beyond the scope of this project,[96] certainly Vēluppiḷḷai's analysis makes significant strides toward explaining a number of grammatical forms described in the text that have baffled historians of Tamil grammar and literature for several generations.[97] To cite but a few examples, Vēluppiḷḷai correctly points out that the *Vīracōḻiyam* is the only Tamil grammar that accounts for the change of *ḻ-* before another consonant.[98] Such euphonic transformations are not found in any literary works written before the *Vīracōḻiyam* but are found in a number of inscriptions.[99] Vēluppiḷḷai also painstakingly counts the number of times that various case signs and postpositions not found in the *Tolkāppiyam* appear in literary texts and inscriptions both before and after the general date assigned to the *Vīracōḻiyam* and concludes that the forms laid out in the Buddhist grammar are attested to far more often in inscriptions than in poetic texts.[100] Vijayavenugopal notices in particular the *Vīracōḻiyam*'s mention of the feminine suffix *-icci*, a suffix not found in the *Tolkāppiyam* but used in an inscription of the tenth-century king, Sundaracola.[101] Whether or not the *Vīracōḻiyam* can best be described as a descriptive grammar of inscriptional Tamil, the uniqueness of certain forms attested to in the text, in conjunction with the text's general program of combining Sanskrit and Tamil methods of grammatical and poetic analysis, would seem to indicate that the *Vīracōḻiyam* formulates a new kind of literary language, one that both departs from the language described and codified by the *Tolkāppiyam* and preserves many of those earlier Tamil linguistic, poetic, and aesthetic formulations.

Drawing on the writings by and about various Buddhist scholar-monks associated in some way with South India from the eleventh century onward and on the changing character of inscriptions and inscriptional language in South India during that same period, two particularly salient points emerge concerning the literary culture in which the *Vīracōḻiyam* was composed. First, new ways of expressing Buddhist identity and sense of community come to the fore in the vocabulary of Coḷiya monks and Ḍamila kingdoms. In the centuries after Buddhadatta and Dhammapāla, Buddhist monks from southernmost India cease to locate themselves solely in terms of monastery or city. Although they continue to write in the name of Mahāvihāra tradition, commentators and grammarians such as Buddhappiya and Kassapa are identified as part of a larger community, a Coḷiya order made coherent through its vision of, perhaps among other things, praxis, a community confident enough of its own identity to criticize those outside the Coḷiya community. Second, alongside this emergence of new ways of imagining Buddhist identity and community, Pallava and Cōḻa epigraphical records attest to the changing status of languages and language choice in medieval literary culture. Just as the *Vīracōḻiyam* proclaims its intent to explain Tamil language and poetic theory in accordance with the rules laid down in Sanskrit texts, so, too, does Tamil take over the inscriptional roles of poetic declaration and royal praise hitherto allotted only to Sanskrit. The literary imagining of a Buddhist community as Coḷiya/Cōḻiya and the raising up of Tamil as a regional literary language with new public functions to perform both suggest a literary context in which the *Vīracōḻiyam*—as a self-consciously Buddhist statement on the nature of Tamil as a language on par with Sanskrit—undertakes significant cultural work.

The Cultural Work of Grammatica

As Irvine argues in his study of European grammatica texts and practices from the fourth through the eleventh centuries, the discipline of linguistic study and interpretation serves a variety of social and cultural functions that extend far beyond the discipline itself. Grammatica not only creates a "model of learning, interpretation, and knowledge that define[s] various regional textual communities"[102] but also internalizes and thus supports certain conceptions and structures of hierarchy and authority that were closely tied, in the European case, to newly emerging regional political orders. Although Irvine's preoccupation with the relationship between grammatica and social/political power structures lies beyond the particular concerns of this project, Irvine's general attempt to trace the broader implications of the grammatica project suggests potentially useful ways of thinking about the nature of the *Vīracōḻiyam* and its relation to the formulation and articulation of religious community. Like the grammatica texts of ninth- and tenth-century England,[103] the *Vīracōḻiyam* constructs a technology for a bilingual textual culture. In the case of the Tamil text, the ability to mediate between two very different literary and linguistic models, to move between linguistic worlds, serves both as a sign of erudition and authority and as a new means of envisioning and articulating religious identity.

The *Vīracōḻiyam* presents a new kind of linguistic and literary mediation in the literary culture of Tamil-speaking South India that had long been multilingual. Even the oldest of the extant Tamil poetic grammars, the *Tolkāppiyam*, is obviously indebted to Sanskrit literary tradition. Although the Caṅkam poetic corpus embodies, in many respects, a uniquely Tamil tradition of literary themes (e.g., the inner love and outer heroic) and conventions (e.g., the five landscape motifs, various kinds of rhyme and meter), the *Tolkāppiyam*, in organizing and codifying the language of the Caṅkam poets, appropriates a range of Sanskrit vocabulary and modes of analysis. Whereas the statement in the preamble to the *Tolkāppiyam*, that the author of the text was "well-versed in *aintiram*" (aintiram *niṟainta*),[104] has given rise to a host of speculations among Tamil scholars regarding a lost "Aindra" school of Sanskrit grammar that rivaled that of Pāṇini,[105] several studies have also demonstrated the extent to which the *Tolkāppiyam* is indebted to Pāṇinian categories of analysis.[106] The *Tolkāppiyam* addresses directly, albeit briefly, for example, the task of transliterating from Sanskrit into Tamil: "The words of northern language (*vaṭa col*), discarding northern letters (*vaṭa eḻuttu*) and adopting [Tamil] letters, become [Tamil] words."[107] "All traditional grammars of Tamil reflect an awareness of Sanskrit grammatical models and theories," notes Zvelebil, "and even the earliest Tamil poetry reflects the fact that these texts did not originate in a vacuum but within the context of a pan-Indian . . . culture."[108] From the *Tolkāppiyam* to the tenth-century treatise on prosody, the *Yāpparuṅkalam* of Amitacākarar, Tamil grammarians, poets, and literary theorists are acutely aware of the Sanskrit literary tradition. The commentary on *Yāpparuṅkalam* verse 5, for example, speaks of "Tamil teachers who follow the way of northern texts" (*vaṭanūl vaḻit tamiḻ āciriyar*).[109] Hart explores the northern elements in the Caṅkam literary corpus itself,[110] and the *Maṇimēkalai*, as discussed previously, arguably develops in sophisticated fashion a complex and nuanced presentation of the aesthetic experience (rasa) of pathos (karuṇa). Given the tradition that assigns the Sanskrit poet and literary critic, Daṇḍin, to the seventh-century Pallava court at Kāñcīpuram,[111] it is perhaps not surprising to encounter glimpses of Sanskrit grammatical and aesthetic principles at work in even the earliest regional literature of southern India.

Yet despite all the evidence for a long history of Sanskrit and Tamil intermingled in South Indian literary culture, the *Vīracōḻiyam*'s bald statements that it will explain Tamil grammar and poetic theory "according to the ancient rules of grammar [sanctioned by] northern texts" and that the principles of poetic ornamentation in particular will be discussed in light of "the statements of Taṇṭi," signal an entirely new sort of Sanskrit influence at work, a brand of self-conscious appropriation and incorporation of Sanskrit analytic terms and frameworks without precedent in Tamil. In a multilingual literary culture, the *Vīracōḻiyam* represents a first self-declared effort at mediating between two literary languages, at attempting to incorporate into Tamil grammatical and literary theory a variety of Sanskrit linguistic and literary forms. The question that obviously arises here is: why? How does the *Vīracōḻiyam*'s self-conscious incorporation of Sanskrit models signal a different sort of grammatica project, and what sort of work does such a project attempt to accomplish? In borrowing more explicitly from Sanskrit literary theory than any other Tamil text before it, what does the *Vīracōḻiyam* seek to achieve?

One possible answer lies in the fact that in its explicit appropriation of Sanskrit terminology and methods of analysis, the *Vīracōḻiyam* seeks to take part in a translocal literary culture through the medium of a local or regional language. Whereas the *Tolkāppiyam* borrows certain aspects of the Pāṇinian grammatical model to explain the linguistic structure and rules governing the use of poetic Tamil, the *Vīracōḻiyam* demonstrates the ways in which the Tamil language participates in the transregional literary culture of Sanskrit. As Rita Copeland argues in her study of medieval European practices of translation and commentary, "by taking over the textual strategies of academic exegesis, vernacular writing can insert itself into the privileged cultural sphere of Latin learning."[112] Although Tamil, by the eleventh century, was certainly not simply a vernacular but a mature literary language, the *Vīracōḻiyam*, like the translations of classical Latin texts into Old French and Old English discussed by Copeland, translates Sanskrit poetic and grammatical theory into Tamil. Through the exegesis of a local or regional literary language, the *Vīracōḻiyam* "inserts itself" into the "privileged cultural sphere" of Sanskrit "learning."

The *Vīracōḻiyam*, for example, ties the Tamil language to the same specific geographical region marked by the *Tolkāppiyam*[113] and to the language sanctioned by a particular king of that geographical region (as noted previously) but shows Tamil to possess, at the same time, the capacities of a translocal language. Echoing the *Tolkāppiyam*'s concern with defining the region of southern India as "the good world where Tamil is spoken," the *Vīracōḻiyam* also overlays Daṇḍin's notion of the two "paths" or literary styles (mārga)—the "Vaidarbha," or "southern way," and the "Gauḍīya," or "eastern way"—onto the linguistic and literary world envisioned by earlier Tamil literature. In a single verse that translates Daṇḍin's *Kāvyādarśa*, i.41–42, nearly word for word, the *Vīracōḻiyam* lists the ten qualities that are central to Vaidarbha (*vitarppaṉ*) style and notes that the opposite (*viparītam*) qualities are characteristic of the Gauḍīya (*kauṭaṉ*) style.[114] Yet unlike the ninth-century Kannada poetic grammar examined by Pollock, the *Kavirājamārgam*, which transfers Daṇḍin's stylistic distinctions onto the Kannada literary world,[115] the *Vīracōḻiyam* offers no such application of Daṇḍin's geographic vision to the Tamil country. The implication of such silence, however, is clear. In more or less directly "translating" Daṇḍin on this issue, the Tamil text demonstrates the *Kāvyādarśa*'s own marked preference for the Vaidarbha, or southern, style. The *Vīracōḻiyam*, having earlier defined itself and the Tamil language it describes with reference to the geographic region extending from "the abode of Kumari to the great Vēṅkaṭam hill"[116]—an unmistakably southern region—identifies itself with the poetic qualities of the Vaidarbha style, providing definitions of its ten essential qualities (guṇa) in the following three verses.[117] Thus aligning itself and the Tamil poetic language it analyzes with the style of the Vaidarbha Sanskrit poets—the only style that really counts for Daṇḍin—the *Vīracōḻiyam* imagines southern India "from Vēṅkaṭam to Kumari" not only as the land where pure or good Tamil is spoken but as the region where good Sanskrit poetry is composed. In the *Vīracōḻiyam*, two literary languages—one regional, the other translocal but at its poetic best in a particular regional style—are brought together, and the regional is shown to be thoroughly compatible with the literary culture of the translocal. Through translating Daṇḍin and appropriating the style discussion without comment, the *Vīracōḻiyam* brings together two literary languages, Sanskrit and Tamil, and the regional Tamil is assumed simply to be compatible with and fully able to participate in the literary culture of the transregional. Vaidarbha, or southern style, poetry equals good poetry, whether written in Sanskrit or Tamil.

The *Vīracōḻiyam* thus imagines Tamil, as a regional literary language, to be equal in status to, equivalent to, even an alternative to, Sanskrit as a literary language choice with transregional application and import. The *Vīracōḻiyam*, in essence, claims for literary Tamil an authority equal to that of Sanskrit and ties the best of Sanskrit poetic style to the southern region of India where, perhaps not coincidentally, Tamil is also spoken. Certain grammatical rules, such as the rather convoluted application of the Pāṇinian nominal affix *-sup* to Tamil forms mentioned previously, show Tamil to be thoroughly compatible, even interchangeable, with Sanskrit. The blending together of Tamil and Sanskrit words defined as the style of rubies and coral (maṇippiravāḷam) at *Vīracōḻiyam* 181 exemplifies in practice the ways in which grammatical forms and poetic styles can be intermingled and exchanged between the two languages. Tamil and Sanskrit meet in the *Vīracōḻiyam* as equals, and the status of Tamil as a merely regional or local language is raised in the process.

The reasons behind this new brand of Sanskritization in a literary culture that had included both Sanskrit and Tamil as language options for more than a millennium are, of course, historically obscure. Just as the *Maṇimēkalai*, a regional text, anticipates an audience of sophisticated literary connoisseurs, so, too, does the *Vīracōḻiyam* address itself to explicitly literary language, to the meters, stanzas, and embellishments of ornate poetic composition; the text represents something more than the mere application of Sanskrit norms to a nonliterate, or vernacular, culture. Noting that the history of literary cultures in South Asia remains largely uncharted, Pollock,[118] as mentioned previously, relates the literary-cultural shift marked by works such as the *Kavirājamārgam* and the *Vīracōḻiyam* to changing political circumstances, to the emergence of new forms of state and power. Speaking of the appearance of regional literatures in the eleventh-century Deccan, he argues that "the creation of a great literature, deeply informed by the superposed model of Sanskrit poetry . . . was part of the creation of a polity with regional sensibilities newly energized."[119] Yet the literary culture of southernmost India had always possessed regional sensibilities, from the preface of the *Tolkāppiyam* and the praise of cities such as Maturai, Kāñcī, and Vañci in the Caṅkam corpus to the three-city structure of the *Cilappatikāram* narrative. Unlike the Kannada *Kavirājamārgam* or the fourteenth-century poetic grammar of Malayalam, the *Līlātilakam*,[120] the *Vīracōḻiyam* styles itself on an earlier regional grammar (the *Tolkāppiyam*) and applies Sanskrit grammatical and poetic categories to that regional theoretical construct. Why the author of the *Vīracōḻiyam*, if guided by "regional sensibilities newly energized," would infuse an already vibrant regional literary tradition with the grammatical endings and poetic embellishments of Sanskritic literary tradition remains somewhat unclear.

One possible answer lies in the nature of earlier Tamil literary theory itself. For all of the theoretical sophistication of the earlier *Tolkāppiyam*, Daṇḍin's notion of poetic ornament based on content or meaning (Tamil *poruḷaṇi*, Sanskrit *arthālaṁkāra*) does inject something truly new and productive into Tamil literary theory. With the exception of an extended discussion of simile (uvamai) in the seventh section of its treatment of poetic content (poruḷ) and a brief definition of the juxtaposition of contradictory terms (*muraṇ*),[121] the *Tolkāppiyam*'s discussion of poetic ornamentation is largely restricted to ornamentation based on sound (*toṭai*) rather than on meaning or content. Noting, as does Daṇḍin himself,[122] that the number of poetic ornaments could be endlessly divided and subdivided,[123] the *Tolkāppiyam* enumerates and defines five methods of ornamentation.[124] With the exception of the juxtaposition of contradictory terms noted previously, all deal exclusively with sound, or, in the terminology of the *Kāvyādarśa* and the *Vīracōḻiyam*, with "word ornaments" (Sanskrit *śabdālaṁkāra*, Tamil *collaṇi*).[125] When the *Tolkāppiyam* does, in fact, turn its attention to poetic content or theme, the text seems far more descriptive of an extant poetic corpus than theoretically generative. The section on traditional usage (marapu) represents this in the extreme, opening with a lengthy discussion of the appropriate terms to denote the male and female varieties of various objects, followed by words that can be used to denote the young offspring of various animals.[126] Even the more theoretical of the chapters dealing with poetic content, such as the first two addressing the general themes of love and war, with their suggestive landscape motifs, emotions, flora, and fauna, either describe or generate the types of poetic anthologies now known as the Caṅkam corpus. By the era of the *Vīracōḻiyam*, however, there existed a substantial body of poetic work in Tamil that extended beyond these thematic boundaries of love and war. Daṇḍin's discussion of poetic ornamentation based on meaning or content, rather than simply sound, represents, in other words, a far more open-ended critical device for the analysis of meaning. The ornaments based on meaning (Tamil poruḷaṇi) introduce new ways of thinking about the content of poetry in Tamil beyond the traditional topics of love, war, and landscape. Daṇḍin provides a fresh lens for interpreting Tamil poetic composition and analysis in theoretically and thematically interesting ways.

That Daṇḍin's work introduces a venue for new, content-driven discussions of poetry in Tamil provides an interesting means of examining the cultural work of his Tamil interpreter. As is discussed at length in chapter 5, the commentary on the *Vīracōḻiyam* illustrates, with an explicit emphasis on content, that Tamil literature is not only on par with Sanskrit, illustrative of its principles of grammar, syntax, meter, and poetic ornamentation, but it is also Buddhist in theme. In providing poetic examples in Tamil for each of Daṇḍin's categories of ornament, the commentary shows the extent to which the local language possesses all the capacities of the dominant translocal language, Sanskrit. Those translocal capacities of Tamil poetic language are continually reinforced in the *Vīracōḻiyam* text and its commentary as both refer repeatedly to Daṇḍin (Taṇṭi, Taṇṭiyār) and northern textual tradition and language (vaṭanūl and vaṭamoḻi).

Whatever causes or catalysts, political, literary, or otherwise, might be assigned to the project of the *Vīracōḻiyam*, clearly the text is composed at the beginning of an era that witnessed substantial and significant changes in the literary cultures of southernmost South Asia. From roughly the ninth through the fourteenth centuries, the poets and literary critics of South India and Sri Lanka engaged in a regional movement of "appropriat[ing] and domesticat[ing] models of language-use from superposed cultural formations,"[127] something that would not happen in the case of northern vernaculars for several more centuries.[128] The number of and relative speed with which translations of Daṇḍin's *Kāvyādarśa* appeared—no less than the profound effect they wielded on local literary cultures—is truly remarkable; it seems as though Daṇḍin's work literally swept through the royal courts of South Asia at the turn of the last millennium. The ninth-century Kannada *Kavirājamārgam* cited previously, for example, closely parallels the *Vīracōḻiyam* in appropriating Daṇḍin to present Kannada as a fully literary language.[129] Although the *Kavirājamārgam* does not use the stylistic term rubies and coral (maṇipravāla), all four of the South Indian literary languages—Kannada, Tamil, Malayalam, and Telugu—develop a literary style mixing regional vocabulary and Sanskrit grammatical forms. As noted previously, such a style is known in Sanskrit texts as one peculiar to the South, and the *Vīracōḻiyam* appears to describe a poetic rubies and coral rather than the prose form found most commonly in Jain and Vaiṣṇava commentaries.[130] In the fourteenth century, the *Līlātilakam* defines a regional version of such a mixed-language style based on "the speech of the Kēraḷas" (*kēraḷabhāṣā*), a precursor to

Malayalam.[131] As in the case of Tamil, literary Sinhala, or "Elu," is attested to long before the era under discussion, beginning with the "graffiti" poetry found at Sīgiriya; the tenth-century *Siyabaslakara*, in the manner of the *Vīracōḻiyam*, offers "an abridged Sinhalese translation" of Daṇḍin's *Kāvyādarśa*[132] and marks the first in a long series of poetic grammars in Sinhala based on Sanskrit, and perhaps even Tamil, models.[133] Telugu texts that combine, in similar fashion, the grammatical and poetic categories of Sanskrit literary culture also appear for the first time during this period, beginning with the composition of Nannayya's retelling of the *Mahābhārata* in the eleventh century.[134]

The *Vīracōḻiyam*, although the first text of its kind in Tamil, is thus composed in an era of rapidly changing attitudes toward language status and language choice in the literary cultures of South India and Sri Lanka, a time in which vernacular and regional literary languages are rethought, reworked, and reimagined in relation to the dominant literary language on the subcontinent, Sanskrit. As noted previously, even Pāli appears to appropriate the literary styles of ornate Sanskrit poetry during this period, as witnessed by a limited number of highly ornate poetic works such as Buddhappiya's *Pajjamadhu*. In the case of Tamil, such changes entail not the transformation of a language previously devoid of its own corpus of literary works and criticism but the raising up of a long-standing regional literary language to translocal status; Tamil is demonstrated to be thoroughly compatible with Sanskrit, evincing its transregional qualities. As Irvine notes in his discussion of the emergence of an English-language textual culture in ninth- and tenth-century Europe that borrowed heavily from the Latin, "the dialogic interplay between Latin and English traditions produced a distinctive kind of grammatical culture."[135] In similar fashion, the "dialogic interplay" between Tamil and Sanskrit evidenced by the *Vīracōḻiyam* ushers in a new sort of grammatical and literary culture in the Tamil-speaking South, a culture that produces new kinds of Sanskrit-influenced poetic and prose works, from Kampaṉ's twelfth-century rendition of the story of Rāma, the *Irāmāvatāram*, to numerous Tamil renderings of the Sanskrit mythological literature (purāṇa), the literature of the Śaiva Siddhānta, and the Vaiṣṇava commentaries of Piḷḷai Lōkācārya and Maṇavāḷamāmuṉikaḷ composed in the fourteenth century. Yet despite the widespread application of the grammatical and literary theory laid out in the *Vīracōḻiyam*, the intermingling of Sanskrit and Tamil in rubies and coral style commentary, or the ornate poetic qualities of Kampaṉ's work, this particular poetic grammar in several ways makes the Tamil appropriation of the rules of Sanskrit grammar and poetic composition a distinctly Buddhist project. The *Vīracōḻiyam* claims the Tamil language and literary culture it describes for the Buddhist community; the new grammatical culture envisioned by the text becomes a means for imagining a new sort of Buddhist identity and community.

Poetic Grammar and Religious Community

Although Pollock is no doubt correct in dismissing the oft-recited historical narrative that attributes the rise of vernacular literatures in the age of the *Vīracōḻiyam* to the rise of Hindu devotional religion,[136] to ignore completely the religious elements in a text such as the *Vīracōḻiyam* in favor of new regional sensibilities fueled by newly emerging polities is to overlook a crucial factor in the project of the text. Just as Buddhist monks with some affiliation with South India are increasingly identified and identify themselves as Coḷiya, the *Vīracōḻiyam* imagines a Buddhist community through outlining the technology of a new grammatical culture that explicitly combines both Sanskrit and Tamil. The discourse of literary language and aesthetics rather than of nation or polity provides the means for envisioning a Buddhist identity that is at once regional and capable of evincing transregional claims. Like Kassapa's assertion of a Coḷiya identity that adheres to the transregional tradition of the Mahāvihāra yet criticizes other regional orders, the *Vīracōḻiyam* asserts the superiority of Tamil as a regional language that adheres to the standards set by translocal Sanskritic theory. The technology of grammatica, in other words, serves to articulate and legitimate a particular vision of religious identity. From the earliest Buddhist adaptations of Pāṇini, such as the *Kātantra* or *Kalāpa* of Śarvavarman and the *Cāndravyākaraṇa* of Candragomin,[137] to Aśvaghoṣa's pioneering appropriation of Sanskrit to imagine the life of the Buddha in ornate poetic style, literary culture, and discourse on grammar and poetics in particular, has provided a means for articulating new visions of Buddhist identity.

The *Vīracōḻiyam* ties its technology of literary culture to a vision of Buddhist community in a number of complex ways. Chief among them are the two passages in the text, the second verse of the preamble and verse 83, which closes the discussion of morphemes (col), that identify the Tamil explained grammatically and poetically by the text as the language of Avalōkitaṉ, a Tamil equivalent for the name of the Buddha-to-be, Avalokiteśvara.[138] The *Vīracōḻiyam* places Avalōkitaṉ at the very center of its project, and it is the Tamil of this Buddha-to-be in particular that is so thoroughly compatible with the language and literary principles of Sanskrit texts. In the second introductory verse, for example, it is said that the text:

> will explain here the beautiful Tamil
> that was uttered for the sake of the abundant earth
> and heard by Akattiyaṉ
> at the side of Avalōkitaṉ of beautiful qualities.[139]

Here, it is Akattiyaṉ (Sanskrit Agastya), the bearer of Sanskrit and Tamil literary culture first mentioned by name in Tamil, perhaps not coincidentally, in the preamble to the earlier Buddhist text, *Maṇimēkalai*, who hears the "beautiful Tamil" of the Buddha-to-be. The sage "whose greatness appears to lie in his command of *both* traditions,"[140] Sanskrit and Tamil, here sanctions the aim of the *Vīracōḻiyam* as stated in the following verse: to explain the grammatical and poetic aspects of Tamil according to the rules of Sanskrit tradition. *Tamil* here would seem to imply not only language but the five categories listed in the introductory verse and treated at length by the text: phonology, morphology, poetic theme, prosody, and ornamentation. Agastya is explicitly made the student of the Buddha-to-be, and his understanding of Tamil and Sanskrit literary culture is thus implicitly a Buddhist one, derived from the teachings of Avalōkitaṉ. The *Vīracōḻiyam* is, in fact, the first in a long line of texts to claim Agastya as a member of a particular religious community, taught by a specific divine being. Any number of medieval treatises, for example, all of which postdate the *Vīracōḻiyam*, maintain that Lord Śiva himself taught Akattiyaṉ Tamil.[141] Akattiyaṉ, unlike the character found in the earlier *Maṇimēkalai*, is no longer linguistically neutral. The *Vīracōḻiyam* associates the bilingual literary culture of the sage with Avalōkitaṉ, with a particular religious identity, and establishes a pattern for claiming Akattiyaṉ as the cultural center of religious community.

The connection between the Tamil poetic language explicated by the *Vīracōḻiyam* and the Buddha-to-be, Avalōkitaṉ, is made even more explicit in the final verse of the chapter on morphology that refers to the "true Tamil of Avalōkitaṉ whose glory shines in a thousand ways" (*āyiram vitattil poliyum pukaḻ avalōkitaṉ meyt tamiḻē*).[142] Here, the "true" Tamil, the Tamil that can be shown to be in complete accord in this particular context with the formation of Sanskrit finite verbs and, more generally, with both Sanskrit grammatical and poetic usage, is the Tamil of a glorious Buddhist figure. Avalōkitaṉ's Tamil is the true and beautiful Tamil taught to Akattiyaṉ, the regional language extending from Vēṅkaṭam to Kumari that evinces all the capacities of a translocal poetic language. Avalōkitaṉ is both source for and sponsor of the bilingual literary culture whose technology the *Vīracōḻiyam* attempts to construct. Literary culture here is also Buddhist culture, literary language Buddhist language, the language of the Buddha-to-be.

In an age when monks such as Buddhappiya and Kassapa identify themselves as Coḷiya, as more orthodox, more loyal to the traditions of the Mahāvihāra than other monks or monastic orders, and others identify them with either the Coḷa or Ḍamila country, the *Vīracōḻiyam* explicitly makes of Tamil a Buddhist language and literary culture. To be literate in Tamil, according to the *Vīracōḻiyam*, is to know the true language of the Buddha-to-be as taught to the sage Akattiyaṉ. The technology of literary culture, so intimately tied to the glorious Avalōkitaṉ, is depicted as a particularly Buddhist project. Like the Coḷiya monks who claim a local identity while pledging allegiance to a translocal authority, so, too, does the *Vīracōḻiyam* focus on the regional—Tamil—in terms of the transregional. Tamil in the *Vīracōḻiyam*, as not only the speech of the king and a specific region of southern India but as the speech of Avalōkitaṉ and the language of poetry, acquires an almost divine status. As in the Jain-authored *Yāpparuṅkalakkārikai*, a tenth-century treatise on prosody attributed to Amitacākarar, the text is addressed to Tamil itself, often in the form of a beautiful woman. Verses variously dedicate themselves to "oh lady of bright forehead" (*vāṇutalē*),[143] "oh lady of flowing hair" (*tāḻkuḻalē*),[144] "oh lady of choice ornaments" (*āyiḻaiyē*),[145] "oh lady speaking sweet words" (*paṉimoḻiyē*),[146] "oh lady wearing golden bangles" (*paintoṭiyē*),[147] and "oh lady wearing bright jewels" (*viḻaṅkiḻaiyē*),[148] to cite but a few examples. Other verses end in praise to the "language" (*moḻi*) in unanthropomorphized form: "oh divine language" (*tēmoḻiyē*),[149] "oh pure language" (*tūmoḻiyē*),[150] and "oh true language" (*vāymoḻiyē*),[151] all glossed by the commentator as "address to a woman" (*makaṭūu muṉṉilai*).[152] Tamil, as a literary language fully comparable to Sanskrit, assumes a life and power of its own. That power, according to the opening verses of the *Vīracōḻiyam*, stems from its origin in the very mouth of Avalōkitaṉ. Poetic language, as constructed by the *Vīracōḻiyam*, is envisioned as the centerpiece of a specifically Buddhist literary culture.

"Whatever else they may be," notes LaCapra, "texts are events in the history of language."[153] The *Vīracōḻiyam*, as a text engaging in discourse about the nature of language itself, lays claim to the very foundation of literary textual history as Buddhist, as a history that has as its point of origin the words of Avalokiteśvara. A Buddhist identity, a vision of Buddhist community, is thus imagined through the discourse of grammar and poetics, tied to a particular vision of literary aesthetics and culture. The regional literary language that can be explicated through the categories of Pāṇini and Daṇḍin is a Buddhist one; in constructing a technology of literary culture, in analyzing the language of Avalōkitaṉ and Akattiyaṉ according to translocal standards, the *Vīracōḻiyam* defines what it is to be a literate Buddhist in a multilingual literary culture.

The religious elements in the *Vīracōḻiyam*, then, far from being merely rhetorical, point to the importance of language and literary aesthetic vision in the imagining of religious identity and community. The project of the *Vīracōḻiyam*—appropriating the literary culture of a translocal prestige language—is envisioned as the analysis of the language spoken by the Buddha-to-be. True Tamil is the Tamil that corresponds entirely to the linguistic and poetic frameworks of Pāṇini and Daṇḍin. Like the Coḷiya or Ḍamila monks who claim adherence to the Mahāvihāra but assert their own positions on doctrine and practice as correct, the *Vīracōḻiyam* constructs a linguistic and literary technology whereby the local completely adheres to the standards of the transregional but also asserts itself in new and forceful ways. As a work of grammatica, the *Vīracōḻiyam* imagines the new literary course it envisions to be tied to the community of Agastya and Avalokiteśvara. The cultural work of imagining religious community does not stop, however, with the beautiful Tamil of Avalōkitaṉ or praise of Tamil as "the woman wearing bright jewels." The commentary on the *Vīracōḻiyam*, written perhaps by Puttamittiraṉ's own disciple, Peruntēvaṉār, envisions a Buddhist community through literary culture by marshaling a community of Tamil texts to illustrate the *Vīracōḻiyam*'s application of Daṇḍin to the *Tolkāppiyam*. The nature of Peruntēvaṉār's commentary and the many ways in which it imagines a particular kind of Buddhist identity through the gathering and interpreting of literary texts is the focus of the following chapter.

5

Imagining Community through Commentary

I used to quote verses I had come across in other Tamil works as occasion arose. One of these is a lament of those who were near the Lord Buddha on his entering the Parinirvāṇa. It is quoted as an illustration by the commentator on *Vīracōḻiyam*:

> Since we can never more see before us the Saint
> who destroyed Darkness with Great Enlightenment
> what shall we do, what shall we do?
>
> Since we can never more hear the Dharma
> expounded by Him with Compassion in saintty [*sic*] words
> what shall we do, what shall we do?
>
> Since we shall never more see the Prince
> whose penance led him straight to the Truth
> what shall we do, what shall we do?

When I read this poem I could not read on and my tongue faltered. Raṅkācāriyar, too, was fully overcome by its pathos, and forgot his self [*sic*] in a feeling of tender sympathy.

U. V. Cāminātaiyar, *The Story of My Life*

As in the case of the *Maṇimēkalai*, Cāminātaiyar's deeply felt response to the poetic content of the *Vīracōḻiyam* commentary reveals something of the depth and complexity of the text, of its literary elegance and moving poetic qualities. Far from simply providing dry explication and illustration of Puttamittiraṉ's Tamil appropriation of northern texts, the commentary on the *Vīracōḻiyam* constitutes a literary work in its own right, an anthology of verse with its own particular vision. Central to that vision in the *Vīracōḻiyam* commentary is a conception of Buddhist community rooted in the technology of literary culture but embodied and enacted through the products of that culture. The commentary on the *Vīracōḻiyam*, in other words, envisions Buddhist community through the gathering together of a significant body of Buddhist poetic literature composed in Tamil, most of which is no longer extant. The language of Avalōkitaṉ, in which Tamil and Sanskrit intermingle grammatically and poetically, is the language of a poetic corpus of praise and devotion to the Buddha, of ethical reflection on the nature of compassion and concern for the welfare of others.

This chapter examines the ways in which the commentary on the *Vīracōḻiyam* both supports and expands the vision of religious community found in the grammar itself and discussed in the preceding chapter. In an era in which other South Indian religious communities were formally anthologizing their bodies of poetic literature, the commentary substantiates the text's vision of literary culture specifically made Buddhist through marshaling the Buddhist poetic corpus composed in Tamil to provide concrete examples of Tamil poetic meters, thematic content, and Sanskrit poetic ornamentation in the manner of Daṇḍin. The *Vīracōḻiyam* and its commentary are, unfortunately, the sole remaining artifacts of that Buddhist Cōḻa-era literary culture of southern India, a literary culture now lost except for the fragments of poetry preserved in the commentary. Indeed, much as the work of the twelfth-century Gujarati Jain monk and literary theoretician, Hemacandra, has been credited with making "extensive contributions to the preservation of many passages of Indian [Sanskrit] poetry and poetics"[1] that would have otherwise been completely lost, so, too, does the commentary on the *Vīracōḻiyam* provide a glimpse of what must have once been a flourishing Buddhist literary culture in Tamil.

The Text

Although the commentator on the *Vīracōḻiyam* never identifies himself by name, Tamil literary tradition holds that Peruntēvaṉār (Sanskrit Mahādeva), a student or disciple of Puttamittiraṉ, composed the commentary on his teacher's poetic grammar.[2] Perhaps because he quotes so copiously from texts such as the *Tirukkuṟaḷ* and the eighth-century *Nālaṭiyār*, both of which are often assumed to be Jain, Zvelebil identifies Peruntēvaṉār as a "Jain scholar";[3] that his primary orientation is a Buddhist one, however, should become clear from the discussion to follow. Peruntēvaṉār's supposed association with Puttamittiraṉ would place him in the late eleventh or early twelfth century. In addition to texts such as the *Tirukkuṟaḷ*, the commentator quotes from the tenth-century Tamil work on prosody, the *Yāpparuṅkalam* attributed to Amitacākarar, and as a rule quotes "books composed only before the 12th c[entury]."[4] Mention of specific events, such as the battle of Koppam cited in the commentary on verse 138,[5] a battle thought to have been waged by the *Vīracōḻiyam*'s patron and namesake, Vīrarācēntira (Sanskrit Vīrarājendra) Cōḻa, in 1061–1062, has led scholars such as Zvelebil to place Peruntēvaṉār in the same general era as Puttamittiraṉ.[6]

Whether or not the *Vīracōḻiyam* commentary can be assigned with any certainty to the student of Puttamittiraṉ, the text represents one of the earliest examples of Tamil prose commentary.[7] On the first two chapters that address the topics of phonology and morphology, the commentary adds little to the substance of the *Vīracōḻiyam* verses themselves. Often providing a word-by-word gloss on the compact syntax of the verse and a number of examples of particular kinds of declensions or compound formations, the commentary restricts itself largely to paraphrase and explication. It is in the final three chapters on poetic content (poruḷ), prosody (yāppu), and ornamentation (alaṅkāram) that the commentary truly embarks on its project of gathering together the pieces of a Buddhist literary culture in Tamil, anticipating and envisioning a community of Buddhist literary connoisseurs fluent in both Tamil and Sanskrit poetic and grammatical theory. Just as the *Tolkāppiyam* codifies or systematizes the language of the Caṅkam poetic corpus, so, too, does the *Vīracōḻiyam*, argues the commentary by example, analyze the language and poetic content of a now lost corpus of Buddhist devotional and narrative literature in Tamil. The commentary demonstrates the extent to which Tamil literature—and Buddhist literature composed in Tamil in particular—partakes of the literary qualities of both Tamil and Sanskrit, linguistically and poetically. In providing examples of the application of the principles of northern textual tradition to Tamil, the commentary establishes not only that Tamil literature is compatible with the rules of Sanskrit grammar and poetic theory but that Buddhist teachings and values as well are best expressed through a combination of Tamil prosody and Sanskrit poetic ornamentation. In anthologizing a corpus of Tamil poetry that both speaks directly to the ideals of Buddhism and draws on a variety of passages that share the values of Buddhism, from hymns of praise to the Buddha and the lament cited previously by Cāminātaiyar to the ethical maxims of the *Tirukkuṟaḷ* and *Nālaṭiyār* and the stories of the Jātakas, the *Vīracōḻiyam* commentary imagines a textual community deeply suffused with the teachings and values, sentiments and ideals, of the Buddha and his followers.

In verse 173, for example, the *Vīracōḻiyam* defines in Tamil three of Daṇḍin's methods of poetic ornamentation: the description of two separate things presented as one (*oruṅkiyal*, Sanskrit *sahokti*), the nonliteral exchange of things or ideas (*parimāṟṟam*, Sanskrit *parivṛtti*), and the expression of benediction (*āci*, Sanskrit *āśiṣ*):

> The ornament oruṅkiyal uses one statement simultaneously to describe two things, [either] actions or nouns denoting qualities.
> Following [that], the ornament parimāṟṟam exchanges meanings [or things] in an unspoken [nonliteral] manner.
> The eminent āci ornament is the expression of the excellence [of a thing] without error.
> Realize [this], oh woman of flowing tresses![8]

The commentary on this verse is quite representative of the larger whole, beginning with simple paraphrasing before moving on to illustrate each point made in Puttamittiraṉ's verse with a diverse set of poetic examples. Such examples, in each case, cover a wide variety of styles and themes, ranging from Caṅkam-style love stanzas that invert the classical appreciation of human love to overt praise of the Buddha's many illustrious qualities. Here, Peruntēvaṉār begins by providing a word-for-word paraphrase of the verse above, expanding each definition slightly and providing synonyms for the key terms: *puṇar nilai* is a synonym for conjoint description (puṇar nilai *eṉiṉum* oruṅkiyal eṉiṉum *okkum*), whereas nonliteral exchange also goes by the name *parivarttaṉai*.[9] Next, examples (*varalāṟu*) of each of the poetic ornaments thus defined are furnished, beginning with an (anonymous) illustration of conjoint description of action (viṉai puṇar nilai) in which the activity of gazing or looking is shared between two very different characters. As discussed later, such quotations, although suffused with the Caṅkam poetic themes of love, invert the classical depictions to focus on human suffering and anguish:

> The young girl of the hills, adorned with flowers [and her] dark eyes full of cunning, becomes one with the hearts of many and ruins [them].
> Through that gaze, what suffering [will befall] the hero who possesses eyes [but] who does not look?[10]

As an example of conjoint description of qualities (*paṇpu* puṇar nilai), the commentator offers yet another anonymous verse in which the lingering glow of twilight is likened to the life of a woman awaiting her lover:

Just as the birds in the flower garden grow weary as dusk falls
[and] do not depart [but] linger, becoming desirous [to remain there],
such is the life of the solitary woman who longs for her lover to come,
emitting sighs of distress.[11]

Each of these first two poetic illustrations, although betraying no particularly Buddhist qualities or characteristics, emphasizes not the Caṅkam joy of lovers in union or in eager anticipation of union but their despair. The Caṅkam motif of the hill country (*kuṟiñci*), for example, highlighted in the first stanza, is most often associated with a euphoric sexual rendezvous,[12] not with the "cunning" glance of a woman who ensnares and "ruins" men. When these Tamil stanzas are compared to Daṇḍin's Sanskrit illustrations of this style of poetic ornamentation, the thematic discrepancies are even more pronounced. *Kāvyādarśa*, ii.354, for example, provides a charming image of springtime exuberance in sharp contrast to the Tamil images of women cunning and despairing in turn. Daṇḍin writes:

Pleasing because of the cuckoo's song and [full of] fragrant breezes,
the days of spring are fulfilled along with the joys of the people.[13]

The Tamil commentator moves in a more obviously Buddhist direction in his next poetic example, illustrative of the nonliteral exchange of things or ideas:

The one who defeated Kāmaṉ [the god of lust] gave a place of shade
to the [river] Gaṅgā and to the one who holds the moon in his matted locks [Śiva];
[he] received [in return] a thousand forms [reflections of the Gaṅgā and the moon],
a gift of the jewels in the hood of the large, lustrous serpent.[14]

This short, anonymous stanza suggests a Buddhist poetic tradition in Tamil that posits the Buddha as the superior of every member of the Hindu pantheon of divinities. Not only does the Buddha as the victor over lust provide protective shade to the holiest of rivers and the moon (both associated with Śiva), but he also enjoys the "largesse" of that mythological serpent of a thousand heads upon whom the entire world rests (Tamil Āticēṭaṉ, Sanskrit Ādiśeṣa), a serpent most often associated with Viṣṇu; in this case, the glorious jewels of Āticēṭaṉ merely reflect the compassionate care of the Buddha.[15]

The final example, illustrating the benedictory means of poetic ornamentation, leads the reader to remember that this grammatical treatise has been named for its royal Cōḻa patron, the heroic king "Vīra"cōḻaṉ, scion of a dynasty that identified itself predominantly with the Hindu god Śiva. Calling to mind the Vaiṣṇava or Bhāgavata king of the *Maṇimēkalai*, who is nowhere said to "convert" to Buddhism, the commentator here asks for Śiva's blessings to bring prosperity to the kingdom:

May the great one with matted locks [Śiva], adorned with serpents and the pale moon,
who has destroyed hatred and illusion,
protect that [royal city] Kōḻi,[16] that is like a budding flower,
[the city of] the royal horse of the incomparable [Cōḻa king] and the tiger.[17]
May the earth and sky prosper![18]

This type of eclectic or non-Buddhist quotation is typical of the *Vīracōḻiyam* commentary. Sandwiched between stanzas praising the Buddha, the compassion of the Buddha-to-be, and describing the transience of love and all human life are poetic illustrations from a wide range of sources that illustrate the theoretical point at hand, praise the deeds of the commentator's patron, and construct a vision of a Tamil-speaking Buddhist community living side by side with other sectarian and literary communities. Just as the *Maṇimēkalai*, in its present-tense narrative, portrays its principal character interacting with non-Buddhist sages and kings, so, too, does the *Vīracōḻiyam* commentary construct a Buddhist literary corpus that explicitly acknowledges the presence of other sectarian communities in the Tamil religious landscape.

Despite the richness and complexity of the commentarial text and the tantalizing glimpses it provides of what must have once been a significant body of Tamil Buddhist poetry now lost, the commentary on the *Vīracōḻiyam* has largely been ignored by historians of South Indian religions and literatures. Zvelebil glances through the commentary for evidence of Tamil literature extant before the twelfth century,[19] and Vijayavenugopal's brief article concerns itself primarily with the supposed influence of Hindu devotional poetry on the fragments of Buddhist hymns cited in the commentary.[20] No one to date has considered the text as a whole, the work of the commentary as both a Buddhist gloss on poetic grammar and a Buddhist literary piece unto itself with a particular vision of literary culture and community. As indicated previously, the complexity and literary elegance of the text suggest multiple layers of meaning, subtle and nuanced ways of imagining and articulating a vision of Buddhist community.

The Commentarial Project

At the most straightforward level, Peruntēvaṉār's commentary simply underscores, reinforcing by explanation and example, the cultural work of grammatica discussed in the previous chapter. Like the verses of the *Vīracōḻiyam* themselves, the commentary raises Tamil from the status of local to transregional literary language. In providing poetic examples in Tamil for each of Taṇṭi's (Daṇḍin's) poetic ornaments, for example, the commentary shows the extent to which the local language possesses all the capacities of the dominant transregional language, Sanskrit. Those translocal qualities of Tamil poetic language are continually reinforced as Peruntēvaṉār refers to Taṇṭi, Taṇṭiyār, northern texts (vaṭanūl), and northern language (vaṭamoḻi) far more often than does Puttamittiraṉ. In gathering together poetic excerpts that exemplify the language of Avalōkitaṉ described by Puttamittiraṉ, the commentary shows Tamil literary culture to be not only perfectly compatible with the Sanskrit but also perfectly compatible with the "pure language" (tūmoḻi), the "divine language" (tēmoḻi), spoken by the Buddha-to-be to the sage Akattiyaṉ. What the *Vīracōḻiyam* claims for Tamil—both in terms of its compatibility with Sanskrit and its origin in the speech of the a Buddha-to-be—the commentary substantiates by example.

Those poetic examples are, in turn, validated by their association with the language of Avalōkitaṉ, Pāṇini, and Daṇḍin. As Pierre Bourdieu notes in his discussion of the production of art and literature, discourse about art authenticates both the object of art and the discourse itself. "Every critical affirmation contains, on the one hand, a recognition of the value of the work that occasions it," writes Bourdieu, ". . . and on the other hand an affirmation of its own legitimacy."[21] Following Bourdieu, one might say that by anthologizing a corpus of Buddhist poetry in Tamil and applying to it the linguistic and poetic rules of both Sanskrit and Tamil, the *Vīracōḻiyam* commentary in effect both affirms the value of that literary corpus as embodying the language of the Buddha-to-be and the principles of poetic ornamentation of Daṇḍin and authenticates its own project of constructing a technology for a bilingual literary culture. The literary works gathered together by Peruntēvaṉār are made a legitimate collection by their inclusion in the commentary, whereas the commentary in turn validates a Buddhist poetic corpus composed in Tamil by offering each as an example of the Tamil spoken by Avalōkitaṉ and explained through the grammatical and poetic discourse of northern textual tradition.

Yet as Anne Blackburn suggests in her detailed study of the *Sārāthadīpanī*, Saraṇaṁkāra's eighteenth-century Sinhala commentary on a Pāli anthology of Buddhist verses, commentary not only anthologizes and preserves particular sets of poetic and narrative works but also "signal[s] monastic erudition . . . that . . . help[s] to identify and sustain authoritative Buddhist monastic voices in a highly competitive religious milieu."[22] Although one cannot say with certainty whether the "lord of Poṉpaṟṟi" and his commentator/student were, indeed, monastic voices, the *Vīracōḻiyam* claims for Buddhism the sophisticated intermingling of Tamil and Sanskrit that it describes. The *Vīracōḻiyam* commentator, in explicating the verses of the grammar and marshaling a wide range of texts in support of such a literary technology, raises an erudite and authoritative Buddhist voice in the multilingual literary culture and multireligious landscape of medieval South India. Like the *Vīracōḻiyam* itself, as a text of many firsts, the commentator displays his expertise in two literary traditions through his very selection of genre, writing a prose commentary on grammar and poetic theory in the manner of Kātyāyana, Patañjali, Bhartṛhari, or Abhinavagupta. By citing a wide variety of poetic texts dealing with devotional and ethical themes, the commentator further provides a site for reflection on topics of concern to a specifically Buddhist community, from the nature of the Buddha and his teachings to the moral vision of his deeds as a Buddha-in-the-making.

As much recent work on commentarial practice in the South Asian context has shown, commentary constitutes a form of argument, a rhetorical means of reinterpreting, refashioning, and relocating the text in changing historical circumstances.[23] Among the things argued for in the *Vīracōḻiyam* commentary is a particular vision of Buddhist community based not only on the intermingling of Tamil and Sanskrit as literary languages explicated by the *Vīracōḻiyam* but on the devotional and ethical themes of the poetic corpus anthologized and legitimated through its inclusion in the commentary itself. In the changing historical and literary circumstances outlined in chapter 4, it is interesting to note that the poetic corpus gathered together, explicated, and authenticated with great erudition by Peruntēvaṉār—and, by extension, its envisioning of community—does not include the *Maṇimēkalai*; with the composition of each text separated historically by perhaps four or five centuries, no vision of community appears to connect these two remnants of Buddhist literature composed in Tamil.

Community Envisioned through Commentary

Although the individual fragments of poetry cited by Peruntēvaṉār do not, in and of themselves, allow much space for interpretation, the entire commentary, when considered as a textual whole, constitutes something of a literary tour de force, a Buddhist anthology in Tamil, a sophisticated and erudite corpus of poetic thoughts and sentiments that in one way or another exemplify Buddhist values and ideals. The range and breadth of the commentator's illustrative reserve is impressive; throughout the final three chapters on poetic theme, prosody, and ornamentation, the commentary cites literally hundreds of stanzas in different meters, with varying thematic content and demonstrating various methods of poetic embellishment or ornamentation. The majority of the quotations—most of them quite short and many limited to stanzas of two or four lines—are drawn from unknown texts no longer extant; the variation in meter and style is sufficient to suggest, however, that the commentator draws on a large number of original sources rather than simply citing different verses from a key text or two. Displaying mastery of the classical poetic tradition of the *Tolkāppiyam*, as well as the literary theory of Taṇṭiyār (Daṇḍin), and extensive knowledge of Tamil literary works from the Caṅkam anthologies to treatises on prosody and poetic versions of the Jātaka stories,[24] the *Vīracōḻiyam* commentary imagines a community of readers sympathetic to Buddhist ideals and values in several ways.

The commentator first lays claim, for example, not simply to Buddhist literary works but to classical and medieval Tamil literary culture more generally, showing himself to be thoroughly competent in all aspects of Tamil grammar, prosody, and poetic content. Several times he refers to the author of the *Tolkāppiyam*, Tolkāppiyaṉār,[25] and twice quotes the earlier treatise on grammar and poetics directly: once while commenting on verses 90–94, which outline the Caṅkam poetic scheme of the five landscapes (tiṇai),[26] and again under verse 171, which defines the three poetic ornaments of representing the quality of an object apart from its natural context or substratum (Tamil *ciṟappu*, Sanskrit *viśeṣa*), of representing several objects that share qualities as equals (Tamil *uṭaṉilai*, Sanskrit *tulyayogitā*), and the expression of contradictory properties in a single object (Tamil muraṇ, Sanskrit *virodha*).[27] In his discussion of the five classical landscape motifs (tiṇai), the commentator expounds at length on the nature of each[28] and elsewhere cites such classical texts as *Puṟanāṉūṟu* and *Kalittokai*.[29] Also quoted several times are verses from the Caṅkam anthology known as *Kuṟuntokai*.[30] That the commentator knows thoroughly the traditions of Tamil grammar and poetics extending into his own era is evidenced by his citing of Amitacākarar by name, the author of the tenth-century work on metrics, *Yāpparuṅkalam*.[31] Elsewhere, while discussing various types of poetic meter under verse 123, Peruntēvaṉār quotes directly from the same author's condensation of his own work, the *Yāpparuṅkalakkārikai*.[32] The commentator on the *Vīracōḻiyam* thus displays his significant erudition in all manner of Tamil poetic composition, citing both literary classics and earlier theoretical works on grammar and poetry.

The *Vīracōḻiyam* commentary also locates its vision of a Tamil literary tradition intermingled with Sanskrit in a particular geographical region, one somewhat different from that envisioned by the text itself. As noted in the preceding chapter, Puttamittiraṉ follows the *Tolkāppiyam* in defining the Tamil-speaking region as extending from "the abode of Kumari to the great Vēṅkaṭam hill" (*vīṟu mali vēṅkaṭam kumarik kiṭai*).[33] Peruntēvaṉār, some three centuries before the appearance of the first grammar of Malayalam (the fourteenth-century *Līlātilakam*), refines the geographical region represented by pure Tamil (centamiḻ) by excluding the area west of the hill country that presently forms the boundary between Tamilnadu and Kerala (*kuṭakam*). The area where pure Tamil is spoken, according to the commentary, is marked by the following four boundaries: "the eastern ocean, Kumari [in the south], the western hill country, and the [northern] Vēṅkaṭam hill" (*kuṇakatal* kumari kuṭakam vēṅkaṭam).[34] In redefining the boundaries of the Tamil linguistic and literary region, the commentary reveals the extent to which Tamil is associated with a particular geographic territory; the local language that possesses translocal capacities is confined, in its purest form (centamiḻ), to a specific area, one that no longer includes, in the commentator's mind, those who live west of the Kuṭakam Hills.

Perhaps most importantly, however, the *Vīracōḻiyam* commentary envisions a community of Buddhists through the gathering together of a corpus of poetic works, ranging from stories of the Buddha-to-be's former lives to hymns of devotion to a compassionate and loving Buddha. In bringing together numerous poetic examples of the literary language spoken by Avalōkitaṉ and compatible with the Sanskritic textual traditions of Pāṇini and Daṇḍin, the commentator imagines a reading or textual community that is also thoroughly Buddhist and conversant in the literary themes and images of non-Buddhist traditions. Even the most mundane of the commentator's examples have Buddhist connotations. Under the initial discussion of metrical feet (*cīr*) in verse 105, for example, the line that is scanned in the commentary reads "I take refuge in the lord of the bodhi tree" (*pōti vēntaṉ caraṇalāl araṇ pukēm*).[35] More often, however, the commentary quotes full stanzas as examples, bringing together a body of Buddhist poetic work in Tamil now lost.

Peruntēvaṉār quotes from or mentions by name a number of times one of the lost "five great ornate poetic works" (aimperuṅkāppiyam) in Tamil, the *Kuṇṭalakēci*. One stanza is quoted for the first time under *Vīracōḻiyam*, verse 107, in the context of explaining varieties of metrical feet:

> He is the ancient [lord] adorned with greatness; he meditated with resoluteness and achieved virtue.
> He spoke of [good] qualities.
> He thought not of his own welfare, but exerted himself for the welfare of others.
> The foot of the lord is foremost among the refuges.[36]

That same verse is cited again under a discussion of meter in verse 121 and again under the following verse.[37] Although the two preceding citations indicate the verse as an example of a metrical stanza known as *kalitturai*,[38] under the definition of another meter (viruttam) in verse 127 it is said that "all ornate poetic works beginning with the *Kuṇṭalakēci* are in viruttam" (*kuṇṭalakēci mutalāṉa kāppiyam ellām viruttamām*).[39] Both the *Kuṇṭalakēci* and a work known as the *Utayaṇaṉ Katai*[40] are noted under verse 144 both for their rigorous poetic style (*vali*) and for their difficult complexity. Here, the *Kuṇṭalakēci* is said to be full of the obscure words and ideas that poets of such a voluminous work (*akalakkavi*) invariably use but that were perhaps more readily understood at the time when the text was originally composed (*aṉṟiyum avai ceyta kālattu accoṟkaḷum poruḷkaḷum viḷaṅki irukkum*).[41] The *Kuṇṭalakēci*, then, was perhaps a composition much like the *Maṇimēkalai*, a long poetic Buddhist narrative in an elegant and difficult literary style, full of complex concepts and vocabulary. Whether or not the text was fully known to the commentator on the *Vīracōḻiyam*,[42] certainly it is presented as a paradigmatic work, as an important ornate poetic creation and an example of an erudite poetic narrative whose meaning may not be entirely clear but whose style and beauty are highly valued. The

Kuṇṭalakēci, as one of the few texts Peruntēvaṉār cites repeatedly by name, in other words, emerges as a centerpiece of the literary anthology compiled by the commentator.

In addition to this repeated mention of one of the five Tamil great poetic works, Peruntēvaṉār also quotes from a large number of devotional hymns to the Buddha, stanzas praising the Buddha's glorious demeanor, his many wonderful qualities, and his compassionate concern for the suffering of all living beings. As in the excerpt selected by Cāminātaiyar for his autobiography and cited previously, other selections focus on the human experience of the Buddha, in that case the profound grief of his followers after his earthly death. The source of each of the many examples of such verses remains unknown. Given the fact that Peruntēvaṉār does cite a number of known works, however (including the *Tolkāppiyam*, the *Yāpparuṅkalam*, and the *Tirukkuṟaḷ*), it is safe to assume that he draws from an extant corpus of Buddhist devotional literature in Tamil and does not simply compose his own examples. For were he to mix both direct citation and imaginative compositions of his own, Peruntēvaṉār would violate Indic commentarial precedent that calls either for self-authored illustrations (Daṇḍin) or citations drawn from readily recognized works of literature (Abhinavagupta). Throughout the verses cited in the commentary whose original source remains lost to us, the Buddha is praised variously as the "protector of precious life" (*ār uyir kāval*),[43] "the king who taught the flawless teachings" (*kōtu illā aṟam pakarnta . . . kōṉ*),[44] "the pure one" (*puṉitaṉ*),[45] "the first lord" (*āti nātaṉ*),[46] and "the light in the shade of the bodhi tree" (*pōti nīḻal cōti*),[47] to cite but a few such epithets of praise. As an example of poetic lines composed of two metrical feet under verse 107, the commentator offers:

> He became the great physician
> of perfect red-lotus feet,
> the great ascetic sitting properly
> under the bodhi tree.[49]

As an example of yet another type of metrical stanza, the commentator offers the following hymn of praise under verse 115:

> You are the one whose good qualities are innumerable.
> You are the one who remembers all people.
> You are the one who graciously dispenses food.
> You are the one who abounds in greatness.
> You are the one who knows the truth.
> You are the one who rejoices in the true dharma.
> You are the one who performs austerities with correctness.
> You are a refuge for those who gather together.[49]

As an example of a variation on the meter in which the *Tirukkuṟaḷ* is composed (*kuṟaṭṭāḻicai*), the commentator cites the following:

> The meritorious one in the shade of the bodhi tree, he whose feet are beautiful,
> is the first cause of the world.[50]

To cite but one more of many such examples, under verse 115 the commentator offers yet another poetic testimony to the Buddha's great understanding and compassion, this time as an illustration of a meter known as *curitakam*:

In order to adore that which abides in
the sage who has realized all
and who sits majestically with compassion in the holy shade of the bodhi tree,
"be single-minded,"
transcend the three evil qualities [lust, anger, and delusion] in order to overcome the bonds of the two classes of moral action [good karma and bad karma],
grow dignified through realizing the four aims in human life,
and live long with joy,
never abandoning anyone in this world.[51]

Such verses of praise and devotion to the Buddha appear again and again throughout the commentary on the *Vīracōḻiyam*. Whether or not Vijayavenugopal is correct in assuming such devotional poems to bear the stamp of Hindu devotional influence,[52] what emerges from the commentary is a corpus of clearly devotional poetry addressed to the Buddha, verses in various types of meter and rhyme, employing different kinds of poetic ornamentation. Buddhist literary output in Tamil by the time of Peruntēvaṉār obviously included not only complex and difficult narratives on the ornate poetic model such as the *Maṇimēkalai* and the *Kuṇṭalakēci* but numerous poetic compositions praising and worshipping the lord of the bodhi tree. In gathering together such verses full of reverence, the commentator anticipates and imagines a reading community for his text that is interested not only in the mechanics of grammar and poetic theory but in proper adoration of the Buddha. The verses that best exemplify the Tamil intermingled with northern language and spoken by Avalōkitaṉ are those that praise the Buddha of compassion, the great physician, the refuge.

Equally ubiquitous throughout the *Vīracōḻiyam* commentary are poetic fragments extolling the compassionate deeds of the Buddha-to-be in his various births. Drawn, perhaps, from a collection of Tamil Jātaka tales,[53] references to the Buddha's former lives emphasize his acts of kindness and generosity. Under verse 107, as an example of a stanza composed in lines of three metrical feet, the commentator quotes a reference to the Buddha-to-be's generous giving of his own eyes to Indra:[54]

Without suffering any malady in that good place,
the meritorious one sitting under the bodhi tree
immediately felt love for the lord of the celestials
who needed eyes.[55]

This same verse is cited later, but not quoted in its entirety, as an example of an ornate stanza composed in a specific poetic meter.[56] Two different stanzas are quoted that depict the story of the Buddha-to-be giving his own flesh to feed a hungry tigress;[57] elsewhere, his compassionate care of those who live in hell (*narakar*) is portrayed, as the Buddha-to-be:

stepped into a great hell of burning flames,
as if [stepping on] a lotus flower,
in order to destroy the formless karma (*aruviṉai*)
of a chosen few [among the hell dwellers].[58]

His concern for the welfare of the serpents (nāgas) is reiterated several times, as the Buddha-to-be teaches the dharma (aṟam) to Garuḍa (Karuṭaṉ), enemy of the serpents, to ease their pain and suffering.[59] Elsewhere, he relieves their suffering[60] and leads the "bejeweled serpents" (*maṇinākar*) along the "path of truth" (*vāymai neṟi*).[61] The glorious and compassionate qualities of the Buddha-to-be in several births are praised in a single verse:

> He controlled his burning anger at Māra in meditation.
> He removed the suffering of many serpents.
> Assuming the form of a fish, he was immersed in truth.
> Assuming the form of a deer, he revealed great qualities.[62]

As noted previously, these poetic fragments preserved in the *Vīracōḻiyam* commentary are all that remain of what once must have been a considerable corpus of Buddhist poetry composed in Tamil. In the chapter on prosody alone (yāppu), over 100 verses with obvious reference to the Buddha or to Buddhist teachings are cited. All are of different meters and styles, in varying degrees of complexity and sophistication, suggesting a wide variety of poetic genres from which Peruntēvaṉār could draw. Many appear to be modeled on classical meters of the Caṅkam poetic corpus, such as the example of *āciriyattāḻicai* meter quoted under verse 120:

> [We] worship your two feet, [you who are] the first lord,
>   [you whose] light the celestial beings graciously came to worship,
>   [you who] banished vileness while dwelling [under] the bodhi tree.[63]

One can only guess at the nature of the full corpus from which such poetry is drawn; the sheer variety of forms and styles indicates, however, a body of poetry of considerable size, age, and sophistication. Beyond these relatively straightforward observations, however, what might such poetic fragments allow one to infer regarding the character of Tamil-speaking Buddhist literary culture during the Cōḻa period?

The exclusive focus on the character of the Buddha-to-be and the Buddha himself in the poetic examples cited previously and throughout the *Vīracōḻiyam* commentary suggests, at the very least, a redefinition of Daṇḍin's concept of the proper poetic subject, namely, the hero (*nāyakam*) who is a courageous royal figure.[64] For Peruntēvaṉār, the only true hero is the Buddha himself, restricting the ideal poetic hero to the central figure of his own particular religious community. In addition to the ethical reflection invited by these and many other references to the former lives and deeds of the Buddha, a topic discussed in detail later, these poetic fragments serve to create a sense of time, a history of sorts that ties the Buddha and his past deeds as Buddha-to-be to the present grammatical and theoretical project of the *Vīracōḻiyam* and the community it envisions. By referring so consistently to the compassionate acts of the Buddha in his former lives, his service to the serpents, the hell dwellers, and the starving tigress, as well as his births as fish and deer, the commentator summons up a vision of the Buddha's past, his lives before enlightenment under the bodhi tree. That Buddhist past, expressed in proper Tamil-Sanskrit grammar and verse, becomes inseparably identified with the "beautiful Tamil" uttered by Avalōkitaṉ and explicated by Puttamittiraṉ and his commentator. The community of readers envisioned in the present of the commentarial text also has a past, a history rooted in acts of self-sacrificing kindness. The poetic corpus of Jātaka references gathered in Peruntēvaṉār's commentary, in other words, grounds the imagined community of the text in time. The Tamil taught to Akattiyaṉ by Avalōkitaṉ and shown to be compatible with Sanskrit rules of grammar and poetic theory is a literary language expressing praise and adoration not only to the enlightened Buddha, who is wise, meritorious, and the greatest of celestial beings (see previous discussion), but to the Buddha-in-the-making, who in the past perfected his qualities of generosity and compassion in specific narrative instances. The literary language of the *Vīracōḻiyam*, the commentary thus implies, is the language of a specifically Buddhist community with its roots in the distant past.

Not only do such fragments of verse addressed to the glories of the Buddha's past lives serve to ground the commentary's vision of community in time, but they also become a means of imbuing, through example, classical Tamil literary conventions and themes with Buddhist values. To cite but one particularly clear case of such redefinition, the commentator quotes several lengthy verses under *Vīracōḻiyam*, verse 102, a verse that defines the poetic theme of the achievements of different social classes, or castes (*vākai*), identified in the *Tolkāppiyam* as the heroic, or outer (puṟam), equivalent of the love, or inner (akam), motif of the desert wasteland (pālai).[65] Puttamittiraṉ's verse is only loosely based on the *Tolkāppiyam*'s elaboration of this theme that emphasizes the classification of caste duties:[66]

> In [the poetic theme of] the achievements of the social classes in union with others
> are the duties of the four castes, the three divisions of time, the destruction on the
>   battlefield, the sweet hillside dance,
> the qualities of strength, manliness, and desire in [the one who possesses] honor,
>   the [four] aims [of human life],
> the martial qualities of protection, renunciation, and the gift,
>   and others.[67]

After providing brief glosses on the first seven characteristics of this poetic theme, the commentator offers the following verse as an example of greatness or honor (*mēṉmai*), a term that he defines as "the ability to endure great injury, to undertake a life of austerities with grace" (*perum pakai* mēṉmai *atu aruḷoṭu puṇarnta akaṟciyām*):

> Grasping a way to save the starving newborn offspring
>   of a tigress who had ceased to give milk,
> [the Buddha-to-be] entangled himself in the sharp-pointed claws of the
>   hunting tigress,
> his flesh sliced off in plunder by the lethal teeth,
> [and] he died for the sake of the young animals [the tigress's offspring].
> This alone is honor, in combination with great compassion,
>   [the honor] that assumes the protection of all life,
>   the great mercy that dwells [under] the green-leafed bodhi tree.[68]

In this reference to the well-known Jātaka stories of the Buddha-to-be's ultimate display of compassion toward others,[69] the *Vīracōḻiyam* offers a unique interpretation of this Caṅkam poetic theme, an extended commentary on honor that is not taken up for any detailed discussion in the *Tolkāppiyam*. In depicting the Buddha-to-be in heroic self-sacrifice, the verse presents an interesting combination of a number of the eighteen "situations" (tuṟai) that are said to evoke this theme in the earlier theoretical text. Whereas the *Tolkāppiyam* suggests, for example, that the qualities of the valiant soldier are brought about by heroic fighting without attachment to the body and self-sacrifice in the fire to make one's enemies feel ashamed,[70] the Buddha-to-be's act of self-sacrifice is utterly compassionate, intended to protect all life. The martial heroics of the classical Tamil corpus are turned toward different ends, imbued with a moral sensibility, a call to selfless action in the service of others, to act compassionately without a thought of the cost to oneself.

This reinterpretation of Caṅkam heroic ideals, the reorientation of classical themes through Buddhist example, is even more emphatic in the example the *Vīracōḻiyam* commentary provides for the theme of "the gift" under verse 102:

> Like the gift unbidden of the great and compassionate lord of the green-leafed
> bodhi tree,
> heroic giving is giving in strength to anyone,
> [as in] the time when [the Buddha] gave his own nourishing blood,
> having split open his own body and given the rich [blood] that poured forth
> to quench the thirst of those who begged assistance but who were without love;
> [as in the Buddha's] giving of [his constructed] body,
> that is to say, the powerful one's illusory body [*māya yākkai*]
> to the dark, cunning woman of the forest.[71]

"The gift" is named in the *Tolkāppiyam* as one of the fourteen "dreadful" (*uṭkuvara*) divisions of a heroic theme describing the king as he captures enemy cattle in war (*veṭci*).[72] After a series of events that includes killing the residents of the village from whom the cattle are to be taken (*ūrkolai*), the king is to give generously (koṭai).[73] The gift is glossed by the editor of the text as "the distribution of the herd of cattle to those in need" (*pakutta niraiyai vēṇṭi irappārkkuk koṭuttal*),[74] "those in need" being the survivors of the raid and ensuing massacre. Although the king is certainly called on here and throughout the extant Caṅkam literary corpus to give generously to his subjects, the king is also one who can seize wealth in violent battle. Generosity is merely an offshoot of power, the *Tolkāppiyam*'s treatment of the gift an admonition of sorts to the literary king to remember to support those who are dependent on his largesse. In classical Tamil literary terms, then, the gift represents the act of a beneficent lord or chieftain who distributes the spoils of his military ventures to those within his kingdom.

Peruntēvaṉār's commentarial example of the gift as a poetic theme also stresses giving—the Buddha's action is, indeed, described here as "heroic giving in strength" (*vīrakkoṭai valappaṭu*)—but the nature of the gift, the giver, and the recipient is utterly transformed, the moral emphasis behind the act of giving subtly refocused. The king as hero is replaced by the heroic giver, identified in the first line of the poem as "the compassionate lord of the green-leafed bodhi tree." The gift itself is not the culmination of any royal conquest but a "gift unbidden," not sought out or expected by its recipients; the Buddha is not a king fulfilling royal duty. Moreover, the gift represents an action far more humane and compassionate than the distribution of stolen or pillaged property. Although the Caṅkam literary king is certainly expected to be a generous benefactor to all within his realm, here the Buddha-to-be offers his own blood to quench the thirst of a band of ungrateful supplicants. Through example, Peruntēvaṉār extends the *Tolkāppiyam*'s literary ideal to its Buddhist extreme, the logical conclusion to the Buddha's emphasis on compassionate concern for others. The warring chieftain, now replaced by the Buddha as the heroic giver, gives selflessly of his own flesh and blood to feed those who pay him no homage, who offer him nothing in return. The hero is transformed from warring but beneficent king to compassionate caregiver, a hero whose weapons are turned only upon himself, a feeder of those in need regardless of their character or merit. In quoting such a verse to illustrate the classical poetic theme of the gift, the commentator appropriates an aspect of Tamil literary culture for Buddhism, offering an utterly self-sacrificing vision of the hero and the heroic ethic. The critical literary apparatus set out in the *Tolkāppiyam* and borrowed in the third chapter on poetic content in the *Vīracōḻiyam* is reimagined by the commentator as a means of expressing Buddhist values.

The commentary on the *Vīracōḻiyam* transforms not only the literary vision of the classical Tamil poetic corpus as articulated in the *Tolkāppiyam* but the principles of poetic ornamentation laid out by Daṇḍin as well. Although claiming, like Puttamittiraṉ, to be following the words of Taṇṭi or Taṇṭiyār through the fifth and final chapter on ornament, Peruntēvaṉār at times departs significantly from the *Kāvyādarśa*, adding or refining categories to lend a particularly Buddhist tone to the set of poetic embellishments. Daṇḍin, for example, lists "that which possesses a mood or sentiment" (*rasavat*) as the eighteenth of his ornaments, and provides examples of eight different varieties, beginning with "the erotic" (*śṛṅgāra*).[75] Peruntēvaṉār translates or transliterates each of the eight—labeled "taste" (*cuvai*)—into Tamil,[76] yet adds a ninth not included in the *Kāvyādarśa*: "the peaceful" or "the quiescent" (Tamil cāntam, Sanskrit śānta), a category of aesthetic experience perhaps first introduced into Sanskrit literary theory, as discussed in chapter 1, by Buddhist and Jain authors. The commentator quotes only a single verse from the *Tirukkuṟaḷ* as an example of "the peaceful":[77]

> How can he whose own life has known pain
> inflict pain on the lives of [other] human beings?

There is little evidence to suggest that including this ninth among the varieties of aesthetic experience is simply a regional or Tamil tradition. Not only does Daṇḍin's *Kāvyādarśa* not include the peaceful, but the twelfth-century Tamil rendering of Daṇḍin's text as an independent treatise, the *Taṇṭiyalaṅkāram*, also lists only eight types of aesthetic awareness.[78] The inclusion of the peaceful as a ninth thus seems to constitute an innovation on the part of the commentator.[79] If the peaceful can, indeed, be identified as a creation of particularly Buddhist (or Jain) critical literary analysis, then the commentator's vision of a literary theory imbued with Buddhist values would seem to supersede the *Vīracōḻiyam*'s explicit assertion that it "explains [the nature of poetic embellishment] according to the statements of Taṇṭi" (taṇṭi coṉṉa karai mali nūliṉ paṭiyē uraippaṉ).[80] Like the *Tolkāppiyam* theme of the gift discussed previously, Daṇḍin's theory of poetic ornamentation can be redefined, revised, and expanded to accommodate the ideals and values of Buddhist literary culture. Grammatical and poetic theory become a means of expressing Buddhist sentiments, of imagining a community of Buddhist readers and listeners bound together by shared literary and ethical values.

Peruntēvaṉār's use of a verse from the *Tirukkuṟaḷ* to illustrate the peaceful as one of nine types of aesthetic experience signals yet another aspect of the commentator's imagining of Buddhist community through literature and literary culture: the ethical or moral vision constructed through seemingly disparate poetic fragments. As discussed previously, the commentary on the *Vīracōḻiyam* gathers together a sizable collection of Tamil Buddhist verses devoted to stories of or references to the Buddha's past lives; such references tend to emphasize the compassionate qualities of the Buddha-to-be, his selfless acts of giving, teaching, and healing. The Buddha-to-be redefines, in the offering of his own blood to the thirsty supplicants "who were without love," the meaning of heroic giving in Tamil literary culture. Yet the commentary often refers to texts not explicitly Buddhist in tone, theme, or teaching, as in the commentary on verse 173 cited previously or in the citation from the *Tirukkuṟaḷ* to illustrate the quiescent under verse 168. The *Tirukkuṟaḷ*, a text of more than 1,300 "moral epigrams"[81] that may or may not be explicitly Buddhist, for example (as discussed in chapter 1), is cited some seventy-two times by the commentator on the *Vīracōḻiyam*, and the *Nālaṭiyār*, a ninth-century book of "moral maxims" often assumed to be Jain,[82] is quoted a number of times, as are several more obscure but similar texts associated with religious communities other than the Buddhist. If Peruntēvaṉār means to imagine a literary culture and religious community explicitly made Buddhist through association with the language of Avalōkitaṉ, why are these texts whose specific communal associations remain unclear cited so many times in the *Vīracōḻiyam* commentary?

One possibility may be that, given the very nature of a text such as the *Tirukkuṟaḷ* as moral maxim or moral epigram, the careful selection of specific verses contributes to the commentator's overall ethical vision. Of the seventy-two quotations from the *Tirukkuṟaḷ* provided by Peruntēvaṉār, for example, a substantial majority (fifty-two) are taken not from the portion of the *Kuṟaḷ* that deals with erotic love (kāmam) but from the first two sections of the text that address the themes of virtue (Tamil aṟam, Sanskrit dharma) and wealth and power (Tamil poruḷ, Sanskrit artha). Of the twenty quotations drawn from the *Kuṟaḷ*'s discussion of erotic love, sixteen are employed to illustrate Daṇḍin's/Peruntēvaṉār's theory of poetic ornament. The effect of such use of *Tirukkuṟaḷ* verses on the nature of love is primarily twofold. First and most obviously, the commentator's selections highlight the pain and anguish of love—rather than its rapturous joys—as envisioned by the *Kuṟaḷ*, particularly in the context of chaste or wedded love (kaṟpu). As an example of the ornament expressing a nonliteral exchange of ideas or things (Tamil parimāṟṟam, Sanskrit parivṛtti), for example, Peruntēvaṉār quotes verse 1183 from the *Tirukkuṟaḷ* section dealing with the pallor (pacalai) brought about by the separation of husband and wife:

> He took [my] beauty and shame
> and gave [me] in exchange [only] sickness and pallor.[83]

The anguish of separation is again the focus of the commentator's illustration of the expression of objection or denial (Tamil *taṭaimoḻi*, glossed by Peruntēvaṉār under verse 151 as "*ākkēpam* [Sanskrit *ākṣepa*] according to Taṇṭiyār").[84] Here, the verse quoted is *Tirukkuṟaḷ*, 1151:

> Tell me only if he is not going;
> of quick return tell [only] those who can survive [such sorrow].[85]

In addition to this emphasis on love as a source of human anguish, the commentator's examples also imbue the various ornaments with sentiments of pain and suffering that contradict directly Daṇḍin's examples of the same embellishments. The *Kāvyādarśa*, for example, illustrates the nonliteral exchange of ideas or things (parivṛtti) not with a verse of grief but with a striking image of kingly glory in battle:

Oh king, having struck blows with your sword,
your arm has captured the long-held and lotus-pale glory of this earth's princes.[86]

Of the more than twenty types of expressions of objection or denial (ākṣepa) described by Daṇḍin (and not elaborated on in the *Vīracōḻiyam* or its commentary), the Sanskrit examples again differ quite significantly from those found in the Tamil text. Rather than highlighting the miseries and anguish of love, Daṇḍin focuses on the pleasures and amusements of erotic attraction, from:

With his five flower arrows, the god of love conquered the entire world;
this is not possible, [but] such is the wondrous power of things![87]

to:

Oh my one of soft voice, why do you place a lotus [near] your ear?
Do you think that your glance will fail to attract me?[88]

In choosing so selectively from the *Tirukkuṟaḷ* such radically different examples of poetic ornamentation, in other words, the commentary on the *Vīracōḻiyam* imagines ordinary human or erotic love as a source of pain rather than joy, as a form of human attachment that leads only to suffering rather than the coy playfulness and happiness suggested by the Sanskrit model of poetic theory in practice. Ornamentation theory and *Tirukkuṟaḷ* example enable the commentator to refocus the Tamil tradition of literary love, to emphasize instead the ultimate pain caused by such worldly attachment.

The commentary's focus on the virtue (aṟam) and wealth (poruḷ) sections of the *Tirukkuṟaḷ* contributes even further to the moral vision of the text. The examples quoted stress, above all else, compassionate concern for others, particularly for the poor and suffering. *Tirukkuṟaḷ*, verse 230, quoted under *Vīracōḻiyam*, verse 112, as an example of a particular type of meter (*kuṟaḷ veṇpā*), for example, declares:

There is no greater pain than death,
but death is sweet if one has nothing to give [as alms to the poor].[89]

As yet another example of the same type of meter, the commentator quotes *Tirukkuṟaḷ*, verse 406, under *Vīracōḻiyam*, verse 125:

The ignorant are like an infertile field.
"They are," but [they] are without use.[90]

Again, as in the case of the love verses discussed previously, the bulk of the *Tirukkuṟaḷ* verses on virtue and wealth cited by the *Vīracōḻiyam* commentator are found in the section on poetic ornamentation, imbuing the poetic adornments with an ethical sense not found in Daṇḍin's work. Among the several types of expression of contradictory properties in a single subject (Sanskrit virodha), Daṇḍin cites as an example:

Who would not be stricken by a woman's body that is of thin waist,
ample thighs, red lips, black eyes, flattened navel, and raised breasts?[91]

As an example of the Tamil equivalent (muraṇ), Peruntēvaṉār quotes a verse (*Tirukkuṟaḷ*, 222) of strikingly different sentiment:

> Even if one is without blame, it is bad to receive;
> even if there is no heaven, it is good to give.[92]

In discussing generally the nature of metaphor (Tamil *uruvakam*, Sanskrit *rūpaka*) under *Vīracōḻiyam*, verse 150, the commentator offers as examples *Tirukkuṟaḷ*, verse 42:

> The householder is protection
> for the ascetics, the poor, and the dead.[93]

and verse 10:

> Only those who clasp the feet of the lord
> cross the ocean of births.[94]

As mentioned before, such moral imperatives to help the poor and the ascetic wanderer, to "clasp the feet of the lord," stand in sharp contrast to Daṇḍin's many examples of metaphor with a singularly erotic flavor, such as:

> Anyone who is bewildered by your face,
> its cheeks red with drink and its eyes [like] lotuses tender with affection,
> is made passionate.[95]

Such a large number of quotations from the *Tirukkuṟaḷ*, in conjunction with verses on similar themes drawn from the *Nālaṭiyār*[96] and other medieval texts of comparable nature,[97] serve to imbue the literary theory outlined in the *Vīracōḻiyam*, and particularly the theory of poetic ornamentation, with moral sensibilities quite foreign to the examples given by Daṇḍin in his *Kāvyādarśa*. In drawing on texts that may or may not be Buddhist, but carefully selected parts of which are in a sense made Buddhist through their association with the language of Avalōkitaṉ and their close proximity in the commentary to verses of devotion to the Buddha, the commentator lays claim to a larger part of Tamil literary culture as compatible with his vision of Buddhist community. In turn, the *Vīracōḻiyam* and its commentary clearly envision a Tamil-speaking Buddhist community living alongside other sectarian communities in the South Indian religious landscape. The moral maxims of the *Tirukkuṟaḷ* that Peruntēvaṉār chooses to highlight are thoroughly in keeping with the compassionate nature of the Buddha emphasized in the more avowedly Buddhist quotations. The commentary, in imagining a Buddhist community through literature that includes works such as the *Tirukkuṟaḷ* and the *Nālaṭiyār*, becomes a site to reflect on issues far wider than mere grammatical categories or poetic theory. Peruntēvaṉār's gloss on the *Vīracōḻiyam* considers not only the nature of the Buddha and his miraculous deeds in his former lives but the ideal ethical or moral orientation of the ordinary person. Peruntēvaṉār, in short, transforms Daṇḍin's discussion of poetic ornamentation into a meditation on the proper way to live. The technology of literary culture becomes a medium for envisioning a community of readers with an explicitly Buddhist devotional orientation and set of values in the context of a complex sectarian and literary milieu in which Buddhists can find common cause with others in the realm of ethics, of moral responsibility.

Peruntēvaṉār embarks on his commentarial project of gathering together a corpus of Buddhist poetry that best exemplifies the pure Tamil of Avalōkitaṉ, made compatible with northern language, in an era when other religious communities in the Tamil-speaking region of southern India were similarly anthologizing and formalizing their poetic corpus. According to the fourteenth-century narrative of Umāpati Civācāriyar, the *Tirumuṟaikaṇṭapurāṇam*, the "Story of the Discovery to the *Tirumuṟai*," the songs of the celebrated Śaiva saints Appar, Campantar, and Cuntarar and others had largely been lost by the time of the eleventh-century Cōḻa king, Apayakulacēkaraṉ. At the insistence of the king, a young Śaiva devotee known as Nampi Āṇṭār Nampi discovers the lost texts, half-eaten by white ants, in a sealed room in the great temple to Śiva at Citamparam, and the king oversees their arrangement into the volumes of the Śaiva canon, the *Tirumuṟai*.[98] Whether or not one reads the *Tirumuṟaikaṇṭapurāṇam* as a historically accurate narrative, in claiming a specific set of Śaiva devotional hymns as very ancient and as associated with the important temple at Citamparam, certainly Umāpati himself, as Karen Prentiss argues, "attempt[s] to create a canon of Tamil devotional literature to Śiva."[99] Similar processes of formalizing a poetic corpus can be seen in the stories surrounding the Vaiṣṇava *Nālāyirativyappirapantam*, "The Holy Collection of Four Thousand Verses." According to the thirteenth-century hagiography, the *Guruparamparāprabhāvam*, "The Splendor of the Succession of Teachers," the poems of the Vaiṣṇava poet-saints were rediscovered and anthologized in the tenth century by the first teacher (*ācārya*) of the community, Nātamuṉi.[100] Both the Śaiva and Vaiṣṇava sources, by narrating stories of rediscovery of ancient texts and reincorporation into the community, attempt to define that community through the formalization or canonization of a particular poetic corpus. Like the commentary on the *Vīracōḻiyam*, in other words, the gathering together of a body of devotional poetry signals the imagining of religious community through literature. Peruntēvaṉār's commentary, like the *Tirumuṟai* attributed to Nampi Āṇṭār Nampi and the *Nālayirativyappirapantam* attributed to Nātamuṉi, fixes a poetic vision to be passed down from generation to generation as the commentary is read and studied. Although the sectarian communities surrounding the Śaiva and Vaiṣṇava anthologies have survived into the modern period, the Tamil-speaking Buddhist community has not; without a living community to read and preserve the anthology of poetry imagined and enacted by Peruntēvaṉār, the poetic fragments in the written commentary are all that remain.

Given the fact that only two Buddhist texts in Tamil have survived in manuscript form, what is perhaps most interesting to note about the anthology of verse assembled by the commentator on the *Vīracōḻiyam*, especially given the legitimating power of age in the stories of the Śaiva and Vaiṣṇava collections, is the complete absence of the *Maṇimēkalai*. Not counted among the rare and difficult poetic works such as the *Kuṇṭalakēci* nor even quoted as an example of the meter (akaval or āciriyam) in which it is composed, the *Maṇimēkalai* is a work unknown to or simply discounted by the commentator on the *Vīracōḻiyam*. Whatever the historical reasons for Peruntēvaṉār's silence in this regard might be—whether the *Maṇimēkalai* was simply a minor work of little importance that has assumed relatively greater significance for scholars today, whether the text was simply lost or forgotten by the eleventh century, or whether the commentator knew of the text but simply rejected it as suitable illustration for some historically unrecoverable reason—what is clear is that the vision of Buddhist community imagined through the technology of literary culture laid out in the *Vīracōḻiyam*, and both expanded on and substantiated by the commentary on the text, does not include the reading community of the *Maṇimēkalai*. Although both texts are composed in Tamil, both are the products of multilingual and highly sophisticated literary cultures, and both are clearly

Buddhist, the *Maṇimēkalai* and the *Vīracōḻiyam* and its commentary anticipate different audiences and imagine different Buddhist communities in different ways.

Yet despite this seemingly sharp disjuncture or discontinuity between the two texts, both the *Maṇimēkalai* and the *Vīracōḻiyam* emphasize similar themes in drawing out their unique visions of the community of Tamil-speakers committed to the teachings and moral example of the Buddha. Although the *Maṇimēkalai* as ornate poetic narrative obviously represents a wholly different genre of text than does the theoretical *Vīracōḻiyam* and its commentary, both texts repeatedly emphasize devotion to the Buddha, and to the eminently moral deeds of the Buddha-to-be, as the central focus of Buddhist life. Both texts also focus intensely on the nature of the ideal human life, drawing on even those Tamil literary texts that are not explicitly Buddhist (e.g., the *Tirukkuṟaḷ*) but that advocate a sense of moral responsibility that can easily fit within a Buddhist framework. In quoting such non-Buddhist Tamil literary works, both the *Maṇimēkalai* and the *Vīracōḻiyam* align themselves with other sectarian communities of similar moral commitment, imagining their respective Buddhist communities living in a religiously diverse world. In the multilingual literary culture of Tamil-speaking South India, whether in the sixth century or the eleventh, ornate and sophisticated literary work provides a powerful medium for articulating a distinct religious identity in a complex sectarian environment, for creating a space for the followers of the Buddha in that diverse and competitive religious world.

Conclusion

Following Peruntēvaṉār's commentary on the *Vīracōḻiyam*, the Buddhist literary record in Tamil falls silent. Although various Buddhist texts continue to be remembered as illustrations of particular moral maxims,[1] examples of difficult and complex poetry,[2] and instances of heretical religious doctrine,[3] no new Buddhist compositions in Tamil appear to have been produced after the eleventh century; at least no such compositions have survived. Buddhist characters continue to make appearances as ill-fated interlocutors as late as the seventeenth and early eighteenth centuries in the "historical" manuscripts composed for and collected by Mackenzie. Several of these manuscripts, for example, detail the deportation of Buddhists from the Tamil country to Burma and Sri Lanka.[4] Coḷiya monks continue to compose in Pāli,[5] and stray references exist in other parts of the Buddhist world to monks who hail from Kāñcīpuram.[6] Bronze Buddhas were produced at Nākapaṭṭiṉam perhaps as late as the seventeenth century.[7] It is quite impossible, however, to infer from such isolated literary references and evidence of artistic manufacture the existence of any true Buddhist community in the Tamil-speaking region of southernmost India.

Yet despite this frustratingly incomplete historical record, the *Maṇimēkalai* and the *Vīracōḻiyam* with its commentary have much to tell us about the communities of Tamil-speaking Buddhists at two distinct moments in time. In the sixth-century literary culture of the *Maṇimēkalai* and that of the *Vīracōḻiyam* some five or six centuries later, both formal literary expression and poetic theory provided a sophisticated arena for the articulation, defense, and contestation of religious identities, ideals, and values. As creatively erudite works of literature—the *Maṇimēkalai* an ornate poetic narrative and the *Vīracōḻiyam* and its commentary theoretical discourses about the nature of literary language—each text concerns itself with envisioning a place for Buddhism in a religiously and linguistically diverse milieu.

As chapters 1 through 3 argue, the *Maṇimēkalai* constitutes a compelling literary whole that both reveals something of its historical audience and itself imagines a Buddhist community yet to come, gathered at the feet of the future Buddha whose earthly birth will take place in a time near at hand. Through careful consideration of the narrative as a literary work produced in the context of a diverse South Indian literary culture, one can infer a reading community for the text composed of literary connoisseurs fluent in languages beyond Tamil, well versed in the world views and literatures of various religious communities, and engaged in the project of articulating religious identity through the medium of sophisticated poetry. Through its focus on the principal role played by the central character's begging bowl, the text's emphasis on the coming of the future Buddha and those moral values that will enable one to see that future Buddha clearly emerge. Participating in wider, early medieval Asian patterns of redrawing the Buddhist world, relocating its centers away from the cities of northern India associated with Gautama Buddha, the *Maṇimēkalai* is ultimately a forward-looking text, concerned with evoking a vision of compassion and care that will lead its audience to participate in that glorious community yet to come.

Chapters 4 and 5 address a very different sort of text, one that at first glance might seem to convey precious little about the nature of Buddhist community in the Tamil-speaking region. Both the *Vīracōḻiyam* and its commentary construct a theoretical vision of a multilingual literary culture, and that literary culture combining Tamil and Sanskrit grammatical and poetic theory is claimed explicitly for Buddhism. Tamil is thus elevated from the level of local literary option to that of translocal prestige language of learning, and the *Vīracōḻiyam* claims as its source of authority the figure of the great Buddha-to-be, Avalokiteśvara. In further carving out a place for Buddhism in the Tamil religious and literary landscape of competing sectarian communities, the commentary on the *Vīracōḻiyam* effectively anthologizes fragments of what once must have been a considerable corpus of Buddhist narrative and devotional poetry composed in Tamil. Expanding on the *Vīracōḻiyam*'s project by substantiating the language of the Buddha-to-be with Tamil literary examples, the commentary envisions a community of readers who share a profound devotion to the Buddha and his many former lives, as well as a moral vision of human kindness and self-sacrificing compassion for the welfare of others. In drawing from texts that are not explicitly Buddhist for many of his moral illustrations, the commentator envisions this community of Buddhists as one among many religious groups in Tamil-speaking literary culture; in quoting so broadly, he both locates and reworks common ethical concerns and claims a part of the literary corpus in Tamil for Buddhism.

At one level, even these complete extant literary remains of Buddhism in the Tamil-speaking region are fragmentary. The commentary on the *Vīracōḻiyam*, by failing to cite even once the *Maṇimēkalai*, emphatically suggests that despite the historian's hope that the two texts might speak to one another, the *Maṇimēkalai* and the *Vīracōḻiyam* do not belong to a single or continuous textual community. Instead, each envisions a reading community unique to its own historical context. Each text reveals a distinct moment in the way Tamil-speaking Buddhist communities represented and imagined themselves in diverse religious and linguistic landscapes.

Yet, at another level, one can also discern certain thematic threads running through the *Maṇimēkalai*, the *Vīracōḻiyam*, and the *Vīracōḻiyam* commentary, shared literary concerns that perhaps speak to common strategies of imagining a place for Buddhism in a diverse religious environment that was dominated by sectarian communities other than the Buddhist. Both texts, for example, quote the celebrated *Tirukkuṟaḷ*, a text whose precise sectarian affiliation remains unclear. Although the verses cited at *Maṇimēkalai*, xxii.59–61, extolling the powers of the virtuous woman and ascribed to "the poet without falsehood" are not among the *Vīracōḻiyam* commentary's numerous quotations from the same text, the fact that both appeal to the moral authority of the *Kuṟaḷ* suggests that important non-Buddhist works in Tamil could be called on in the project of imagining a place for Buddhism in a diverse and competitive milieu. Buddhist ideals and principles, such quotations argue, are thoroughly built on classical Tamil literary tradition, very much in keeping with the message of the *Tirukkuṟaḷ* text (and others like it quoted in the *Vīracōḻiyam* commentary) that have long held a place of honor in Tamil-speaking literary culture.

That the *Kuṟaḷ* is, in fact, a text obviously concerned with conveying a sense of moral responsibility or proper ethical conduct also points to another common strategy shared by the *Maṇimēkalai* and the *Vīracōḻiyam* commentary: to imagine a place for Buddhism in the Tamil-speaking region through emphasis on care and compassion rather than through insistence on exclusive devotion to the figure of the Buddha. Although both texts are suffused with an ethos of devotion to the Buddha's many glorious qualities, from the hymns of praise put in the mouths of the narrative text's main characters to the many fragments of devotional hymns quoted in the commentary, each text envisions a Buddhist community living among sectarian groups with other devotional affiliations. What Buddhism can offer in such a context of religious diversity, both the *Maṇimēkalai* and the *Vīracōḻiyam* suggest, is a profound ethic of compassion for others that extends beyond the maxims of the *Tirukkuṟaḷ* or the images of generous Caṅkam kings. The king of Pukār in the *Maṇimēkalai*, for example, can remain a follower of Viṣṇu; what is important is that he convert his royal prison into an abode for ascetics. The queen can grieve for her murdered son, but she is forgiven for her attempts to kill the heroine and is eventually led to see the virtue in showing compassion to all beings. Likewise, the *Vīracōḻiyam* commentator asks that his royal patron's Hindu god shower blessings upon the kingdom, but at the same time, through illustrative example, provides an image of kingship absolutely self-sacrificing in its generosity.

Given the consummately literary nature of these texts, the *Maṇimēkalai* and the *Vīracōḻiyam* also suggest something of the power of the aesthetic in the shaping of their religious visions. Close attention to each text reveals aesthetic concerns to be absolutely central to the articulation of religious identity. The *Maṇimēkalai*, for example, draws on both the Sanskrit and Tamil theories of emotional experience to evoke a heightened sense of pathos or empathy in its audience; that empathy for the suffering of others, cultivated through the application of poetic/aesthetic theory and embodied in the character of the wondrous begging bowl, becomes the means for winning the right to participate in the liberating community of the future. In the case of the *Vīracōḻiyam* and its commentary, discourse about the nature of poetic language and its application is appropriated by the Buddha-to-be Avalōkitaṉ and made an explicitly Buddhist discourse; Daṇḍin's theory of poetic ornamentation is transformed by Peruntēvaṉār's commentary into an ethical reflection on the right way to live in the world among other human beings. In each of these texts, literary and aesthetic theory express religious sentiments and allegiances. To engage in the aesthetic pleasure of reading or listening to the text is to imagine two distinctly Buddhist visions of the world, visions of Buddhist community flourishing in a diverse landscape of languages and sectarian commitments.

Despite the lack of hard historical data concerning the audiences of the *Maṇimēkalai* or the *Vīracōḻiyam*, the consideration of these complex and sophisticated products of literary culture as profoundly religious expressions hopefully suggests new avenues for the pursuit of historical work in South Asian religions. From close readings of the texts, done with eyes consciously focused on the literary culture in which each is embedded, one can begin to infer something of the reading community of the text in a historically responsible way. Literary works such as the *Maṇimēkalai*, the *Vīracōḻiyam*, and the *Vīracōḻiyam* commentary attest to specific moments in the history of the imagination that are crucial to the articulation and enactment of religious community. Ornate poetic narrative, even poetic theory itself, draws attention to various kinds of cultural practices in the absence of archaeological or inscriptional evidence and offers fresh insight into the long and complex historical processes of debate, selection, transmission, and recreation that constitute religious community.

Notes

Introduction

1. Fred Clothey, *The Many Faces of Murukaṉ: The History and Meaning of a South Indian God*, Religion and Society, no. 6 (New York: Mouton, 1978), 116.

2. Little is known about the Ājīvikas, except for what can be deduced from often derogatory references to the tradition in non-Ājīvika texts. They are most commonly characterized as rejecting the ubiquitous Indic conception of karma in favor of a doctrine of "fate" (*niyati*). The most complete study of this tradition is A. L. Basham's *History and Doctrines of the Ājīvikas: A Vanished Indian Religion* (London: Luzac, 1951; Reprint, Delhi: Motilal Banarsidass, 1981). For a discussion of the Ājīvikas as they appear in classical and medieval Tamil literature, see R. Vijayalakshmy, *Tamiḻakattil Ācīvakarkaḷ* (Madras: International Insitute of Tamil Studies, 1988).

3. The term appears in a number of places, including the ninth-century Vēḷvikuṭi copperplate inscription; see Robert Sewell, *The Historical Inscriptions of Southern India*, ed. S. Krishnaswami Aiyangar, Madras University Historical Series, no. 5 (Madras: University of Madras, 1932), 21.

4. See Iravatham Mahadevan, *Corpus of Tamil-Brāhmī Inscriptions* (Madras: Tamilnadu State Department of Archaeology, 1970).

5. Caṅkam literature, literature of the "community" or "assembly" (Sanskrit *saṅgha*), refers to a collection of six anthologies (*tokai*) and nine long poems (*pāṭṭu*) composed in Tamil during the early centuries of the common era. Addressing themes of love and war, these poems are noted for their unique style and aesthetic, and deal largely with nonreligious, or secular, topics. For a brief overview of the tradition, see Kamil V. Zvelebil, *Lexicon of Tamil Literature*, Handbuch der Orientalistik, Zweite Abteilung: Indien, vol. 9, ed. J. Bronkhorst (Leiden: E. J. Brill, 1995), 108–110.

6. Richard H. Davis, "The Story of the Disappearing Jains: Retelling the Śaiva-Jain Encounter in Medieval South India," in *Open Boundaries: Jain Communities and Cultures in Indian History*, ed. John E. Cort (Albany: State University of New York Press, 1998), 214.

7. K. A. Nilakanta Sastri, *Development of Religion in South India* (Madras: Orient Longman, 1963), for example, begins his survey with what he terms the "integration of cults" in the "classical," or "Caṅkam," age, then describes the rise of the devotional (bhakti) movements, and proceeds through the development of Hindu "religious institutions" and the eventual rise of "reform and modern Hinduism." Throughout, he refers to both Buddhism and Jainism several times as "heretical creeds." More recently, Indira Viswanathan Peterson, in her *Poems to Śiva: The Hymns of the Tamil Saints* (Princeton, N.J.: Princeton University Press, 1989), 11, notes in regard to the emergence of the first Śaiva devotional poets in the seventh century, "The mythology and cultural contexts of the Hindu gods were more congenial to the spirit of a new personal religion in the framework of Tamil civilization than Buddhism and Jainism could be."

8. Leslie C. Orr, "Jain and Hindu 'Religious Women' in Early Medieval Tamilnadu," in *Open Boundaries: Jain Communities and Cultures in Indian History*, ed. John E. Cort (Albany: State University of New York Press, 1998), 187–212. See also Orr, *Donors, Devotees, and Daugh-*

ters of God: Temple Women in Medieval Tamilnadu (New York: Oxford University Press, 2000).

9. James Ryan, "Erotic Excess and Sexual Danger in the *Cīvakacintāmaṇi*," in *Open Boundaries: Jain Communities and Cultures in Indian History*, ed. John E. Cort (Albany: State University of New York Press, 1998), 81. See also Ryan, "The 'Civakacintamani' in Historical Perspective" (Ph.D. Diss., University of California, Berkeley, 1985).

10. Paula Richman, *Women, Branch Stories, and Religious Rhetoric in a Tamil Buddhist Text*, Foreign and Comparative Studies/South Asia Series, no. 12 (Syracuse, N.Y.: Maxwell School of Citizenship and Public Affairs, Syracuse University, 1988).

11. Indira Viswanathan Peterson, "*Śramaṇas* against the Tamil Way: Jains as Others in Tamil Śaiva Literature," in *Open Boundaries: Jain Communities and Cultures in Indian History*, ed. John E. Cort (Albany: State University of New York Press, 1998), 173.

12. Richard Davis, "Disappearing Jains."

13. Ibid., 223.

14. Peter Schalk, "The Oldest Buddhist Artefacts Discovered in Tamiḻakam," in *Being Religious and Living Through the Eyes: Studies in Religious Iconography and Iconology: A Celebratory Publication in Honour of Professor Jan Bergman*, ed. Peter Schalk and Michael Strausberg, Acta Universitatis Upsaliensis: Historia Religionum, no. 14 (Uppsala, Sweden: Faculty of Theology, Uppsala University, 1998), 307–327; Schalk, "The Controversy About the Arrival of Buddhism in Tamiḻakam," *Temenos* 30 (1994):197–232; Schalk, "On the Beginning of Buddhism in Tamiḻakam," *Temenos* 29 (1993):157–163; and Schalk, "On the Beginning of Buddhism in Tamiḻakam," in *Studies in South Indian History and Culture: Professor V. R. Ramachandra Dikshitar Centenary Volume*, ed. R. Nagaswamy (Madras: V. R. Ramachandra Dikshitar Centenary Committee, 1977), 249–254. See also Schalk et al., *Pauttamum Tamiḻum: Inventory, Investigation and Interpretation of Sources Pertaining to Buddhism Among Tamiḻar in Pre-Colonial Tamiḻakam and Īḻam (Ilaṅkai)*, Acta Universitatis Upsaliensis: Historia Religionum, vol. 15 (Uppsala, Sweden: Uppsala University, 2001).

15. Schalk, "Oldest Buddhist Artefacts," 319–325.

16. See *Indian Archaeology: A Review* (New Delhi: Archaeological Survey of India) for 1961–1962 (26–27), 1962–1963 (13), 1963–1964 (20), 1964–1965 (24–25), 1965–1966 (24), 1969–1970 (35), 1970–1971 (32–35), and 1972–1973 (30, 32); R. Nagaswamy, *Kaveripoompattinam: A Guide* (Madras: State Department of Archaeology, Government of Tamilnadu, 1973); and R. Subrahmanyam, "Kañchīpuram Excavations," *Journal of the Andhra Historical Research Society* 34/1–4 (1974–1975):23–31. For the most exhaustive list of archaeological and artistic remains of Buddhism in Tamilnadu compiled to date, see K. Sivaramalingam, *Archaeological Atlas of the Antique Remains of Buddhism in Tamilnadu* (Madras: Institute of Asian Studies, 1997).

17. T. A. Gopinatha Rao, "Bauddha Vestiges in Kanchipuram," *Indian Antiquary* 44 (June 1915):127–129.

18. Schalk, "Oldest Buddhist Artefacts," 309–310.

19. Buddhadatta, *The Clarifier of Sweet Meaning (Madhuratthavilāsinī): Commentary on the Chronicle of the Buddhas (Buddhavaṁsa) by Buddhadatta Thera*, trans. I. B. Horner (London: Pali Text Society, 1978), 299; Buddhadatta, *Buddhadatta's Manuals, or Summaries of the Abhidhamma: Abhidhammāvatāra and Rūpārūpavibhāga*, vol. 1, ed. A. P. Buddhadatta (London: Humphrey Milford, for Pali Text Society, 1915), 138.

20. See, for example, Dhammapāla, *Paramatthadīpanī: Theragāthā-Aṭṭhakathā, the Commentary of Dhammapālācariya*, vol. 3, ed. F. Woodward (London: Luzac, for Pali Text Society, 1959), 210, and Dhammapāla, *Therīgāthā-Aṭṭhakathā (Paramatthadīpanī VI)*, ed. William Pruitt (Oxford: Pali Text Society, 1998), 273.

21. K. R. Norman, *Pāli Literature: Including Canonical Literature in Prakrit and Sanskrit of All the Hīnayāna Schools of Buddhism*, A History of Indian Literature, vol. 7, fascicle 2 (Wiesbaden: Otto Harrassowitz, 1983), 134.

22. R. A. L. H. Gunawardana, *Robe and Plough: Monasticism and Economic Interest in Early Medieval Sri Lanka*, Association for Asian Studies: Monographs and Papers, no. 35 (Tuscon: University of Arizona Press, for Association for Asian Studies, 1979), 263.

23. Buddhaghosa, *Manorathapūraṇī: Commentary on the Aṅguttara Nikāya*, vol. 5, ed. Hermann Kopp et al. (London: Luzac, for Pali Text Society, 1956), 98.

24. These medieval references to Tamil-speaking South India are taken up for further discussion in chapter 4.

25. Xuanzang [Hsuan-tsang], *Si-Yu-Ki: Buddhist Records of the Western World*, vol. 2, trans. Samuel Beal (London: Kegan Paul, Trench, Trubner, 1884; Reprint, Delhi: Motilal Banarsidass, 1981), 227–234.

26. Ibid., 229.

27. "Buddha Relic of the 12th Century Found," *Motilal Banarsidass Newsletter: A Monthly of Indological Bibliography* 21/12 (1999):9.

28. T. Ramachandran, "The Nagapattinam and Other Buddhist Bronzes in the Madras Government Museum," *Bulletin of the Madras Government Museum* 7/1 (1954): 1–150.

29. Such sources of information on the Buddhist presence in Nākapaṭṭiṉam are taken up for further discussion in chapter 3.

30. The inscription is located to the right of the inner sanctum of the Ādivarāha cave temple; see A. Krishna Sastri, *Two Statues of Pallava Kings and Five Pallava Inscriptions in a Rock-Temple at Mahabalipuram*, Memoirs of the Archaeological Survery of India, no. 26 (Calcutta: Government of India, Central Publication Branch, 1926), 5.

31. Four lines are quoted in the commentary on the ninth-century Jain poetic narrative known as the *Nīlakēci*, verse 190; A. Chakravarti, ed. and trans., *Neelakesi: The Original Text and the Commentary of Samaya-Divakara-Vamana-Muni*, vol. 2 (Kumbakonam, India: By the author, 1936), 71.

32. Nineteen verses of the text are preserved in the fifteenth-century poetic anthology known as *Puṟattiraṭṭu*; see I. Iḷaṅkumaraṉ, ed., *Puṟattiraṭṭu* (Tinnevelly: South India Saiva Siddhanta Works Publishing Society, 1972).

33. H. C. Norman, ed., *The Commentary on the Dhammapada*, vol. 2 (London: Henry Frowde, for Pali Text Society, 1906–1915; Reprint, London: Luzac, for Pali Text Society, 1970), 217–227; Dhammapāla, *Therīgāthā-Aṭṭhakathā*, 97–106.

34. See Caṇmukacuntara Mutaliyār, ed., *Civañāṉacittiyār parapakkam mūlamum Cattuvappirakācar uraiyum* (Madras: By the editor, 1894), 83, 117.

35. Ibid., 84.

36. Totagamuvē Śrī Rāhula "speaks of the *Ḍemala Jātaka-gaṭapada*," a Tamil glossary on the Jātakas, in his *Pañcikāpradīpiya*; see K. D. Somadasa, *Catalogue of the Hugh Nevill Collection of Sinhalese Manuscripts in the British Library*, vol. 4 (London: British Library, 1990), 373.

37. Richman's contention that the *Maṇimēkalai* was written for an audience "relatively ignorant of Buddhism" (*Branch Stories*, 10) is taken up for further discussion in chapter 1.

38. Steven Collins, *Nirvana and Other Buddhist Felicities: Utopias of the Pali Imaginaire*, Cambridge Studies in Religious Traditions, no. 12 (Cambridge: Cambridge University Press, 1998).

39. José Ignacio Cabezón and Roger R. Jackson, ed., " Editor's Introduction," in *Tibetan Literature: Studies in Genre*, (Ithaca, N.Y.: Snow Lion, 1996), 17.

40. Vinay Dharwadker, "Orientalism and the Study of Indian Literature," in *Orientalism and the Postcolonial Predicament: Perspectives on South Asia*, ed. Carol A. Breckenridge and Peter van der Veer (Delhi: Oxford University Press, 1994), 160–163.

41. Ibid., 177–180.

42. Brian Stock, *The Implications of Literacy* (Princeton, N.J.: Princeton University Press, 1983), 522–524.

43. Benedict Anderson, *Imagined Communities: Reflections on the Origin and Spread of Nationalism*, 2d ed. (London: Verso, 1991).

44. Sheldon Pollock, "The Cosmopolitan Vernacular," *Journal of Asian Studies* 57/1 (1998): 9.

Chapter 1

1. For a general discussion of the rediscovery of Tamil literature in the late nineteenth and early twentieth centuries, see Kamil V. Zvelebil, *Companion Studies to the History of Tamil Literature*, Handbuch der Orientalistik, Zweite Abteilung: Indien, no. 5, ed. Jan Gonda (Leiden: E. J. Brill, 1992), 144–222.

2. U. V. Cāminātaiyar, *The Story of My Life: An Autobiography of Dr. U. V. Swaminatha Iyer*, vol. 2, trans. Kamil V. Zvelebil (Madras: Institute of Asian Studies, 1994), 515–526, describes vividly his efforts to decode the meaning of the *Maṇimēkalai*.

3. References to the text of the *Maṇimēkalai* are drawn from Cāttaṉār, *Maṇimēkalai*, ed. U. V. Cāminātaiyar (Madras: Mahamahopadhyaya Dr. U. V. Swaminathaiyer Library, 1981), and Cāttaṉār, *Maṇimēkalai*, ed. N. M. Vēṅkaṭacāmi Nāṭṭār and A. C. Turaicāmi Piḷḷai (Tinnevelly: South India Saiva Siddhanta Works Publishing Society, 1992). In cases where the texts are in disagreement, I follow Cāminātaiyar. For an exhaustive list of the published editions of the *Maṇimēkalai* to date, see Kamil V. Zvelebil, *Lexicon of Tamil Literature*, Handbuch der Orientalistik, Zweite Abteilung: Indien, vol. 9, ed. J. Bronkhorst (Leiden: E. J. Brill, 1995) 411-412.

4. So described in line 97 of the preface to the text.

5. *Kātai*, at times *katai*: from the Sanskrit *kathā*, meaning story or narrative, or *gāthā*, meaning poem or division of a poem containing a narrative. See *Tamil Lexicon*, vol. 2 (Madras: University of Madras, 1982), 864.

6. The *Maṇimēkalai* has been translated and summarized many times over the past century, beginning with Julien Vinson's partial translation and paraphrase into French, *Légendes Bouddhistes et Djainas: Traduites du Tamoul*, 2 vols. (Paris: Maisonneuve, 1900). For a list of translations to date, see Zvelebil, *Lexicon of Tamil Literature*, 412–413. Zvelebil does not mention the recent translation, Cāttaṉār, *Manimekhalai: Girdle of Gems*, trans. K. Guruswamy and S. Srinivasan (Madras: Mahamahopadhyaya Dr. U. V. Swaminathaiyer Library, 1994).

7. Paula Richman, *Women, Branch Stories, and Religious Rhetoric in a Tamil Buddhist Text*, Foreign and Comparative Studies/South Asia Series, no. 12 (Syracuse, N.Y.: Maxwell School of Citizenship and Public Affairs, Syracuse University, 1988), 2–3, provides an explanation of the aptness of this term as well as a table outlining the principal "branch stories" and their relation to the contents of the main narrative.

8. Umberto Eco, *Six Walks in the Fictional Woods*, Charles Eliot Norton Lectures, 1993 (Cambridge: Harvard University Press, 1994), 13–15.

9. Richman, *Branch Stories*, 157–158, provides a concise summary of the various positions on this question. The pairing of poet and king perhaps suggests a context of royal patronage for both the *Maṇimēkalai* and the *Cilappatikāram*; the relationship of the two texts and the contents of their respective prefaces is taken up for discussion in chapter 2.

10. Zvelebil, *Lexicon of Tamil Literature*, 128.

11. E. S. Varatarāja Ayyar, *Tamiḻ ilakkiya varalāṟu* (Madras: Aṇṇāmalaip Palkalaik Kaḻakam, 1957), 148. As Richman, *Branch Stories*, 160, correctly points out, early dating is characteristic "among Tamil scholars of a more traditional bent."

12. Shu Hikosaka, *Buddhism in Tamilnadu: A New Perspective* (Madras: Institute of Asian Studies, 1989), 93–94.

13. A. Vēluppiḷḷai, "Historical Background of the *Maṇimēkalai* and Indigenization of Buddhism," in *A Buddhist Woman's Path to Enlightenment: Proceedings of a Workshop on the Tamiḻ Narrative*

Maṇimēkalai, *Uppsala University, May 25–29, 1995*, Acta Universitatis Upsaliensis: Historica Religionum, vol. 13, ed. Peter Schalk (Uppsala, Sweden: Uppsala University, 1997), 53–94.

14. Rendering the *Maṇimēkalai* a post-Dignāga or seventh-century text. See, for example, S. Kuppuswami Sastri, "Problems of Identity in the Cultural History of Ancient India," *Journal of Oriental Research* 1/2 (1927):191–201; K. G. Sesha Aiyar, "The Date of Maṇimēkalai," *Journal of Oriental Research* 1/4 (1927):321–329; and Hermann Jacobi, "Über das Alter der *Maṇimēkhalai*," in *Kleine Schriften*, vol. 2, ed. Bernhard Kolver (Wiesbaden: Franz Steiner Verlag GMBH, 1970), 293–310.

15. S. N. Kandaswamy, *Buddhism as Expounded in Maṇimēkalai* (Annamalainagar, India: Annamalai University, 1978), 29–74, epitomizes this approach, although he also relies on linguistic evidence (see later). After a convincing analysis of the phonemic, grammatical, semantic, and lexical changes evident in the *Maṇimēkalai*, when compared to classical Caṅkam poetic language (5–19), Kandaswamy launches into a lengthy discussion of dating based on the relative presence or absence of such things as the name Akattiyaṉ (Agastya; 20), "glimpses of Tantric Buddhism" (60), and the "theory of momentariness" (73).

16. *Tirukkuṟaḷ mūlamum Parimēlaḻakar uraiyum* (Tinnevelly: South India Saiva Siddhanta Works Publishing Society, 1991), verses 54–55, 24. The verses, as translated by P. S. Sundaram (*The Kural* [New York: Penguin, 1990], 24), read:

> What can excel a woman
> Who is rooted in chastity?
>
> She whose husband is her only God
> Says, "Rain" and it rains.

Richman (*Branch Stories*, 109–110) discusses this quotation at some length, noting the ambiguity of the verbal form *toḻaḷ*, literally "not worshipping." The correct interpretation of the verse, in the narrative context in which it is quoted, is debated. Does it imply "the rain will fall at the command of a woman who worships either (1) no other gods until she worships her husband or (2) no god except her husband" (109)? The significance of this quotation from the *Tirukkuṟaḷ* is taken up for further discussion in chapter 2.

17. Kandaswamy, *Buddhism*, 5–19. As noted previously, Kandaswamy's analysis of grammatical and morphophonemic variation clearly places the *Maṇimēkalai* after the Caṅkam poetic anthologies that date from the early centuries of the common era.

18. For an introduction to the *Tēvāram*, the poems of the first three Tamil Śaiva saints (Nāyaṉār, "leaders")—Appar, Cuntarar, and Campantar—see Indira Viswanathan Peterson, *Poems to Śiva: The Hymns of the Tamil Saints* (Princeton, N.J.: Princeton University Press, 1989).

19. Kamil V. Zvelebil, *The Smile of Murugan on Tamil Literature of South India* (Leiden: E. J. Brill, 1973), 13, discusses the "semantic shift" from akaval, meaning "call," "summon," or "song" to āciriyam (from Sanskrit *ācārya*), meaning "teaching," "sermon," or "explanation," as indicating, perhaps, a gradual shift from the oral, bardic poetry of the Caṅkam corpus to the more "learned *Kunstdichtung*" of the Buddhists and Jains.

20. Kamil V. Zvelebil, *Classical Tamil Prosody: An Introduction* (Madras: New Era, 1989), 47.

21. Ibid., 77.

22. Sheldon Pollock, review of *Genres litteraires en Inde*, ed. Nalini Balbir, *Journal of the American Oriental Society* 115/4 (1995):687.

23. Traditionally, the Sanskrit dramas *Raghuvaṁśa*, *Kumārasambhava*, *Śiśupālavadha*, *Kirātārjunīya*, and *Naiṣadha*.

24. Commentary on verse 387 in U. V. Cāminātaiyar, ed., *Naṉṉūl mūlamum Mayilainātar uraiyum* (Madras: Kabir, 1946; Reprint, Madras: Mahamahopadhyaya Dr. U. V. Swaminathaiyer Library 1995), 212.

25. Zvelebil, *Companion Studies*, 73, note 126. Richman, *Branch Stories*, 10, describes the "jewel" analogy learned even today by school children in Tamilnadu: Mother Tamil wears *Maṇimēkalai* as her jeweled girdle, *Cilappatikāram* as her anklet, *Vaḷaiyāpati* as her bangle, *Kuṇṭalakēci* as her earring, and *Cīvakacintāmaṇi* as her necklace.

26. *Encyclopedia of Tamil Literature*, s.v., vol. 1, "Literary Genres in Tamil: A Diachronic Study," by Annie Mrithulakumari Thomas, 343–347, provides a detailed discussion of the medieval treatises on literary genre (*pāṭṭiyal*). The traditional ninety-six poetic genres are also listed and the most important briefly discussed in Zvelebil, *Prosody*, 84–101.

27. Taṇṭi, *Taṇṭiyalaṅkāram Cuppiramaṇiyatēcikar uraiyuṭaṉ*, ed. K. Irāmaliṅkat Tampirāṉavarkaḷ (Tinnevelly: South India Saiva Siddhanta Works Publishing Society, 1938; Reprint, 1997). How closely the Tamil version follows the Sanskrit has been the subject of scholarly debate; for a summation of the various points of view, see Zvelebil, *Lexicon of Tamil Literature*, 653. For more on the relation of the Sanskrit work of Daṇḍin to its Tamil interpretations, see Anne Monius, "The Many Lives of Daṇḍin: The *Kāvyādarśa* in Sanskrit and Tamil," *International Journal of Hindu Studies* 4/2 (2000):1–37.

28. See Richman, *Branch Stories*, 158–160, for a discussion of the problems inherent in trying formally to assign the *Maṇimēkalai* to the Sanskrit-derived genre of ornate poetry (kāvya).

29. Richman, *Branch Stories*, 159.

30. For an introduction to the poetic themes of the classical Caṅkam poetic corpus as outlined in the earliest Tamil grammatical text, the *Tolkāppiyam*, see A. K. Ramanujan, *The Interior Landscape: Love Poems from a Classical Tamil Anthology* (Bloomington: Indiana University Press, 1967; Reprint, New Delhi: Oxford University Press, 1994), especially the "Afterward," 97–115; A. K. Ramanujan, *Poems of Love and War, from the Eight Anthologies and the Ten Long Poems of Classical Tamil* (New York: Columbia University Press, 1984); and Takanobu Takahashi, *Tamil Love Poetry and Poetics*, Brill's Indological Library, vol. 9, ed. Johannes Bronkhorst (Leiden: E. J. Brill, 1995).

31. Iḷaṅkō Aṭikaḷ, *Cilappatikāram mūlamum Arumpata uraiyum Aṭiyārkkunallār uraiyum*, ed. U. V. Cāminātaiyar (Madras: Mahamahopadhyaya Dr. U. V. Swaminathaiyer Library, 1978), 6–8.

32. As opposed to disconnected poems (*taṉicceyyuḷ*) collected into anthologies (tokai) and now known as the Caṅkam literary corpus. See Kamil V. Zvelebil, *Tamil Literature*, Handbuch der Orientalistik, Zweite Abteilung: Indien, vol. 2, no. 1, ed. Jan Gonda (Leiden: E. J. Brill, 1975), 110.

33. According to Vidya Dehejia, "The Persistence of Buddhism in Tamilnadu," *Marg* 39/4 (1988):55, Buddhist images continued to be produced at Nākapaṭṭiṉam as late as the seventeenth century.

34. Zvelebil, *Tamil Literature*, 22–23, provides an account of "the establishment and spread of this deplorable ideology." In his *Companion Studies*, 147, Zvelebil adds:

> Cāmināta Tēcikar (17th–18th cent.), in the commentary on the *Ilakkaṇakkottu* . . . condemns the following books as unnecessary, indeed inferior writings which one should not read wasting [*sic*] one's time: "*Cintāmaṇi, Cilappatikāram, Maṇimēkalai, Caṅkappāṭṭu, Koṅkuvēḷ mākkatai, Pattupāṭṭu, Eṭṭuttokai, Patiṉeṅkīḻkkaṇakku, Irāmaṉkatai, Nalaṉkatai, Ariccantiraṉ katai*, etc." This list virtually contains almost all the best achievements of Tamil literature! On the other hand, the names of the quoted books show that, even at the beginning of the 18th century, the great classics were known at least to some scholars even if they were prohibited by influential fanatics like Cāmināta Tēcikar.

35. Cāminātaiyar, *My Life*, vol. 2, 370.

36. Ibid., 477–478.

37. Anglo-American reader-response criticism has shifted attention away from the historical audience addressed by an author situated in a specific place and time toward the ideal or model

reader or audience anticipated by the text itself. In addition to Eco's concept of the model author and its counterpart, the model reader (see Eco, *Six Walks*), a variety of terms describing such a textually anticipated reader have emerged over the last two decades, each carrying slightly different shades of meaning: the *mock reader* (Walker Gibson, "Authors, Speakers, Readers, and Mock Readers," in *Reader-Response Criticism: From Formalism to Post-Structuralism*, ed. Jane P. Tompkins [Baltimore: Johns Hopkins University Press, 1980], 1–6); the *implied reader* (Wolfgang Iser, *The Implied Reader: Patterns of Communication in Prose Fiction from Bunyan to Beckett* [Baltimore: Johns Hopkins University Press, 1974]); the *narratee* (Gerald Prince, "Introduction to the Study of the Narratee," in *Reader-Response Criticism: From Formalism to Post-Structuralism*, ed. Jane P. Tompkins [Baltimore: Johns Hopkins University Press, 1980], 7–25); and so on. Elizabeth Freund, *The Return of the Reader: Reader-Response Criticism* (London: Methuen, 1987), 7, lists ten such terms, from Eco's *model reader* to Holland's *literant*.

38. Eco, *Six Walks*, 13.

39. Ibid., 13–14.

40. Ibid., 24: "They must appear together because the model author and the model reader are entities that become clear to each other only in the process of reading, so that each one creates the other."

41. Ibid., 15, defines the model author and reader as follows: "The model author . . . is a voice that speaks to us . . . that wants us beside it. This voice is manifested as a narrative strategy, as a set of instructions which is given to us step by step and which we have to follow when we decide to act as the model reader." For more on Eco's conception of the model reader as he or she who follows the "set of instructions" encoded in the narrative style and strategies of the text itself, see Eco, *The Role of the Reader* (Bloomington: Indiana University Press, 1979).

42. See later for further discussion of why the audience assumed by modern literary criticism, that of the lone reader gazing at the printed page, is perhaps the least applicable to the premodern South Asian context.

43. J. A. B. van Buitenen, trans., *The Mahābhārata*, vol. 3 (Chicago: University of Chicago Press, 1978), 29.

44. For the Pāli version of the story, see Mahānāma, *The Mahāvaṁsa*, ed. Wilhelm Geiger (London: Henry Frowde, for Pali Text Society, 1908), 7–9. For an English translation of this story of the Buddha's visit to the "Island of the Serpents" (Nāgadīpa), see Mahānāma, *The Mahāvaṁsa, or the Great Chronicle of Ceylon*, trans. Wilhelm Geiger and Mabel Haynes Bode (London: Henry Frowde, for Pali Text Society, 1912; Reprint, New Delhi: Asian Educational Services, 1993), 5–8.

45. The stories of these two sages appear to be unique to the *Maṇimēkalai*.

46. A phrase coined by Hans Robert Jauss, *Toward an Aesthetic of Reception*, Theory and History of Literature, vol. 2, trans. Timothy Bahti (Minneapolis: University of Minnesota Press, 1982), 22. As he explains the importance of this concept for understanding the history of literature: "The coherence of literature as an event is primarily mediated in the horizon of expectations of the literary experience of contemporary and later readers, critics and authors."

47. Unlike the other Tamil Buddhist ornate poetic work (now lost), the *Kuṇṭalakēci*. Stories of the young girl, Kuṇḍalakesī, also known as Bhaddā Kuṇḍalakesā, who falls in love with and marries a murderous thief, eventually discovers her husband's treachery, kills him, and becomes a female ascetic (*bhikkhunī*), are found in numerous places in Theravāda literature, including the Pāli commentaries on the *Dhammapada* (A. C. Norman, *The Commentary on the Dhammapada*, vol. 2 [London: Henry Frowde, for Pali Text Soxiety, 1906–1915; Reprint, London: Luzac, for Pali Text Society, 1970], 217–227) and the *Therīgāthā* (Dhammapāla, *Therīgāthā-Aṭṭhakathā* [*Paramatthadīpanī VI*], ed. William Pruitt [Oxford: Pali Text Society, 1998], 97–106).

48. *Cilappatikāram*, chapter 5, *intiraviḻa ūr eṭutta kātai*, "The Story of the Celebration of the Indra Festival in the City," provides a more complete description of the city's lavish prepara-

tions. For an English translation of this passage, see Iḷaṅkō Aṭikaḷ *The Cilappatikāram of Iḷaṅkō Aṭikaḷ: An Epic of South India*, trans. R. Parthasarathy (New York: Columbia University Press, 1993), 46–56.

49. The festival of spring (vasantotsava) was orginally celebrated on the full-moon day of the month of Caitra (March–April) but is now said to take place on the full-moon day of Phālguna (February–March); see Harṣa, *Priyadarśikā: A Sanskrit Drama by Harsha*, Columbia Indo-Iranian Series, no. 10, trans. G. K. Nariman, et al. (New York: Columbia University Press, 1923), 98–99. According to *Cilappatikāram*, i.5.64, the Indra festival was also held during the month of *cittirai* (Caitra); see Iḷaṅkō Aṭikaḷ, *Cilappatikāram*, 140.

50. Bharata, *Nāṭyaśāstra of Bharatamuni, with the Commentary Abhinavabhāratī by Abhinavaguptācārya*, Parimal Sanskrit Series, no. 4, vol. 1, ed. R. S. Nagar (Delhi: Parimal, 1981), 22–25.

51. Kālidāsa, *The Mālavikāgnimitra: A Sanskrit Play by Kālidāsa, with the Commentary of Kāṭayavema*, Bombay Sanskrit Series, no. 6, ed. Shankar Pāṇḍurang (Bombay: Government Central Book Depot, 1889), 2–3. Here, the stage manager (*sūtradhāra*) reports that the audience has demanded to see this work by Kālidāsa at the spring festival (vasantotsava).

52. Kālidāsa, *The Abhijñānaśākuntalam of Kālidāsa, with the Commentary of Rāghavabhaṭṭa, Various Readings, Introduction, Literal Translation, Exhaustive Notes, and Appendices*, ed. M. R. Kale (Bombay: Oriental, 1902; Reprint, Delhi: Motilal Banarsidass, 1994), 204. Here, the heavenly nymph, Sānumatī, wonders why the festival preparations have not yet commenced in the royal palace, because the festival season (*ṛtūtsava*) has already begun.

53. Harṣa, *The Ratnāvalī of Śrīharshadeva*, ed. Nārāyaṇa Bālakriṣṇa and Kāśināth Pāṇḍurang 2d ed. (Bombay: Nirṇaya-Sāgara, 1890), 2. Here again, the stage manager reports that various kings assembled for the celebration of the spring festival have requested a performance of this play.

54. See Harṣa, *Priyadarśikā*, 4–6. The circumstances of the stage manager's announcement of the production are identical to those found in the opening lines of the *Ratnāvalī*.

55. Harṣa, *Nāgānanda of Śrīharṣa*, ed. and trans. Raghunath Damodar Karmarkar (Bombay: Visvanath, 1923), 1. The stage manager here repeats more or less the same formulaic announcement found in *Ratnāvalī* and *Priyadarśikā*, yet the occasion this time is the Indra festival (indrotsava).

56. The story of Mātavi, Kōvalaṉ, and Kōvalaṉ's virtuous wife, Kaṇṇaki, is told in the *Cilappatikāram*. The *Maṇimēkalai* narrative here seems to assume audience familiarity with the situation of the main protagonists; it is perhaps this abrupt entree into the flow of narrative events that first led medieval Tamil commentators, beginning with Aṭiyārkkunallār in the thirteenth century, to suggest that the two texts be taken together as illustrations of the four human aims (*puruṣārtha*): wealth and power, desire, and virtue (*Cilappatikāram*) and liberation (*Maṇimēkalai*). For a discussion of the shortcomings of such an assessment of the "twin" texts, see chapter 2, as well as Richman, *Branch Stories*, Appendix A, especially 159–160.

57. Literally, "protector or upholder of the dharma (aṟam)," perhaps intended as a Tamil translation of the Pāli/Sanskrit name Dhammapāla/Dharmapāla.

58. The *Akitta-jātaka* also mentions a park in the neighborhood of Kāvīrapaṭṭana (e.g., Kāvirippūmpaṭṭiṉam or Pukār) in the Ḍamila (Tamil) kingdom where the Buddha-to-be resided for a time in deep meditation. See V. Fausbøll, ed., *The Jātaka Together with its Commentary: Being Tales of the Anterior Births of Gotama Buddha*, vol. 4 (London: Trubner, 1887), 238.

59. John S. Strong, "*Gandhakuṭī*: The Perfumed Chamber of the Buddha," *History of Religions* 16/4 (1977):390–406.

60. Richman, *Branch Stories*, 28, discusses the "intensity . . . of passion" suggested by the literary elephant in rut.

61. Maṇimēkalā appears in a number of Jātaka stories, rescuing the shipwrecked Buddha-to-be as he swims in the sea. A sea goddess by that name is also found in a number of folktales,

rituals, and dances from Southeast Asia. Maṇimēkalā's appearance in Buddhist and non-Buddhist sources from across Asia is discussed further in chapter 3.

62. Richman, *Branch Stories*, 53. See chapters 4 and 5 of Richman's work, 53–100, for a discussion of the ways in which Cāttaṉār works the classic Tamil literary themes of desert landscape and love into a poetic discourse on life's impermanence. Richman also provides a detailed description and graphic illustration of the cosmology described in the *Maṇimēkalai* text.

63. Ibid., 69–71.

64. Ibid., 24, interprets the sequence of events that follows on the island of Maṇipallavam as an initiation of sorts, as "the structural equivalent of an initiation into the life of an almswoman."

65. Mahānāma, *Mahāvaṁsa*, 7–9.

66. The appearance of various treasures on the anniversary of the Buddha's birth and enlightenment is a theme alluded to rather enigmatically in a number of Pāli and Sanskrit sources. For a brief discussion of the four "treasure-urns" (*cattāro* or *cattāro nidhayo*) of the Buddha and their appearance in relation to the birth of a Buddha-to-be or some similarly momentous event, see Buddhadatta, *The Clarifier of Sweet Meaning (Madhuratthavilāsinī): Commentary on the Chronicle of the Buddhas (Buddhaavaṁsa) by Buddhadatta Thera*, trans. I. B. Horner (London: Pali Text Soxiety, 1978), xlv–xlvii. Faxian (Fa-hsien), the fifth-century Chinese pilgrim to India and Sri Lanka, notes a story of "miraculous appearance" that he first heard at the Mahāvihāra: the Buddha's almsbowl appears every hundred years or so at various locations and will continue to do so until the future Buddha Maitreya appears to claim it. See Faxian [Fa-hsien], *A Record of Buddhistic Kingdoms: Being an Account of the Chinese Monk Fa-Hsien of Travels in India and Ceylon* (AD *399–414) in Search of Buddhist Books of Discipline*, trans. James Legge (London: Dover, 1886; Reprint, New Delhi: Munshiram Manoharlal, 1991), 109–110. Faxian's story of the begging bowl is further discussed in chapter 3.

67. Richman interprets this image of the inexhaustible begging bowl as a depiction of "maternal nurturing," as a means of justifying the practice of female renunciation to a society largely repulsed by the idea. See Richman, *Branch Stories*, 33; Richman, "The Portrayal of a Female Renouncer in a Tamil Buddhist Text," in *Gender and Religion: On the Complexity of Symbols*, ed. Caroline Walker Bynum et al. (Boston: Beacon, 1986), 143–165; and Richman, "Gender and Persuasion: The Portrayal of Beauty, Anguish, and Nurturance in an Account of a Tamil Nun," in *Buddhism, Sexuality, and Gender*, ed. José Ignacio Cabezón (Albany: State Univesity of New York Press, 1992), 111–136. Dennis Hudson, "The Courtesan and Her Bowl: An Esoteric Reading of the *Maṇimēkalai*," in *A Buddhist Woman's Path to Enlightenment: Proceedings of a Workshop on the Tamil Narrative* Maṇimēkalai, *Uppsala University, May 25–29, 1995*, Acta Universitatis Upsaliensis: Historica Religionum, vol. 13, ed. Peter Schalk (Uppsala, Sweden: Uppsala University, 1997), 169–180, interprets the bowl as analogous to the bowl of Mohinī and symbolic of Buddhist Vajrayāna cultic activity in Kāñcīpuram. Perhaps a more straightforward way of understanding this image of Amutacurapi tirelessly relieving the pain and hunger of the suffering is to consider it within a larger framework of a general Buddhist emphasis on healing. The notion of suffering as concrete, physical disease, and the power of the Buddha to act as "Great Physician" in a literal sense, is a ubiquitous theme in Buddhist cultures that has thus far been little examined. Paul Demiéville's short study, *Buddhism and Healing: Demiéville's Article* "Byō" *from* Hōbōgirin, trans. Mark Tatz (Lanham, Md.: University Press of America, 1985), provides a useful overview of images of medicine and healing in Buddhist literature, as well as Buddhist monastic theories of health, illness, and healing.

68. The specificity of the date of the Buddha's return is quite remarkable and is discussed further in chapter 3. For a brief discussion of the passages in the *Maṇimēkalai* that deal with the date and time of the Buddha's appearance on earth, see Ruth Walldèn, "Notes on Some Dates of the Buddha in the *Maṇimēkalai*," in *Die Datierung des historischen Buddha [The Dating*

of the Historical Buddha], Symposium zur Buddhismusforschung, vol. 4, no. 2, ed. Heinz Bechert (Gottingen: Vandenhoeck and Ruprecht, 1992), 200–207.

69. See Richman, *Branch Stories*, 123–142, for an interpretation of this portion of the text as a vehicle for Cāttaṉār's criticism of both brahmins and their Vedic deities. Hudson, "Courtesan and Her Bowl," 185–189, analyzes the Āputtiraṉ story as a vehicle for explaining the manner in which Vajrayāna liturgies were transmitted from South India to Java (20). Āputtiraṉ and his connection to Southeast Asia will be taken up in yet another light in chapter 3.

70. Cāvakam perhaps represents a Tamil form of the name Java.

71. See Richman, *Branch Stories*, 101–121, for an interpretation of the ascetics' stories of Maruti and Vicākai as a discourse on the powers of disciplined women and the king's duty to protect female renouncers. Visākhā is presented in Pāli narratives as the paradigmatic lay disciple of the Buddha, renowned for her generosity to the Saṅgha; for a brief summary of the various stories told about her in Pāli, see G. P. Malalasekera, *Dictionary of Pāli Proper Names*, vol. 2 (London: John Murray, for Government of India, 1938), 899–904.

72. xxiv.105–140 is repeated verbatim, with one small exception, at xxx.48–81; the single variation is the addition of two extra lines at xxx.60–61. Perhaps this repetition suggests that the author is quoting another text, a versified rendition of the doctrine of interdependent origination in Tamil.

73. One of three ancient Tamil capital cities, according to the Caṅkam poems, and the seat of the Cēraṉ rulers. Nagaswamy presents a plausible argument for identifying the ancient Vañci with modern-day Karūr in the Trichy district of Tamilnadu. See R. Nagaswamy, *Roman Karūr: A Peep into Tamils' Past* (Madras: Brahad Prakashan, 1995). For an overview of the place of Vañci in Tamil literary sources, see C. S. Cheluva Aiyar, "Vañcimānakar, or the Great City Called Vañci," *Journal of Oriental Research* 2 (1928):113–134.

74. The text itself does not explain the manner in which the ten teachers encountered by Maṇimēkalai can be reduced to five different systems.The five systems described are suggested by *Manimekhalai* (*The Dancer with the Magic Bowl*), trans. Alain Daniélou (New York: New Directions, 1989; Reprint, New York: Penguin, 1993), 141, and Cāttaṉār, *Manimekalai: Girdle of Gems*, trans. Guruswamy and Srinivasan, 257.

75. The bulk of the secondary scholarship on the *Maṇimēkalai* has, in fact, read this chapter as historical document. See, for example, Nellai K. Subramanian, "Sankhya Philosophy in Manimekalai and Neelakeci," in *Proceedings of the Fifth International Conference-Seminar of Tamil Studies*, vol. 2, ed. M. Arunachalam (Madras: International Association of Tamil Research, 1982), 12/2–12/26; S. S. Suryanarayanasastri, "The Manimekalai Account of the Sankhya," *Journal of Indian History* 8/3 (1929):322–327; Ruth Walldèn, "Materialism as Expounded in the *Maṇimēkalai*, the *Nīlakēci*, and the *Civañāṉacittiyār*," in *Orientalia Suecana*, ed. Trygrove Kronholm (Stockholm: Almovist and Wiksell International, 1991), 246–251; and Ruth Walldèn, "The Presentation of Sāṁkhya in the *Maṇimēkalai*," in *Kalyāṇamitrārāgaṇam: Essays in Honour of Nils Simonsson*, ed. Eivind Kahrs (Oslo: Norwegian University Press, 1986), 303–312.

76. This story appears twice in the Jātaka collection, in the *Saṅkha-jātaka* (Fausbøll, *Jātaka*, vol. 4, 15–22) and in the story of Mahājanaka (Fausbøll, *Jātaka*, vol. 6, 30–68). Two additional stories are found in the *Paññāsa* or "apocryphal" Jātaka collection from Southeast Asia: the *Samuddaghosa-jātaka* and the story of Candakumāra. See Padmanabh S. Jaini, ed., *Paññāsa Jātaka or Zimme Paṇṇāsa* (*in the Burmese Recension*), Pali Text Society Text Series, no. 172, vol. 1 (London: Pali Text Society, 1981), 64–82, 259–269.

77. This discussion was first sparked by the recovery of the Sanskrit *Nyāyapraveśa* text in the early decades of the twentieth century. For an introduction to the principal players in this debate, see Kuppuswami Sastri, "Problems of Identity"; S. Kuppuswami Sastri, "Aṟavaṇavaṭikaḷ (Ācārya-Dharmapāla?) Again," *Journal of Oriental Research* 2 (1928):79–83; Sesha Aiyar, "Date of Maṇimēkalai"; S. Krishnaswami Aiyangar, *Manimekhalai in Its Historical Setting* (London:

Luzac, 1928), 54–107; and N. Aiyaswami Sastri, "Maṇimekhalai's Contributions to Indian Logic," *Journal of Oriental Research* 11/2 (1937):116–128. If the Tibetan tradition that places Dignāga in Kāñcīpuram in the era of the *Maṇimēkalai*'s composition can be taken seriously (see Tāranātha, *Tāranātha's History of Buddhism in India*, ed. Debiprasad Chattopadhyaya, trans. Lama Chimpa and Alaka Chattopadhyaya [Delhi: Motilal Banarsidass, 1990], 181), it would seem far more likely that the *Maṇimēkalai* and the *Nyāyapraveśa* each represent different formulations of a system of inferential logic current in Kāñcī at that time rather than either being a direct translation of the other.

78. Hikosaka, *Buddhism in Tamilnadu*, 135–137.

79. See U. V. Cāminātaiyar, *Caṅkat tamiḻum piṟkālat tamiḻum* (Madras: Mahamahopadhyaya Dr. U. V. Swaminathaiyer Library, 1978), 137.

80. The meter, known as *kaṭṭalaik kalitturai*, is a difficult one widely used in the late classical/early medieval period, employed in works ranging from the Śaiva *Tēvāram* to the Jain *Cīvakacintāmaṇi* (Zvelebil, *Prosody*, 75–77).

81. Discussed in chapter 17 of the text entitled, "Explanation of the Soil of Wisdom" (*paññābhūminiddesa*; Buddhaghosa, *Visuddhimaggo with Paramatthamañjūsaṭīkā*, Pali Granthamala, no. 3, vol. 3, ed. Revatadhamma [Varanasi: Varanaseya Sanskrit Vishvavidyalaya, 1969], 1171–1368, and Buddhaghosa, *The Path of Purification* [*Visuddhimagga*], trans. Bhikkhu Ñāṇamoli [Kandy, Sri Lanka: Buddhist Publication Society, 1991], 525–604).

82. Completely absent from chapter 30 of the *Maṇimēkalai*, for example, is any indication of the doctrine of emptiness (*śūnyatā*) applied to interdependent origination, as found in Nāgārjuna's *Mūlamadhyamakakārikā*, trans. Kenneth K. Inada (Tokyo: Hokuseido, 1970).

83. A number of sources tell the story of Buddhaghosa and Buddhadatta meeting in midocean, as Buddhaghosa's ship heads for Sri Lanka and the Mahāvihāra to complete the work of translation and codification that Buddhadatta, en route home to India, had begun. For a traditional account of the writing of the *Visuddhimagga*, see Wilhelm Geiger and C. Mabel Rickmers, trans., *Cūlavaṁsa: Being the More Recent Part of the Mahāvaṁsa*, vol. 1 (London: Oxford University Press, for Pali Text Society, 1929–1930; Reprint, New Delhi: Asian Educational Services, 1992), 22–26. The meeting of the two monks is described in the introductions and epilogues of a number of their own works, as well as in the twelfth-century commentary on Buddhadatta's *Vinayavinicchaya* (quoted in A. P. Buddhadatta, "The Great Author of Summaries—Contemporary of Buddhaghosa," *University of Ceylon Review* 3/1 [1945]:34) and in the (fifteenth-century?) text from Burma, the *Buddhaghosuppatti* (see James Gray, ed. and trans., *Buddhaghosuppatti, or the Historical Romance of the Rise and Career of Buddhaghosa*, vol. 2 [London: Luzac, 1892], 17–18). In the latter text, it is said that Sakka, king of the gods, arranged for the two to meet without their ships colliding; Buddhadatta then reports that he has left the work of translation unfinished and hands to Buddhaghosa the iron stylus and stone that had initially been given to him by Sakka.

84. For an assessment of Buddhadatta's work as that of a "great poet," see A. P. Buddhadatta, "Great Author," 34–40, as well as B. M. Barua's response in "Buddhadatta and Buddhaghosa: Their Contemporaneity and Age," *University of Ceylon Review* 3/2 (1945):77–88. The commentary on the thirteenth-century Śaiva text, *Civañāṉacittiyār parapakkam*, preserves a single quatrain from the (now lost) Buddhist text called *Cittāntattokai*, literally "Collection of *Siddhāntas* or Doctrines"; *tokai*, in classical literary Tamil, refers specifically to a poetic anthology (e.g., *Kuṟuntokai, Kalittokai*), thus suggesting that this "Collection of [Buddhist] Doctrines" was a work in verse. See Caṇmukacuntara Mutaliyār, ed., *Civañāṉacittiyār parapakkam mūlamum Catuvappirakācar uraiyum* (Madras: By the editor, 1894), 117. The first two lines of the excerpt, as well as the name *Cittāntattokai*, also appear earlier in the text (83).

85. For the most complete discussions of this chapter to date, see Kandaswamy, *Buddhism*, 313–397, and Hikosaka, *Buddhism in Tamilnadu*, 95–118. Although Kandaswamy follows the

Tamil text closely, Hikosaka skips over many points to dwell at length on topics, such as the five "bundles" (*pañcaskandha*) that receive minimal attention (two lines, xxx.189–190) in the *Maṇimēkalai*. Aṟavaṇaṉ introduces interdependent origination as "the teaching benevolently given by countless Buddhas in the past" (xxx.14–15), reiterated most recently by the Buddha "who defeated Māra and became a victor" (xxx.11). After summarizing the entire doctrine in thirty-five short lines (xxx.16–50), Aṟavaṇaṉ then defines each of the links in the causal chain in turn. In his discussion of ignorance (Tamil pētaimai, Sanskrit *avidyā*), he notes an unusual configuration of possible births (Tamil *kati*, Sanskrit *gati*); his list includes rebirth as a "brahman" (Tamil *piramaṉ*, Sanskrit *brahma*) (xxx.57–58), a birth peculiar to this particular Buddhist text. The definitions of each of the twelve links are in their own way quite unique. Volition (Tamil ceykai, Sanskrit *saṁskāra*, Pāli *saṅkhāra*) is defined quite straightforwardly as good and bad karma (xxx.55–81), and "consciousness" (Tamil *uṇarvu*, Sanskrit *vijñāna*, Pāli *viññāṇa*) is likened to "the awareness of a sleeping man" (xxx.82–83). The discussion of the cyclic arising and cessation of the twelve links, the four groups, and the three junctions among them closely resembles that found in the *Visuddhimagga* (xvii.2); the "three categories of birth" (*mūṉṟu vakaip piṟappu*) correspond to Buddhaghosa's three realms (*dhātu*), while the grouping of the twelve elements in the causal chain according to the three times of past, present, and future and the discussion of the three rounds (*tivaṭṭāni*) also follow a tradition similar to that of the *Visuddhimagga* (xvii.284–287). The text then quickly defines the Four Noble Truths and five aggregates (Sanskrit *skandha*, Pāli *khandha*) in terms of the twelve causal links (xxx.179–190). Having outlined the principal classifications of the causal sequence, the text then moves to discuss the various ways in which the elements of interdependent origination are to be investigated, analyzed, and understood. Such methods of investigation, although common to all discussions of interdependent origination, are explained in particular ways and with specific examples not found elsewhere in Buddhist discussions of the same topic. The discussion of "designation" (Tamil *vaḻakku*, Pāli *paññatti*) at xxx.191–216, for example, reiterates a common formulation of designations that refer to names of things (*nāma*-paññatti) found in Pāli commentarial literature but differs in its presentation of four designations of concept (*attha*-paññatti). Although the four methods (*naya*) outlined at xxx.217–234 parallel Buddhaghosa's discussion in *Visuddhimagga* xvii.309–313, the four questions and answers (*viṉāviṭai*) are discussed in terms similar to those found in the *Milindapañha* but with different examples chosen to illustrate the various categories.

86. Geoffrey Samuel, "The Gesar Epic of East Tibet," in *Tibetan Literature: Studies in Genre*, ed. José Ignacio Cabezón and Roger R. Jackson (Ithaca, N.Y.: Snow Lion, 1996), 366.

87. Robert Chalmers, ed., *The Majjhima-Nikāya*, vol. 2 (London: Henry Frowde, for Pali Text Society, 1898), 97–105, and Norman, *Commentary on the Dhammapada*, vol. 3, 169–170, and vol. 4, 231–232. The story of the Buddha's conversion of Aṅgulimāla in a previous existence is also told in the *Mahāsutasoma-jātaka*; see Fausbøll, *Jātaka*, vol. 5, 456–511. For an English rendering of Aṅgulimāla's story drawn from several of these sources, see Eugene Watson Burlingame, trans., *Buddhist Legends: Translated from the Original Pali Text of the Dhammapada Commentary*, Harvard Oriental Series, no. 30 (Cambridge: Harvard University Press, 1921), 6–14.

88. Norman, *Commentary on the Dhammapada*, vol. 1, 26. The tale of Maṭṭhakuṇḍali also appears in Dhammapāla, *Paramatthadīpanī: Being the Commentary on the Vimāna-Vatthu*, ed. E. Hardy (London: Henry Frowde, for Pali Text Society, 1901), 322–330.

89. Discussions of the beneficial root conditions (kusalamūla) and their unbeneficial (akusala) counterparts of greed (lobha), ill will (dosa) and ignorance (moha), in the context of their identification with the first of the twenty-four conditional relations (*hetupaccaya*), can be found at any number of places in the Pāli philosophical literature, including Buddhaghosa's *Visuddhimagga*, xvii.66–70. For an introduction to the topic in English, see Nyanatiloka, *Buddhist Dictionary: Manual of Buddhist Terms and Doctrines* (Kandy, Sri Lanka: Buddhist Publication Society, 1988),

119–120, 134–140; Ledi Sayadaw, "The Patthanuddesa Dipani, or The Buddhist Philosophy of Relations," in *The Manuals of Buddhism: The Expositions of the Buddha-dhamma*, ed. Union Buddha Sāsana Council (Bangkok: Mahamakut, 1978), 61–120; and H. Saddhātissa, "The Six Root-Conditions," *One Vehicle* (1984):135–138.

90. Ētu/hetu might be translated into English in any number of ways, as "cause," "prerequisite," or "condition." The Pāli literature likewise employs a number of synonyms for the term; as Buddhaghosa points out in the *Visuddhimagga* at xvii.68: "The words condition, cause, reason, source, originator, producer, etc., are one in meaning though different in the letter" (Buddhaghosa, *Path of Purification*, 543).

91. See Anne E. Monius and Rangarajan Vijayalakshmy, "*Ētunikaḻcci* in the *Maṇimēkalai*: The Manifestation of Beneficial Root 'Causes' and Renunciation," in *A Buddhist Woman's Path to Enlightenment: Proceedings of a Workshop on the Tamiḻ Narrative* Maṇimēkalai, *Uppsala University, May 25–29, 1995*, Acta Universitatis Upsaliensis: Historica Religionum, vol. 13, ed. Peter Schalk (Uppsala, Sweden: Uppsala University, 1997), 261–275, for a fuller examination of the ways in which Abhidhamma and commentarial texts define the term.

92. Ledi Sayadaw, "On the Philosophy of Relations," *Journal of the Pali Text Society* (1915–1916):34.

93. In Robert Caesar Childers, *A Dictionary of the Pali Language* (London: Kegan Paul, Trench, Trubner, 1909), 530. Here Childers cites the authoritative Theravādin scholar, Subhuti: "Subh. writes to me . . . that *upanissaya* means *bhāgya* (destiny, luck), and is a synonym of *hetu*."

94. Buddhadatta's commentary on *Buddhavaṁsa*, II.59, explains, for example, "*tattha manussattan ti manussabhāve yeva ṭhatvā buddhataṁ patthentassa patthanā samijjhati, na nāgajāti-ādisu ṭhitānaṁ. Kasmā ti ce? Ahetukabhāvato*" (*Madhuratthavilāsinī nāma Buddhavaṁsaṭṭhakathā of Bhadantācariya Buddhadatta Mahāthera*, ed. I. B. Horner [London: Humphrey Milford, for Pali Text Society, 1946], 91). Horner translates this passage in Buddhadatta, *Clarifier of Sweet Meaning*, 132, as: "Therein *human existence* means: the aspiration of one who is aspiring to Buddhahood succeeds only when he is in human status, not of those born as nāgas and so forth. And why is that? Because of the absence of the (three skilled) root causes." This constitutes Buddhadatta's opening remark on the *Buddhavaṁsa* stanza that lists the eight prerequisites for Buddhahood: human existence (manussattam); being born as a male (*liṅgasampatti*); cause, meaning a reason for becoming an arahant or worthy one (hetu); seeing a teacher (*satthāradassanam*); going forth, that is, living among ascetics (*pabbajā*); attainment of special qualities (*guṇasampatti*); an act of merit (*adhikāro*); and possession of great resolve (*chandatā*; Buddhadatta, *Madhuratthavilāsinī*, 91–92). This list of eight is repeated in the *Buddhavaṁsa* commentary (Buddhadatta, *Madhuratthavilāsinī*, 271) and occurs in many other places, including the introduction to the Jātaka collection (see Fausbøll, *Jātaka*, vol. 1, 44). Note that hetu is also tied to the attainment of liberation through the third of the prerequisite conditions; as Buddhadatta explains, only for a man who possesses a cause or reason (hetu) for becoming a worthy one (arahant) does the aspiration to become a Buddha succeed and for no other (*hetu ti purisassa pi tasmiṁ attabhāve arahattappattiyā hetusampannass' eva patthanā samijjhati na itarassa*; Buddhadatta, *Madhuratthavilāsinī*, 91).

95. *Tamil Lexicon*, vol. 1, 521–522.

96. *tavattiṟam pūṇṭu tarumam kēṭṭup*
pavattiṟam aṟuka eṉap pāvai nōṟṟaṉaḷ eṉ (xxx.263–264)

[Thus] having heard the dharma and having taken to asceticism,
the young girl made a vow to eradicate the [karmic effects] of birth.

97. At xxviii.151–154, Mācāttuvāṉ, Kōvalaṉ's father and thus Maṇimēkalai's grandfather, tells Maṇimēkalai that Aṟavaṇaṉ has gone to Kāñcī because that is the place where her ētus are to become fully manifest:

Because the conditions for your dharma (*aṟattiṟku* ētu), flowering creeper,
[will become manifest] in the great city of Kacci,
[Aṟavaṇaṉ] himself [went] there.

98. *kassa nu kho ahaṁ paṭhamaṁ dhammaṁ deseyyaṁ?* See Hermann Oldenberg, ed., *The Vinaya Piṭakam: One of the Principal Buddhist Holy Scriptures in the Pāli Language*, vol. 1 (London: Williams and Norgate, 1879), 7. This formulaic question is repeated throughout the stories of past Buddhas found in the *Buddhavaṁsa* and its commentary; see, for example, Buddhadatta, *Madhuratthavilāsinī*, 18, 133.

99. Norman, *Commentary on the Dhammapada*, vol. 1, 26.

100. Ibid., vol. 1, 27.

101. Malalasekera, *Dictionary of Pāli Proper Names*, vol. 1, 23. The monks who gather together in the introduction to the *Mahāsutasoma-jātaka* (Fausbøll, *Jātaka*, vol. 5, 456–457), for example, discuss in terms of wonder and awe the peaceful conversion of Aṅgulimāla before hearing the parallel story, in the Buddha's incarnation as Mahāsutasoma, of his conversion of a cannibalistic king. In the introduction to the *Mahākaṅha-jātaka* (Fausbøll, *Jātaka*, vol. 4, 180–181), the monks wonder, in similar fashion, at the Buddha's compassionate efforts to convert such seemingly "hard cases" as Aṅgulimāla. In the story of Devadatta found in the *Dhammapada* commentary, a disease-ridden Devadatta begs to be taken to see the Buddha with the verse: "Toward the murderer Devadatta, toward the thief Aṅgulimāla, and toward Dhanapāla and Rāhula, [the Buddha maintained] complete tranquility of mind" (Norman, *Commentary on the Dhammapada*, vol. 1, 146).

102. Translated from the twelfth-century Sinhala text, *Amavatura*, by R. Spence Hardy in his *A Manual of Buddhism, in its Modern Development*, Chowkhamba Sanskrit Studies, vol. 56 (London: Patridge and Oakey, 1853; Reprint, Varanasi: Chowkhamba Sanskrit Series Office, 1967), 250.

103. Norman, *Commentary on the Dhammapada*, vol. 3, 230–236.

104. Ibid., vol. 3, 235.

105. Ibid., vol. 3, 235–236.

106. Ibid., vol. 1, 290–297.

107. Ibid., vol. 1, 292.

108. Dhammapāla, *Commentary on Vimāna-Vatthu*, and Dhammapāla, *Elucidation of the Intrinsic Meaning So Named: The Commentary on the Vimāna Stories* (*Paramattha-dīpanī nāma Vimānavatthu-aṭṭhakathā*), trans. Peter Masefield and N. A. Jayawickrama (Oxford: Pali Text Society, 1989). In several ways these *Vimānavatthu-aṭṭhakathā* stories, particularly those dealing with women, might be said to provide a close narrative parallel to the *Maṇimēkalai*. Most of the stories follow a similar formula: the woman performs an act of kindness to the Buddha in one of his many lives; as a result, she is reborn in the realm of the Thirty-Three (Tāvatiṁsa); one of the chief disciples of the Buddha asks her how she managed to be reborn in such a high state; and the disciple sees that the woman is ready to hear the dharma and thus teaches her. In the case of Maṇimēkalai, it is her feeding of the sage, Cātucakkaraṉ (x.24–41, xxi.181–187), that has generated the character of her present birth in which her ētus mature and become manifest. Dhammapāla's commentary on the *Visālakkhivimāna* story (Dhammapāla, *Commentary on Vimāna-Vatthu*, 169–172) points explicitly to the difference between the doing of a good deed and its "ripening" in a later existence: "I was possessed of virtue, but it has thus far not ripened" (*yañ ca sīlavatī āsiṁ na taṁ tāva vipaccati*; Dhammapāla, *Commentary on Vimāna-Vatthu*, 171). The commentary on the *Pabhassaravimāna* story (Dhammapāla, *Commentary on Vimāna-Vatthu*, 178–181) tells the tale of a woman who has the opportunity to hear the dharma from Mahāmoggallāna but passes it by; this theme of the missed opportunity is also found in the *Maṇimēkalai* at x.33–34, where Maṇimēkalai, in her former life as Ilakkumi, chides her then-

husband, Irākulan̲, for not paying proper attention to the words of the sage, Cātucakkaran̲: "By not worshiping the flower[-like] feet of [this sage] who has descended from the heavens, your tongue has become impoverished." Although the content of the individual stories in the *Vimāna* commentary bears little resemblance to the content of the Tamil narrative, the simple point I make here is that the basic narrative structure revolving around the emergence of a woman's capacity to hear the dharma is not unique to the *Maṇimēkalai*.

109. Dhammapāla, *Commentary on Vimāna-Vatthu*, 63. The passage is translated by Masefield and Jayawickrama (Dhammapāla, *Vimāna Stories*, 91) as follows: "Now the elder Sāriputta emerged from the cessation upon which he had been entered for the (last) seven days and, surveying (the world) wondering towards whom he might that day act sympathetically, saw Puṇṇa entered within the net of his cognition; surveying him wondering whether he had faith and whether he would be able to act hospitably towards him he came to know his condition of faith, his ability to act hospitably and his (ability) to acquire great excellence."

110. Note that Maṇimēkalā seems only to be interested in those who are karmically ready for her help: Kōvalan̲'s ancestor and Maṇimēkalai of the ripened ētu. The goddess displays no interest in rescuing King Kiḷḷi's shipwrecked infant son, and as if to underscore the child's unworthiness in relation to the shipwrecked Buddha-to-be, Maṇimēkalā floods the city of Pukār while the distraught king searches in vain for his missing son (see xxix.1–35). Aṟavaṇan̲, in telling the stories of the rescue of the Buddha-to-be, the death of the king's child, and the subsequent submerging of Pukār in the passage cited, weaves one narrative into the other to the extent that all three scenes appear almost to comprise a single episode.

111. It is interesting to note, in relation to the goddess's initiatory powers, the close parallels between the story of Maṇimēkalā/Maṇimēkalai and that of Uppalavaṇṇā, the female elder (*therī*) with whom the goddess is identified in several Jātaka stories (see the stories of Saṅkha [Fausbøll, *Jātaka*, vol. 4, 22] and Mahājanaka [Fausbøll, *Jātaka*, vol. 6, 68]; in the *Paññāsa-jātaka* collection, see the stories of Samuddaghosa [Jaini, *Paññāsa Jātaka*, vol. 1, 78] and Candakumāra [Jaini, *Paññāsa Jātaka*, vol. 1, 267]). Uppalavaṇṇā's name is frequently mentioned in Pāli literature (see Malalasekera, *Dictionary of Pāli Proper Names*, vol. 1, 418–421), and her full story is found in Dhammapāla's commentary on the *Therīgāthā* (Dhammapāla, *Therīgāthā-Aṭṭhakathā*, 177–191), the *Dhammapada* commentary (Norman, *Commentary on the Dhammapada*, vol. 2, 48–52), and Buddhaghosa's commentary on the *Aṅguttāra-Nikāya* (Buddhaghosa, *Manorathapūraṇī: Commentary on the Aṅguttara Nikāya*, vol. 1:1, ed. Hermann Kopp et al. [London: Luzac, for Pali Text Society, 1924], 345–356). Like the goddess Maṇimēkalā and her human namesake, Uppalavaṇṇā is said to be exceedingly beautiful. The Burmese recension of her story makes a particular point of this; like Maṇimēkalai, who disarms the god of love and drives men to distraction (iii.20–25), of the young Uppalavaṇṇā it is said: "The brahmins, as soon as they saw her, went mad; one put a handful of rice on top of his head, another made a mistake and put it into a hole in the floor, and another put it inside his ear, another under his armpit" (Captain T. Rogers, trans., *Buddhaghosha's Parables* [London: Trubner, 1870], 188–191). Both Uppalavaṇṇā and Maṇimēkalai are inappropriately pursued throughout their respective narratives by lust-driven men (Norman, *Commentary on the Dhammapada*, vol. 2, 48–52, narrates the story of Uppalavaṇṇā's rape); each is tied to a male character named Rāhula (Tamil Irākulan̲) in previous births (Mary E. Lilley, ed., *Khuddaka Nikāya: Apadāna*, vol. 2 [London: Oxford University Press, for Pali Text Society, 1927], 551, and *Maṇimēkalai*, ix.42–47, x.20–43, and xxi.47–62). Both beautiful girls are also told to take up the life of a Buddhist renunciant by a concerned parent (*Maṇimēkalai*, ii.55–57; Buddhaghosa, *Manorathapūraṇī*, vol. 1:1, 355–356; and Norman, *Commentary on the Dhammapada*, vol. 2, 48–49). Like Maṇimēkalai, whose ascetic power (*tapas*) is mature (*ūḻtarutavattaḷ*), who wields arrows made of curses (*cāpacaratti*; v.16), and who stands equipped with the power of Maṇimēkalā's three mantras (x.80–91), Uppalavaṇṇā is said to be chief among those who have acquired extraordinary powers (*iddhi*; Buddhaghosa,

Manorathapūraṇī, vol. 1:1, 356). Like the goddess of the Tamil narrative, Uppalavaṇṇā is also said to have acquired the authority to initiate followers into Buddhist practice (Buddhaghosa, *Manorathapūraṇī*, 1:1, 323). Both Maṇimēkalai and Uppalavaṇṇā serve, or will serve in the future, as chief disciples of the Buddha (*Maṇimēkalai*, xxi.178–179; Uppalavaṇṇā is identified as the Buddha's chief female disciple throughout the Jātakas and the *Buddhavaṁsa* commentary). Although it remains unclear just how far the parallel elements in these two narrative cycles might be pushed, the Maṇimēkalā/Uppalavaṇṇā connection might further elucidate the Tamil goddess's role as Maṇimēkalai's namesake, first Buddhist teacher, and guide.

112. This three-stage process of spiritual realization also resembles in structure the story of the Buddha's three watches under the bodhi tree during the course of his enlightenment, a story referred to many times throughout the Pāli commentarial literature (e.g., Buddhadatta, *Madhuratthavilāsinī*, 8, 190, 289). The Buddha is said first to realize the nature of his past lives (an insight Maṇimēkalai achieves before the Buddha's jeweled seat on Maṇipallavam), with that realization giving rise in turn, in the Tamil text, to lack of attachment to those previous lives. The second watch is marked by the so-called purified god (deva) vision, a realization of the nature of the lives of other beings that might perhaps be construed as a parallel to Maṇimēkalai's growing understanding and compassion for others (adosa). Finally, during the third watch of the night, the Buddha is said to realize the truth of interdependent origination, just as Maṇimēkalai's instruction from Aṟavaṇaṉ closes with an exposition of that doctrine, yielding a state of knowledge (amoha).

113. *Paṟṟu*, a synonym here for *kāmam*, used throughout the text as a Tamil equivalent for attachment (lobha).

114. *Ceṟṟam*, a synonym here for *vekuḷi*, used throughout the text as a Tamil equivalent for ill will (dosa).

115. *Mayakkam*, used throughout the text as a Tamil equivalent for ignorance (moha).

116. Discussed at length in the literature on "conditional relations" (*paccaya*). See U. Narada, trans., *Conditional Relations* (*Paṭṭhāna*), 2 vols. (London: Pali Text Society, 1969–1981; Reprint, 1992).

117. Preface, lines 95–98: "When the king, Iḷaṅkō, graciously requested [so], Cāttaṉ, the prosperous grain merchant, made known [the story of] the renunciation of Maṇimēkalai in thirty songs (pāṭṭu), with the aid of eloquent Tamil."

118. Hikosaka, *Buddhism in Tamilnadu*, 46.

119. Although the term in modern Tamil clearly means "song," its precise connotations in Cāttaṉār's day are not clear. The characteristics of pāṭṭu are not explained in any detail in the oldest extant Tamil grammar, the *Tolkāppiyam*; it may simply have indicated a certain type of classical verse. See Thomas, "Literary Genres," 340.

120. The ninth-century commentary on this line, *Arumpata urai*, glosses this as "a poetic work combining verse and prose" (*pāṭṭum uraiyum kalantuvanta kāviyam*; Iḷaṅkō Aṭikaḷ, *Cilappatikāram*, 5).

121. Zvelebil, *Companion Studies*, 150–151, for example, characterizes the presence of writing in Tamil culture in the premodern era as follows:

> Although writing in Tamil India must have been known and employed at least from the very beginning of the common era, Tamil has remained until relatively very recently a civilisation which could by and large be characterized as oral/semi-oral, with a language typical for its diglossia (formal/standard: informal/non-standard), and its literacy, in the sense of systematic selfconscious use of writing, limited to a very narrow elite strata of traditional scholars, some members of the priestly communities, some administrators and members of royal bureaucracies, and professional scribes.

122. Sudipta Kaviraj, "Writing, Speaking, Being: Language and the Historical Formation of Identities in India," in *Nationalstaat und Sprachkonflikte in Süd- und Südostasien*, Beiträge zur Südasienforschung, no. 149, ed. Dagmar Hellmann-Rajanayagam and Dietmar Rothermund (Stuttgart: Franz Steiner Verlag, 1992), 28.

123. Nancy K. Florida, *Writing the Past, Inscribing the Future: History as Prophecy in Colonial Java* (Durham, N.C.: Duke University Press, 1995), 11.

124. Ibid., 12.

125. James N. Baker, "The Presence of the Name: Reading Scripture in an Indonesian Village," in *The Ethnography of Reading*, ed. Jonathan Boyarin (Berkeley: University of California Press, 1993), 98–138.

126. Cāminātaiyar, *My Life*, vol. 2, 374.

127. Ibid., vol. 1, 83–84.

128. For an introduction to reader-response theory, see Jane P. Tompkins, ed., *Reader-Response Criticism: From Formalism to Post-Structuralism* (Baltimore: Johns Hopkins University Press, 1980), and Susan Suleiman and Inge Crosman, eds., *The Reader in the Text: Essays on Audience and Interpretation* (Princeton, N.J.: Princeton University Press, 1980). Since the publication of these seminal collections, much of the work of reader-response critics has focused on placing the once abstract reader into his or her specific historic, sociopolitical context. See, for example, Peter Verdonk and Jean Jacques Weber, eds., *Twentieth-Century Fiction: From Text to Context* (London: Routledge, 1995), and Andrew Bennett, ed., *Readers and Reading* (New York: Longman, 1995).

129. Tompkins, *Reader-Response Criticism*, ix.

130. Although meyppāṭu as a technical literary term would not seem to be entirely synonymous with rasa and Sanskrit rasa theory certainly later developed in ways that are not mirrored in the Tamil application of meyppāṭu, the list found in the *Tolkāppiyam* bears striking resemblance to the eight rasas discussed by Bharata in his *Nāṭyaśāstra*: the humorous (Tamil *nakai*, Sanskrit *hāsya*), the pitiable (Tamil aḻukai, Sanskrit karuṇa), the loathesome (Tamil *iḷivaral*, Sanskrit *bībhatsa*), the awesome (Tamil *maruṭkai*, Sanskrit *adbhuta*), the terrifying (Tamil *accam*, Sanskrit *bhayānaka*), the heroic (Tamil *perumitam*, Sanskrit *vīra*), the furious (Tamil *vekuḷi*, Sanskrit *raudra*), and the erotic (Tamil *uvakai*, Sanskrit *śṛṅgāra*). See *Tolkāppiyam: Iḷampūraṇar uraiyuṭaṉ: Poruḷatikāram* (Tinnevelly: South India Saiva Siddhanta Works Publishing Society, 1977), verse 247, 361–362, and Bharata, *Nāṭyaśāstra*, vol. 1, 293–336. Note that the order given previously is that found in the *Tolkāppiyam*; Bharata's order is slightly different, beginning with the erotic and ending with the awesome. The extent to which the *Tolkāppiyam* models its presentation of heightened emotional experience on the Sanskrit is unclear; the Tamil text defines meyppāṭu as "the description of an object so vivid that one enjoys it with hair bristling, by shedding tears, etc." (*Tolkāppiyam: Iḷampūraṇar uraiyuṭaṉ: Poruḷatikāram*, verse 505, 537; translation taken from P. S. Subrahmanya Sastri, *Tolkāppiyam, the Earliest Extant Tamil Grammar: Porul-Atikāram–Tamil Poetics* [Madras: Kuppuswami Sastri Research Institute, 1956], verse 507, vol. 3, 67.) Later commentators use the *Tolkāppiyam*'s verses on meyppāṭu to discuss the Sanskrit poetics of direct bodily experience (bhāva), lasting mood (*sthāyibhāva*), and aesthetic experience (Sanskrit rasa, Tamil *cuvai*). Particularly relevant is Pērāciriyar's thirteenth-century commentary; see *Tolkāppiyam Pērāciriyar uraiyuṭaṉ: Poruḷatikāram* (Tinnevelly: South India Saiva Siddhanta Works Publishing Society, 1966), verse 249, 1–3. For more on the relationship between the Tamil and Sanskritic notions of emotional experience generated by literature, see John Ralston Marr, *The Eight Anthologies: A Study in Early Tamil Literature* (Madras: Institute of Asian Studies, 1985), 56–64; G. Sundaramoorthy, *Early Literary Theories in Tamil, in Comparison with Sanskrit Theories* (Madurai: Sarvodaya Ilakkiya Pannai, 1974), 78–92; and P. Thirugnanasambandhan, *The Concept of Alamkara Sastra in Tamil* (Madras: Samskrita Academy, 1977). The topic of meyppāṭu has largely been ignored by scholars of Tamil literature (e.g., Zvelebil includes only a

four-line entry in his *Lexicon of Tamil Literature*, 436), often dismissed as a later addition to the *Tolkāppiyam* under the noxious, or at least corrupting, influence of Sanskrit. Marr, *Eight Anthologies*, 56, for example, claims: "this whole *iyal* [chapter on meyppāṭu] would seem to depend on Sanskrit dramatic theory. . . . From the point of view of Tamil it is an accretion, and may well have been added later to *Tol[kāppiyam]*."

131. Eco, *Six Walks*, 27.

132. Edwin Gerow, *Indian Poetics*, A History of Indian Literature, vol. 5, fascicle 3, ed. Jan Gonda (Wiesbaden: Otto Harrassowitz, 1977), 249.

133. Ibid., 247.

134. Ānandavardhana, *Dhvanyālokaḥ Śrīmadabhinavaguptopādaviracita Locana sahitaḥ satipaṇa Prakāsa Hindīvyākhyopetaś ca*, Vidyābhavana Saṁskṛta Granthamālā, no. 97 (Benares: Caukhambā Vidyābhavana, 1963), 39–40: *sahṛdayānām iti yeṣāṁ kāvyānuśīlanābhyāsavaśāt viśadībhūte manomukure varṇīyatanmayībhavanayogyatā te svahṛdayasaṁvādabhājaḥ sahṛdayāḥ*. Translation from Ānandavardhana, *The Dhvanyāloka of Ānandavardhana with the Locana of Abhinavagupta*, Harvard Oriental Series, no. 49, trans. Daniel H. H. Ingalls, Jeffrey Moussaieff Masson, and M. V. Patwardhan (Cambridge: Harvard University Press, 1990), 70.

135. *Tolkāppiyam: Iḷampūraṇar uraiyuṭaṉ: Poruḷatikāram*, verse 271, 393.

136. For a general introduction to Indian poetic theory, in addition to Gerow's *Indian Poetics*, see V. K. Chari, *Sanskrit Criticism* (Honolulu: University of Hawaii Press, 1990); G. Vijayawardhana, *Outlines of Sanskrit Poetics*, Chowkhamba Sanskrit Studies, no. 76 (Varanasi: Chowkhamba Sanskrit Series Office, 1970); and A. K. Warder, *The Science of Criticism in India*, Adyar Library General Series, no. 7 (Madras: The Adyar Library and Research Centre, 1978).

137. The discussion of heightened emotional experience in *Tolkāppiyam* is relatively short, comprising only twenty-seven stanzas. Perhaps not surprisingly, given the text's emphasis on love themes, the bulk of the discussion focuses on the erotic.

138. George L. Hart III, *The Poems of Ancient Tamil: Their Milieu and Their Sanskrit Counterparts* (Berkeley: University of California Press, 1975), and Hart, *The Relation Between Tamil and Classical Sanskrit Literature*, A History of Indian Literature, vol. 10, fascicle 2, ed. Jan Gonda (Wiesbaden: Otto Harrassowitz, 1976). In both works Hart argues for a view of the Sanskrit and Tamil literary traditions as continually engaged in processes of dialogue and exchange, going so far as to suggest that Tamil influenced certain Sanskrit poetic ideals, based on his analysis of shared poetic conventions (e.g., the themes of messenger and lovers separated by the monsoon), shared poetic meters (e.g., the Ārya, which Hart maintains is not native to Sanskrit), and shared techniques of poetic suggestion.

139. Among the many studies of the *Maṇimēkalai* to date, only David Shulman's brief article ("Cāttaṉār's Dream Book," in *A Buddhist Woman's Path to Enlightenment: Proceedings of a Workshop on the Tamiḻ Narrative* Maṇimēkalai, *Uppsala University, May 25–29, 1995*, Acta Universitatis Upsaliensis: Historica Religionum, vol. 13, ed. Peter Schalk [Uppsala, Sweden: Uppsala University, 1997], 241–260) has made any attempt to discuss the text's effect on its audience. Shulman interpets the *Maṇimēkalai* as a series of interlocking dream sequences, as "a book about the structure, the inner dynamics, and the potentialities of awareness" (245).

140. The *Tolkāppiyam*, as noted previously, discusses the various emotional/aesthetic experiences (meyppāṭu), landscape (tiṇai), and poetic themes of love and war, but there exists no theoretical discussion in classical Tamil of the particular sort of narrative/philosophical text exemplified by the *Maṇimēkalai*.

141. As at xviii.130–133:

> Even if my heart loses all control and goes out to him,
>   even if he holds my bangle[-laden] arm,
> it is not proper to deny him, he who was my husband.

142. Buddhadatta, *Madhuratthavilāsinī*, 92–94.

143. Compare this to the portrayal of Maṇimēkalai's entry into the Buddhist life in the *Cilappatikāram* (xxx.24–28); there, Mātavi shaves off her daughter's beautiful, long, flower-bedecked hair.

144. David Shulman, *The King and the Clown in South Indian Myth and Poetry* (Princeton, N.J.: Princeton University Press, 1985), 72.

145. In the *Cilappatikāram*, it is Kavunti, the Jain nun, who is said to cast a curse born of the power of her penance (x.245: *cāpaviṭai ceytu tavap perum ciṟappiṉ*); see *Cilappatikāram*, 264.

146. Eco, *Six Walks*, 49–73. The technique of using lengthy descriptive passages to create "space," to cause the audience to linger and reflect before the advent of significant events in the narrative, is one employed several times in the text of the *Maṇimēkalai*. Before Maṇimēkalai and her friend, Cutamati, witness the crystal pavilion and its magnificent Buddha pedestal in the Uvavaṉam park, for example, the text provides a long description of the people whom they encounter along the way, as well as the flora and fauna of the park itself (iii.86–iv.24). Maṇimēkalai's encounter with her paternal grandfather, Mācāttuvāṉ, and her entry into Kāñcīpuram and subsequent receiving of instruction from Aṟavaṇaṉ, are all preceded by a sixty-three-line description of the city of Vañci and its surrounding moat.

147. Richman, *Branch Stories*, 167–174, presents three different Pāli versions of the story (from the *Manorathapūraṇī*, Dhammapāla's commentary on the *Therīgāthā*, and the *Dhammapada-aṭṭhakathā*). When Gotamī's son dies, she wanders about looking for someone who can revive the boy. Finally, she encounters the Buddha, who asks her to collect a mustard seed from every home in which no one has ever died. Going from house to house and eventually realizing that not one is free of death, Gotamī comprehends that all life is transient and that all beings are destined to suffer and die. Eventually, she joins the order of Buddhist nuns.

148. For one interpretation of some of the stylistic differences between the Pāli and Tamil stories, see Richman, *Branch Stories*, 79–100.

149. That all must die is the basic message of the Buddha to Kisāgotamī. In the *Dhammapada-aṭṭhakathā* version of the story, for example, the verse given is (Norman, *Commentary on the Dhammapada*, vol. 2, 287):

> Death seizes and bears away that man who is possessed with longing
> for sons and herds of cattle,
> like a great flood [overtaking] a sleeping village.

150. The audience at this point has already learned that Maṇimēkalai's existence comprises three distinct periods or phases: in her past lives, actions were performed in ignorance of their ultimate consequences; her present life constitutes a period of dawning understanding; and in future lives, she will be reborn again and again as a man in Magadha, the Buddha's country, where she will eventually serve as his chief disciple (xxi.173–179).

151. Abhinavagupta's *Abhinavabhāratī* (commentary on Bharata's *Nāṭyaśāstra*), translated in J. L. Masson and M. V. Patwardhan, *Aesthetic Rapture: The Rasādhyāya of the Nāṭyaśāstra*, vol. 1 (Poona: Deccan College, 1970), 33.

152. *Tolkāppiyam: Iḷampūraṇar uraiyuṭaṉ: Poruḷatikāram*, verse 271, 393.

153. Ānandavardhana, *Dhvanyāloka*, 50; translated by Ingalls et al., *Dhvanyāloka*, 81.

154. Martha C. Nussbaum, *Love's Knowledge: Essays on Philosophy and Literature* (New York: Oxford University Press, 1992), 165.

155. J. Hillis Miller, "Narrative," in *Critical Terms for Literary Study*, 2d ed., ed. Frank Lentricchia and Thomas McLaughlin (Chicago: University of Chicago Press, 1995), 66–79.

156. Robert Alter, *The World of Biblical Literature* (New York: Basic Books, 1992), 45.

157. Like all Tamil and Sanskrit ornate poetic works, the *Maṇimēkalai* elicits any number of moods, with a single emotion, in this case pathos, predominating.

158. *Tolkāppiyam: Iḷampūraṇar uraiyuṭaṉ: Poruḷatikāram*, verse 249, 364–365.

159. *Pacalai*, a technical literary term in old Tamil that refers to the pale complexion of a woman suffering the loss of separation from her husband or lover. *Index des mots de la litterature tamoule ancienne*, Publications de l'institut français d'indologie, no. 37, vol. 3 (Pondichéry: Institut Français d'Indologie, 1970), 938, lists more than fifty occurrences of this term in the Caṅkam poetic anthologies.

160. See Richman, *Branch Stories*, 3.

161. As Shulman (*King and the Clown*, 72) notes in his brief remarks on Āputtiraṉ, modern commentators on the text have noted that the scene in which Āputtiraṉ digs up the bones of his former body on the island of Maṇipallavam is particularly "laden with pathos."

162. See Anne E. Monius, "Literary Theory and Moral Vision in Tamil Buddhist Literature," *Journal of Indian Philosophy* 28/2 (2000):195–223.

163. From *antaram*, "sky," literally "she who lives in the sky." The bards sing the praises of such a being at *Cilappatikāram*, xiii.104. Although the term, in later Tamil literature, becomes synonymous with the goddess Durgā, it is unclear that that identification can be made here.

164. The precise meaning of this term is somewhat obscure, but perhaps it means "guardian of the Vindhyā hills," from the verb "to drive off" (*kaṭi*). This, combined with the use of "she who lives in the sky" mentioned previously, perhaps constitutes a reference to the goddess in her form as Vindhyavāsinī. See David Kinsley, *Hindu Goddesses: Visions of the Divine Feminine in the Hindu Religious Tradition* (Berkeley: University of California Press, 1988), 107, and Cynthia Ann Humes, "Vindhyavāsinī: Local Goddess Yet Great Goddess," in *Devī: Goddesses of India*, ed. John Stratton Hawley and Donna Marie Wulff (Berkeley: University of California Press, 1996), 49–76.

165. *Tolkāppiyam Iḷampūraṇar uraiyuṭaṉ: Poruḷatikāram*, verse 249, 364–365.

166. xvii.62–66:

> In the Tamiḻ land, on the island of Campu,
> there is a city of virtue where ascetics dwell
> and where wealthy people, whose riches are constant,
> help those who are helpless.
> Even though [it will take] many days [to get there] by overland travel,
> [go and] enter that city!

167. See *Tolkāppiyam Pērāciriyar uraiyuṭaṉ: Poruḷatikāram*, 9, and U. V. Cāminātaiyar, ed., *Puṟanāṉūṟu mulam* (Madras: Mahamahopadhyaya Dr. U. V. Swaminathaiyer Library, 1936; Reprint, 1993), verse 252, 133. Translation by Ramanujan, *Poems of Love*, 175.

168. Cāminātaiyar, *Puṟanāṉūṟu*, verse 248, 132. Translation by Ramanujan, *Poems of Love*, 178.

169. R. Irākavaiyaṅkār, *Kuṟuntokai viḷakkam* (Aṇṇāmalai, India: Aṇṇāmalaip Palkalaik Kaḻakam, 1993), verse 97, 162. Translated by Martha Ann Selby in Norman Cutler and Paula Richman, eds., *A Gift of Tamil: Translations from Tamil Literature in Honor of K. Paramasivam* (New Delhi: Manohar and American Institute of Indian Studies, 1992), 12.

170. Quoted in *Tolkāppiyam: Iḷampūraṇar uraiyuṭaṉ: Poruḷatikāram*, 365; see also Cāminātaiyar, *Puṟanāṉūṟu*, verse 255, 134. Translated by Ramanujan, *Poems of Love*, 176.

171. Richman, *Branch Stories*, 53–78.

172. *Tolkāppiyam: Iḷampūraṇar uraiyuṭaṉ: Poruḷatikāram*, verse 77, 127–135.

173. Ibid., verses 53–54, 64–69. Verse 54 lists the following four situations suggestive of improper love: (1) the lover's mounting of a palm-stem horse to proclaim his grief, (2) the old age of one of the lovers, especially the woman, (3) the state of complete loss of sanity due to a violent passion, and (4) forced sexual union in such a state.

174. Paul Ricoeur, *Oneself as Another*, trans. Kathleen Blamey (Chicago: University of Chicago Press, 1992), 115.

175. The academic study of Buddhist ethics is a rapidly growing field, as witnessed by the success of the on-line periodical, *Journal of Buddhist Ethics* (http://jbe.la.psu.edu/). For an overview of the field as a whole, see Frank E. Reynolds, "Buddhist Ethics: A Bibliographic Essay," *Religious Studies Review* 5/1 (1979):40–48, and a more recent update of Reynolds' work, Charles Hallisey, "Recent Works on Buddhist Ethics," *Religious Studies Review* 18/4 (1992):276–285. Writers such as Ricoeur address the relationship between narrative and ethics in a wholly western context; the role of narrative literature as a medium for Buddhist ethical inquiry has thus far been little explored. See Charles Hallisey and Anne Hansen, "Narrative, Sub-Ethics, and the Moral Life: Some Evidence from Theravāda Buddhism," *Journal of Religious Ethics* 24/2 (1996):305–327.

176. Martha C. Nussbaum, *Poetic Justice: The Literary Imagination and Public Life* (Boston: Beacon, 1995), xvi, for example, argues for the relevance of literature in thinking about moral choices because engagement with a literary work presupposes a capacity to reflect on and appreciate the lives of others: "I defend the literary imagination precisely because it seems to me an essential ingredient of an ethical stance that asks us to concern ourselves with the good of other people whose lives are distant from our own."

177. This ethical question, the problem of finding value and meaning in human action in a world conditioned by forces beyond human control, takes precedence in the *Maṇimēkalai* over any concern with the specifics of ontology or liberation; the text is strikingly lacking, for example, in terms so often associated with the Buddhist quest for enlightenment, terms such as *bodhisatta*, nibbāna, or arahant. The very structure of the overall text itself, as discussed previously—the fact that in the story of "the renunciation of Maṇimēkalai" the renunciatory vow takes place only in the final two lines of the narrative—suggests that the world of everyday human affairs and interactions is the arena that most concerns the *Maṇimēkalai*, not the rarefied existence of the ascetic few.

178. George L. Hart III, "Archetypes in Classical Indian Literature and Beyond," in *Syllables of Sky: Studies in South Indian Civilization in Honour of Velcheru Narayana Rao*, ed. David Shulman (Delhi: Oxford University Press, 1995), 167.

179. Ānandavardhana, *Dhvanyāloka*, 368–369; translation by Ingalls et al., *Dhvanyāloka*, 437.

180. Ānandavardhana, *Dhvanyāloka*, 200; translation by Ingalls et al., *Dhvanyāloka*, 226.

181. Ānandavardhana, *Dhvanyāloka*, 570.

182. Ibid., 570–580.

183. V. Raghavan's study of equanimity as a ninth category of aesthetic experience, *The Number of Rasas*, Adyar Library Series, vol. 21 (Madras: Adyar Library and Research Center, 1975), notes (23–24) that "the Buddhist and Jain poets and dramatists might have been responsible for the introduction of religious and philosophical poems and plays, for making Śānta the Aṅgin or Leading Rasa of the Ādhikārika-itivṛtta or main theme." Raghavan quotes (23) the lines from Aśvaghoṣa's *Saundarananda* that claim that the great poetic work (mahākāvya) was composed for the sake of peace (*upaśānti*) and liberation (mokṣa), and mentions the same author's *Buddhacarita* as among the earliest poetic works evoking peace or equanimity (śānta; 36). J. L Masson and M. V. Patwardhan, *Śāntarasa and Abhinavagupta's Philosophy of Aesthetics*, Bhandarkar Oriental Series, no. 9 (Poona: Bhandarkar Oriental Research Institute, 1969), provide a far more detailed analysis of Abhinavagupta's understanding of equanimity (śānta) as the most significant of aesthetic experiences.

184. In similar fashion, Āputtiraṉ, who in many ways represents a paradigm of generosity and benevolent rule, once failed to think about the impact of his actions on others when he

committed suicide on Maṇipallavam. Uncovering the bones of those who sought to rescue Āputtiraṉ from the island, Tīvatilakai accuses the man now reborn as King Puṇṇiyarācaṉ of Cāvakam:

> You took your [own] life.
> You took the lives of the others who came afterward [in search of you],
> pitying your life.
> Are you not the murderer who has become king? (xxv.172–174)

185. See ii.68, xvi.84–85, and xxv.77–78, for example.

186. As in the stories of Kāyacaṇṭikai, Ilakkumi's feeding of Cātucakkaraṉ, the Nāgas' concern with what they will eat if they refrain from killing, the drought in Kāñcīpuram, Āputtiraṉ's service to the poor of Maturai, the hunger in Cāvakam until Āputtiraṉ is reborn there, and the repeated appeals to the prince and king to rule justly to ensure regular rainfall.

187. "Great Physician" is a common epithet of the Buddha throughout Buddhist literature in all languages, including the *Maṇimēkalai*; at ix.61, for example, he is called "doctor" (*maruttuvaṉ*).

188. That Puṇṇiyarācaṉ hastily puts his minister in charge of the affairs of the kingdom and goes off to Maṇipallavam anyway contributes to a certain moral ambiguity in his character. As noted previously, on Maṇipallavam the king is also chided for the deaths of those who came looking for him after he committed suicide in his birth as Āputtiraṉ. Like Kāñcaṉaṉ, Āputtiraṉ is a consummately human character, torn between his own despair, his gradual awakening to spiritual interests, and his earthly duties as king. Both characters would appear to acknowledge the inherent difficulties of acting in the interest of others when all human beings are drawn to act in their own self-interest. Shulman (*King and Clown*, 64–75) focuses on this conflicted nature of his kingship, as the character is torn between his duty to rule and a growing predilection for asceticism.

189. Cāminātaiyar, *Puṟanāṉūṟu*, verse 186, 101. Translation by Ramanujan, *Poems of Love*, 158.

190. Here, Maṇimēkalai refers to her previous existence as the wife of Utayakumaraṉ/Irākulaṉ.

191. *Uyir*, meaning "life" or "breath," in this Buddhist context is difficult to define precisely; in later Hindu literature, it comes to be mean "soul."

192. Iraṅkal here might also be understood as "feeling" or "pity" for others.

193. See xi.30–36. Here, Tīvatilakai, the guardian of the miraculous almsbowl, explains to Maṇimēkalai that those fortunate enough to gain knowledge of former births before the Buddha's seat are "rare in this world."

194. Geoffrey Galt Harpham, "Ethics," in *Critical Terms for Literary Study*, ed. Frank Lentricchia and Thomas McLaughlin, 2d ed. (Chicago: University of Chicago Press, 1995), 404.

195. As Nussbaum, *Love's Knowledge*, 15, points out in the case of classical Greek drama, the recitation or performance of a text in a communal setting in broad daylight creates an experience quite unlike the dark and "splendid isolation" of the modern theater-goer.

196. Bharata, *Nāṭyaśāstra*, vol. 3, 242:

> *jitendriyajñānavatī nānāśilpavicakṣaṇā*
> *dakṣiṇādhamahālakṣyā bhītānāṁ parisāntvanī*
> *nānāśāstrārthasaṁpannā gambhīryaudāryaśālinī*
> *sthairyatyāgaguṇopetā jñeyā prakṛtir uttamā*

Translation by Masson and Patwardhan, *Aesthetic Rapture*, vol. 1, 41; at vol. 2, 56, note 335, the authors suggest correcting *dakṣiṇādhamahālakṣyā* to *dakṣiṇā mahālakṣyā*.

Chapter 2

1. Brian Stock, in his study of the impact of literacy on eleventh-century European culture (*The Implications of Literacy* [Princeton, N.J.: Princeton University Press, 1983], 522), uses the term "textual communities" to describe "groups of people whose social activities are centered around texts, or, more precisely, around a literate interpreter of them. . . . [T]he group's members must associate voluntarily; their interaction must take place around an agreed meaning for the text. Above all, they must make the hermeneutic leap from what the text says to what they think it means; the common understanding provides the foundation for changing thought and behavior." Stock's phrase is particularly useful in the case of the *Maṇimēkalai*, where the text is the only source of evidence for a historical community.

2. Jacques Le Goff, *The Medieval Imagination*, trans. Arthur Goldhammer (Chicago: University of Chicago Press, 1988), 5.

3. Umberto Eco theorizes this connection between the literary and the historical in his discussion of the narrative "wood" as a public interpretive space shaped by the model author of the text. In the narrative wood, the reader must make "reasonable" choices, interpretive decisions grounded in the text's own narrative strategies, signals, and signs. "Since a wood is created for everybody," he writes, "I must not look there for facts and sentiments which concern only myself. Otherwise . . . I am not interpreting a text but rather *using* it" (*Six Walks in the Fictional Woods*, Charles Eliot Norton Lectures, 1993 [Cambridge: Harvard University Press, 1994], 9–10). In another essay, Eco discusses possible interpretations of the line in Wordsworth's poem, "I wander lonely as a cloud," that reads: "A poet could not but be gay." How can one be sure here whether *gay* means "happy" or "homosexual"? "[A] sensitive and responsive reader," writes Eco, " . . . has the duty to take into account the state of the lexical system at the time of Wordsworth. . . . If I want to *interpret* Wordsworth's text I must respect his cultural and linguistic background." As Eco extends his argument, if the text of the poem were found in a bottle—completely cut off from any historical context, in other words—the reader must consider all possible meanings of the word in the context of what the text itself says; in that case, the reader is "not speaking about the author's intentions but about the text's intention, or about the intention of the Model Author that I am able to recognize in terms of textual strategy" (Umberto Eco, with Richard Rorty, et al., *Interpretation and Overinterpretation*, ed. Stefan Collini [Cambridge: Cambridge University Press, 1992], 68–69). In other words, what Eco suggests here is that interpretation grounded in the rules embedded in the text itself is legitimate. All such interpretations, whether ancient or contemporary, together constitute the history of the reception of the text.

4. Dominick LaCapra, *Rethinking Intellectual History: Texts, Contexts, Language* (Ithaca, N.Y.: Cornell University Press, 1983), 44.

5. Jane P. Tompkins, "The Reader in History: The Changing Shape of Literary Response," in *Reader-Response Criticism: From Formalism to Post-Structuralism*, ed. Jane P. Tompkins (Baltimore: Johns Hopkins University Press, 1980), 210, sums up this attitude quite succinctly: "The first requirement of a work of art in the twentieth century is that it should *do* nothing."

6. *Identity* is a term ubiquitous in literary criticism and modern discourses of race, gender, and nationality but one that is seldom defined or used with precision. For the purposes of this project, *identity*, specifically *religious identity*, can simply be taken to mean an awareness of continuity between oneself and a larger community, an identification with a larger religious tradition and the community imagined or envisioned by that tradition. For various definitions of the term and an overview of the use of *identity* in recent decades, see Philip Gleason, "Identifying Identity: A Semantic History," *Journal of American History* 69/4 (1983):910–931, and Norman N. Holland, "Unity Identity Text Self," in *Reader-Response Criticism: From Formalism to Post-Structuralism*, ed. Jane P. Tompkins (Baltimore: Johns Hopkins University Press, 1980), 118–133.

7. Benedict Anderson, *Imagined Communities: Reflections on the Origin and Spread of Nationalism*, 2d ed. (London: Verso, 1991), 6, employs the phrase "imagined political community" to define the concept of nation: "It is *imagined* because the members of even the smallest nation will never know most of their fellow-members, meet them, or even hear of them, yet in the minds of each lives the image of their communion." Anderson briefly extends the idea of the imagined community to the realm of religion, noting that "the great sacral cultures . . . incorporated conceptions of immense communities . . . imaginable largely through the medium of sacred language and written script" (12–13).

8. Whether or not this is the same Cāttaṉ to whom the *Maṇimēkalai* is attributed is, of course, uncertain. Of significance here is the fact that the prefaces of both the *Maṇimēkalai* and the *Cilappatikāram* tie the texts together through the appearance of the characters Cāttaṉ and King Iḷaṅkō.

9. This and all references to the *Cilappatikāram* are drawn from Iḷaṅkō Aṭikaḷ, *Cilappatikāram mūlamum Arumpata uraiyum Aṭiyārkkunallār uraiyum*, ed. U. V. Cāminātaiyar (Madras: Mahamahopadhyaya Dr. U. V. Swaminathaiyer Library, 1978).

10. T. V. Gopal Iyer, ed., *Tēvāram: Hymnes Śivaites du pays Tamoul*, Publications de l'institut français d'indologie, no. 68, vol. 1 (Pondichéry: Institut Français d'Indologie, 1984), 195. All later references to the *Tēvāram* are taken from this edition. Translated by Indira Viswanathan Peterson, *Poems to Śiva: The Hymns of the Tamil Saints*, (Princeton, N.J.: Princeton University Press, 1989), 189.

11. From the poem "Aṟputattituvantāti," translated in part by Norman Cutler, *Songs of Experience: The Poetics of Tamil Devotion* (Bloomington: Indiana University Press, 1987), 119.

12. This is supported not only by commentarial tradition but also by the fact that Nīlakēci's first opponent is a Buddhist teacher named Kuṇṭalakēci (see A. Chakravarti, ed. and trans., *Neelakesi: The Original Text and the Commentary of Samaya-Divakara-Vamana-Muni* [Kumbakonam, India: By the author, 1936], vol. 1, 141–145; vol. 2, 57–86).

13. This pairing is made by Umāpati Civācāriyar in his fourteenth-century account of the writing of the *Periyapurāṇam*, the *Tiruttoṇṭarpurāṇa varalāṟu*; see Chandralekha Vamadeva, *The Concept of* Vaṉṉaṉpu *'Violent Love' in Tamil Śaivism, with Special Reference to* Periyapurāṇam, Uppsala Studies in the History of Religions, no. 1 (Uppsala, Sweden: Uppsala University, 1995), 95.

14. The Buddhists' supposed fondness for luxurious robes, tasty food (especially meat), and fine wine receives as much, if not more, hostile attention from the *Nīlakēci* than the doctrine of "no soul" (*anattā*).

15. Iyer, *Tēvāram*, vol. 1, 399, translated in Peterson, *Poems to Śiva*, 276. Peterson (270–282) provides a brief overview of the life and poetry of Campantar, the poet-saint who devotes the tenth stanza in each of his hymns to vitriolic attacks against Jain (and sometimes Buddhist) monks. Peterson's "*Śramaṇas* Against the Tamil Way: Jains as Others in Tamil Śaiva Literature," in *Open Boundaries: Jain Communities and Cultures in Indian History*, ed. John E. Cort (Albany: State University of New York Press, 1998), 163–185, provides the most thoughtful analysis of the attitudes of the earliest Śaiva poets toward their (primarily Jain) opponents; this topic is taken up for further discussion later.

16. Although the *Mattavilāsa* is clearly attributed to Mahendravarman (or Śrīmahendravikramavarman) in the stage manager's opening remarks (see "The Text and Translation of *Mattavilāsa Prahasanam* [A Farce of Drunken Sport]," in Michael Lockwood and A. Vishnu Bhat, ed. and trans., *Metatheater and Sanskrit Drama* [Madras: Tambaram Research Associates, 1994], 2), the authorship of the *Bhagavadajjukam* has given rise to more controversy. Lockwood and Bhat, making use of both epigraphical and internal textual evidence, offer a convincing argument that the play is, indeed, the work of the Pallava king (see Lockwood and

Bhat, "The Farce of the Drunken Courtesan," in *Metatheater and Sanskrit Drama*, 3–13). Lockwood and Bhat's discussion of "metatheater" in relation to Sanskrit drama and the texts and translations of Mahendravarman's two satires are bound together in one volume but paged separately. Quotations from the dramas will be cited with the play title and page number according to the pagination for that particular text within the larger volume.

17. Lockwood and Bhat's introductions to their translations of the two plays in *Metatheater and Sanskrit Drama*, as well as Michael Lockwood, *Māmallapuram and the Pallavas* (Madras: Christian Literature Society, 1982), provide useful discussions of the literary talents of the Pallava king.

18. Mahendravarman's own religious affiliation is unclear. The Tamil Śaiva tradition, based on verses found in the *Periyapurāṇam*, remembers him as a Jain who was converted to Śaivism by the saint, Appar, who was himself an ex-Jain. The Pallava king who subsequently persecutes the Jains remains unnamed, however, in Cēkkiḻār's text. See Cēkkiḻār, *Tiruttoṇṭarpurāṇam Periyapurāṇam*, ed. V. Kaliyāṇacuntaraṉār and M. Pālacuppiramaṇiyamutaliyār (Madras: Cēkkiḻār Ārāycci Maiyam, 1993), 482–483.

19. Lockwood and Bhat, *Metatheater and Sanskrit Drama*, "Bhagavadajjukam," 30.

20. See the story of the god, Pācaṇṭa Cāttaṉ, who assumes the body of the dead child of Mālati, in *Cilappatikāram*, chapter 9, "The Story of the Narration of the Nature of the Dream."

21. One kāvatam equals a distance of approximately ten miles.

22. "Bhagavadajjukam," 20.

23. Ibid., 25; Lockwood and Bhat, *Metatheater and Sanskrit Drama*, "Mattavilāsa," 69.

24. "Bhagavadajjukam," 29.

25. Ibid., 23.

26. "Mattavilāsa," 66.

27. Ibid., 67.

28. Ibid., 63

29. Ibid., 64.

30. Ibid., 64.

31. Of the more than 150 satirical dramas listed in Suram Srinivasulu, *Hāsya and Prahasana: A Critical Study* (Guntur, India: Navodaya, 1989), Appendix I, the majority, and nearly all those composed in the premodern era, are believed to have been written in southern India. The satire, as a genre of Sanskrit drama, has been littled studied; S. Ramaratnam, *Prahasana in Sanskrit Literature* (Mysore: Kavyalaya, 1987), provides the best overview. According to Ramaratnam's survey, Sanskrit satire appears to have enjoyed popularity at distinct periods separated by many centuries. After the appearance of Mahendravarman's two plays in the seventh century, for example, there is no evidence that any more satirical dramas were written until the twelfth century; the genre appears to have been favored again in the seventeenth and eighteenth centuries.

32. As Lockwood and Bhat's observations concerning the Keralan tradition of interpreting the satirical drama in deeply religious, allegorical terms suggest ("Bhagavadajjukam," 9), literary cultures change dramatically over time. Despite the obvious fun made of allegorical interpretation in the *Mattavilāsa* passage concerning Kāñcī as a Vedic sacrificial altar cited previously, the sarcasm of the texts, the web of intertextual references and allusions that sustains the puns and parodies, would appear to have been forgotten long ago. K. K. Malathi Devi, *Prahasana in Sanskrit Literature and Kerala Stage* (Delhi: Nag, 1995), 160–173, discusses the performance of the *Mattavilāsa* and the *Bhagavadajjukam* in Kerala.

33. Such an emphasis is rather unusual because the Ājīvikas, for example, are often singled out in hostile texts for their principle of fate (Sanskrit niyati). "Fate" (*ūḻ* in classical Tamil) receives only a brief mention in the *Maṇimēkalai* (xxvii.164), and the bulk of the Ājīvika's discourse is devoted to the various types of "atoms" and their respective colors.

34. Because of his bad karma coming into force there,
oh king whose white umbrella surpasses [the beauty and majesty of] the moon,
your son, Utayakumaraṉ, did not leave [the public rest house].
[His bad karma] brought [Maṇimēkalai] there to the public rest house (*ampalam*),
led [your son] there in the pitch blackness of midnight,
summoned the semidivine being with the sharp sword who was Kāyacaṇṭikai's husband,
confused the mind of [that] vengeful being [into thinking that] this man here, [Utayakumaraṉ], had come to see the woman [who was his wife],
and cut down this man here, [your son], in the public rest house through the sword in the [vidyādhara's] hand.

35. Titthāyatana is taken to mean "the sphere or fold of a sect" in the Pali Text Society's dictionary (T. W. Rhys Davids and William Stede, *The Pali Text Society's Pali-English Dictionary* [London: Pali Text Society, 1921–1925; Reprint, 1992], 302). Kotatsu Fujita, "The Doctrinal Characteristics of *Karman* in Early Buddhism," in *Indological and Buddhist Studies: Volume in Honour of Professor J. W. de Jong on His Sixtieth Birthday*, ed. L. A. Hercus, et al. (Canberra: Faculty of Asian Studies, 1982), 149, translates tīṇi titthāyanāni as the "three grounds of the sectarian tenets"; Shwe Zan Aung, translator of Ledi Sayadaw, "Some Points in Buddhist Doctrine," *Journal of the Pali Text Society* (1913–1914):117–118, suggests the three "harbours of error."

36. Richard Morris, ed., *The Aṅguttara-nikāya*, vol. 1 (London: Henry Frowde, for Pali Text Society, 1885), 173. Fujita ("*Karman* in Early Buddhism," 149) offers the following English translation of the relevant passage based on F. L. Woodward, trans., *The Book of Gradual Sayings*, vol. 1 (London: Pali Text Society, 1932), 157:

> There are, monks, certain recluses and brahmins who speak thus, who hold this view: "Whatsoever pleasure (*sukha*), pain (*dukkha*) or neither-pain-nor-pleasure (*adukkhamasukha*) this person experiences, all that is due to previous action (*pubbekatahetu*)." There are, monks, certain recluses and brahmins who speak thus, who hold this view: "Whatsoever pleasure, pain nor neither-pain-nor-pleasure this person experiences, all that is due to the creation of a supreme deity (*issaranimmānahetu*)." There are, monks, certain recluses and brahmins who speak thus, who hold this view: "Whatsoever pleasure, pain or neither-pain-nor-pleasure this person experiences, all that is without a cause, without condition (*ahetu-appacayā*)."

The *Maṇimēkalai* dispenses quickly with the last two views. The story of Cāṅkalaṉ (whose name pointedly derives from Viṣṇu's mighty bow, *śāṅga*) and Kōtamai emphasizes the futility of looking to the divine to intervene in the processes of karma; as Campāpati explains to the grieving mother, to maintain that the gods can bring back life is merely "the hypocritical [rationalization] of cruel people who say that killing is a virtue" (vi.162–163). Indeed, the entire temple of the cosmic place (cakkiravāḷak kōṭṭam) is constructed by Mayaṉ to commemorate the gathering of the gods to convince Kōtamai of the limitations of their powers (vi.190–202). Tuvatikaṉ, the painting on the pillar, bluntly says that "only the ignorant (*aṟiyār*) say that god can protect [one] from the pain of bad karma" (xxi.63–64), and Aṟavaṇaṉ ends his discourse on interdependent origination by reminding Maṇimēkalai that no one can intervene in the cycle of bondage and liberation (xxx.250–251). The last of the three wrong views, that experience is unconditioned by any cause at all, is singled out for special ridicule in the *Maṇimēkalai*. The exponent of such a doctrine, the Pūtavāti or Bhūtavādin of xxvii.266–283, is the only one of the ten Vañci teachers to appear twice in the narrative: first in the predictions of Tuvatikaṉ at xxi.103–112, where the painting foretells Maṇimēkalai's contempt for his ideas, and second, in chapter twenty-seven, where the Bhūtavādin is the only teacher with whom Maṇimēkalai engages directly in debate (after she laughs at him in contempt).

37. *Naṟṟiṇai* 216–219, in H. Veṅkaṭarāmaṉ, ed., *Naṟṟiṇai mūlamum uraiyum* (Madras: Mahamahopadhyaya Dr. U. V. Swaminathaiyer Library, 1989), 392–400.

38. U. V. Cāminātaiyar, ed., *Puṟanāṉūṟu mūlam* (Madras: Mahamahopadhyaya Dr. U. V. Swaminathaiyer Library, 1993), poem 278, stanzas 4–5, 143.

39. This concern with spiritual or magical power in the text has been little explored in the secondary literature, and I am indebted to Professor Alexander M. Dubianski of the Institute of Asian and African Countries, Moscow State University, for several illuminating conversations on this topic. Although the definitive interpretation of the *Cilappatikāram* has yet to be published, a list of the available secondary sources, as well as the various editions and translations of the text, can be found in Kamil V. Zvelebil, *Lexicon of Tamil Literature*, Handbuch der Orientalistik, Zweite Abteilung, no. 9, ed. J. Bronkhorst (Leiden: E. J. Brill, 1992), 144–148. This work does not mention the recent translation, Iḷaṅkō Aṭikaḷ, *The Cilappatikāram of Iḷaṅkō Aṭikaḷ: An Epic of South India*, trans. R. Parthasarathy (New York: Columbia University Press, 1993).

40. *Cilappatikāram*, preface, lines 61–62.

41. *Maṇimēkalai*, preface, lines 95–98.

42. Both the *Maṇimēkalai* and the *Cilappatikāram* share a substantial amount of imagery and vocabulary not found in other works of Tamil literature of the same or earlier historical period. The principal characters common to both texts, for example–Kōvalaṉ and Kaṇṇaki, Mātavi and Maṇimēkalai–appear in no other Tamil works. The same holds true for the Indra monastery (Tamil *intiravikāram*, Pāli *vihāra*; *Cilappatikāram*, x.14, xxvii.92; *Maṇimēkalai*, xxvi.55, xxviii.70), the lengthy descriptions of the festival in honor of Indra (*Cilappatikāram*, v; *Maṇimēkalai*, i), and the detailed discussions of the many arts of the courtesan (e.g., *Cilappatikāram*, iii; *Maṇimēkalai*, ii.18–32) to cite but a few examples.

43. *Cilappatikāram* 10–11. Aṭiyārkkunallār also maintains here that the *Maṇimēkalai* preceeded the *Cilappatikāram*, an observation that few subsequent scholars have taken seriously (see Zvelebil, *Lexicon of Tamil Literature*, 115).

44. The epilogue, line 4, says that the story deals with virtue, wealth, and love, and lines 17–18 contend that the *Cilappatikāram* really ends with the story told in the *Maṇimēkalai*.

45. Richman, *Women, Branch Stories, and Religious Rhetoric in a Tamil Buddhist Text*, Foreign and Comparative Studies/South Asia Series, no. 12 (Syracuse, N.Y.: Maxwell School of Citizenship and Public Affairs, Syracuse University, 1988), 158–160.

46. The connection between the *Cilappatikāram* tragedy and spiritual liberation in the *Maṇimēkalai* is made most explicit in the story of Maṇimēkalai's grandfather, Mācāttuvāṉ (*Maṇimēkalai*, xxviii.93–100):

> Listen, oh lady!
> Having heard of the suffering and death [of your] father and mother
> [and of] the destruction of the prosperous city [of Maturai] because of [their] bad karma,
> I became worthy of the compassionate dharma of the Buddha.
> Realizing that the householder's life is delusory,
> and realizing conclusively that neither wealth nor the body are even the least bit permanent,
> I undertook great austerities.

A few lines later, at xxviii.141–147, Mācāttuvāṉ reveals that he and his son, Kōvalaṉ, will achieve liberation on the same day (in the future) at the feet of the coming Buddha.

47. Indra instructs the goddess: "End the sorrow of he who suffers in the vast sea, [he who is] the lord at the foot of the bodhi tree, the first being."

48. R. Vijayalakshmy, *Tamiḻakattil Ācīvakarkaḷ* (Madras: International Institute of Tamil Studies, 1988), 41–68, discusses the use of the term ūḻ in Tamil literature. Although both ūḻ

and vinai are used synonymously in modern Tamil to denote karma, such an identification of terms occurred after the composition of the *Maṇimēkalai*; as noted previously, the Ājīvika teacher encountered by Maṇimēkalai uses ūḻ to distinguish fate from viṉai, or karma (xxvii.164).

49. The compound ūḻviṉai occurs infrequently in the *Maṇimēkalai* and clearly is used to mean matured or ripened karma, as at vi.152 and xx.123.

50. To return, for example, to the account of Utayakumaraṉ's death given at xxii.193–203 and cited previously, the prince's bad karma (tīviṉai) is shown to be a force at work in creating the many circumstances that lead to the murder; it not only compels Utayakumaraṉ himself to stay in the rest house but also propels Maṇimēkalai and Kāñcaṉaṉ into their respective roles.

51. The community or sectarian context to which the *Cilappatikāram* belongs is far less clear than in the case of the *Maṇimēkalai*. The *Maṇimēkalai*'s overtly doctrinal arguments and biting sarcasm are largely absent from the *Cilappatikāram*, and the latter's characters worship a variety of deities, from village goddesses and the mighty Durgā to Buddha, Śiva, and the image of Viṣṇu at Śrīraṅkam. Kavunti, the female ascetic who accompanies Kōvalaṉ and Kaṇṇaki on their arduous journey to Maturai, would appear to be a Jain, judging from her physical description (x.98–99) and her fast unto death (xxvii.83); as Zydenbos notes, however, Kavunti reveals a regard for family life and an almost wistful satisfaction for the love between husband and wife that seems odd for a committed Jain renunciant (Robert J. Zydenbos, "The Jaina Nun Kavunti," *Bulletin d'études indiennes* 5 [1987]:387–417). Kavunti worships a sage outside Śrīraṅkam who praises a lord or being of omniscience, power, and love who might be claimed by any number of religious communities (x.170–207). In short, it is difficult to affix a label such as *Jain* or *Buddhist* to the worldview expressed in the *Cilappatikāram*, although given the position of the *Maṇimēkalai* vis-à-vis this text, discussed later, *Buddhist* would seem to be among the least satisfactory of labels.

52. For more on the gods and goddesses of Pāli canonical and commentarial literature, see J. R. Haldar, *Early Buddhist Mythology* (New Delhi: Manohar, 1977), 70–128.

53. *Cilappatikāram*, xxvii.1.

54. As Kaṇṇaki informs Maṇimēkalai at xxvi.36–37, time spent in heaven as a goddess will not diminish in any way the bad karma brought about by her fiery act of vengeance on the king and people of Maturai.

55. A minister of the king who seized an innocent gold merchant, Caṅkamaṉ, and put him to death. Caṅkamaṉ's wife (now reborn as Kaṇṇaki), in utter despair, hurled herself from a mountain peak. See *Cilappatikāram*, xxiii.137–176, and *Maṇimēkalai*, xxvi.14–32.

56. The two characters are not given names in the *Cilappatikāram* text.

57. Mālati visits the temple of the wishing tree of the immortals, the temple of the white elephant, the temple of the handsome white god, the temple of the sun, the temple of the guardian deity of Pukār (unnamed here but identified as Campāpati in the *Maṇimēkalai*), the temple of the deity with the spear (Murukaṉ), the temple of Indra's thunderbolt, the temple of the Nikkantas (Nirgranthas or Jains), and the temple of the moon (ix.11–13).

58. Identified by Parthasarathy (*Cilappatikāram of Iḷaṅkō Aṭikaḷ*, 379) in his glossary as "Pācaṇṭaṉ Aiyaṉār, a village god learned in texts on heretical religions."

59. David Shulman, *Tamil Temple Myths: Sacrifice and Divine Marriage in the South Indian Śaiva Tradition* (Princeton, N.J.: Princeton University Press, 1980), 138–144, provides an excellent discussion of the relationship between female power, marriage, and womanly virtue in Tamil literature.

60. Kamil V. Zvelebil, *Tamil Literature*, Handbuch Orientalistik, Zweite Abteilung: Indien, vol. 2, no. 1, ed. Jan Gonda (Leiden: E. J. Brill, 1975), 111, note 6.

61. *Maṇimēkalai*, iii.5–6. Here, Maṇimēkalai sheds tears at the tragedy of her "parents"; at xxvi.2–4, the image of Kaṇṇaki is said to be that of Maṇimēkalai's "mother." Just as Cutamati describes Maṇimēkalai at v.13–17 as an ascetic of mature spiritual powers (tapas), so, too, is

Kaṇṇaki identified by an oracle at *Cilappatikāram*, xii.48, as the "sprout" (*koḻum*) of former austerities (*ceyta tavam*).

62. Much like the *Rāmāyaṇa* story found in various renditions throughout India and South and Southeast Asia, cutting across religious or sectarian lines; see Paula Richman, ed., *Many Rāmāyaṇas: The Diversity of a Narrative Tradition in South Asia* (Berkeley: University of California Press, 1991). The *Cilappatikāram* story survives in a variety of forms (Sally A. Noble, "The Tamil Story of the Anklet: Classical and Contemporary Tellings of the *Cilappatikāram*" [Ph.D. Diss., University of Chicago, 1990]), from the classical Tamil telling to the liturgical songs of the Pattiṉi cult in Sri Lanka (Gananath Obeyesekere, *The Cult of the Goddess Pattini* [Chicago: University of Chicago Press, 1984; Reprint, Delhi: Motilal Banarsidass, 1987]) and the modern oral versions studied by Beck (Brenda E. F. Beck, "The Study of a Tamil Epic: Several Versions of the *Silappadikaram* Compared," *Journal of Tamil Studies* 1 [September 1972]:23–38).

63. *Tirukkuṟaḷ mūlamum Parimēlaḻakar uraiyum* (Tinnevelly: South India Saiva Siddhanta Works Publishing Society, 1991), verses 54–55, 24. As noted in the previous chapter, Richman provides a detailed discussion of the quotation as it occurs in the midst of the story of Maruti, narrated to the king before he is told the tragic news of Utayakumaraṉ's death. Maruti, like Maṇimēkalai, has been wronged by a prince of the city and is told by a great semidivine being (*mā perum pūtam*) that she has lost the power to command the rains because she has been worshiping gods other than her husband; the guardian deity tells her that she must follow the life of a chaste wife if she is to regain such power. See Richman, *Branch Stories*, 109–111.

64. See, for example, the comments of Albert Schweitzer ("There hardly exists in the literature of the world a collection of maxims in which we find so much lofty wisdom") given in Zvelebil, *Tamil Literature*, 123, note 77. Reverend G. U. Pope, who began his missionary work in Mylapore (Madras), a spot often associated with the author of the *Tirukkuṟaḷ*, was fascinated by possible connections between the author of the Tamil text and the Christian legends placing Saint Thomas in the same region at roughly the same time: "The East and West have influenced one another in a very real and not yet thoroughly understood way from the earliest times. It is undoubtedly a noteworthy fact that from this Mayilāpūr, on which the eyes of Christendom have ever rested as the one sacred spot in India of Apostolic labour, comes the one Oriental book, much of whose teaching is an echo of the 'Sermon on the Mount'" (see G. U. Pope, ed. and trans., *The Sacred Kurral of Tiruvalluva-Nayanar with Introduction, Grammar, Translation, Notes, Lexicon, and Concordance* [London: Henry Frowde, 1886; Reprint, New Delhi: Asian Educational Services, 1990], iii).

65. For a summary of the available secondary literature on the *Tirukkuṟaḷ*, see Zvelebil, *Lexicon of Tamil Literature*, 669–671. Not cited by Zvelebil is Norman Cutler's valuable article on the *Kuṟaḷ*'s commentarial tradition, "Interpreting *Tirukkuṟaḷ*: The Role of Commentary in the Creation of a Text," *Journal of the American Oriental Society* 112/4 (1992):549–566.

66. Chakravarti, *Neelakesi*, vol. 2, 124, 143. The first instance quotes *Kuṟaḷ*, verse 292, that a falsehood can be taken as true if it produces an undeniably good result; the second quotes verse 261, defining penance (*tavam*) as bearing one's own pain without inflicting pain on others.

67. Subramania Gopalan, "Dhammapada and Tirukkuṟaḷ: A Comparative Study," in *Pāli Buddhism*, ed. Frank J. Hoffman and Mahinda Deegalle (Richmond, U.K.: Curzon, 1996), 57–77, attempts a comparative look at the *Tirukkuṟaḷ* and the Buddhist *Dhammapada*.

68. See Richman's discussion in *Branch Stories*, 109–111.

69. Ibid., 110.

70. Richard Valantasis, "Constructions of Power in Asceticism," *Journal of the American Academy of Religion* 63/4 (1995):799.

71. Martha C. Nussbaum, *Poetic Justice: The Literary Imagination and Public Life* (Boston: Beacon, 1995), 1–2.

72. See, for example, Richman's excellent discussion of the manner in which the *Maṇimēkalai* transforms the Caṅkam desert landscape (*pālai*) into "a meditation on life's impermanence" (*Branch Stories*, 58–78).

73. That the king is a Bhāgavata (Vaiṣṇava) is evident in the long passage at xix.51–114, in which the king likens the dance of a peacock, peahen, and swan to the dancing of Kṛṣṇa, his brother, and his favorite consort (known as Nappiṉai; lines 61–66), and then mistakes a dark green bamboo tree for Kṛṣṇa and a *katampu* tree with white flowers for Kṛṣṇa's elder brother (lines 75–77).

74. That the *Maṇimēkalai* does not direct its sarcastic remarks at various characters for their views of reality, ritual, or the divine, but rather concentrates on a perceived lack of moral integrity, suggests that the points of departure among various traditions (at least from a Buddhist perspective) were quite different in early medieval South India than in the modern study of religion. The *Maṇimēkalai* does not set its Buddhist vision of the world over and against that of the Jain or Bhāgavata on the basis of the superiority of the Buddha over the Jina or Lord Viṣṇu but rather focuses on right attitude, on proper modes of living. A text such as the *Maṇimēkalai* presents a valuable opportunity for rethinking the criteria for distinguishing one religious tradition or community from another, for re-evaluating the grounds on which sectarian identities are defined and defended in historical context.

75. *Local* in this case does not mean "vernacular" in the sense of regional spoken dialect. By the time of the *Maṇimēkalai*'s composition, Tamil was—whatever the form of the language spoken in southern India might have been—a highly developed literary language, as witnessed by the Caṅkam poetic corpus, the *Tolkāppiyam*, the *Tirukkuṟaḷ*, and works such as the *Cilappatikāram*. The language choice on the part of the author is thus a choice between the literary languages of the cultural elite, each envisioning different, and overlapping, reading communities.

76. Sheldon Pollock, "Literary History, Region, and Nation in South Asia: Introductory Note," *Social Scientist* 23/10–12 (1995):3.

77. Anderson, *Imagined Communities*, 12. Although Anderson grounds his notion of the immense religious community in the use of a translocal language (i.e., Arabic = Islam), "Tamil" literary culture, as discussed throughout this chapter, is fundamentally multilingual. "Tamil," as the *Tolkāppiyam* quote cited later indicates, encompasses a region of southern India where Tamil is perhaps the dominant spoken language, but where, as argued previously, the choices of literary language are several.

78. *Tolkāppiyam: Eḻuttatikāram, Iḷampūraṇar uraiyuṭaṉ* (Tinnevelly: South India Saiva Siddhanta Works Publishing Society, 1955; Reprint, 1996), 10:

vaṭa vēṅkaṭam teṉ kumari
āyiṭait
tamiḻ kūṟu nallulakattu

Although Tamil may be characterized as a cosmopolitan language, in use not only in South India but also in Sri Lanka and Southeast Asia, this earliest of Tamil grammars does not consider the poetic language it describes to be transregional in scope. In the *Tolkāppiyam* and in the Buddhist *Vīracōḻiyam* discussed in following chapters, Tamil inhabits a particular region, a carefully bounded space.

79. H. C. Norman, ed., *The Commentary on the Dhammapada*, vol. 2 (London: Henry Frowde, for Pali Text Society, 1906–1915; Reprint, London: Luzac, for Pali Text Society, 1970), 217–227; *Therīgāthā-Aṭṭhakathā* (*Paramatthadīpanī VI*), ed. William Pruitt (Oxford: Pali Text Society, 1998), 99–108.

80. As noted previously, four lines are quoted in the commentary on *Nīlakēci*, 190; see Chakravarti, *Neelakesi*, vol. 2, 71. The same four lines are also quoted in Caṇmukacuntara

Mutaliyār, ed., *Civañāṉacittiyār parapakkam mūlamum Cattuvapirakācar uraiyum* (Madras: By the editor, 1894), 125, and the text is cited as *Vimpacārakatai*.

81. For a summary of the Pāli stories surrounding King Bimbisāra, see G. P. Malalasekera, *Dictionary of Pāli Proper Names*, vol. 2 (London: John Murray, for Government of India, 1938), 285–289.

82. *Encyclopedia of Tamil Literature*, s.v., vol. 1, "Jainism and Tamil Literature," by R. Vijayalakshmy, 205–206.

83. Ibid., vol. 1, 202. See also R. Vijayalakshmy's *A Study of the Perunkatai: An Authentic Version of the Story of Udayana* (Madras: International Institute of Tamil Studies, 1981), and U. V. Cāminātaiyar, *The Story of Udayana*, trans. T. R. Rajagopala Aiyar (Madras: Mahamahopadhyaya Dr. U. V. Swaminathaiyer Library, 1983).

84. Vijayalakshmy, "Jainism and Tamil Literature," 210.

85. Peterson, *Poems to Śiva*, Appendix D, 343–348.

86. Sheldon Pollock, "Philology, Literature, Translation," in *Translating, Translations, Translators: From India to the West*, Harvard Oriental Series: Opera Minora, vol. 1, ed. Enrica Garzilli (Cambridge: Department of Sanskrit and Indian Studies, Harvard University, 1996), 114.

87. Anderson, *Imagined Communities*, 2–13.

88. Christina Schaffner, "Editorial," in *Cultural Functions of Translation*, ed. Christina Schaffner and Helen Kelly-Holmes (Clevedon, U.K.: Multilingual Matters, 1995), 3.

89. Ibid., 3.

90. For a discussion of "foreignising" and "domesticating" as "the two main translation strategies," see Lawrence Venuti, "Translation and the Formation of Cultural Identities," in *Cultural Functions of Translation*, ed. Christina Schaffner and Helen Kelly-Holmes (Clevedon, U.K.: Multilingual Matters, 1995), 9–25.

91. Rita Copeland, *Rhetoric, Hermeneutics, and Translation in the Middle Ages: Academic Traditions and Vernacular Texts* (Cambridge: Cambridge Univesity Press, 1991), 222.

92. Pollock, "Philology, Literature, Translation," 114–115, 117–118.

93. Velcheru Narayana Rao, "Coconut and Honey: Sanskrit and Telugu in Medieval Andhra," *Social Scientist* 23/10–12 (1995):27.

94. Shu Hikosaka discusses the "glossarial problems" posed by the *Maṇimēkalai*'s use of both Tamil translations and transliterations of Sanskrit terms, particularly in the chapter dealing with Buddhist logic, in *Buddhism in Tamilnadu: A New Perspective* (Madras: Institute of Asian Studies, 1989), 135–137; see 160–164 for a discussion of the "nativization" of Buddhism "at the linguistic level."

95. *Index des mots de la litterature tamoule ancienne*, Publications de l'institut françois d'indologie, no. 37, vol. 2 (Pondichéry: Institut Français d' indologie, 1967–1970), 729. *Tarumam* (from the Sanskrit dharma) occurs more frequently as a synonym for the Tamil aṟam in the *Maṇimēkalai* than in any previous text (see *Index des mots*, vol. 2, 716).

96. *Index des mots*, vol. 2, 487. Note that *karumam* (from the Sanskrit karma) in the *Maṇimēkalai* occurs only in compound, as in "collection of karma" (*karumat tokuti*) used at xxx.112 as a synonym for "becoming" (*bhava*) in the context of interdependent origination.

97. The defeat of Māra is an episode common to many versions of the Buddha's life story, including several of his previous existences. See, for example, the *Nidānakathā* or introduction to the *Jātaka* collection (V. Fausbøll, ed., *The Jātaka Together with Its Commentary: Being the Tales of the Anterior Births of Gotama Buddha*, vol. 1 [London: Kegan Paul, Trench, Trubner, 1877–1897], 63, 71–74) and the *Khadiraṅgāra-jātaka*, in which the Buddha-to-be overcomes Māra's fiery efforts to thwart his almsgiving (Fausbøll, vol. 1, 226–234).

98. From the story of the Buddha-to-be born as King Sivi, who offers his own eyes to Sakka, disguised as a blind brahmin (Fausbøll, vol. 4, 401–412).

99. See the story of the Buddha's intervention in a Nāga war (Mahānāma, *The Mahāvaṁsa*, 7–9).

100. Fausbøll, vol. 1, 51. As in the *Maṇimēkalai*, human deformities disappear, the inhabitants of hell suffer no more, the rains fall abundantly, and all beings live in peace and harmony.

101. The principal exception to this, among the main branch stories, is the long tale of Āputtiraṉ. If the *Maṇimēkalai* draws upon other sources for the basic story, the nature of those sources is unclear. When compared to the other branch stories full of "Tamilized" Indo-Āryan names (see later), the name Āputtiraṉ itself presents an interesting combination of an old Tamil word (*ā* for "cow") and a Sanskrit term (*puttiraṉ* for Sanskrit *putra* or "son").

102. As when Vicākai exhorts her cousin, Tarumatattaṉ (Dharmadatta), a merchant who has amassed great wealth: "Immeasurable wealth does not last! . . . Perform generous acts (tāṉam)!" (xxii.136–138).

103. For the story of Visākhā, see Norman, *Commentary on the Dhammapada*, vol. 1, 151–154. In Morris, *Aṅguttāra-nikāya* (vol. 1, 26), Visākhā is referred to as "first among donors" (*dāyikānaṁ aggā*). Note that whereas Visākhā represents the paradigmatic lay patron of the monastic order, Vicākai, in the Tamil version of the story, remains unmarried; only in a future birth will she marry her beloved cousin, Tarumatattaṉ (xxii.97–98).

104. The *Saṅkha-jātaka* (Fausbøll, vol. 4, 15–22) and the *Mahājanaka-jātaka* (Fausbøll, vol. 6, 30–68), as well as the apocryphal *Samuddaghosa-jātaka* (Padmanabh S. Jaini, ed., *Paññāsa Jātaka or Zimme Paṇṇāsa (in the Burmese Recension)*, Pali Text Society Text Series, no. 172 [London: Pali Text Society, 1981], vol. 1, 64–82) and the *Candakumāra-jātaka* (Jaini, *Paññāsa Jātaka*, vol. 1, 259–269).

105. See chapter 1, note 111.

106. Note that in the *Maṇimēkalai*, xxix.14–33, the story of the rescue of Kōvalaṉ's (and thus Maṇimēkalai's) ancestor from the sea clearly makes Maṇimēkalai a direct descendent of the Buddha-to-be who was saved by Maṇimēkalā. Given this identification of Maṇimēkalai as a direct descendent of the Buddha-to-be and Rāhula's status as the son of the Buddha, both Maṇimēkalai and Irākulaṉ/Rāhula might, indeed, be taken as half-siblings.

107. Mary E. Lilley, ed., *Khuddaka Nikaya: Apadāna*, vol. 2 (London: Oxford University Press, for Pali Text Society, 1927), 551.

108. Richman, *Branch Stories*, 57.

109. Ibid., 95. This work (85) also provides a graphic illustration of this "urn-shaped" universe.

110. *Tamil Lexicon*, vol. 3 (Madras: University of Madras, 1982), 1382.

111. Ibid., vol. 5, 2816–2817.

112. Suggesting that in the multilingual literary culture of early medieval South India, the local literary language was viewed as the most potent for evoking the emotional awareness central to both the ethical vision of the *Maṇimēkalai* and its ornate poetic form. For reasons that remain historically unclear, Pāli remained underdeveloped as a literary language; the translocal medium for South Asian Buddhist poetry and drama was, from the time of Aśvaghoṣa's *Buddhacarita*, Sanskrit.

113. George L. Hart III and Hank Heifetz, *The Forest Book of the* Rāmāyaṇa *of Kampaṉ* (Berkeley: University of California Press, 1988), 7.

114. Although written some thousand years after the composition of the *Maṇimēkalai*, Civvākkiyar's seventeenth-century appreciation of the emotional force of Māṇikkavācakar's ninth-century poetry to Śiva, the *Tiruvācakam*, offers a succinct appraisal of the emotional power of Tamil verse that is perhaps not entirely irrelevant to the age of the *Maṇimēkalai*:

We have not seen hearts melt
and eyes flow with tears
when people read the Vedas,
but when they read the *Tiruvācakam*
even once, black stony hearts will melt
and tears will flow
as from springs in the sands.

(Quoted in A. K. Ramanujan, *Hymns for the Drowning: Poems for Viṣṇu by Nammāḻvār* [Princeton, N.J.: Princeton University Press, 1981]). Horton's discussion of the persistent view of Japanese literary culture, that the Japanese language possesses the greater power to express human feelings, even after the full-scale adoption of Chinese forms of writing and written expression in the early medieval period, perhaps suggests a certain parallel to the Tamil-Pāli/Sanskrit case in southern India (see H. Mack Horton, "Japanese Spirit and Chinese Learning: Scribes and Storytellers in Pre-modern Japan," in *The Ethnography of Reading*, ed. Jonathan Boyarin [Berkeley: University of California Press, 1993], 156–179).

115. Taken from Norman, *Commentary on the Dhammapada*, vol. 2, 270–275.

116. Ibid., vol. 2, 272.

117. Ibid., vol. 2, 272. Kisāgotamī is described here as one who has not seen death before (*sā adiṭṭhapubbamaraṇatāya*).

118. Ibid., vol. 2, 274: *Tassā evaṁ cintayamānāya puttasinehamudukaṁ hadayaṁ thaddhabhāvaṁ agamāsi.*

119. Or perhaps they simply remain unspoken by the author. What the emotional content of a simple declarative sentence in Pāli, such as "he died," might have been for an audience of readers/listeners is unclear. It is certain, however, that the *Maṇimēkalai* elaborates considerably on the human experience of grief and despair; what might have been understood in the more terse Pāli rendering of the story is spelled out in detail in the Tamil.

120. Richman, *Branch Stories*, 43, suggests this translation of "binding with language" (*pāṭaiyil piṇittu*), that is to say, winning the Nāgas over with his mastery of their language.

121. That language choice becomes overtly politicized is indicated by the fact that the first Pallava inscriptions written in Tamil appear only late in the sixth century; all prior inscriptions are written in either Sanskrit or Prākrit (see T. V. Mahalingam, *Kāñcīpuram in Early South Indian History* [New Delhi: Asia Publishing House, 1969], 16).

122. The resurgence of interest in Tamil language and literature in the modern era and its impact on nationalist and caste-centered political movements have been well documented by Eugene F. Irschick, *Politics and Social Conflict in South India: The Non-Brahmin Movement and Tamil Separatism, 1916–1929* (Berkeley: University of California Press, 1969), 275–310, and Sumathi Ramaswamy, *Passions of the Tongue: Language Devotion in Tamil India, 1891–1970* (Berkeley: University of California Press, 1997).

123. Karen Pechilis Prentiss, *The Embodiment of Bhakti* (New York: Oxford University Press, 1999), 68–76; Peterson, "*Śramaṇas* Against the Tamil Way," 163–185; Glenn E. Yocum, "Buddhism Through Hindu Eyes: Śaivas and Buddhists in Medieval Tamilnad," in *Traditions of Contact and Change: Selected Proceedings of the XIVth Congress of the International Association for the History of Religions*, ed. Peter Slater and Donald Wiebe (Waterloo, Ontario: Wilfrid Laurier University Press, 1983), 143–162; and R. Champakalakshmi, "Religious Conflict in the Tamil Country: A Re-appraisal of Epigraphic Evidence," *Journal of the Epigraphic Society of India* 5 (1978):69–81.

124. Although the phrase "geography of exclusion" has most commonly been used in reference to the alienating and divisive features of the western industrial city, the nature of such features—concern with establishing boundaries, separating the pure from the defiled, and con-

trolling "space"—is equally applicable to the literary landscape defined and defended by the Tamil devotional poets. For more on geographies of exclusion, see David Sibley, *Geographies of Exclusion: Society and Difference in the West* (London: Routledge, 1995).

125. Although the discussion to follow necessarily limits itself to the early Śaiva poets' presentation of the Buddhists (and Jains) as linguistically inept, the poets' full-scale frontal assault on the "foreign heretics" over issues of lifestyle, healing, ethical views, and attitudes toward divinity and Vedic sacrifice is a complex topic that warrants much further investigation. An equally fertile topic for further study is the relationship among the poetic works produced by Buddhists, Jains, and Hindu devotional poets in the early medieval period; although the poet-saints denounce their non-Hindu counterparts as foreigners, their poetry shares much in terms of vocabulary, imagery, and style with the literary works of those they condemn. A clearer appreciation of the ways in which Jains, Buddhists, Śaivas, and Vaiṣṇavas draw on a shared pool of images to often strikingly similar ends will certainly advance scholarly understandings of the manner in which religious communities define and set themselves apart, the ways in which boundaries between communities are envisioned and enacted. Richard Davis' conception of the "productive encounter" between Śaivas and Jains in the Tamil-speaking context represents a thoughtful move in this direction; see Davis, "The Story of the Disappearing Jains: Retelling the Śaiva-Jain Encounter in Medieval South India," in *Open Boundaries: Jain Communities and Cultures in Indian History*, ed. John E. Cort (Albany: State University of New York Press, 1998), 213–224.

126. Iyer, *Tēvāram*, hymn III–39, verse 2, vol. 1, 318.

127. Note particularly the description of the unwashed Jain monk who lumbers along the street "like an elephant in distress" (*Maṇimēkalai*, iii.86–91).

128. Iyer, *Tēvāram*, hymn III–39, verse 2, vol. 1, 318. Translated by Peterson in *Poems to Śiva*, 278.

129. Iyer, *Tēvāram*, hymn III–39, verse 4, vol. 1, 318.

130. Ibid., verse 11, vol. 1, 319.

131. Ibid., hymn III–69, verse 11, vol. 1, 348. Translated by Peterson in *Poems to Śiva*, 176.

132. Iyer, *Tēvāram*, hymn II–47, verse 11, vol. 1, 195.

133. Ibid., hymn III–47, verse 11, vol. 1, 326.

134. Ibid., hymn III–120, verse 11, vol. 1, 399.

135. Ibid., hymn VII–62, verse 8, vol. 2, 458. Translated by Peterson in *Poems to Śiva*, 323–324.

136. Iyer, *Tēvāram*, hymn VII–88, verse 8, vol. 2, 491.

137. Ibid, hymn VII–65, verse 2, vol. 2, 462.

138. Peterson, "*Śramaṇas* Against the Tamil Way," 172–173.

139. Appar in Iyer, *Tēvāram*, hymn V–48, verse 6, vol. 2, 159. Translated by Peterson in *Poems to Śiva*, 259.

140. The history of the Jains and Jain literary culture in Tamil-speaking South India, from the earliest Brāhmī inscriptions to the present day, is a long and complex one that has thus far been little studied. For a brief introduction to Jain literature composed in Tamil, see A. Chakravarti, *Jaina Literature in Tamil*, Jñānapīṭha Mūrtidevī Granthamālā, English Series, no. 3 (New Delhi: Bhāratīya Jñānapīṭha, 1974). In the Buddhist case, the centuries immediately preceding the age of Appar and Campantar represent an era of linguistic reform marked by Buddhist translation of vernacular commentaries into Māgadhī or Pāli. Buddhadatta and Buddhaghosa, according to legend, dedicated their monastic lives to rendering the local into the transregional, to making the "commentary . . . composed in the language of Sīharadīpa" intelligible to "the monks beyond the island" (Buddhaghosa, *Samantapāsādikā: Buddhaghosa's Commentary on the Vinaya Piṭaka*, vol. 2, ed. J. Takakusu and M. Nagai [London: Oxford University Press, for Pali Text Society, 1924–1976], 2). In that same text (*Samantapāsādikā*, vol. 1, 255), Buddhaghosa also dismisses Tamil as an example of an unrefined or tribal language (*milakkhakam*).

141. Peterson, *Poems to Śiva*, 15–16.

142. That literary culture and language choice play an important role in the shaping of religious identity can be clearly charted in the literary renaissance spurred by the introduction of Christianity to Tamil South India in the eighteenth and nineteenth centuries, a more historically accessible test case that bears some interesting parallels to the Buddhist material under discussion. The literary output of early Christian converts among the higher castes, such as the Veḷḷāḷa, is impressive, with works produced in a wide range of traditional literary genres on a variety of Christian themes (*Encyclopedia of Tamil Literature*, s.v., vol. 1, "Christianity and Tamil Literature," by G. John Samuel and L. R. John, 391–409). Vētanāyaka Cāstiri (Vedanayaga Sastri), the most influential of the early nineteenth-century Christian poets, produced more than 120 works, among them the "Bethlehem *Kuṟavañci*" (*Pettalakēṅkuṟavañci*), making use of a dramatic form (the *kuṟavañci*) popular in the Tañcāvūr Maratha court of the time. Like the temple of the cosmic place in the *Maṇimēkalai*, the "Bethlehem *Kuṟavañci*" emphasizes an appropriate cosmological model (one character juggles the planets of the solar system while describing their respective orbits); like the poetry of the Śaiva poet-saints, Vedanayaga Sastri vilifies his chief rivals, the Catholics, whenever possible. As in the *Maṇimēkalai*, where the courtesan embodies a certain definition of art and culture (see the long list of Mātavi's talents at ii.18–36) that is ultimately rejected by the text, so, too, does Vedanayaga Sastri's literary work condemn the culture of the female temple servants (*devadāsī*) in favor of a new, Christian lifestyle. His "Garland of Prayer Songs" (*Jepamāla*), a Tamil translation of the German Protestant hymnal, offers an interesting parallel to the *Maṇimēkalai*'s translation techniques discussed previously, adding new emotional and psychological content to the rather staid European songs. I thank Indira Peterson, currently working on a monograph-length study of the kuṟavañci dramas, for her insights into this literary genre. Kṛṣṇa Piḷḷai borrows the form and style of the Śaiva *Tēvāram* in his *Iraṭcaṇiya Maṉōkaram*, providing another example of a literary piece using classical forms to articulate the vision of a new religious community (Samuel and John, "Christianity and Tamil Literature," 401). Literature, particularly poetry, serves as the medium for the expression and imagining of a new Christian identity and community, one that is tied both to Bethlehem and to the court of Tañcāvūr, to the Bible and to local literary culture.

Chapter 3

1. Jacques Le Goff, *The Medieval Imagination*, trans. Arthur Goldhamner (Chicago: University of Chicago Press, 1988), 3.

2. Ibid., 5.

3. Ibid., 12.

4. Ibid., 80.

5. Ibid., 80.

6. Steven Collins, "*Nirvāṇa*, Time, and Narrative," *History of Religion* 31/3 (1992):246.

7. For more on the Pāli texts, such as the *Anāgatavaṁsa*, that deal explicitly with the nature and characteristics of the coming Buddha's earthly reign (and are labeled "prophetic texts" by K. R. Norman, *Pāli Literature: Including Canonical Literature in Prakrit and Sanskrit of All the Hīnayāna Schools of Buddhism*, History of Indian Literature, vol. 7, fascicle 2 [Wiesbaden: Otto Harrassowite, 1983], 160–162), see the discussion later in this chapter.

8. This is in keeping with the general rule that all Buddhas-to-be must take their penultimate birth in Tuṣita heaven. There, all the deities of the world implore him to be born on earth when the time is ripe for another Buddha to appear. See, for example, H. C. Norman, ed., *The Commentary on the Dhammapada*, vol. 1 (London: Henry Frowde, for Pali Text Society, 1906–1915; Reprint, London: Luzac, for Pali Text Society, 1970), 84.

9. Literally "in twice eight with twice eight hundred year(s)" (*īr eṇṇūṟṟōṭu īr eṭṭu āṇṭil*). The era or year to which this number refers is unclear and is discussed later.

10. Furthermore, if the story of Vicākai found at xxii.82–158 can, as suggested in chapter 2, be taken as a Tamil rendering of the story of the pious laywoman, Visākhā, it is interesting to note that Visākhā plays an important role in the reign of the future Buddha Metteyya in the Pāli prophetic text, the *Anāgatavaṁsa*. Verses 63–64 of that twelfth-century work state that Visākhā, along with a woman named Yasavatī, will renounce, along with 84,000 other women and men, at the command of Metteyya. See J. Minayeff, ed., "Anāgata-vaṁsa," *Journal of the Pali Text Society* (1886):47.

11. The empty pedestal, amidst the fragrant flowering gardens of Maṇipallavam, calls to mind the perfumed chamber (gandhakuṭī) prepared for the absent Buddha; see John S. Strong, "*Gandhakuṭī*: The Perfumed Chamber of the Buddha," *History of Religions* 16/4 (1977):390–406.

12. The text's orientation toward future events, particularly the implicit emphasis on preparing oneself to participate in the living Buddha's community, might explain Aṟavaṇaṉ's repetition of the teaching concerning ignorance (pētaimai) and good and bad karma (ceykai) at xxiv.111–140 and xxx.51–81. In both passages, the emphasis is on the attainment of good births, births that would enable one to accumulate the merit necessary to appear before the future Buddha and obtain liberation.

13. Alan Sponberg, "Introduction," in *Maitreya, the Future Buddha*, ed. Alan Sponberg and Helen Hardacre (Cambridge: Cambridge University Press, 1988), 2.

14. Ibid., 3.

15. V. Fausbøll, ed., *The Jātaka Together with Its Commentary: Being Tales of the Anterior Births of Gotama Buddha*, vol. 6 (London: Kegan Paul, Trench, Trubner, 1877–1897), 594.

16. Buddhaghosa, *The Path of Purification* (*Visuddhimagga*), trans. Bhikkhu Ñāṇamoli (Kandy, Sri Lanka: Buddhist Publication Society, 1991), i.135.

17. Jan Nattier, "The Meanings of the Maitreya Myth: A Typological Analysis," in *Maitreya, the Future Buddha*, ed. Alan Sponberg and Helen Hardacre (Cambridge: Cambridge University Press, 1988), 23–47, offers four basic categories of Maitreya myth: (1) those of the "here/later" variety that speak of a golden age to appear later on earth; (2) those of the "there/later" type that focus on rebirth during Maitreya's reign in Tuṣita heaven; (3) those of the "there/now" variety, emphasizing a mystical encounter with the Buddha-to-be in Tuṣita heaven; and (4) those of the "here/now" type, tranformed into an ideology of rebellion in parts of premedieval China.

18. The celestial Buddhas and Buddhas-to-be of the Sanskrit Maitreya traditions seem far removed from the Buddhas past and future envisioned by the *Maṇimēkalai* and are, therefore, not considered here. Sudhana's vision of the celestial Maitreya multiplied among the towers of Vairocana, as described in the *Gandavyūhasūtra*, to cite but one example, bears nothing in common with the brief descriptions of the coming Buddha found in the *Maṇimēkalai* (see Thomas Cleary, trans., *Entry into the Realm of Reality: A Translation of the Gandavyuha, the Final Book of the Avatamsaka Sutra* [Boston: Shambala, 1989], 328–378). For an overview of the relevant Pāli literature, see Padmanabh S. Jaini, "Stages in the Bodhisattva Career of the Tathāgata Maitreya," in *Maitreya, the Future Buddha*, ed. Alan Sponberg and Helen Hardacre (Cambridge: Cambridge University Press, 1988), 54–90, and Norman, *Pāli Literature*, 160–162.

19. J. Estlin Carpenter et al., ed., *Dīgha Nikāya*, vol. 3 (London: Henry Frowde, for Pali Text Society, 1911), 58–79.

20. Buddhadatta, *Madhuratthavilāsinī nāma Buddhavaṁsaṭṭhakathā of Bhadantācariya Buddhadatta Mahāthera*, ed. I. B. Horner (London: Humphrey Milford, for Pali Text Society, 1946), 252.

21. J. Minoyeff, ed., "Gandha-vaṁsa," *Journal of the Pali Text Society* (1886):60–61.

22. For later elaborations of the Metteyya story, see H. Saddhātissa, ed. and trans., *The Birth Stories of the Ten Bodhisattas and the* Dasabodhisattuppattikathā (London: Pali Text Society, 1975), and François Martini, ed. and trans., "Dasa-Bodhisatta-Uddesa," *Bulletin de l'École Française d'Extrême Orient* 36/2 (1937):287–390.

23. Mahānāma, *The Mahāvaṁsa*, ed. Wilhelm Geiger (London: Henry Frowde, for Pali Text Society, 1908), 265.

24. In its broadest outline, this scene echoes the story of the shipwrecked Buddha-to-be in the *Mahājanaka-jātaka* who, after his rescue, renounces his kingdom and wealth and becomes a monk (Fausbøll, *Jātaka*, vol. 6, 30–68).

25. A similar family connection to the future Buddha Metteyya can be seen in the *Mahāvaṁsa* passage cited above (Mahānāma, *Mahāvaṁsa*, 265), although the Buddha himself is in no way identified with the family of King Duṭṭhagāmaṇi. The passage states that the king's father and mother will be reborn as Metteyya's parents, Duṭṭhagāmaṇi's younger brother will serve as second disciple, and the king's son will be reborn as the Buddha's son.

26. The *Mahāvaṁsa*, generally assigned to the fifth or sixth century CE, thus marks a tradition of identifying the future Buddha with the current king that is roughly contemporaneous with the era of the *Maṇimēkalai*'s composition.

27. For a discussion of this process of identification in the case of Sinhala kings, see John Clifford Holt, *Buddha in the Crown: Avalokiteśvara in the Buddhist Traditions of Sri Lanka* (New York: Oxford University Press, 1991), 53–62.

28. See iii.149–150, where the good people of Pukār surround Maṇimēkalai and proclaim:

> Any mother who would cause [a daughter]
> of such beautiful appearance
> to undertake austerities
> is a cruel woman and an unfit mother!

29. Found in the collection of apocryphal Jātakas; see Padmanabh S. Jaini, *Paññāsa Jātaka or Zimme Paṇṇāsa (in the Burmese Recension)*, Pali Text Society Series, no. 172, vol. 2 (London: Pali Text Society, 1981), 396–402.

30. At which point the current Buddha, known as "Lord Former Dīpaṅkara" (*porāṇadīpaṅkaro bhagavā*), launches into a discussion of the eight prerequisites for successfully aspiring to Buddhahood. It is interesting to note that the third of the conditions, called simply hetu in other lists, is here explicitly termed "the three causes" (*tihetukam*), referring even more directly, it would seem, to the manifestations of the three beneficial root conditions of nonattachment, nonenmity, and nondelusion. See Jaini, *Paññāsa-Jātaka*, vol. 2, 399.

31. Ibid., vol. 2, 400.

32. Minayeff, "Anāgatavaṁsa," 50:

> *sukho vipāko puññānaṁ buddhaseṭṭhassa tādino*
> *tassa tejena pupphānaṁ acinteyyo pavāyati*

33. *Maṇimēkalai*, iii.3–4:

> *māmalar nāṟṟam pōl maṇimēkalaikku*
> *ētunikalcci etirntuḷatu.*

34. See N. Ross Reat, ed. and trans., *The Śālistamba Sūtra* (Delhi: Motilal Banarsidass, 1993). The *Śālistamba Sūtra*, a text of unknown antiquity that survives only in Tibetan and Chinese translations, deals in detail with the doctrine of interdependent origination. The entire teaching is given not by the Buddha Śākyamuni but by the Buddha-to-be Maitreya. In verse 47 (72–73), Maitreya explicitly ties knowledge of interdependent origination to future Buddhahood: "Whosoever . . . understands conditioned arising perfectly, for him the Tathāgata . . . predicts unsurpassable perfect, complete enlightenment (saying): 'He will become a perfect, complete Buddha!'"

35. Glossed in the commentary as "countless hundreds of thousands of rainy seasons" (*anekavassakoṭiyo*; Minayeff, "Anāgatavaṁsa," 41).

36. Carpenter, *Dīgha-Nikāya*, vol. 3, 74–75.

37. Nattier, "Meanings of the Maitreya Myth," 31.

38. For a discussion of Kassapa's probable dates, see Kassapa, *Mohavicchedanī Abhidhammamātikatthavaṇṇanā by Kassapatthera of Coḷa*, ed. A. P. Buddhadatta and A. K. Warder (London: Luzac, for Pali Text Society, 1961), x–xii.

39. Wilhelm Geiger, ed., *Cūlavaṁsa: Being the More Recent Part of the Mahāvaṁsa*, vol. 1 (London: Humphrey Milford, for Pali Text Society, 1925), 19.

40. Although Faxian quite consciously puts the story to follow in the mouth of an Indian monk (see the following), it is interesting to note in connection with the Chinese pilgrim that the emergence of an eschatological Maitreya cult in China in the fourth through sixth centuries—in which Maitreya's arrival on earth to save his devoted followers from suffering was believed to be imminent—coincides roughly with the date of the composition of the *Maṇimēkalai*. For a survey of the Chinese messianic texts of the early medieval period, see E. Zürcher, "'Prince Moonlight': Messianism and Eschatology in Early Medieval Chinese Buddhism," *T'oung Pao* 68/1–3 (1982):1–75, and Michel Strickmann, *Mantras et mandarins: le bouddhisme tantrique en Chine* (Paris: Gallimard, 1996), 59–126.

41. See Koichi Shinohara, "The Story of the Buddha's Begging Bowl: Imagining a Biography and Sacred Places," in *Sacred Biography and Sacred Place: Explorations in the Formation of Religious and Social Identity in Asia*, ed. Neil McMullin (Toronto: University of Toronto Press, forthcoming), 14–15. Other translations available include Faxian [Fa-hsien], *A Record of Buddhistic Kingdoms: Being an Account of the Chinese Monk Fa-Hsien of Travels in India and Ceylon* (AD *399–44) in Search of Buddhist Books of Discipline*, trans. James Legge (London: Dover, 1886; Reprint, New Delhi: Munshiram Manoharlal, 1991), and Faxian [Fa-hsien], *Travels of Fah-Hian and Sung-Yun, Buddhist Pilgrims from China to India* (*400* A.D. *and 418* A.D.), trans. Samuel Beal (London: Trubner, 1869; Reprint, New Delhi: Asian Educational Services, 1993), 159–164.

42. Faxian notes that an exact number of years between each change of location was given in the monk's recitation, but he has fogotten it. Beal (Faxian, *Travels of Fah-Hian*, 161) translates Faxian's general number as "in somewhat like a hundred years," whereas Legge (Faxian, *Record of Buddhistic Kingdoms*, 109) takes the term to mean "after so many hundred years." R. A. Giles (Faxian [Fa-hsien], *The Travels of Fa-hsien (399–414* A.D.*), or Record of the Buddhistic Kingdoms* [Cambridge: Cambridge University Press, 1923], 74) reads "after a great number of years"; a more condensed rendering of Faxian's text translates "after several centuries" (*A Record of the Buddhist Countries by Fa-hsien* [Peking: Chinese Buddhist Association, 1957], 85).

43. Shinohara, "Buddha's Begging Bowl," 14. The mountain, translated as "Pinna" by Beal (Faxian, *Travels of Fah-Hian*, 162) and "Anna" by Legge (Faxian, *Record of Buddhistic Kingdoms*, 109–110), is identified by both as a mountain at the foot of Mount Meru, home to the four deities (devas) who are said to guard the almsbowl.

44. Shinohara, "Buddha's Begging Bowl," 15.

45. Ibid., 15.

46. Zürcher, "Prince Moonlight," 31, interprets Faxian's account to mean that the story of the bowl's travels through the Buddhist world is "based on Indian tradition." The Chinese messianic texts of the period assign various dates to the coming of Maitreya and to the coming of the great Buddha-in-the-making, Candraprabhakumāra; see Zürcher, "Prince Moonlight," 18–24.

47. Himanshu P. Ray, *The Winds of Change: Buddhism and the Maritime Links of Early South Asia* (Delhi: Oxford University Press, 1994), 128.

48. C. Sivaramamurti, "Amaravati Sculptures in the Madras Government Museum," *Bulletin of the Madras Government Museum, New Series* 4 (1942):178.

49. Shinohara, "Buddha's Begging Bowl," 1–2.

50. For a discussion of the early medieval Chinese texts that tie the disappearance of the bowl relic to the decline of the Buddha's teachings and its reappearance on earth to the arrival

of Maitreya, see Françoise Wang-Toutain, "Le bol du Buddha: Propagation du bouddhisme et legitimité politique," *Bulletin de l'École Française d'Extrême-Orient* 81 (1994):59–82. As her subtitle suggests, Wang-Toutain interprets the bowl in Chinese narrative as a symbol of the propagation of Buddhist teachings, as well as a source of political legitimation for a succession of Chinese royal dynasties.

51. Identified by both Beal (Faxian, *Travels of Fah-Hian*) and Legge (Faxian, *Record of Buddhistic Kingdoms*) as modern Peshawar.

52. Xuanzang [Hsuan-tsang], *Si-yu-ki: Buddhist Records of the Western World*, vol. 2, trans. Samuel Beal (London: Kegan Paul, Trench, Trubner, 1884; Reprint, Delhi: Motilal Banarsidass, 1981), 278–279. In a note (277, note 92), Beal assumes that Xuanzang "did not visit [the kingdom of Po-la-sse] personally; he writes from report." Faxian, or more appropriately, the Indian monk whom Faxian cites, does not mention Po-la-sse as a future site for the Buddha's almsbowl, perhaps indicating a variety of competing visions of the Buddhist world drawn through the movement of the bowl relic in the early medieval period.

53. Shinohara, "Buddha's Begging Bowl," 15–16.

54. Mahānāma, *Mahāvaṁsa*, 133–139.

55. Ibid., 159.

56. Ibid., 272.

57. The sole exception to this is *Cūlavaṁsa*, xxxviii.189–198 (Geiger, *Cūlavaṁsa*, vol. 1, 15–16). Dharmaratna Herath, in his study of the political significance of the tooth relic for the kings of Sri Lanka, speculates that although the story of Devānaṁpiyatassa suggests "that some political importance was attached to the Bowl Relic during the early centuries" of Buddhism in Sri Lanka, by the time of the founding of the kingdom of Polonnaruva in the eleventh century, "the Tooth Relic superseded both the Bowl Relic and the Dhammacakka as symbols of political significance" (Dharmaratna Herath, *The Tooth Relic and the Crown* [Colombo: By the author, 1994], 91–94).

58. Marco Polo, *The Book of Ser Marco Polo the Venetian Concerning the Kingdoms and Marvels of the East*, vol. 2, trans. Henry Yule (London: John Murray, 1926), 319–320.

59. Dennis Hudson, in "The Courtesan and Her Bowl: An Esoteric Buddhist Reading of the *Maṇimēkalai*," in *A Buddhist Woman's Path to Enlightenment: Proceedings of a Workshop on the Tamil Narrative* Maṇimēkalai, *Uppsala University, May 25–29, 1995*, Acta Universitatis Upsaliensis: Historica Religionum, vol. 13, ed. Peter Schalk (Uppsala, Sweden: Uppsala University, 1997), 151–190, for example, offers an "esoteric" reading of the text that interprets the bowl as symbolic of Buddhist cultic rites parallel to those of the Bhāgavatas.

60. Xuanzang, *Buddhist Records of the Western World*, vol. 2, 98.

61. Geiger, *Cūlavaṁsa*, vol. 2, 474, 515.

62. Ibid., 515.

63. Collins, "*Nirvāṇa*, Time, and Narrative," 245.

64. Ibid., 246.

65. See Buddhadatta, *The Clarifier of Sweet Meaning* (*Madhuratthavilāsinī*): *Commentary on the Chronicle of the Buddhas* (*Buddhavaṁsa*), *by Buddhadatta Thera*, trans. I. B. Horner (London: Pali Text Society, 1978), xlv–xlvii. For an overview of the sources discussing the great treasures, see Vimalakīrti, *The Holy Teachings of Vimalakīrti* (*Vimalakīrtinirdeśa*), trans. Étienne Lamotte (French) and Sara Boin (English) (London: Pali Text Society, 1976), 167–168, note 34. According to some sources, Lamotte notes, the four treasures "are already in existence and are made use of by the local inhabitants, every seven years, on the seventh day of the seventh month" (167).

66. Faxian, *Travels of Fah-Hian*, 37, and Faxian, *Record of Buddhistic Kingdoms*, 35. Legge here explains in a note that "the king thought that his [karmic] virtue from the past was not yet sufficient to give him possession of the bowl."

67. Faxian, *Travels of Fah-Hian*, 38.

68. Shinohara, "Buddha's Begging Bowl," 16.

69. Mahānāma, *Mahāvaṁsa*, 272.

70. Geiger, *Cūlavaṁsa*, vol. 1, 15–16. As Herath, *Tooth Relic and the Crown*, 88, notes, the tooth relic eventually replaces the Buddha image and the bowl relic in the rain-making ritual.

71. Polo, *Book of Ser Marco Polo*, vol. 2, 320.

72. *Encyclopedia of Religion*, s.v., "Relics," by John S. Strong, 281: "[Relics] are clearly symbols of death and impermanence; they are what is left after the saints and founders of the tradition are no more. Yet . . . they also make manifest the continuing presence and life of these absent beings."

73. Shinohara, "Buddha's Begging Bowl," 16.

74. Faxian states explicitly that he told the Indian monk that he wished to put in writing the story about the movement of the bowl and the coming of Maitreya; the Indian monk responded by saying, "This is no sacred book, but only what I have learnt by memory, and repeat verbally" (Faxian, *Travels of Fah-Hian*, 164).

75. John S. Strong, *The Experience of Buddhism: Sources and Interpretations* (Belmont, Calif.: Wadsworth, 1995), 42.

76. Collins, "*Nirvāṇa*, Time, and Narrative," 246.

77. Faxian, *Travels of Fah-Hian*, 161: "When Fah Hian was residing in this country [Sri Lanka], he heard a religious brother from India, seated on a high throne, reciting a sacred book and [narrating the story of the bowl]."

78. Where Faxian himself claims to have seen the bowl, in the city of Puruṣapura; see Faxian, *Travels of Fah-Hian*, 36–38.

79. An obvious reference to Faxian's homeland.

80. Sri Lanka, where Faxian claims to have heard the story of the bowl.

81. In a sixth-century Chinese text attributed to Narendrayaśas, the Buddha predicts that the Buddha-to-be, Candraprabhakumāra (Yueguang), will be born as a great ruler who worships the bowl relic, brings it to the Chinese kingdom of Sui from Kashgar, and thus establishes the Buddhist dharma in his kingdom "on a grandiose scale"; see Zürcher, "Prince Moonlight," 25–26.

82. As argued by Wang-Toutain in "Le bol du Buddha."

83. Shinohara, "Buddha's Begging Bowl."

84. For a general discussion of the classical Caṅkam corpus that supplies many of the names and cities of its central characters, see Kamil V. Zvelebil, *Tamil Literature*, Handbuch der Orientalistik, Zweite Abteilung: Indien, vol. 2, no. 1, ed. Jan Gonda (Leiden: E. J. Brill, 1975), 80–109. The division of the *Cilappatikāram* into three books (*kāṇṭam*), each corresponding to one of the capital cities, has given rise to the claim that the text is the "first Tam[il] 'national' 'epic'"; see Kamil V. Zvelebil, *Lexicon of Tamil Literature*, Handbuch der Orientalistik, Zweite Abteilung: Indien, vol. 9, ed. J. Bronkhorst (Leiden: E. J. Brill, 1995), 146.

85. U. V. Cāminātaiyar, ed., *Pattuppāṭṭu mūlamum Nacciṉārkkiṉiyar uraiyum* (Tañcāvūr, India: Tamiḻp Palkaik Kaḻakam, 1986), 513–563.

86. Kāvirippūmpaṭṭiṉam, or Pukār, is also depicted as the site of a beautiful garden where the Buddha-to-be once cultivated meditative insight (*jhānābhiññaṁ nibbattesi*) in the *Akitti-jātaka*; see Fausbøll, *Jātaka*, vol. 4, 238.

87. Cāminātaiyar, *Pattuppāṭṭu*, 288–433.

88. As when Āputtiraṉ finds purpose in feeding the poor of Maturai after being cast out by his adopted brahmin community for showing compassion to a cow about to be sacrificed (xiii.104–115).

89. As at xiv.9–15, where Cintātēvi, whose "temple of the arts" lies in Maturai, hands the wondrous bowl over to Āputtiraṉ.

90. Cāminātaiyar, *Pattuppāṭṭu*, 133–134.

91. This story constitutes the central narrative of the third and final book of the *Cilappatikāram*, the *Vañcikkāṇṭam*.

92. The *Maṇimēkalai* mentions only briefly the "southern Potiyil [mountain]" (*teṉṟicaip potiyil*; xvii.24) as the mountain to which the loving couple, Kāñcaṉaṉ and Kāyacaṇṭikai, travel from their majestic city in the north. South India's Mount Potiyil, also known as Potalaka, becomes the focus of increasing Chinese interest from the sixth century onward, however, as the abode of Avalokiteśvara.

93. *Tolkāppiyam: Eḻuttatikāram, Iḷampūraṇar uraiyuṭaṉ* (Tinnevelly: South India Saiva Siddhanta Works Publishing Society, 1955; Reprint, 1996), 10.

94. The exact measure of distance indicated by the yojana has been a matter of some dispute, according to Monier Monier-Williams, *A Sanskrit-English Dictionary* (Oxford: Oxford University Press, 1899; Reprint, Delhi: Motilal Banarsidass, 1986), 858. With estimates ranging from two and one-half to nine miles, Monier-Williams sides in favor of the longer distance.

95. A mountainous island of naked ascetics located somewhere between South India and maritime Southeast Asia is depicted in a number of Chinese Buddhist sources. Yijing (I-tsing), the seventh-century pilgrim, for example, tells of a bountiful island of naked people (whom he does not particularly claim for Buddhism); see Yijing [I-tsing], *A Record of the Buddhist Religion as Practiced in India and the Malay Archipelago* (A.D. *671–695) by I-Tsing*, trans. J. Takakusu (Delhi: Munshiram Manoharlal, 1966), xxx–xxxi. The Chinese biography of a South Indian monk, Vajrabodhi, compiled in the tenth century, makes a similar, if more abbreviated, mention of "the country of naked people"; see Chou Yi-Liang, "Tantrism in China," *Harvard Journal of Asiatic Studies* 8/3–4 (1945):274, 318.

96. See Richman's discussion of this narrative in *Branch Stories*, 37–52.

97. See, for example, Xuanzang's *Buddhist Records of the Western World*, vol. 2, 236: "The country was originally (called) Pao-chu (Ratnadvīpa), because of the precious gems found there."

98. Given the linguistic possibility of *Cāvakam* as a Tamil form of *Java* or the more commonly found Sanskrit term *Yava*, and the association of camphor with the island (see later), the Cāvakam of the *Maṇimēkalai* has long been identified by Tamil scholars with the island of Java in the Indonesian archipelago. If the term refers specifically to the island currently known as Java is, of course, uncertain.

99. *Tavaḷam* (Sanskrit *dhavala*), here translated as "camphor," can also mean "white." As Jean Filliozat persuasively notes in his article, "The Oldest Sea-Routes of the Tamil Trade," *Bulletin of the Institute of Traditional Cultures, Madras* (July-December 1976):25–26, however, "white" as a translation makes little sense here, as "the mountains of Cāvakam are not white, they never receive snow and even if they are constituted of chalk, the whiteness of the chalk is not apparent on the external surface." Malaya and Sumatra have long been identified in Chinese and Arab sources as the center of a flourishing Asian camphor trade; see, for example, K. A. Nilakanta Sastri, "Takua-Pa (Siam) Tamil Inscription," *Journal of Oriental Research, Madras* 6/4 (1933):308–309.

100. As discussed by David Shulman in *The King and the Clown in South Indian Myth and Poetry* (Princeton, N.J.: Princeton University Press, 1985), 64–75.

101. A thorough exploration of the economic, political, and cultural ties between South and Southeast Asia in the early medieval period lies beyond the scope of this project. Much of the scholarship to date on the subject has focused either on the role of India as a premodern colonial power of sorts in Southeast Asia or on the continuity of local Southeast Asian cultures in the face of "Indianization" or "Hinduization." For a general discussion of the history of Indian contacts with Southeast Asian cultures and kingdoms, see Nicholas Tarling, ed., *The Cambridge History of Southeast Asia, Volume One: From Early Times to c. 1800* (Cambridge: Cambridge University Press, 1992; Reprint, 1999); G. Coedès, *The Making of South East Asia*, trans. H. M.

Wright (Berkeley: University of California Press, 1966); Paul Wheatley, *The Golden Khersonese* (Kuala Lumpur: University of Malaya Press, 1961); David G. Marr and A. C. Milner, eds., *Southeast Asia in the 9th to 14th Centuries* (Singapore and Canberra: Institute of Southeast Asian Studies, Singapore, and the Research School of Pacific Studies, Australian National University, 1990); and O. W. Wolters, *History, Culture, and Region in Southeast Asian Perspective* (Singapore: Institute for Southeast Asian Studies, 1982). Ray, *Winds of Change*, argues for the particular role of Buddhist monastic establishments in nurturing and sustaining trade between South and Southeast Asian ports.

102. Cāminātaiyar, *Pattupāṭṭu*, 550: *kaṭārattil uṇṭāṉa nukarum poruḷkaḷum.*

103. Cited in K. A. Nilakanta Sastri, *History of Sri Vijaya*, Sir William Meyer Lectures, 1946–1947 (Madras: University of Madras, 1949), 26. For a brief overview of the *Tivākaram*, see Zvelebil, *Lexicon of Tamil Literature*, 702.

104. Nilakanta Sastri, *History of Sri Vijaya*, 26. Coedès raises objections to the identification of Kāḻakam with Kedah; for a discussion of the controversy, see Wheatley, *Golden Khersonese*, 279, where Wheatley concludes that despite the validity of Coedès's argument, "no one can disagree with Nilakanta Sastri's conclusion that the word *Kāḷagam* stands for the name of a place having trade relations with Kaveripaṭṭinam."

105. *Cilappatikāram*, xiv.106–112.

106. Nilakanta Sastri, *History of Sri Vijaya*, 26. Wheatley, *Golden Khersonese*, 182, although not agreeing entirely with Nilakanta Sastri's insistence that Toṇṭi refers to a Malaysian locale, does concur that "the itemized products are certainly those of the Archipelago so that, whether or not we accept [Nilakanta Sastri's] argument in full, the passage does reflect some Indian acquaintance with the lands of South-East Asia."

107. V. Trenckner, ed., *The Milindapañho: Being Dialogues Between King Milinda and the Buddhist Sage Nāgasena*, James G. Forlong Series, vol. 5 (London: Royal Asiatic Society, 1928), 359. As Norman, *Pāli Literature*, 110, notes: "Nothing is known certainly about the origin of this text." Norman dates the *Milinda-pañha* to anywhere between the second century B.C.E. and the fifth century C.E., with the upper limit based on Buddhaghosa's direct knowledge of the text.

108. Perhaps a Pāli term for China. "Cīna" or "Cīnaraṭṭha" is also mentioned in a list of countries and peoples in Mary E. Lilley, ed., *Khuddaka Nikāya: Apadāna*, vol. 2 (London: Oxford University Press, for Pali Text Society, 1927), 359.

109. A substantial amount of ink has been spilled in the effort to identify which lands constitute this "land of gold." Suvaṇṇabhūmi has been identified by scholars with locations ranging from Lower Burma (G. P. Malalasekera, *Dictionary of Pāli Proper Names*, vol. 2 [London: John Murray, for Government of India, 1938], 1262–1263) to Sumatra.

110. As Norman, *Pāli Literature*, 111, notes, despite the controversies surrounding the origin of the text, its supposed "Greek connection," and its date of composition, it is clear that "all the geographical details [in the text] relate to North India." For a rough map of "Milinda's India," see Bhikkhu Pesala, trans., *The Debate of King Milinda: An Abridgment of the Milinda Pañha*, Buddhist Traditions, vol. 14 (Delhi: Motilal Banarsidass, 1991), viii.

111. Fausbøll, *Jātaka*, vol. 4, 15, and vol. 6, 34.

112. According to the introduction to the Pāli Jātakas, Majjhimadesa extends from Kajaṅgala, beyond which is Mahāsāla, to the river Salalavatī in the southeast, the town of Satakaṇṇika in the southwest, the brahmin village of Thūṇa in the west, and the Usīraddhaja mountain in the north (Fausbøll, *Jātakas*, vol. 1, 49).

113. L. De la Vallée Poussain and E. J. Thomas, eds., *Niddesa, Volume One: Mahāniddesa*, vol. 1 (London: Humphrey Milford, for Pali Text Society, 1916), 154–155.

114. N. A. Jayawickrama, ed., *Buddhavaṁsa and Cariyāpiṭaka*, Pali Text Society Text Series, no. 166 (London: Pali Text Society, 1974).

115. Buddhadatta concludes his commentary on the *Buddhavaṁsa* with an exposition of the eight differences that exist among the twenty-five Buddhas; such differences amount to variations in life span, height, family, time spent striving for enlightenment, the extent of the rays emanating from the Buddha, the vehicle used to depart the palace, the type of tree under which enlightenment is attained, and the span of the legs of the Buddha as he sits in a cross-legged position. See Buddhadatta, *Madhuratthavilāsinī*, 296–300. I. B. Horner provides a useful discussion of the formulaic nature of each of the *Buddhavaṁsa* stories in her introduction to *The Minor Anthologies of the Pali Canon, Part III: Chronicle of the Buddhas (Buddhavaṁsa) and Basket of Conduct (Cariyāpiṭaka)* (London: Pali Text Society, 1975), xix–lii.

116. A miracle performed by the Buddha to refute heretical teachers, in which he causes opposite forces or phenomena to appear in tandem (e.g., fire and water).

117. Buddhadatta, *Madhuratthavilāsinī*, 298.

118. Thanks are due to Professor R. A. L. H. Gunawardana of the Department of History, University of Peradeniya, Sri Lanka, for his insights on this topic of the early medieval reimagining of the Buddhist world.

119. Norman, *Pāli Literature*, 115, dates the *Dīpavaṁsa* to roughly the fourth century; to Mahānāma, the supposed author of the *Mahāvaṁsa*, he assigns a date later than Buddhaghosa (118, note 98), roughly the sixth century C.E. (132).

120. *Sujanappasādasaṁvegatthāya*. This phrase is found at the end of each chapter of the text.

121. Norman, *Pāli Literature*, 118. See as well Wilhelm Geiger, *The Dīpavaṁsa and the Mahāvaṁsa and Their Historical Development in Ceylon*, trans. E. M. Coomaraswamy (Colombo: Government Printer, 1908), 16–17.

122. Mahānāma, *Mahāvaṁsa*. See the twelfth chapter on "the virtue of various countries" (*nānādesapasādo*), 94–99.

123. Mahānāma, *Mahāvaṁsa*, 94.

124. Buddhaghosa, *Manorathapūraṇī: Commentary on the Aṅguttara Nikāya*, vol. 2, ed. Herman Kopp, et al. (London: Luzac, for Pali Text Society, 1924–1956), 36–37.

125. Faxian, *Travels of Fah-Hian*, 165–166.

126. Ibid., 150–151.

127. Ibid., 152.

128. Ibid., 153.

129. Xuanzang, *Buddhist Records of the Western World*, vol. 2, 229.

130. Ibid., 233. Mount Potalaka consistently marks South India as an important site in the Buddhist world for medieval Chinese authors. The tenth-century biography of the Tantric master Vajrabodhi, for example, depicts the monk as "a native of Malaya . . . in South India, . . . a district located near Potalaka Mountain, where Avalokiteśvara's palace was situated" (Yi-Liang, "Tantrism in China," 272).

131. Yijing, *Record of the Buddhist Religion*, 215.

132. Ibid., 45–47, describes the "grander" preparations for "fast-day" in "the ten islands of the Southern Sea"; to cite another example, Yijing also describes how the use of a cloth for kneeling among the monks of the "Southern Sea islands" causes Indian monks to smile (111).

133. See, for example, G. Coedès, *The Indianized States of Southeast Asia*, ed. Walter F. Vella, trans. Susan Brown Cowing (Honolulu: East-West Center Press, 1968), 81–82.

134. Yijing, *Record of the Buddhist Religion*, xxx.

135. Ibid., 184.

136. Shih Pao-ch'ang, *Lives of the Nuns: Biographies of Chinese Buddhist Nuns from the Fourth to Sixth Centuries*, trans. Kathryn Ann Tsai (Honolulu: University of Hawaii Press, 1994).

137. Ibid., 15–16.

138. Ibid., 53–54, 70, 86. A boatload of nuns from Sri Lanka is said to arrive, brought by "a foreign boat captain named Nan-t'i." The arrival of the foreign nuns is said to allow the Chinese women's monastic community (saṅgha) to receive full ordination for the first time from both the assembly of monks and the assembly of nuns.

139. Summarized by Zürcher in "Prince Moonlight," 47–59.

140. Le Goff, *Medieval Imagination*, 13.

141. Ibid., 60–66.

142. K. V. Subrahmanya Aiyer, "The Larger Leiden Plates (of Rajaraja I)," *Epigraphia Indica* 22/6 (1934):241–242.

143. See T. Ramachandran, "The Nagapattinam and Other Buddhist Bronzes in the Madras Government Museum," *Bulletin of the Madras Government Museum*, 7/1 (1954):1–150.

144. The significance of the Śailendra name has been much debated in the scholarly literature; see, for example, Coedès, *Indianized States*, 88–89.

145. See Walter Elliot, "The Edifice Formerly Known as the Chinese or Jaina Pagoda at Negapatam," *Indian Antiquary* 7 (1878):224–227. Subramaniam identifies Elliot's Chinese pagoda with the temple built by "the king of South India" (Narasiṁha Pōtavarmaṉ) for the emperor of China in the eighth-century Chinese text, *Kieou T'ang*; see T. N. Subramaniam, *The Pallavas of Kanchi in South-East Asia*, Suvarnabhumi and Tamilnadu, no. 1 (Madras: Swadeshimitram, 1967), 10.

146. See James Gray, ed. and trans., *The Kalyānī Inscriptions Erected by King Dhammaceti at Pegu in 1476 A.D.: Text and Translation* (Rangoon: Government Press, 1892), 28. For more Buddhist sources that mention the monasteries of Nākapaṭṭiṉam, see S. Paranavitana, "Negapatam and Theravāda Buddhism in South India," *Journal of the Greater India Society* 11/1 (1944):23–31.

147. Dates for this inscription, which does not itself mention any regnal year or calendrical era, range over a number of centuries, but there appears to be a general scholarly consensus placing it in the fourth to fifth centuries CE. For a list of the various arguments for particular dates, see Coedès, *Indianized States*, 278, note 38.

148. Sheldon Pollock, "The Sanskrit Cosmopolis, 300–1300 C.E.: Transculturation, Vernacularization, and the Question of Ideology," in *Ideology and Status of Sanskrit: Contributions to the History of the Sanskrit Language*, Brill's Indological Library, vol. 13, ed. Jan E. M. Houben (Leiden: E. J. Brill, 1996), 230.

149. Ibid., 230.

150. Xuanzang, *Buddhist Records of the Western World*, vol. 2, 249.

151. Huili [Hwui Li], *The Life of Hiuen-Tsiang by the Shaman Hwui Li*, trans. Samuel Beal (London: Kegan Paul, Trench, Trubner, 1911), 139–140.

152. Buddhappiya, *Upāsakajanālaṅkāra: A Critical Edition and Study*, ed. H. Saddhatissa (London: Luzac, for Pali Text Society, 1965), 357–358.

153. C. M. Fernando, trans., *The Nikāya-saṅgrahaya* (Colombo: H. C. Cottle, Government Printer, 1908), 13–14.

154. *Tamil Lexicon*, vol. 3 (Madras: University of Madras, 1982), 1492, indicates that *cīṉam* appears as one of fifty-six countries (Tamil *tēcam*, Sanskrit *deśa*) in the commentary on the thirteenth-century Jain grammatical treatise, *Naṉṉūl*, and as a language in the lexicon, *Tivākaram*, cited previously.

155. See, for example, K. A. Nilakanta Sastri, *The Cōḻas*, 2d ed., Madras University Historical Series, no. 9 (Madras: University of Madras, 1955; Reprint, 1984), 21–23.

156. For a variety of scholarly efforts both to decipher specific aspects of the monument and to interpret the edifice as a whole, see Soekmono, *Chandi Borobudur: A Monument of Mankind* (Amsterdam: UNESCO, 1976); Jan J. Boeles, *The Secret of Borobudur* (Bangkok: By the author,

1985); and Luis O. Gomèz and Hiram W. Woodward, Jr., eds., *Barabuḍur: History and Significance of a Buddhist Monument*, Berkeley Buddhist Studies Series, no. 2 (Berkeley, Calif.: Asian Humanities Press, 1981).

157. B. C. Chhabra, "Expansion of Indo-Aryan Culture During Pallava Rule, as Evidenced by Inscriptions," *Journal of the Asiatic Society of Bengal, Letters* 1 (1935):55–56: "In the very numerous inscriptions, on copper and stone, left by the rulers of the Pallava dynasty, no reference is made to relations, friendly or hostile, with the countries overseas. . . . The epigraphical documents of Further India and Indonesia are almost equally reticent about any connexion with India proper."

158. Pollock ("Sanskrit Cosmopolis") attributes the power and attraction of Sanskrit as a literary language throughout the Southeast Asian world to two principal factors: (1) its ability as a language to make "*translocal* claims . . . not so much because of its numinous qualities . . . but because of its aesthetic qualities, its ability somehow to make reality more real" (239) and (2) its deeply literary qualities that enabled one "to say things . . . that were not yet sayable in any of the other languages" (241).

159. Ibid., 235.

160. Ibid., 238.

161. For a survey of Old Javanese literature from the tenth through the fifteenth centuries, from the Sanskrit themes of the earliest poetic works (*kakawin*) to the emergence of more local themes and images, see J. Gonda, *Old Javenese Literature*, Handbuch der Orientalistik, Dritte Abteilung, Dritte Band: Literaturen, no. 1 (Leiden: E. J. Brill, 1976), 187–245. C. Hooykaas, in *The Old-Javanese Rāmāyaṇa Kakawin, with Special Reference to the Problem of Interpolation in Kakawins*, Verhandelingen van het Koninklijk Instituut voor Taal-, Land- en Volkenkunde, deel 16 ('s-Gravenhage, The Netherlands: Martinus Nijhoff, 1955), and *The Old-Javanese Rāmāyaṇa: An Exemplary Kakawin as to Form and Content*, Verhandelingen der Koninklijke Nederlandse Akademie van Wetenscappen, Afd. Leteerkunde, deel 65, no. 1 (Amsterdam: N. V. Noor-Hollandsche Uitgevers Maatschappij, 1958), explores the Sanskritic features of the Old Javanese *Rāmāyaṇa*, as well as its possible inspiration, the seventh-century Sanskrit work known as the *Bhaṭṭikāvya*. For a more general survey of Javanese literature in the pre-Muslim period, see Theodore G. T. Pigeaud, *Literature of Java, Volume I: Synopsis of Javanese Literature, 900–1900* A.D., Koninklijk Instituut voor Taal-, Land- en Volkenkunde, no. 9 (The Hague: Martinus Nijhoff, 1967).

162. Gonda, *Old Javanese Literature*, 187.

163. In addition to Yijing's depiction of "Śrībhoja" as a place where Sanskrit grammar (śabdavidyā) was taught (cited previously), Lokesh Chandra provides a general discussion of Java, Sumatra, and Bali as the Southeast Asian centers of Sanskrit literary culture ("Sanskrit Studies in Classical Indonesia," *Indologica Taurinensia* 6 [1978]:113–123).

164. Mpu Prapañca, *Deśawarṇana* (*Nāgarakṛtāgama*) *by Mpu Prapañca*, Verhandelingen van het Koninklijk Instituut voor Taal-, Land- en Volkenkunde, vol. 169, trans. Stuart Robson (Leiden: Koninklijk Instituut voor Taal-, Land- en Volkenkunde, 1995), 93. Robson also notes (148–149, note 1d) that the character mentioned immediately after Śrī Buddhāditya, one Śrī Mutali Sahṛdaya, is also probably of South Indian origin, *mutali* being a Tamil title indicating a member of the Veḷḷāḷa or land-owning caste.

165. Sylvain Lévi, *Mémorial Sylvain Lévi*, ed. Paul Hartmann (Paris: Rue Cujas, 1937), 382.

166. Ibid., 391. Lévi goes on to provide the tale of the shipwrecked future Buddha in the Sanskrit *Mahāvastu* as a counterproof to his argument. Although the Buddha-to-be is saved from drowning by a goddess of the sea who has been neglectful of her duties, as in the Tamil and Pāli sources, the goddess is not named in Sanskrit. Lévi concludes, therefore, that the compiler of the *Mahāvastu* "is writing beyond the pale of the goddess Maṇimekhalā" (391).

167. Fausbøll, *Jātakas*, vol. 6, 30–68, and vol. 4, 15–22, respectively.

168. *Maṇimēkalai*, xxix.14–31; see previous discussion above. Note also that the *Maṇimēkalai* presents this episode as central to both the naming of Maṇimēkalai and her resolve to become a renunciant.

169. Nandasena Mudiyanse, "Buddhist Writings in Tamil and Relevant Sinhalese Adaptations," *Journal of Oriental Research, Madras* 38/3 (1969):19.

170. B. Guṇasēkara, trans., *The Rājāvaliya, or a Historical Narrative of Siṅhalese Kings from Vijaya to Vimala Dharma Sūrya II* (Colombo: George J. A. Skeen, Government Printer, 1900), 23–24.

171. L. D. Barnett, *Alphabetical Guide to Sinhalese Folklore from Ballad Sources* (Bombay: British India Press, 1917), 61: "Maṇi-mekhalāva" is said to be both sea goddess and the one who "restored to Pattini her ring." Gananath Obeyesekere, *The Cult of the Goddess Pattini* (Chicago: University of Chicago Press, 1984; Reprint, Delhi: Motilal Banarsidass, 1987), records not only songs of Maṇimekhalā's saving of Kāvēri merchants from drowning in the sea (148–149) but also relates the story of Maṇimekhalai's birth as the result of a tryst between Mādevi (Mātavi) and Pālaṅga (Kōvalan̲; 238).

172. Jaini, *Paññāsa-Jātaka*, vol. 2, 519.

173. Ibid., vol. 2, 528.

174. Ibid., vol. 1, 76. Note the association of Maṇimēkalā with the Indra festival of Pukār in the *Maṇimēkalai*: "At that time, the goddess, Maṇimēkalā, had come [to the city of Pukār] to witness the tumult of the Indra festival" (v.94–96).

175. Jaini, *Paññāsa-Jātaka*, vol. 1, 262.

176. Elizabeth Wray et al., *Ten Lives of the Buddha: Siamese Temple Paintings and Jataka Tales* (New York: Weatherhill, 1979), plates 6 and 8.

177. Frank E. Reynolds, "*Rāmāyaṇa*, *Rāma Jātaka*, and *Ramkien*: A Comparative Study of Hindu and Buddhist Traditions," in *Many Rāmāyaṇas: The Diversity of a Narrative Tradition in South Asia*, ed. Paula Richman (Berkeley: University of California Press, 1991), 59.

178. See *Ramayana: Masterpiece of Thai Literature Retold from the Original Version Written by King Rama I of Siam*, 2d ed. (Bangkok: Mrs. Chalermkwan Jumsai Publisher, 1967), 17–18; René Nicolas, "Le Ramayana Siamois (Analysé)," *Extrême-Asie: Revue Indochinoise Illustrée* 19 (Janvier 1928):301–302; and Judith M. Jacob, trans., *Reamker (Rāmakerti): The Cambodian Version of the Rāmāyaṇa*, Oriental Translation Fund, New Series, vol. 45 (London: Royal Asiatic Society, 1986), 287.

179. See Nhung Hicks, trans., *Cambodian Folktales in Vietnamese* (Ho Chi Minh City, forthcoming).

180. Chan Moly Sam, "Muni Mekhala: The Magic Moment in Khmer Court Dance," in *Text, Context, and Performance in Cambodia, Laos, and Vietnam*, Selected Reports in Ethnomusicology, vol. 9, ed. Amy Catlin et al. (Los Angeles: Department of Ethnomusicology, University of California, Los Angeles, 1992), 93–113. For a description of the dance performed in 1967 "in answer to the wishes of the peasants of the Kingdom who are worried about the continuing drought in some provinces," see "At the Palace, Sacred Dances to Bring Rain (5th July)," *Kambuja: Monthly Illustrated Review* 3/29 (1967):20–23.

181. V. Raghavan, for example, in his *The Ramayana in Greater India*, Rao Kamalashankar Pranshankar Trivedi Memorial Lectures, 1973 (Surat, India: South Gujarat University, 1975), sees Tamil influence throughout the whole of the Thai Rāmāyaṇa, right down to the spellings of certain names in the text. "All the young women are called Naṅg," he notes, "and this may be the Tamil word *Naṅgai*" (65). S. Singaravelu traces similarities and divergences in various episodes of the story of Rāma as told in Sanskrit, Tamil, Thai, and Malay ("A Comparative Study of the Sanskrit, Tamil, Thai, and Malay Versions of the Story of Rāma with Special Reference to the Process of Acculturation in the Southeast Asian Versions," *Journal of the Siam Society* 56/2 [1968]:137–185), and elsewhere finds evidence that the story of Maiyarāb in the

Thai *Rāmāyaṇa* derives from an episode in Tamil folklore ("The Episode of Maiyarāb in the Thai Rāmakien and Its Possible Relationship to Tamil Folklore," *Indologica Taurinensia* 13 [1985–1986]:297–312).

182. Padmanabh S. Jaini, "The Apocryphal Jātakas of Southeast Asian Buddhism," *Indian Journal of Buddhist Studies* 1/1 (1989):25–26.

183. G. Coedès, ed. and trans., *Inscriptions du Cambodge*, Collection du textes et documents sur l'Indochine, vol. 3, no. 4 (Paris: E. de Brocard, 1952), 90. Here, the brahmin known as Kauṇḍinya, having received a bow from Aśvatthāma, marries Somā, the daughter of a Nāga king. According to Coedès, *Indianized States*, 38, the union of Kauṇḍinya and Somā "was still commemorated at the court of Angkor at the end of the thirteenth century in a rite mentioned by the Chinese envoy Chou Ta-kuan."

184. Coedès, *Indianized States*, 37–38.

185. G. Coedès, "La legende de la *nāgī*," *Bulletin de l'École Française d'Extrême-Orient* 11/3–4 (1911):391.

186. Ibid., 391. For more on the legend of the royal prince united with a serpent princess to found a royal dynasty, see V. Golobew, "Les legendes da la Nāgī et de l'Apsaras," *Bulletin de l'École Française d'Extrême-Orient* 24/3–4 (1924):501–510; Jean Przyluski, "La princesse a l'odeur de poisson et la Nāgī dans les traditions de l'Asie Orientale," in *Études Asiatiques*, vol. 2, ed. G. Van Oest (Paris: Publications de l'École Française d'Extrême-Orient, 1925), 265–284; and R. C. Majumdar, *Kambuja-Deśa or an Ancient Colony in Cambodia* (Philadelphia: Institute for the Study of Human Issues, 1980), 17–20.

187. As various scholars have attempted to establish. Both Filliozat and Wheatley, for example, look to Tamil sources (e.g., Kāraikkālammaiyār's sixth-century hymn to Śiva and Māṇikkavācakar's ninth-century *Tiruvācakam*) to explain the Cambodian identification of Śiva as "Lord of the Mountain," beginning with the ninth-century inscription of Jayavarman II. See Jean Filliozat, "New Researches on the Relations Between Indian and Cambodia," *Indica* 3/1 (1966):95–106, and Paul Wheatley, "The Mount of the Immortals: A Note on Tamil Cultural Influence in Fifth-Century Indochina," *Oriens Extremus* 21/1 (1974):97–109.

188. Preface, lines 11–12: "the goddess Kāviri appeared as the water vessel of the great sage, Akattiyaṉ, overturned." For more mythological stories that trace Agastya/Akattiyaṉ as the source of the river Kāviri and as the husband of the goddess Kāviri, see David Shulman, *Tamil Temple Myths: Sacrifice and Divine Marriage in the South Indian Śaiva Tradition* (Princeton, N.J.: Princeton University Press, 1980), 65–69, 270–272.

189. *Maṇimēkalai*, i.3. Akattiyaṉ is further portrayed as the student of Avalōkitaṉ (Avalokiteśvara) in the introduction to the eleventh-century Tamil Buddhist treatise on grammar and poetics, the *Vīracōḻiyam*, discussed in chapters 4 and 5.

190. For a general discussion of both the texts and traditions attributed to Akattiyaṉ and the available secondary literary, see Zvelebil, *Lexicon of Tamil Literature*, 13–16, and Kamil V. Zvelebil, *Companion Studies to the History of Tamil Literature*. Handbuch der Orientalistik, Zweite Abteilung: Indien, no. 5, ed. Jan Gonda (Leiden: E. J. Brill, 1992), 235–261. Also useful, if somewhat dated, are K. N. Sivaraja Pillai, *Agastya in the Tamil Land* (Madras: University of Madras, 1930; Reprint, New Delhi: Asian Educational Services, 1985), and K. A. Nilakanta Sastri, "Agastya," *Overgedrukt uit het Tijdschrift voor Ind. Taal-, Land-, en Volkenkunde* 76/4 (1936):471–545.

191. Shulman, *Tamil Temple Myths*, 8.

192. Coedès, *Indianized States*, 52, for example, notes the fifth-century inscriptions of a certain King Mūlavarman on a sanctuary dedicated to Agastya in present-day Borneo.

193. Chhabra, "Expansion of Indo-Aryan Culture," 60–61, notes, for example, that Agastya in Java "appears as a companion of Śiva, but also enjoys undivided adoration, especially in the later period." The oldest dated inscription from East Java, the stone inscription of Kañjuraha or

Dinaja of 760 CE, records the erection of a temple to the sage Agastya; see Himansu Bhusan Sarkar, *Corpus of the Inscriptions of Java* (*Corpus Inscriptionum Javanicarum*) (*up to 928* A.D.), vol. 1 (Calcutta: Firma K. L. Mukhopadhyay, 1971), 25–29. More than twenty-five Javanese images of Agastya are now housed in Dutch and Javense museums (*Encyclopedia of Tamil Literature*, s.v., vol. 1, "Contact of the Tamils with the Southeast Asian Countries," by K. D. Swaminathan, 67).

194. J. Gonda, *The Indian Religions in Pre-Islamic Indonesia and Their Survival in Bali*, Handbuch der Orientalistik, volume 2, part 1: Religionen (Leiden: E. J. Brill, 1975), 3.

195. Thomas Stamford Raffles provides the best summation of the various roles assumed by Aji Saka in the Javanese stories; most "agree in attributing to him the first introduction of letters, government, and religion" (*The History of Java*, vol. 2 [London: John Murray, 1830], 72).

196. Gonda, *Old Javanese Literature*, 207–208.

197. The first such instance of ornate court poetry is the Old Javanese *Rāmāyaṇa*, "now almost generally assumed to have been written in the Central Javanese period" (Gonda, *Old Javanese Literature*, 225).

198. The *Tivākaram*, the eighth-century Tamil lexicon noted previously, for example, includes Cāvakam among the seventeen countries where the Tamil language is spoken; cited in S. J. Gunasegaram, "Early Tamil Cultural Influences in South East Asia," *Tamil Culture* 6/4 (1957):322.

199. Richman, *Branch Stories*, 7, quotes the seventeenth-century Śaiva poet, Civappirakācar, on the difficulties of the text: "How can one grasp the intricacy of the text about Maṇimēkalai?"

Chapter 4

1. Vidya Dehejia, *Art of the Imperial Cholas* (New York: Columbia University Press, 1990), xiv.

2. Ibid., xiii.

3. Martin Irvine, *The Making of Textual Culture: 'Grammatica' and Literary Theory, 350–1100*, Cambridge Studies in Medieval Literature, no. 19 (Cambridge: Cambridge University Press, 1994), 1.

4. Ibid., 1.

5. All of Pollock's most recent articles touch on this subject in one way or another; see the list of his works in the accompanying bibliography.

6. The *Vīracōḻiyam* of Puttamittiraṉ and its commentary (attributed to his student, Peruntēvaṉār) have been published in a number of editions. The earliest is that of C. V. Tāmōtaram Piḷḷai, *Vīracōḻiyam* (Madras, 1881); also available are two editions of Puttamittiraṉ, *Vīracōḻiyam mūlamum Peruntēvaṉār iyaṟṟiya uraiyum*, ed. K. R. Kōvintarāja Mutaliyār (Madras: Pavāṉantar Kaḻakam, 1942; Reprint, Tinnevelly: South India Saiva Siddhanta Works Publishing Society, 1970). Page numbers in this chapter and the next refer to the 1970 edition of Kōvintarāja Mutaliyār. As K. Nachimuthu, "A Critical Edition of Vīracōḻiyam," *KOLAM* 2 (July 1998) (online, available: http://www.rrz.uni-koeln.de/phil-fak/indologie/kolam/kolam2/nacciol.html) notes, significant discrepancies exist among the extant manuscripts of the *Vīracōḻiyam* and its commentary; his critical edition of the text is forthcoming. Although the *Vīracōḻiyam* has never been rendered into any European language, both the text and the commentary are slated for analysis and translation into English as part of the French Institute of Pondicherry's recently inaugurated and ambitious project "aimed at the compilation of a Tamil Grammatical Encyclopaedia"; see Amitacākarar, *The Verses on the Precious Jewel Prosody Composed by Amitacākarar with the Commentary of Kuṇacākarar*, Publications du département d'indologie, no. 79, ed. and trans. Ulrike Niklas (Pondichéry: Institut Français, 1993), i.

7. Kamil V. Zvelebil, *Classical Tamil Prosody: An Introduction* (Madras: New Era, 1989), 75–76.

8. See, for example, her *Tiruviraṭṭai maṇimālai*, included in the traditional anthology of Śaiva hymns known as the *Tirumuṟai*; in Kāraikkālammaiyār, *Chants dévotionnels tamouls de Kāraikkālammaiyār*, Publications de l'Institut Français d'Indologie, no. 1, 2d ed., ed. Kārāvēlane (Pondichéry: Institut Français d'Indologie, 1982), 49–58.

9. See, for example, his *Kantarantāti* sung in praise of Lord Skanda at Tiruccentūr (Kamil V. Zvelebil, *Lexicon of Tamil Literature*, Handbuch der Orientalistik, Zweite Abteilung: Indien, vol. 9, ed. S. Bronkhorst [Leiden: E. J. Brill, 1995] 72).

10. As Zvelebil, *Lexicon of Tamil Literature*, 706, notes, the number of verses varies according to the manner in which each commentator on the *Tolkāppiyam* separates them.

11. A total of ninety-eight of the *Vīracōḻiyam*'s verses are devoted to poetic theory, and only eighty-three to phonology and morphology combined.

12. The rather vague reference to Sanskrit as "language of the north" (*vaṭamoḻi*), which might well include Prākrits and Sanskrit, is discussed by N. Sanjeevi in "Vaṭamoḻi : Sanskrit? in Ancient Tamil Literature," *Annals of Oriental Research, University of Madras* 24/1 (1972):1–11. Sanjeevi concludes, after a survey of the references to the language of the north (vaṭamoḻi) and the texts of the north (vaṭanūl) in the Caṅkam corpus, the *Cilappatikāram*, and the *Maṇimēkalai*, that "language of the north" does, indeed, refer to Sanskrit literature and particularly to the Sanskrit treatises of brahminic tradition.

13. T. P. Meenakshisundaran, *Foreign Models of Tamil Grammar*, Dravidian Linguistics Association, no. 15 (Trivandrum: Department of Linguistics, University of Kerala, 1974), provides the most exhaustive treatment of the place of Sanskrit in the *Vīracōḻiyam*'s first two chapters on phonology and morphology.

14. The *Tolkāppiyam*'s twenty-one-verse discussion of the production of speech sounds (*piṟappiyal*), for example, is condensed by the author of the *Vīracōḻiyam* into a single verse (number 6, 6); see *Tolkāppiyam: Eḻuttatikāram, Iḷampūraṇar uraiyuṭaṉ* (Tinnevelly: South India Saiva Siddhanta Works Publishing Society, 1955; Reprint, 1996), verses 83–103, 54–63. All subsequent citations from the chapter on phonemes (*eḻuttatikāram*) are taken from this edition.

15. *Vīracōḻiyam*, verse 10, 8; *Tolkāppiyam: Eḻuttatikāram*, verse 110, 69.

16. *Vīracōḻiyam*, verse 12, 9–10.

17. *Tolkāppiyam: Eḻuttatikāram*, verse 62, 43:

cakarak kiḷaviyum avaṟṟōr aṟṟē
a ai au eṉum mūṉṟalam kaṭaiyē

18. *Vīracōḻiyam*, verse 7, 7:

āvi aṉaittum ka ca ta na pa ma variyum va vil
ēviya eṭṭum ya va āṟum ña nāṉkum el lā ulakum

19. *Tolkāppiyam: Eḻuttatikāram*, verse 64, 45:

ā e
o eṉum mū uyir ñakārattu uriya

20. *Vīracōḻiyam*, verse 7, 7, as shown previously.

21. Meenakshisundaran, *Foreign Models*, 277.

22. See *Vīracōḻiyam*, 70–76.

23. Aṭikaḷāciriyar, ed., *Tolkāppiyam: Collatikāram, Iḷampūraṇar urai*, Tamiḻp Palkalaik Kaḻakam Veḷiyīṭu, no. 101 (Tañcāvūr, India: Tamiḻp Palkalaik Kaḻakam, 1988), verse 152, 142. All subsequent citations from the chapter on morphemes (*collatikāram*) are taken from this edition.

24. Pāṇini, *The Aṣṭādhyāyī of Pāṇini*, vol. 1, ed. and trans. Śrīśa Chandra Vasu (Allahabad, India: Panini Office, 1891–1897; Reprint, Delhi: Motilal Banarsidass, 1988), i.4.14, 173.

25. *Vīracōḻiyam*, verse 33, 29:

oruvaṉ orutti oṉṟiṉ
ēṟiya cu . . . eṅkum aḻiyum
ūḻiya cu

26. Aṭikaḷāciriyar, *Tolkāppiyam: Collatikāram*, verses 406–415, 297–308.

27. *Vīracōḻiyam*, verses 44–49, 48–55.

28. Ibid., verse 81, 84.

29. The *Vīracōḻiyam* presents various definitions and examples of love and heroic themes in several variations in the third chapter, and the fourth runs through various types of metrical feet, meters, and stanzas. In the latter, several Sanskrit meters are introduced, such as the *taṇṭakam* (Sanskrit *daṇḍaka*) in verse 129 (*Vīracōḻiyam*, 176), that are not known to the earlier *Tolkāppiyam*. For an overview of poetic meter and stanza structure in Tamil, see Zvelebil, *Prosody*, and Ulrike Niklas, "Introduction to Tamil Prosody," *Bulletin de l'École Française d'Extrême-Orient* 77 (1988):165–227.

30. *Vīracōḻiyam*, verse 141, 198.

31. The contents of Daṇḍin's *Kāvyādarśa* have been thoroughly examined in the annals of western Indology. This foundational treatise on Sanskrit poetic ornamentation is discussed in virtually every study of the history of Indian poetics (see, e.g., Edwin Gerow, *Indian Poetics*, History of Indian Literature, vol. 5, fasc. 3, ed. Jan Gonda [Wiesbaden: Otto Harrassowitz, 1977], 226–233). The main contents of the *Kāvyādarśa* are as follows: benediction and introductory remarks on the nature of language and literature (i.1–9), the definition and classification of ornate poetry (i.10–39), the poetic styles (*mārga*) and their characteristic qualities (guṇa; i.40–102), purposes and sources of poetry (i.103–105), the poetic ornaments themselves (ii.1–368, iii.1–124), defects of poetic composition (iii.125–185), and concluding remarks (iii.186–187). In discussing each of the poetic ornaments, general definitions are followed by poetic examples, examples that are believed to have been composed by the author himself. About the author, Daṇḍin, virtually nothing is known for sure, although the tradition that places him in the seventh-century Pallava court of Narasiṁhavarman I (630–668 C.E.) perhaps holds some truth, given the obvious influence his work wielded among southern intellectuals in the Tamil-, Kannada-, Sinhala-, and Malayalam-speaking regions (see later).

32. *Vīracōḻiyam*, verse 146, 201, and *Kāvyādarśa*, i.41–42 (Daṇḍin, *The Kāvyādarśa of Śrī Daṇḍin*, Bibliotheca Indica, vol. 40, ed. Paṇḍita Premachandra Tarkabāgīśa [Calcutta: Asiatic Society of Bengal, 1863; Reprint, Osnabrück, Germany: Biblio Verlag, 1981], 38): (1) cohesion (Tamil *cilīṭṭam*, Sanskrit *śleṣa*), (2) dignity (Tamil *utāratai*, Sanskrit *udāratvam*), (3) grace (Tamil *kānti*, Sanskrit *kānti*), (4) lucidity (Tamil *pulaṉ*, equivalent to Sanskrit *prasāda*), (5) evenness (Tamil *camatai*, Sanskrit *samatā*), (6) transference of qualities (Tamil *camāti*, Sanskrit *samādhi*), (7) explicitness of meaning (Tamil *poruṭṭeḷivu*, equivalent to Sanskrit *arthavyakti*), (8) "rigor" through mixing of compounds (Tamil *ōkam*, Sanskrit *ojas*), (9) absence of harshness (Tamil *cukumāratai*, Sanskrit *sukumāratā*), and (10) sweetness (Tamil *iṉpam*, equivalent to Sanskrit *mādhuryya*).

33. *Vīracōḻiyam*, verses 150–153, 206–220, and discussion that follows; Daṇḍin, *Kāvyādarśa* ii.1–368, 96–319.

34. Kamil V. Zvelebil, *Tamil Literature*, Handbuch der Orientalistik, Zweite Abteilung: Indien, vol. 2, no. 1, ed. Jan Gonda (Leiden: E. J. Brill, 1975), 236, note 12. Although, as is argued later, the *Tolkāppiyam* by no means represents a "pure" Tamil grammatical system uninfluenced by Sanskrit, and by Pāṇini in particular, Zvelebil is correct in noting that the *Vīracōḻiyam* signals the beginning of a newly self-conscious and explicit borrowing from the Sanskritic paradigm.

35. As at verses 141, 147, and 160.

36. For a comparative discussion of the *Kāvyādarśa*, the *Vīracōḻiyam*, and the *Taṇṭiyalaṅkāram*, see Anne E. Monuis, "The Many Lives of Daṇḍin: The *Kāvyādarśa* in Sanskrit and Tamil," *International Journal of Hindu Studies* 4/2 (2000):1–37.

37. According to Zvelebil (*Tamil Literature*, 163, note 217), the earliest reference to the style of rubies and coral occurs prior to the composition of the *Vīracōḻiyam*, in Jinasena's ninth-century Sanskrit commentary on the Jain work, *Sadkhaṇḍāgama*. In the eleventh century, Abhinavagupta's *Abhinavabhāratī* notes Bharata's assertion that dramatic dance (*nāṭya*) can be performed in a language mixing Sanskrit and local speech, and Abhinavagupta likens this to the rubies and coral style current in the south (*dakṣiṇapatha maṇipravāla*).

38. *Vīracōḻiyam*, verse 180, 283:

iṭaiyē vaṭa eḻuttu eytil viraviyal . . .
. . . maṇippiravāḷam nal teyvac colliṉ

39. Thus the name of the text, *Vīracōḻiyam*; see *Vīracōḻiyam*, preamble, 1.

40. As summarized by Zvelebil, *Lexicon of Tamil Literature*, 587.

41. Ibid., 587.

42. K. A. Nilakanta Sastri, *The Cōḻas*, 2d ed., Madras Univesity Historical Series, no. 9 (Madras: University of Madras, 1955; Reprint, 1984), 275.

43. G. Vijayavenugopal, in "Some Buddhist Poems in Tamil," *Journal of the International Association of Buddhist Studies* 2/2 (1979):93, for example, simply posits that "this grammar, being written by a Buddhist, was widely used in the Buddhist monasteries by those who learnt Tamil." That assumption is echoed by Shu Hikosaka (*Encyclopedia of Tamil Literature*, s.v., vol. 1, "History of Buddhism in Tamiḻnāṭu," 196) who maintains: "The influence of *Vīracōḻiyam* spread beyond the shores of India to Ceylon when Buddhists there studied Tamil along with Sanskrit and Pāli in the fourteenth-fifteenth centuries when Cōḻa kings of Tamiḻnāṭu established their sway over the island." M. Shanmugam Pillai, in attempting to characterize the *Vīracōḻiyam* as a "contrastive-transfer grammar" (see later), maintains that "Puttamittiraṉ wrote a Contrastive-Transfer Grammar for Tamil with Sanskrit, to teach Tamil to Buddhists who came from [a] Sanskrit background" ("*Vīracōḻiyam*—the Earliest Contrastive-Transfer Grammar in Tamil," in *Buddhism in Tamilnadu: Collected Papers*, ed. R. S. Murthy and M. S. Nagarajan [Madras: Institute of Asian Studies, 1998], 341–342).

44. Shu Hikosaka, *Buddhism in Tamilnadu: A New Perspective* (Madras: Institute of Asian Studies, 1989), 158, for example, devotes only half a paragraph to the text.

45. P. S. Subrahmanya Sastri, *History of Grammatical Theories in Tamil and Their Relation to the Grammatical Literature in Sanskrit* (Madras: *Journal of Oriental Research*, 1934), 231. Rajam Ramamurti, in "What Happens When Foreign Grammatical Terms Are Used to Describe an Indigenous Language? A South Dravidian Situation," *International Journal of Dravidian Linguistics* 12/2 (1983):340, describes the *Vīracōḻiyam* and its seventeenth-century successor, the *Pirayōkavivēkam*, in somewhat more dispassionate terms but concludes that "when Sanskrit terms are used to describe Tamil, the first and foremost distortion that happens on the Tamil side is the total negligence of the descriptive nature of Tamil grammatical terminology." Meenakshisundaran, *Foreign Models*, although betraying a certain orientation toward Sanskrit as "foreign" through his very title, compares the *Vīracōḻiyam* to both the *Pirayōkavivēkam* and the *Ilakkaṇaviḷakam*. N. Kumaraswami Raja, "Sanskrit Influence on Vi:raco:ḻiyam (A Medieval Tamil Grammar)," *International Journal of Dravidian Linguistics*, 13/2 (1983):209–212, "deals with the unwarranted influence of Sanskrit on the Tamil grammar, Vi:raco:ḻiyam" (209) by "demonstrat[ing] the author's blind following of Sanskritic tradition" (210). He concludes with an indictment of Puttamittiraṉ's knowledge of Sanskrit: "The moral of the story is that when a model is followed for writing grammars, it should be done with a good understanding of the implications of the model that is being followed" (212).

46. Shanmugam Pillai's ("*Vīracōḻiyam*") assumption here, that such a grammar necessarily serves as a teaching tool, seems unwarranted, given the significant number of regional-language grammars produced in the medieval period that standardize the local literary language through the application of Sanskritic categories. The fourteenth-century Malayalam grammar, the *Līlātilakam*, for example, formalizes the regional literary language by describing it in Sanskrit. For more on this topic, see Monius, "Many Lives of Daṇḍin," and later.

47. A. Vēluppiḷḷai, "*Viiracoozhiyam* as a Grammar for Inscriptional Tamil," in *Proceedings of the Second International Conference Seminar of Tamil Studies*, vol. 1, ed. R. E. Asher (Madras: International Association of Tamil Research, 1971), 348. Vēluppiḷḷai's case for the text as an inscriptional grammar is taken up for further consideration later.

48. See Kenneth R. Hall, *Trade and Statescraft in the Age of the Cōḻas* (New Delhi: Abhinav, 1980).

49. Burton Stein, *Peasant, State and Society in Medieval South India* (New Delhi: Oxford University Press, 1980), especially 63–89.

50. David Shulman, *The King and the Clown in South Indian Myth and Poetry* (Princeton, N.J.: Princeton University Press, 1985), 10.

51. Sheldon Pollock, "The Sanskrit Cosmopolis, 300–1300 C.E.: Transculturation, Vernacularization, and the Question of Ideology," in *Ideology and Status of Sanskrit: Contributions to the History of the Sanskrit Language*, Brill's Indological Library, vol. 13, ed. Jan E. M. Houben (Leiden: E. J. Brill, 1996), 243.

52. *Vīracōḻiyam*, verse 7, 7.

53. Clifford Geertz, *Negara: The Theatre State in Nineteenth-Century Bali* (Princeton, N.J.: Princeton University Press, 1980), 5.

54. Indira Viswanathan Peterson, *Poems to Śiva: The Hymns of the Tamil Saints* (Princeton, N.J.: Princeton University Press, 1989), 276.

55. Ibid., 231.

56. Cēkkiḻār, *Tiruttoṇṭarpurāṇam Periyapurāṇam*, ed. V. Kaliyāṇacuntaraṉār and M. Pālacuppiramaṇiyamutaliyār (Madras: Cēkkiḻār Ārāycci Maiyam, 1993), verse 2828, 750. The complete story is told in verses 2799–2829 (743–751). For a discussion and full translation of the narrative, see K. A. Nilakanta Sastri, "An Episode in the History of Buddhism in South India," in *B. C. Law Volume*, ed. D. R. Bhandarkar, et al. (Calcutta: Indian Research Institute, 1945), 35–49.

57. Recounted in K. V. Subrahmanya Aiyer, "The Larger Leiden Plates (of Rājarāja I)," *Epigraphia Indica* 22/6 (1934):230–231.

58. Kaṭavuḷamāmuṉivar, *Tiruvātavūrarpurāṇam*, ed. S. Kantacuvāmiyaiyar and Cuppāyamutaliyār (Kāñcīpuram: S. Kantacuvāmiyaiyar, 1888), 123–148. For a discussion of this episode in the hagiography of Māṇikkavācakar, see Yocum, "Buddhism Through Hindu Eyes," 143–162.

59. Buddhadatta, *Buddhadatta's Manuals or Summaries of the Abhidhamma: Abhidhammāvatāra and Rūpārūpavibhāga*, vol. 1, ed. A. P. Buddhadatta (London: Humphrey Milford, for Pali Text Society, 1915–1928), 138:

> *Kāveri-paṭṭane ramme, nānārāmo 'pasobhite*
> *Kelāsa-sikharākhāra-pāsāda-patimaṇḍite*
> *kārite Kaṅhadāsena, dassanīye manorame,*
> *vihāre*

60. Ibid., vol. 1, 138: *uragapura-nivāsikena ācariyena bhadanta-buddhadattena kato abhidhammāvatāro nāmāyan*

61. K. R. Norman, *Pāli Literature: Including Canonical Literature in Prakrit and Sanskrit of All the Hīnayāna Schools of Buddhism*, History of Indian Literature, vol. 7, fascicle 2 (Wiesbaden: Otto Harrassowitz, 1983), 151.

62. See, for example, Anuruddha, "Paramatthavinicchaya by Anuruddha," ed. A. P. Buddhadatta, *Journal of the Pali Text Society* 10 (1985):218, where the compiler of the text indicates where Anuruddha composed it: *seṭṭhe Kañcipure raṭṭhe Kāvīranagare.* A similar trend can be seen in the colophon of the twelfth-century *Upāsakajanālaṅkāra*, attributed to one Ānanda of Kotmalē in Sri Lanka; the colophon says that Buddhappiya composed his text while residing in a monastery known as Perampalli (Tamil *perumpaḷḷi*, or "great monastery") built by a Paṇḍya ruler known as Coḷagaṅga (Buddhappiya, *Upāsakajanālaṅkāra: A Critical Edition and Study*, ed. H. Saddhatissa (London: Luzac, for Pali Text Society, 1965), 357–358.

63. Norman, *Pāli Literature*, 147, 172. On 172, note 397, Norman notes that there may be two Kassapas rather than one because the *Gandhavaṁsa* does not include the *Vimativinodanī* among the works of Kassapa.

64. Kassapa, *Mohavicchedanī Abhidhammamātikatthavaṇṇanā by Kassapatthera of Coḷa*, ed. A. P. Buddhadatta and A. K. Warder (London: Luzac, for Pali Text Society, 1961), 358.

65. C. S. Upasak, ed., *The Sāsanavaṁsa* (Patna, India: Nava Nālandā Mahāvihāra, 1961), 31.

66. Norman, *Pāli Literature*, 2, assigns it to the nineteenth century.

67. Quoted in Amaradasa Liyanagamage, "A Forgotten Aspect of the Relations Between the Sinhalese and the Tamils," *Ceylon Historical Journal* 25/1–4 (1978):115. Buddhappiya unfortunately does not elaborate further on his relationship to the "Ḍamila country."

68. Norman, *Pāli Literature*, 158.

69. Buddhappiya, "The *Pajjamadhu*: A Poem in Praise of the Buddha," ed. R. Gooneratne, *Journal of the Pali Text Society* (1887):1–17. Asha Das, "The Pajjamadhu—A Critical Study," *Journal of the Department of Pali, University of Calcutta* 5 (1989–1990):35–72, provides another edition of the text, as well as a discussion of the poem's style and vocabulary.

70. Quoted in Liyanagamage, "Forgotten Aspect," 134.

71. S. Paranavitana, ed. and trans., *Epigraphia Zeylanica, Being Lithic and Other Inscriptions of Ceylon*, vol. 4 (London: Humphrey Milford, for Government of Ceylon, 1943), 71–72.

72. See R. A. L. H. Gunawardana, *Historiography in a Time of Ethnic Conflict: Constructions of the Past in Contemporary Sri Lanka* (Colombo: Social Scientists' Association, 1995), for a summary of the major positions taken in the debate.

73. Peterson, *Poems to Śiva*, 13–14, for example, describes the Cōḻa period as "the great age of Tamil Śaivism as the 'official' religion of the Tamils."

74. R. A. L. H. Gunawardana, "The People of the Lion: The Sinhala Identity and Ideology in History and Historiography," *Sri Lanka Journal of the Humanities* 5/1 (1979):3–36. For a critical review of Gunawardana's thesis, based on alternative interpretations of the same Sinhalese texts, see K. N. O. Dharmadasa, "The People of the Lion: Ethnic Identity, Ideology, and Historical Revisionism in Contemporary Sri Lanka," *Ethnic Studies Report* 10/1 (1992):37–159, and K. N. O. Dharmadasa,"The Roots of Sinhala Ethnic Identity in Sri Lanka: The Debate on 'The People of the Lion' Continued," *Ethnic Studies Report* 14/2 (1996):137–170.

75. The relevant *Vimativinodanī* passage is transliterated from Sinhala script by P. V. Bapat, "Vimati-Vinodani, a Vinaya Commentary and Kundalkesi-Vatthu, a Tamil Poem," *Journal of Indian History* 45 (1967):689. Bapat follows the text of Kassapa, *Vimativinodani*, ed. Beratuduwe Dhammadhara Tissa Thero (Colombo: Luxman, 1935), 99–100.

76. Bapat, "Vimati-Vinodani," 691.

77. Norman, *Pāli Literature*, 171–172.

78. Wilhelm Geiger, ed., *Cūlavaṁsa: Being the More Recent Part of the Mahāvaṁsa*, vol. 2 (London: Humphrey Milford, for Pali Text Society, 1925), 468–469.

79. Kassapa, *Mohavicchedanī*, 1.

80. Liyanagamage, "Forgotten Aspect," 134.

81. Buddhappiya, *Upāsakajanālaṅkāra*, 357–358.

82. *Cūlavaṁsa*, vol. 2, 515.

83. Buddhaghosa, *Samantapāsādikā: Buddhaghosa's Commentary on the Vinaya Piṭaka*, ed. J. Takakusu and M. Nagai, vol. 2 (London: Oxford University Press, for Pali Text Society, 1924–1976), 2.

84. K. Indrapala, "Buddhism Among the Tamils A.D. 1000–1500," in *Proceedings of the Fifth International Conference-Seminar of Tamil Studies*, vol. 2, ed. M. Arunachalam (Madras: International Association of Tamil Studies, 1981), 12/31.

85. R. A. L. H. Gunawardana, *Robe and Plough: Monasticism and Economic Interest in Early Medieval Sri Lanka*, Association for Asian Studies: Monographs and Papers, no. 35 (Tucson: University of Arizona Press, for Association for Asian Studies, 1979), 264.

86. Pollock, "Sanskrit Cosmopolis," especially 209–213, 216.

87. A. G. Menon, "The Use of Sanskrit in South Indian Bilingual Royal Inscriptions: Social, Political and Religious Implications," in *Ideology and Status of Sanskrit: Contributions to the History of the Sanskrit Language*, Brill's Indological Library, vol. 13, ed. Jan E. M. Houben (Leiden: E. J. Brill, 1996), 249–263.

88. Richard Pischel, *Comparative Grammar of the Prākrit Languages*, trans. Subhadra Jha (Delhi: Motilal Banarsidass, 1981), 9, quoted by Pollock, "Sanskrit Cosmopolis," 210.

89. Pollock, "Sanskrit Cosmopolis," 211.

90. Ibid., 213.

91. Ibid., 216. Menon, "Use of Sanskrit," 260, further notes that Tamil soon takes over from Sanskrit the role of expressing royal genealogy in textual and not just inscriptional form: "In a 12th cent. Tamil text known as Kalinkattupparani, composed to praise the victory of the Coḷa king Kulottunga I, the function of the Sanskrit portion of the bilingual inscriptions is taken over by literary Tamil. The tenth chapter tracing the ancestry of Kulottunga I describes him as an incarnation of Rāma and Kṛṣṇa."

92. Pollock, "Sanskrit Cosmopolis," 198–199.

93. Pollock, "Literary History, Indian History, World History," *Social Scientist* 23/10–12 (1995):116. Note that here Pollock uses the term *inscription* in its broadest sense, as simply "writing down" a lasting record.

94. Ibid., 139, note 6.

95. Vēluppiḷḷai, "*Viiracoozhiyam*," 348. Meenakshisundaran, *Foreign Models*, 34, makes the same point in passing.

96. S. Agesthialingom and S. V. Shanmugam provide an exhaustive linguistic treatment of inscriptional Tamil in their *The Language of Tamil Inscriptions 1250–1350 A.D.*, Annamalai University, Department of Linguistics, no. 23 (Annamalainagar, India: Annamalai University, 1970).

97. Subrahmanya Sastri, *History of Grammatical Theories*, is confounded by the "failure" of Puttamittiraṉ to account for certain literary forms found in texts that predate the *Vīracōḻiyam*. On 184, for example, Subrahmanya Sastri discusses the forms of the present participle given at *Vīracōḻiyam* verse 66, 74. Although the grammar lists *-kiṟa-* among the possible particles used to form a present active participle, yielding a form such as "doing" (*ceykiṟa*) that is still common in modern Tamil, Subrahmanya Sastri notes that he cannot comprehend why Puttamittiraṉ "failed to mention the form *ceykiṉṟa* which was frequently used in the works that were written before his time."

98. *Vīracōḻiyam*, verse 15, 13, explains that *ḻ* followed by *t* is changed to *ṭ*, as is the initial *t* of the following word; in some cases, the second *ṭ* is dropped. Verse 18 (15) states that: if *ḻ* is followed by *n*, the *ḻ* is dropped; *ḻ* followed by a voiceless consonant is changed to *ṭ* or *ṇ*; *ḻ* followed by *m* becomes *ṇ*.

99. Vēluppiḷḷai, "*Viiracoozhiyam*," 346.

100. Ibid., 347.

101. Vijayavenugopal, "Some Buddhist Poems," 93.

102. Irvine, *Textual Culture*, 1.

103. Ibid., 405–460.

104. *Tolkāppiyam: Eḻuttatikāram*, 10.

105. For a general discussion of the possible Sanskrit sources of the *Tolkāppiyam* other than Pāṇini, see P. S. Vedachala Iyer, "The Sources of Tolkāppiyam," *Journal of Oriental Research, Madras* 7/1 (1933):53–58.

106. Subrahmanya Sastri, *History of Grammatical Theories*; Ramamurti, "Foreign Grammatical Terms," especially 336.

107. Aṭikaḷāciriyar, *Tolkāppiyam: Collatikāram*, verse 395, 288.

108. Kamil V. Zvelebil, *Companion Studies to the History of Tamil Literature*, Handbuch der Orientalistik, Zweite Abteilung: Indien, no. 5, ed. J. Bronkhorst (Leiden: E. J. Brill, 1992), 251.

109. Amitacākarar, *Yāpparuṅkalam paḻaiya viruti uraiyuṭaṉ*, ed. I. Iḷaṅkumaraṉ (Tinnevelly: South India Saiva Siddhanta Works Publishing Society, 1973), 48.

110. George L. Hart III, *The Poems of Ancient Tamil: Their Milieu and Their Sanskrit Counterparts* (Berkeley: University of California Press, 1975), especially 51–80.

111. For a discussion of the problems in dating Daṇḍin, as well as a summary of his life story according to traditional sources, see Dharmendra Kumar Gupta, *A Critical Study of Daṇḍin and His Works* (Delhi: Meharchand Lachhmandas, 1970), 61–97.

112. Rita Copeland, *Rhetoric, Hermeneutics, and Translation in the Middle Ages: Academic Traditions and Vernacular Texts* (Cambridge: Cambridge University Press, 1991), 6.

113. *Vīracōḻiyam*, verse 8, 7, follows the *Tolkāppiyam* preamble in stating that learned Tamil is spoken from "the abode of Kumari to the great Vēṅkaṭam hill" (*vīṟu mali vēṅkaṭam kumarik kiṭai mēviṟṟu eṉṟu kūṟum tamiḻ*). The *Vīracōḻiyam* commentator alters slightly the geographical region associated with the Tamil language; see the discussion to follow in chapter 5.

114. *Vīracōḻiyam*, verse 146, 201:

> *īṇṭum cilīṭṭam utāratai kānti pulaṉ camatai*
> *tūṇṭum camāti poruṭṭeḷivu ōkam cukumāratai*
> *īṇṭum iṉpattoṭu pattu āvi eṉṉum vitarppaṉ kauṭaṉ*
> *vēṇṭum ivaṟṟai viparītam āka viḷaṅkiḻaiyē*
>
> Cohesion, dignity, grace, lucidity, evenness,
> transference of qualities, explicitness of meaning, vigor [arising from
> admixture of compounds], absence of harshness,
> together with sweetness—these are the ten breaths of Vitarppaṉ [literary style].
> The opposite of these becomes Kauṭaṉ [literary style],
> oh lady wearing bright jewels!

Daṇḍin, *Kāvyādarśa* i.41–42, 38, simply changes the order in which the ten qualities are listed.

115. Sheldon Pollock, "The Cosmopolitan Vernacular," *Journal of Asian Studies* 57/1 (1998): 21–25. On 24, for example, Pollock notes the way in which "'southern' Kannada literature is marked [in the *Kavirājamārgam*] by the prevalence of local (*dēsi*) words" while "northern poetry [is marked] by the prevalence of unmodified Sanskrit loans (*samasamskṛta*)."

116. *Vīracōḻiyam*, verse 8, 7.

117. *Vīracōḻiyam*, verses 147–149, 202–206.

118. Pollock, "Literary History, Indian History," 112:

> We understand little about the particular circumstances within which certain kinds of speech come to count as "literary" language; we have few accounts of how notions of "the literary" change over time and place; few attempts have been made to compare and analyze the differ-

ent narratives of the development of such literary languages; far fewer, to relate literary-language choice or change and narratives of literary history to their most salient conditions, the acquisition and maintenance of social and political power.

119. Ibid., 126.

120. See Rich Freeman, "Rubies and Coral: The Lapidary Crafting of Language in Kerala," *Journal of Asian Studies* 57/1 (1998):38–65. A summary of the contents of the text can be found in K. N. Ezhuthachan, *The History of Grammatical Theories in Malayalam*, Dravidian Linguistics Association, no. 17 (Trivandrum, India: Department of Linguistics, University of Kerala, 1975), 61–129.

121. *Tolkāppiyam: Iḷampūraṇar uraiyuṭaṉ: Poruḷatikāram* (Tinnevelly: South India Saiva Siddhanta Works Publishing Society, 1977), verse 400, 462.

122. Daṇḍin, *Kāvyādarśa*, ii.1, 96: "who can recite them in their totality" (*kas tān kārtsnena vakṣyati*)?

123. *Tolkāppiyam: Iḷampūraṇar uraiyuṭaṉ: Poruḷatikāram*, verses 393–408, 459–471, comprise the discussion of ornamentation (toṭai). Verse 406 boldly states that learned scholars claim the number of ornaments to be 13,699; verse 407 then adds that the number would become countless if scholars were to further divide it (*terintaṉar virippiṉ varampila ākum*).

124. These are: (1) alliteration (*moṉai*), (2) rhyme of the second syllable (etukai), (3) juxtaposition of contradictory terms (muraṇ), (4) end rhyme (*iyaipu*), and (5) overlengthening of syllables (*aḷapeṭai*).

125. In *Vīracōḻiyam*, the treatment of poetic ornaments based on sound is rather terse, consisting of only three verses (verses 177–179, 269–283).

126. *Tolkāppiyam: Iḷampūraṇar uraiyuṭaṉ: Poruḷatikāram*, 553–555.

127. Pollock, "Literary History, Indian History," 116.

128. Kṛttibās Ojhā's Bengali rendition of the *Rāmāyaṇa*, for example, was first composed in the late fourteenth or early fifteenth century (Dusan Zbavitel, *Bengali Literature*, History of Indian Literature, vol. 9, fasc. 3, ed. Jan Gonda [Wiesbaden: Otto Harrassowitz, 1976], 148–149). The devotional verses of sixteenth-century devotional poets such as Kabīr respresent the first works of Hindi literature (Ronald Stuart McGregor, *Hindi Literature of the Nineteenth and Early Twentieth Centuries*, History of Indian Literature, vol. 8, fasc. 2, ed. Jan Gonda [Wiesbaden: Otto Harrassowitz, 1974], 62). Kashmiri literature is said to begin with Avtāra Bhaṭṭa's *Bāṇāsurakathā* in the fifteenth century (Braj B. Kachru, *Kashmiri Literature*, History of Indian Literature, vol. 8, fasc. 4, ed. Jan Gonda [Wiesbaden: Otto Harrassowitz, 1981], 14).

129. Pollock, "Cosmopolitan Vernacular."

130. For a detailed survey of the Tamil Vaiṣṇava literature composed in the style of rubies and coral, see K. K. A. Venkatachari, *The Manipravala Literature of the Śrī Vaiṣṇava Ācāryas* (Bombay: Ananthacarya Research Institute, 1978); for a brief discussion of the Tamil Jain texts written in this mixed Sanskrit-Tamil style, see *Encyclopedia of Tamil Literature*, s.v., vol. 1, "Jainism and Tamil Literature," by R. Vijayalakshmy, 211–213.

131. Freeman, "Rubies and Coral," 39; Ezhuthachan, *Grammatical Theories*, 61–129; and R. Leeladevi, *History of Malayalam Literature* (Trivandrum, India: Educational Supplies Depot, 1977), 18–29.

132. G. Vijayawardhana, "Siya-Bas-Lakara and a Theory of Suggestion," *University of Ceylon Review* 22/1–2 (1964):21.

133. The thirteenth-century *Sidat Sangarāva*, for example, has been said to follow the *Vīracōḻiyam* "in grammatical terminology and methods of enunciation of rules" (C. E. Godakumbura, *Sinhalese Literature* [Colombo: Colombo Apothecaries, 1955], 318). James de Alwis translates the text into English as *The Sidath Sangarawa: A Grammar of the Singhalese Language* (Colombo: William Skeen, 1852).

134. For more on early literary works in Telugu and their relation to Sanskrit paradigms, see Velcheru Narayana Rao, "Coconut and Honey: Sanskrit and Telugu in Medieval Andhra," *Social Scientist* 23/10–12 (1995): 41–55, and S. Nagaraju, "Emergence of Regional Identity and Beginnings of Vernacular Literature: A Case Study of Telugu," *Social Scientist* 23/10–12 (1995):8–23.

135. Irvine, *Textual Culture*, 405.

136. Pollock, "Sanskrit Cosmopolis," 244: "As for South Asia, it is largely an illusion, albeit one widely shared, that the literization—for some, indeed, the *invention*—of regional languages was due to subaltern *bhaktas*. This is false not only for South India (in Karnataka, for example, old Kannada literature is courtly, suffused with Sanskrit, and unintelligible to those ignorant of Sanskrit); but also in the north, where some of the earliest regional-language texts are composed by courtly Muslims." Given the significant corpus of Tamil literature that predates the poetry of the Śaiva and Vaiṣṇava poet-saints—from the Caṅkam poetic anthologies to the *Cilappatikāram* and the *Maṇimēkalai*—it would be similarly difficult to date the rise of Tamil literature to the seventh- through ninth-century hymns of the *Tēvāram*.

137. M. Winternitz, *History of Indian Literature*, vol. 3, part 2, trans. Subhadra Jhā (Delhi: Motilal Banarsidass, 1967), 439–443.

138. Although the linguistic move from the Sanskrit Avalokiteśvara/Avalokita to Tamil Avalōkitaṉ poses no particular challenges, whether or not Avalōkitaṉ in a Tamil context implies all the qualities of the Sanskrit Buddha-to-be is impossible to determine. The name Avalōkitaṉ appears nowhere else in Tamil, and as is evident from the discussion to follow, the *Vīracōḻiyam* provides little additional information as to nature of this character.

139. *Vīracōḻiyam*, preamble, 1:

> *āyum kuṇattu avalōkitaṉ pakkal akattiyaṉ kēṭṭu*
> *ēyum puvaṉikku iyampiya taṉ tamiḻ īṅku uraikka*

140. David Shulman, *Tamil Temple Myths: Sacrifice and Divine Marriage in South Indian Śaiva Tradition* (Princeton, N.J.: Princeton University Press, 1980), 8.

141. Zvelebil, *Companion Studies*, 239–250.

142. *Vīracōḻiyam*, verse 83, 86.

143. Ibid., verse 6, 6; verse 7, 7.

144. Ibid., verse 27, 25; verse 79, 82; verse 84, 89; verse 173, 266.

145. Ibid., verse 57, 64; verse 119, 157.

146. Ibid., verse 68, 75.

147. Ibid., verse 123, 165.

148. Ibid., verses 145–146, 201.

149. Ibid., verse 1, 2; verse 29, 27; verse 40, 41; verse 115, 139; verse 131, 177.

150. Ibid., verse 10, 8; verse 13, 10; verse 93, 91; verse 111, 132.

151. Ibid., verse 43, 46.

152. Ibid., 3, for example.

153. Dominick LaCapra, *Rethinking Intellectual History: Texts, Context, Language* (Ithaca, N.Y.: Cornell University Press, 1983), 65.

Chapter 5

The epigraph to this chapter, from Cāminātaiyar's autobiography, cites the commentary on *Vīracōḻiyam*, verse 119 (158), and is used to illustrate a particular kind of poetic meter (*veḷi viruttam*):

> *maruḷ aṟutta perum pōti mātavaraik kaṇṭilamāl eṉ cey kōyāṉ*
> *aruḷ irunta tirumoḻiyāl aṟavaḻakkam kēṭṭilamāl eṉ cey kōyāṉ*
> *poruḷ aṟiyum maruntavattup puravalaraik kaṇṭilamāl eṉ cey kōyāṉ*

1. Gary A. Tubb, "Hemacandra and Sanskrit Poetics," in *Open Boundaries: Jain Communities and Cultures in Indian History*, ed. John E. Cort (Albany: State University of New York Press, 1998), 53.

2. As in chapter 4, all references are taken from Kōvintarāja Mutaliyār's 1970 edition of the *Vīracōḻiyam* (Puttamittiraṉ, *Vīracōḻiyammūlamum Peruntēvaṉār iyaṟṟiya uraiyum*, ed. Kōvintarāja Mutaliyār [Madras: Pavāṉantar Kaḻakam, 1942; Reprint, Tinnevelly: South India Saiva Siddhanta Works Publishing Society, 1970]).

3. Kamil V. Zvelebil, *Lexicon of Tamil Literature*, Handbuch der Orientalistik, Zweite Abteilung: Indien, vol. 9, ed. J. Bronkhorst (Leiden: E. J. Brill, 1995), 555.

4. Ibid., 555.

5. *Vīracōḻiyam*, 195.

6. Kamil V. Zvelebil, *Tamil Literature*, Handbuch der Orientalistik, Zweite Abteilung: Indien, vol. 2, no. 1, ed. J. Bronkhorst (Leiden: E. J. Brill, 1975), 192.

7. For a discussion of the advent of prose commentary in Tamil during the early medieval period, see Zvelebil, *Tamil Literature*, 195–196. The majority of the early commentaries are on grammatical texts, such as Iḷampūraṇar's eleventh-century gloss on the *Tolkāppiyam*, Cēṉāvaraiyar's thirteenth-century commentary on the same, and Mayilainātar's fourteenth-century gloss on *Naṉṉūl*.

8. *Vīracōḻiyam*, verse 173, 266:

tuppār oruṅkiyal tūya viṉai paṇpu iraṇṭu poruṭ(ku)
oppā oru collu vaippa tuyar parimāṟṟam atu
ceppār poruḷ māṟiṭal tikaḻ āciyiṉ cīrmai coliṉ
tappāta ācīr vacaṉam eṉa uṇar tāḻkuḻalē

9. These are, in fact, the two terms used in the twelfth-century Tamil interpretation of Daṇḍin's *Kāvyādarśa*, the *Taṇṭiyalaṅkāram* (Taṇṭi *Taṇṭiyalaṅkāram Cuppiramaṇiyatēcikar uraiyutaṉ*, ed. K. Irāmaliṅkat Tampirāṉavarkaḷ [Tinnevelly: South India Saiva Siddhanta Works Publishing Society, 1938; Reprint, 1997], verses 86–87, 178–180).

10. *Vīracōḻiyam*, commentary on verse 173, 266:

pūkkāl puṉainta puṉavar maṭamakaḷ
nōkkāl nōkkuṇṭārai nōvatu eṉ—nōkkātē
kaḷḷam niṟaiyum karum kaṇṇāl kaṭṭu aḻittāḷ
uḷḷam niṟaiyōṭu oruṅku

The same verse is quoted, also as an example of joint description based on verbal action, under verse 153, 219.

11. Ibid., 266:

pūṅkāvil puḷ oṭuṅkum puṉmālaip pōḻtu uṭaṉē
nīṅkāta vemmaivāy nīṇṭaṉavāl—tām kātal
vaikkum tuṇaivar varum avati pārttu āvi
uykkum tamiyār uyir

12. See George L. Hart III's discussion in *The Poems of Ancient Tamil: Their Milieu and Their Sanskrit Counterparts* (Berkeley: University of California Press, 1975) , 216–221.

13. Daṇḍin, *The Kāvyādarśa of Śrī Daṇḍin*, Bibliotheca Indica, vol. 40, ed. Paṇḍita Premachandra Tarkabāgīśa (Calcutta: Asiatic Society of Bengal, 1863; Reprint, Osnabrück, Germany: Biblio Verlag, 1981), ii.354, 308:

kokilālāpasubhagāḥ sugandhivanavāyavaḥ
yānti sārdhaṁ janānandair vṛddhiṁ surabhivāsarāḥ

14. *Vīracōḻiyam*, commentary on verse 173, 266:

> *kāmaṉai veṉṟāṉ caṭaimatiyum kaṅkaiyum*
> *tāmam niḻal oṉṟu tām koṭuttu–nāmap*
> *paru vāḷ araviṉ paṇamaṇikaḷ tōṟum*
> *uruvu āyiram peṟṟuḷa*

In other words, the river and the moon are reflected in the mythical jewels ensconced in the serpent's hood; the serpent in this case is understood by Kōvintarāja Mutaliyār (441) to be the mythological thousand-headed serpent on whose hood all of creation rests (Tamil Āticēṭaṉ, Sanskrit Ādiśeṣa).

15. The ornament of nonliteral exchange is also illustrated by a verse from the *Tirukkuṟaḷ* that is taken up for discussion later.

16. Uṟaiyūr, a capital city of the Cōḻas. The name Kōḻi, literally meaning "chicken," refers to a mythological incident in which a cock is said to have defeated an elephant (*Tamil Lexicon*, vol. 2 [Madras: University of Madras, 1982], 1200).

17. The tiger serves as an emblem of the Cōḻa dynasty.

18. *Vīracōḻiyam*, commentary on verse 173, 266:

> *mikai cērnta nākamum veṇ matiyum tammil*
> *pakai tīrnta māl caṭaiyōṉ kāppa–mukai malar ak*
> *kōḻi aṉupamaṉaṉ kōram puli vāḻi*
> *vāḻiya maṇ talattu vāṉ*

The same verse is also quoted as an example of benediction in the commentary under verse 153, 219.

19. Zvelebil, *Tamil Literature*, 117, notes, for example, that the postclassical anthology known as the "Eighteen Shorter Texts" is referred to as *Patiṉeṇkīḻkkaṇakku* in the commentary on *Vīracōḻiyam*, verse 145; Zvelebil also cites the commentary on *Vīracōḻiyam*, verse 151, as evidence for the existence of a now-lost poem of 900 stanzas in praise of a Tamil king (128).

20. G. Vijayavenugopal, "Some Buddhist Poems in Tamil," *Journal of the International Association of Buddhist Studies* 2/2 (1979): 95, poses the question: "Now the question is, which was the model? Did the Buddhists and Jains follow the Hindu bhakti [devotional] movement and compose poetry on those lines, or vice versa?"

21. Pierre Bourdieu, *The Field of Cultural Production: Essays on Art and Literature*, ed. Randal Johnson (Cambridge: Polity, 1993), 35–36.

22. Anne Blackburn, "The Play of the Teaching in the Life of the *Sāsana*: *Sārāthadīpanī* in Eighteenth-Century Sri Lanka" (Ph.D. Diss., University of Chicago, 1995), 2.

23. See, for example, Martha Ann Selby, "Desire for Meaning: Providing Contexts for Prākrit *Gāthās*," *Journal of Asian Studies* 55/1 (1996):81–93. Selby, in this study of the Māhārāṣṭrī Prākrit collection of verses (*gāthā*) known as the *Gāthāsaptaśatī*, notes the several ways in which Ānandavardhana's and Mammaṭa's use of the verses as exemplars of particular forms of suggestion (*dhvani*) "were honestly rhetorical," revealing the extent to which "both writers were highly skilled in argument" (87). Laurie L. Patton, in "Making the Canon Commonplace: Ṛg-Vidhāna as Commentarial Practice," *Journal of Religion* 77/1 (1997):1–19, shows the ways in which commentary may compete with canonical text by interpreting and using images and words to very different ends.

24. Peruntēvaṉār departs from Daṇḍin's model of exposition by citing known poetic works as examples of the various ornaments. Whereas Daṇḍin composes his own verse examples in the *Kāvyādarśa*, the *Vīracōḻiyam* commentator draws on an existing body of Tamil poetry. Is it possible that Peruntēvaṉār follows here the Kashmiri tradition of Abhinavagupta, who cites

Sanskrit poetic works from the *Mahābhārata* to Kālidāsa's *Kumārasambhava* in his commentary (*Locana*) on the *Dhvanyāloka* of Ānandavardhana?

25. As at *Vīracōḻiyam*, 32, in the commentary on verse 34 on cases (vēṟṟumai), and at 86 and 88, in the commentary on verse 83 dealing with finite verbal forms (*kiriyā*).

26. Ibid., 92. The quotation is from *Tolkāppiyam: Iḷampūraṇar uraiyuṭaṉ: Poruḷatikāram* (Tinnevelly: South India Saiva Siddhanta Works Publishing Society, 1977), verse 21, 19:

ennilam maruṅkil pūvum puḷḷum
annilam poḻutoṭu vārā āyiṉum
vanta nilattiṉ payatta ākum

The flower and bird of one region and season,
when not found in that region and season [ascribed to them],
[must be considered] as belonging to that [region and season] in which they appear.

Translation adapted from S. Ilakkuvanār, trans., *Tholkāppiyam (in English) with Critical Studies* (Madurai: 'Kuṛaḷ Veṛi', 1963), 155.

27. *Vīracōḻiyam*, 264. The quotation is from *Tolkāppiyam: Iḷampūraṇar uraiyuṭaṉ: Poruḷatikāram*, verse 400, 462: "That which differs in word and meaning is muraṇ" (*moḻiyiṉum poruḷiṉum muraṇutal muraṇē*).

28. *Vīracōḻiyam*, commentary on verses 90–94, 92–98. Here, it is impossible to know whether the long poetic explications of each of the five landscapes are the work of Peruntēvaṉār himself or are quotations from some source no longer extant.

29. As in the commentary on *Vīracōḻiyam*, verse 176, 268–269.

30. Ibid., 137 and 153, for example.

31. See *Vīracōḻiyam*, commentary on verse 123, 166, where the commentator quotes *Yāpparuṅkalam*, verse 93 (Amitacākarar, *Yāpparuṅkalam paḻaiya viruti uraiyuṭaṉ*, ed. I. Iḷaṅkumaraṉ [Tinnevelly: South India Saiva Siddhanta Works Publishing Society, 1973], 363), and attributes the text to Amutacākaraṉār.

32. *Vīracōḻiyam*, 168. The quotation is taken from the first two lines of verse 36 of the *Kārikai* (Amitacākarar, *The Verses on the Precious Jewel Prosody Composed by Amitacākarar with the Commentary of Kuṇacākarar*, Publications du département d'indologie, no. 79, ed. and trans. Ulrike Niklas [Pondichéry: Institut Français, 1993], 294–295).

33. *Vīracōḻiyam*, verse 8, 7.

34. Commentary on *Vīracōḻiyam* verse 8, 7.

35. Ibid., 123.

36. Ibid., 125. The commentator here does not cite the source of the quotation, but it is nearly identical to a verse attributed to the *Kuṇṭalakēci* in the fifteenth-century anthology, *Puṟattiraṭṭu* (I. Iḷaṅkumaraṉ, ed., *Puṟattiraṭṭu* [Tinnevelly: South India Saiva Siddhanta Works Publishing Society 1972], 2). The verse as it appears in the *Vīracōḻiyam* commentary reads:

muṉṟāṉ perumaikku aṇiṉṟāṉ muṭivu eytuka āṟu
naṉṟē niṉaintāṉ kuṇa moḻintāṉ taṉakku eṉṟu
oṉṟāṉum uḷḷāṉ piṟarkkē uṟuti cūḻntāṉ
aṉṟē iṟaivaṉ avaṉ tāḷ caraṇaṅkaḷ aṉṟē

37. *Vīracōḻiyam*, 164–165.

38. A stanza consisting of four lines of five feet each, as well as particular patterns of rhyme and alliteration; see Kamil V. Zvelebil, *Classical Tamil Prosody: An Introduction* (Madras: New Era, 1989), 75.

39. *Vīracōḻiyam*, 175. For a full explanation of viruttam, "the grand metre of classical narrative poetry," and its many subtypes, see Zvelebil, *Prosody*, 77–83. This discrepancy between the

unattributed verse claimed as an example of kalitturai meter and the blanket claim that the *Kuṇṭalakēci* is composed entirely in viruttam meter is difficult to explain. Perhaps the medieval compiler of the *Puṟattiraṭṭu* was incorrect in assigning the verse cited previously to the *Kuṇṭalakēci*; perhaps the verse comes from an introductory section praising the Buddha that was deliberately cast in a different meter and not considered part of the poem proper by the *Vīracōḻiyam* commentator.

40. Literally, "The Story of Utayaṇaṉ," perhaps a reference to the tenth-century Tamil Jain version of the story of Udayana commonly known as the *Peruṅkatai* or "Great Story." For more on this text, see R. Vijayalakshmy, *A Study of the Peruṅkatai: An Authentic Version of the Story of Udayana* (Madras: International Institute of Tamil Studies, 1988).

41. *Vīracōḻiyam*, 201.

42. Other than the one verse cited previously and identified by the compiler of the *Puṟattiraṭṭu*, it is not at all clear whether any other of Peruntēvaṉār's many uncited quotations are drawn from the *Kuṇṭalakēci*. Kamil V. Zvelebil, *Companion Studies to the History of Tamil Literature*, Handbuch der Orientalistik, Zweite Abteilung: Indien, vol. 5, ed. Jan Gonda (Leiden: E. J. Brill, 1992), 70, assumes, for example, that the commentary must draw many stanzas from such an obviously important Buddhist literary work.

43. *Vīracōḻiyam*, 114.

44. Ibid., 127.

45. Ibid., 157.

46. Ibid., 161.

47. Ibid., 183.

48. Ibid., 124:

poruntu pōtiyil
irunta mātavar
tiruntu cēvaṭi
maruntum ākumē

49. Ibid., 141:

eṇṇiṟanta kuṇattōy nī
yāvarkku mariyōy nī
uṇṇ iṟainta aruḷōy nī
uyar pāra niṟaittōy nī
meyp poruḷai aṟintōy nī
meyy aṟamiṉ kaḷittōy nī
ceppariya tavattōy nī
cērvārkkuc cārvu nī

50. Ibid., 157:

pōti niḻalil puṉitaṉ polam kaḻal
āti ulakiṉ karaṇ

51. Ibid., 143:

aruḷ viṟṟirunta tiruniḻal pōti
muḻutu uṇar muṉivaṉ nil paravutum toḻutaka
oru maṉam eyti iruviṉaip piṇi viṭa
muppakai kaṭantu nālvakaip poruḷ uṇarnta
ōṅku nīr ulaku iṭai yāvarum
nīṅkā iṉpamoṭu nīṭu vāḻka eṉavē

52. Vijayavenugopal, "Some Buddhist Poems," 96, for example, notes: "the verses quoted in the commentary on Vīracōḻiyam reveal the influence of Tamil bhakti poetry on Buddhist literary activity." His evidence for such a conclusion, however, is quite general; among the "similarities" cited are the eulogizing of the Buddha's qualities and references to Buddhist "mythology."

53. K. D. Somadasa, *Catalogue of the Hugh Nevill Collection of Sinhalese Manuscripts in the British Library*, vol. 4 (London: British Library, 1990), 373.

54. This episode, in which the future Buddha, born as King Sivi, offers his eyes to Saka, disguised as a blind brahmin, is also referred to at *Maṇimēkalai*, vi.61–72; the Pāli version can be found in V. Fausbøll, ed., *The Jātaka Together with Its Commentary: Being Tales of the Anterior Births of Gotama Buddha*, vol. 4 (London: Kegan Paul, Trench, Trubner, 1877–1897), 401–412.

55. *Vīracōḻiyam*, 125:

viṇṇavar nāyakaṉ vēṇṭak
kaṇṇ iṉi taḷitta kātal
puṇṇiyaṉ irunta pōti
nal iṭai nōy naliyāvē

56. Ibid., 165.

57. Ibid., 140, 142.

58. Ibid., 142:

aruviṉai cila keṭa oru peru naraku iṭai
ericuṭar maraimalar eṉa viṭum aṭiyiṉai

59. Ibid., 140.

60. Ibid., 142.

61. Ibid., 144.

62. Ibid., 141:

kaṟpuṭai māraṉaik kāy ciṉam tavirttaṉai
poṟpuṭai nākar taṉ tuyaram pōkkiṉai
mīṉ uru āki meymmaiyil paṭintaṉai
māṉ uru āki vāṉ kuṇam iyaṟṟiṉai

63. Ibid., 161:

pōti mēviṉai puṉmai akaṟṟiṉai
cōti vāṉavar toḻa eḻuntaruḷiṉai
āti nātaṉ niṉ aṭi iṇai paravutum

64. Daṇḍin, *Kāvyādarśa*, begins his definition of a great poetic work (mahākāvya) at i.15 by indicating the necessity of a hero (nāyakam).

65. *Tolkāppiyam: Iḷampūraṇar uraiyuṭaṉ: Poruḷatikāram*, verse 73, 108–109.

66. Ibid., verse 74, 109–116.

67. *Vīracōḻiyam*, verse 102, 113:

nāl kulap pakkam mukālam kaḷavaḻi nal kuravai
āṟṟal vallāṉ vēṭkaiyār pakkam mēṉmaiyārum poruḷē
tōṟṟiya kāval tuṟavu koṭai paṭaiyāḷar pakkam
māṟṟiya oṟṟumaiyōṭu maṟṟum ivai vākaiyilē

68. Ibid., 114:

puṉiṟṟup paci uḻanta pulip piṇavu taṉātu
mulaimaṟā akkuḻavi vāṅki vāyppaṭut
tirai eṉak kavarntatu nōkki aṅka

vēr iḷam kuḻaviṉ ceṉṟu kāṇa
kūr ukir vayamāṉ pulavu vēṭṭut tuṭaṅkiya
vāḷ eyiṟṟuk koḷḷaiyiṉ taṅkiṉaṉ katuvap
pācilaip pōti mēviya perum takai
yār uyir kāval pūṇṭa
pēr aruḷ puṇarccip perumai tāṉē

69. This story of the tigress is unknown in the Pāli Jātaka collection but is found in a number of Sanskrit sources, including Āryaśūra's *Jātakamālā*; see Āryaśūra, *Once the Buddha Was a Monkey: Ārya Śūra's* Jātakamālā, trans. Peter Khoroche (Chicago: University of Chicago Press, 1989), 5–9.

70. *Tolkāppiyam: Iḷampūraṇar uraiyuṭaṉ: Poruḷatikāram*, verse 75, 116:

pullā vāḻkkai vallāṇ pakkamum
ollār nāṇap periyavark kaṇṇic
colliya vakaiyiṉ oṉṟōṭu puṇarntut
toll uyir vaḻaṅkiya avip pali yāṉum

71. *Vīracōḻiyam*, 115:

pācaṭaip pōtip pēr aruḷ vāmaṉ
varaiyā īkai pōla yāvirum
koṭaippaṭṭu vīrakkoṭai valappaṭumiṉ
muṉ oru muṟait taṉ uḻai iranta
aṉpilarkkā vēṇṭaḷavum paruka
eṉpu toṟum kaḻippiṟṟaṉ mey tiṟantu ākkik
kurutik koḻum patam koṭuttatum aṉṟik
karu cimiḻ paṭṭa kaḷḷap puṟaviṉ
māya yākkai colliyatu āṟṟaṉ
uṭampu niṟuttuk koṭuttatum aṉṟi

72. *Tolkāppiyam: Iḷampūraṇar uraiyuṭaṉ: Poruḷatikāram*, verses 59–60, 74–75.

73. Ibid., verse 61, 75–76.

74. Ibid., 79.

75. Daṇḍin, *Kāvyādarśa*, ii.275, ii.280–292.

76. *Vīracōḻiyam*, 256–258: the erotic (Tamil *ciruṅkāram*, Sanskrit śṛṅgāra), the heroic (Tamil *vīram*, Sanskrit vīra), the terrible (Tamil *accam*, Sanskrit bhayānaka), the loathesome (Tamil *iḻippu*, Sanskrit bībhatsa), the awesome (Tamil *viyappu*, Sanskrit adbhuta), the piteous (Tamil *avalam*, Sanskrit karuṇa), the furious (Tamil *uruttiram*, Sanskrit raudra), and the comic (Tamil *muṟukiya nakai*, Sanskrit hāsya). Note that Peruntēvaṉār substitutes several new terms for the categories of aesthetic experience listed at *Tolkāppiyam: Iḷampūraṇar uraiyuṭaṉ: Poruḷatikāram*, verse 247, 361: for the loathesome, iḻippu in lieu of iḷivaral; for the awesome, viyappu in lieu of maruṭkai; for the piteous, avalam instead of aḻukai; and for the furious, uruttiram instead of vekuḷi.

77. *Vīracōḻiyam*, 258. The verse quoted in number 318 of the *Tirukkuṟaḷ*:

taṉṉ uyirkku iṉṉāmai tāṉ aṟivāṉ eṉ kolō
maṉṉ uyirkku iṉṉā ceyal

78. Taṇṭi, *Taṇṭiyalaṅkāram*, verses 69–70, 144–150.

79. As discussed previously, Peruntēvaṉār was perhaps quite familiar with Sanskrit literary culture beyond the work of Daṇḍin. Abhinavagupta, for example, argues at length in his commentary on Ānandavardhana's *Dhvanyāloka* not only for the inclusion of "the quiescent" among the categories of aesthetic awareness but also that the ninth "is the most important of all the rasas"; see Ānandavardhana, *The Dhvanyāloka of Ānandavardhana with the Lacana of*

Abhinavagupta, Harvard Oriental Series, no. 49, trans. Daniel H. H. Ingalls, et al. (Cambridge: Harvard University Press, 1990), 520–526.

80. *Vīracōḻiyam*, verse 141, 198.

81. As described by G. U. Pope in the introduction to his edition and translation of the text, *The Sacred Kurral of Tiruvallava-Nayanar with Introduction, Grammar, Translation, Notes, Lexicon, and Concordance* (London: H. Frowde, 1886; Reprint, New Delhi: Asian Educational Services, 1990), vi.

82. Zvelebil, *Tamil Literature*, 122–123.

83. Quoted under *Vīracōḻiyam*, verse 153, 219:

cāyalum nāṇum avar koṇṭār kaimmāṟā
nōyum pacalaiyum tantu

84. Ibid., 211.

85. Ibid., 210:

cellāmai uṇṭēl eṉakku urai maṟṟu niṉ
val varavu vāḻvārkku urai

86. Daṇḍin, *Kāvyādarśa*, ii.356, 309:

śastraprahāraṁ dadatā bhujena tava bhūbhujām
cirārjitaṁ hṛtaṁ teṣāṁ yaśaḥ kumudapāṇḍuram

Translation adapted from Edwin Gerow, A *Glossary of Indian Figures of Speech* (Paris: Mouton, 1971), 203–204.

87. Daṇḍin, *Kāvyādarśa*, ii.121, 165:

anaṅgaḥ pañcabhiḥ puṣpair viśvam vyajayateṣubhiḥ
ity asaṁbhāvyam atha vā vicitrā vastuśaktayaḥ

Translation adapted from Gerow, *Indian Figures of Speech*, 125.

88. Daṇḍin, *Kāvyādarśa*, ii.123, 166:

kutaḥ kuvalayaṁ karṇe karoṣi kalabhāṣiṇi
kim apaṅgam aparyāptam asmin karmaṇi manyase

Translation adapted from Gerow, *Indian Figures of Speech*, 127.

89. *Vīracōḻiyam*, 133:

cātaliṉ iṉṉātatu illai iṉitu atū um
ītal iyaiyāk kaṭai

90. Ibid., 170:

uḷar eṉṉum māttiraiyar allāl payavāk
kaḷar aṉaiyar kallātavar

91. Daṇḍin, *Kāvyādarśa*, ii.336, 296:

tanumadhyaṁ pṛthuśroṇi raktauṣṭham asitekṣaṇam
natanabhi vapuḥ strīṇāṁ kaṁ na hanty unnatastanam

92. *Vīracōḻiyam*, 217:

nallāṟu eṉiṉum koḷal tītu mēl ulakam
ill eṉiṉum ītalē naṉṟu

93. Ibid., 208:

> *tuṟantārkkum tuvvātavarkkum iṟantārkkum*
> *ilvāḻvāṉ eṉpāṉ tuṇai*

94. Ibid., 208:

> *piṟavip perum kaṭal nīntuvar nīntār*
> *iṟaivaṉ aṭi cērātār*

95. Daṇḍin, *Kāvyādarśa*, ii.75, 143:

> *madapāṭalagaṇḍena raktanetrotpalena te*
> *mukhena mugdhaḥ so 'py eṣa jano rāgamayaḥ kṛtaḥ*

96. Such as *Nālaṭiyār*, 185, quoted under *Vīracōḻiyam*, verse 112 (135), as an example of a type of *veṇpā* meter:

> *uṟupuṉal tantu ulaku ūṭṭi aṟumiṭattum*
> *kal ūṟṟu uḻi ūṟum āṟē pōl celvam*
> *palarkku āṟṟik keṭṭu ulantak kaṇṇum cilarkku āṟṟic*
> *ceyvar ceyal pālavai*

> The river pours forth a mighty stream and feeds the world;
> and when it is dried up, if men dig in its bed, streams gush out!
> So good men, when rich, give to many;
> and, when ruined, give still at least to some, and do what should be done.

Text and translation from G. U. Pope, ed. and trans., *The Nāladiyār or Four Hundred Quatrains in Tamil* (Oxford: Clarendon, 1893; Reprint, New Delhi: Asian Educational Services, 1984), 118–119.

97. Such as the *Nāṉmaṇikkaṭikai* quoted by the commentator (130), described by Zvelebil (*Tamil Literature*, 120) as an early medieval Vaiṣṇava text that "vehemently preaches vegetarianism and abstention from taking life."

98. Indira Viswanathan Peterson, *Poems to Śiva: The Hymns of the Tamil Saints* (Princeton, N.J.: Princeton University Press, 1989), 15–16; Karen Pechilis Prentiss, *The Embodiment of Bhakti* (New York: Oxford University Press, 1999), 143–144. The relevant portions of the *Tirumuṟaikaṇṭapurāṇam* are translated into English by David Shulman in "Poets and Patrons in Tamil Literature and Literary Legend," in *The Powers of Art: Patronage in Indian Culture*, ed. Barbara Stoler Miller (Delhi: Oxford University Press, 1992), 101–102.

99. Karen Pechilis Prentiss, "A Tamil Lineage for Śaiva Siddhānta Philosophy," *History of Religions* 35/3 (1996):250.

100. For a translation of the relevant portions of the text, see John Carman and Vasudha Narayanan, *The Tamil Veda: Piḷḷaṉ's Interpretation of the Tiruvāymoḻi* (Chicago: University of Chicago Press, 1989), 5–6.

Conclusion

1. As in I. Iḷaṅkumaraṉ, ed., *Puṟattiraṭṭu* (Tinnevelly: South India Saiva Siddhanta Works Publishing Society, 1972), where verses from the *Kuṇṭalakēci* are quoted as examples of virtue, power, and love.

2. As in the comment made by the seventeenth-century Śaiva poet, Civappirakācar, and quoted in Paula Richman, *Women, Branch Stories and Religious Rhetoric in a Tamil Buddhist Text*, Foreign and Comparative Studies/South Asia Series, no. 12 (Syracuse, N.Y.: Maxwell School of

Citizenship and Public Affairs, Syracuse University, 1988), 7: "How can one grasp the intricacy of the text about Maṇimēkalai?"

3. As in the fourteenth-century Śaiva work, *Civañāṉacittiyār parapakkam*, and its commentary, both of which refute the teachings of a number of Buddhist philosophical schools, including the Sautrāntika (Tamil *cauttirāntikaṉ*) and the Yogācāra (Tamil *yōkācāraṉ*). See Caṇmukacuntara Mutaliyār, ed., *Civañāṉacittiyār parapakkam mūlamum Cattuvappirakācar uraiyum* (Madras: By the editor, 1894).

4. T. V. Mahalingam, *Mackenzie Manuscripts: Summaries of the Historical Manuscripts in the Mackenzie Collection, Volume One (Tamil and Malayalam)*, 2d ed. (Madras: University of Madras, 1972), 99.

5. As in the case of Buddhappiya's *Upāsakajanālaṅkāra: A Critical Edition and Study*, ed. H. Saddhatissa (London: Luzac, for Pali Text Society, 1965).

6. As in the fourteenth-century Old Javanese text cited earlier, the *Nāgarakṛtāgama*. See Mpu Prapañca, *Deśawarṇana (Nāgarakṛtāgama) by Mpu Prapañca*, trans. Stuart Robson, Verhandelingen van het Koniklijk Instituut voor Taal-, Land- en Volkenkunde, vol. 169 (Leiden: Koninklijk Instituut voor Taal-, Land- en Volkenkunde, 1995). H. Dhammaratana, *Buddhism in South India*, Wheel Publications, vols. 124–125 (Kandy, Sri Lanka: Buddhist Publication Society, 1968), 17, provides a tantalizing but unsubstantiated reference to "an eminent poet of Java writing in the 14th century . . . [who] mentions that at this time Buddhism and Vaishnavism had got so mixed up that it was difficult to distinguish one from the other," whereas Shu Hikosaka, *Buddhism in Tamilnadu: A New Perspective* (Madras: Institute of Asian Studies, 1989), 88, mentions a fourteenth-century inscription from Korea that "tells us of an Indian monk called Dhyānabhadra, who visited Kāñcipuram, where he listened to a discourse on the *Avataṁsaka-sūtra*." Hikosaka provides no direct evidence of this claim.

7. Vidya Dehejia, "The Persistence of Buddhism in Tamilnadu," Marg 39/4 (1988):55.

Bibliography

Agesthialingom, S., and S. V. Shanmugam. *The Language of Tamil Inscriptions 1250–1350* A.D. Annamalai University, Department of Linguistics, no. 23. Annamalainagar, India: Annamalai University, 1970.

Ahir, D. C. *Buddhism in South India.* Bibliotheca Indo-Buddhica Series, no. 112. Delhi: Sri Satguru Publications, 1992.

Aiyaswami Sastri, N. "Maṇimekhalai's Contributions to Indian Logic." *Journal of Oriental Research* 11/2 (1937):116–128.

Alter, Robert. *The World of Biblical Literature.* New York: Basic Books, 1992.

Amitacākarar. *Yāpparuṅkalam paḻaiya viruti uraiyuṭaṉ.* Edited by I. Iḷaṅkumaraṉ. Tinnevelly: South India Saiva Siddhanta Works Publishing Society, 1973.

——. *The Verses on the Precious Jewel Prosody Composed by Amitacākarar with the Commentary of Kuṇacākarar.* Publications du département d'indologie, no. 79. Edited and translated by Ulrike Niklas. Pondichéry: Institut Français, 1993.

Ānandavardhana. *Dhvanyālokaḥ Śrīmadabhinavaguptopādaviracita Locana sahitaḥ satipaṇa Prakāsa Hindīvyākhyopetaś ca.* Vidyābhavana Saṁskṛta Granthamālā, no. 97. Benares: Caukhambā Vidyābhavana, 1963.

——. *The Dhvanyāloka of Ānandavardhana with the Locana of Abhinavagupta.* Harvard Oriental Series, no. 49. Translated by Daniel H. H. Ingalls, Jeffrey Moussaieff Masson, and M. V. Patwardhan. Cambridge: Harvard University Press, 1990.

Anderson, Benedict. *Imagined Communities: Reflections on the Origin and Spread of Nationalism.* 2d ed. London: Verso, 1991.

Anuruddha. "Paramatthavinicchaya by Anuruddha." Edited by A. P. Buddhadatta. *Journal of the Pali Text Society* 10 (1985):155–226.

Āryaśūra. *Once the Buddha Was a Monkey: Ārya Śūra's* Jātakamālā. Translated by Peter Khoroche. Chicago: University of Chicago Press, 1989.

Aṭikaḷāciriyar, ed. *Tolkāppiyam: Collatikāram, Iḷampūraṇar urai.* Tamiḻp Palkalaik Kaḻakam Veḷiyīṭu, no. 101. Tañcāvūr, India: Tamiḻp Palkalaik Kaḻakam, 1988.

Baker, James N. "The Presence of the Name: Reading Scripture in an Indonesian Village." In *The Ethnography of Reading,* edited by Jonathan Boyarin, 98–138. Berkeley: University of California Press, 1993.

Bapat, P. V. "Vimati-Vinodani, a Vinaya Commentary and Kundalkesi-Vatthu, a Tamil Poem." *Journal of Indian History* 45 (1967):689–694.

Barnett, L. D. *Alphabetical Guide to Sinhalese Folklore from Ballad Sources.* Bombay: British India Press, 1917.

Barua, B. M. "Buddhadatta and Buddhaghosa: Their Contemporaneity and Age." *University of Ceylon Review* 3/2 (1945):77–88.

Basham, A. L. *History and Doctrines of the Ājīvikas: A Vanished Indian Religion.* London: Luzac, 1951. Reprint, Delhi: Motilal Banarsidass, 1981.

Beck, Brenda E. F. "The Study of a Tamil Epic: Several Versions of the *Silappadikaram* Compared." *Journal of Tamil Studies* 1 (September 1972):23–38.

Bennett, Andrew, ed. *Readers and Reading*. New York: Longman, 1995.

Bharata. *Nāṭyaśāstra of Bharatamuni, with the Commentary Abhinavabhāratī by Abhinavaguptācārya*. Parimal Sanskrit Series, no. 4. 4 vols. Edited by R. S. Nagar. Delhi: Parimal, 1981.

Blackburn, Anne. "The Play of the Teaching in the Life of the *Sāsana: Sārāthadīpanī* in Eighteenth-Century Sri Lanka." Ph.D. Diss., University of Chicago, 1995.

Blackburn, Stuart, et al., eds. *Oral Epics in India*. Berkeley: University of California Press, 1989.

Boeles, Jan J. *The Secret of Borobudur*. Bangkok: By the author, 1985.

Bourdieu, Pierre. *The Field of Cultural Production: Essays on Art and Literature*. Edited by Randal Johnson. Cambridge: Polity, 1993.

"Buddha Relic of the 12th Century Found." *Motilal Banarsidass Newsletter: A Monthly of Indological Bibliography* 21/12 (1999):9.

Buddhadatta. *Buddhadatta's Manuals, or Summaries of the Abhidhamma: Abhidhammāvatāra and Rūpārūpavibhāga*. 2 vols. Edited by A. P. Buddhadatta. London: Humphrey Milford, for Pali Text Society, 1915–1928.

——. *Madhuratthavilāsinī nāma Buddhavaṁsaṭṭhakathā of Bhadantācariya Buddhadatta Mahāthera*. Edited by I. B. Horner. London: Humphrey Milford, for Pali Text Society, 1946.

——. *The Clarifier of Sweet Meaning (Madhuratthavilāsinī): Commentary on the Chronicle of the Buddhas (Buddhavaṁsa) by Buddhadatta Thera*. Translated by I. B. Horner. London: Pali Text Society, 1978.

Buddhadatta, A. P. "The Great Author of Summaries—Contemporary of Buddhaghosa." *University of Ceylon Review* 3/1 (1945):34–40.

Buddhaghosa. *Manorathapūraṇī: Commentary on the Aṅguttara Nikāya*. 5 vols. Edited by Hermann Kopp et al. London: Luzac, for Pali Text Society, 1924–1956.

——. *Samantapāsādikā: Buddhaghosa's Commentary on the Vinaya Piṭaka*. 8 vols. Edited by J. Takakusu and M. Nagai. London: Oxford University Press, for Pali Text Society, 1924–1976.

——. *Visuddhimaggo with Paramatthamañjūsaṭīkā*. 4 vols. Pali Granthamala, no. 3. Edited by Revatadhamma. Varanasi: Varanaseya Sanskrit Vishvavidyalaya, 1969.

——. *The Path of Purification (Visuddhimagga)*. Translated by Bhikkhu Ñāṇamoli. Kandy, Sri Lanka: Buddhist Publication Society, 1991.

Buddhappiya. "The *Pajjamadhu*: A Poem in Praise of the Buddha." Edited by R. Gooneratne. *Journal of the Pali Text Society* (1887):1–17.

——. *Upāsakajanālaṅkāra: A Critical Edition and Study*. Edited by H. Saddhatissa. London: Luzac, for Pali Text Society, 1965.

Burlingame, Eugene Watson, trans. *Buddhist Legends: Translated from the Original Pali Text of the Dhammapada Commentary*. Harvard Oriental Series, nos. 28–30. Cambridge: Harvard University Press, 1921.

Cabezón, José Ignacio, and Roger R. Jackson. "Editor's Introduction." In *Tibetan Literature: Studies in Genre*, edited by José Ignacio Cabezón and Roger R. Jackson, 11–37. Ithaca, N.Y.: Snow Lion, 1996.

Cāminātaiyar, U. V. *Caṅkat tamiḻum piṟkālat tamiḻum*. Madras: Mahamahopadhyaya Dr. U. V. Swaminathaiyer Library, 1978.

——. *The Story of Udayana*. Translated by T. R. Rajagopala Aiyar. Madras: Mahamahopadhyaya Dr. U. V. Swaminathaiyer Library, 1983.

——, ed. *Pattuppāṭṭu mūlamum Nacciṉārkkiṉiyar uraiyum*. Tañcāvūr, India: Tamiḻp Palkaik Kaḻakam, 1986.

——, ed. *Puṟanāṉūṟu mūlam*. Madras: Mahamahopadhyaya Dr. U. V. Swaminathaiyer Library, 1936. Reprint, 1993.

——. *The Story of My Life: An Autobiography of Dr. U. V. Swaminatha Iyer.* 2 vols. Translated by Kamil V. Zvelebil. Madras: Institute of Asian Studies, 1994.

——, ed. *Naṉṉūl mūlamum Mayilainātar uraiyum.* Madras: Kabir, 1946. Reprint, Madras: Mahamahopadhyaya Dr. U. V. Swaminathaiyer Library, 1995.

Carman, John, and Vasudha Narayanan. *The Tamil Veda: Piḷḷaṉ's Interpretation of the Tiruvāymoḻi.* Chicago: University of Chicago Press, 1989.

Carpenter, J. Estlin, et al., eds. *Dīgha Nikāya.* 3 vols. London: Henry Frowde, for Pali Text Society, 1890–1911.

Cāttaṉār. *Manimekalai.* Translated by A. S. Panchapakesa Ayyar. Madras: Alliance, 1947.

——. *Maṇimēkalai.* Edited by U. V. Cāminātaiyar. Madras: Mahamahopadhyaya Dr. U. V. Swaminathaiyer Library, 1981.

——. *Manimekhalai.* Translated by G. U. Pope. Reprint, Madras: Pioneer Books Services, 1987.

——. *Maṇimēkalai.* Edited by N. M. Vēṇkaṭacāmi Nāṭṭār and A. C. Turaicāmi Piḷḷai. Tinnevelly: South India Saiva Siddhanta Works Publishing Society, 1992.

——. *Manimekhalai (The Dancer with the Magic Bowl).* Translated by Alain Daniélou. New York: New Directions, 1989. Reprint, New York: Penguin, 1993.

——. *Manimekhalai: Girdle of Gems.* Translated by K. Guruswamy and S. Srinivasan. Madras: Mahamahopadhyaya Dr. U. V. Swaminathaiyer Library, 1994.

Cēkkiḻār. *Tiruttoṇṭarpurāṇam Periyapurāṇam.* Edited by V. Kaliyāṇacuntaraṉār and M. Pālacuppiramaṇiyamutaliyār. Madras: Cēkkiḻār Ārāycci Maiyam, 1993.

Chakravarti, A., ed. and trans. *Neelakesi: The Original Text and the Commentary of Samaya-Divakara-Vamana-Muni.* 2 vols. in 1. Kumbakonam, India: By the author, 1936.

——. *Jaina Literature in Tamil.* Jñānapīṭha Mūrtidevī Granthamālā, English Series, no. 3. New Delhi: Bhāratīya Jñānapīṭha, 1974.

Chalmers, Robert, ed. *Majjhima-Nikāya.* 4 vols. London: Henry Frowde, for Pali Text Society, 1888–1925.

Champakalakshmi, R. "Religious Conflict in the Tamil Country: A Re-appraisal of Epigraphic Evidence." *Journal of the Epigraphic Society of India* 5 (1978):69–81.

Chandra, Lokesh. "Sanskrit Studies in Classical Indonesia." *Indologica Taurinensia* 6 (1978):113–123.

Chari, V. K. *Sanskrit Criticism.* Honolulu: University of Hawaii Press, 1990.

Cheluva Aiyar, C. S. "Vañcimānakar, or the Great City Called Vañci." *Journal of Oriental Research* 2 (1928):113–134.

Chhabra, B. C. "Expansion of Indo-Aryan Culture During Pallava Rule, as Evidenced by Inscriptions." *Journal of the Asiatic Society of Bengal, Letters* 1 (1935):1–64.

Childers, Robert Caesar. *A Dictionary of the Pali Language.* London: Kegan Paul, Trench, Trubner, 1909.

Cleary, Thomas, trans. *Entry into the Realm of Reality: A Translation of the Gandavyuha, the Final Book of the Avatamsaka Sutra.* Boston: Shambala, 1989.

Clothey, Fred. *The Many Faces of Murukaṉ: The History and Meaning of a South Indian God.* Religion and Society, no. 6. New York: Mouton, 1978.

Coedès, G. "La legende de la *nāgī.*" *Bulletin de l'École Française d'Extrême-Orient* 11/3–4 (1911):391–393.

——, ed. and trans. *Inscriptions du Cambodge.* Collection du textes et documents sur l'Indochine, vol. 3. Paris: E. de Brocard, 1952.

——. *The Making of South East Asia.* Translated by H. M. Wright. Berkeley: University of California Press, 1966.

——. *The Indianized States of Southeast Asia.* Edited by Walter F. Vella. Translated by Susan Brown Cowing. Honolulu: East-West Center Press, 1968.

Collins, Steven. "*Nirvāṇa*, Time, and Narrative." *History of Religion* 31/3 (1992):215–246.

——. *Nirvana and Other Buddhist Felicities: Utopias of the Pali Imaginaire*. Cambridge Studies in Religious Traditions, no. 12. Cambridge: Cambridge University Press, 1998.

Copeland, Rita. *Rhetoric, Hermeneutics, and Translation in the Middle Ages: Academic Traditions and Vernacular Texts*. Cambridge: Cambridge Univesity Press, 1991.

Cuppiramaṇiyaṉ, C. V. *Vīracōḻiyam: oru tiṟaṉāyvu–mūlamum karuttum*. Madras: Tamiḻp Patippakam, 1977.

Cutler, Norman. *Songs of Experience: The Poetics of Tamil Devotion*. Bloomington: Indiana University Press, 1987.

——. "Interpreting *Tirukkuṟaḷ*: The Role of Commentary in the Creation of a Text." *Journal of the American Oriental Society* 112/4 (1992):549–566.

Cutler, Norman, and Paula Richman, eds. *A Gift of Tamil: Translations from Tamil Literature in Honor of K. Paramasivam*. New Delhi: Manohar and American Institute of Indian Studies, 1992.

Daṇḍin. *The Kāvyādarśa of Śrī Daṇḍin*. Bibliotheca Indica, vol. 40. Edited by Paṇḍita Premachandra Tarkabāgīśa. Calcutta: Asiatic Society of Bengal, 1863. Reprint, Osnabrück, Germany: Biblio Verlag, 1981.

Das, Asha. "The Pajjamadhu—A Critical Study." *Journal of the Department of Pali, University of Calcutta* 5 (1989–1990):35–72.

Davis, Richard H. "The Story of the Disappearing Jains: Retelling the Śaiva-Jain Encounter in Medieval South India." In *Open Boundaries: Jain Communities and Cultures in Indian History*, edited by John E. Cort, 213–224. Albany: State University of New York Press, 1998.

de Alwis, James, trans. *The Sidath Sangarawa: A Grammar of the Singhalese Language*. Colombo: William Skeen, 1852.

Dehejia, Vidya. "The Persistence of Buddhism in Tamilnadu." *Marg* 39/4 (1988):53–74.

——. *Art of the Imperial Cholas*. New York: Columbia University Press, 1990.

Demiéville, Paul. *Buddhism and Healing: Demiéville's Article* "Byō" *from* Hōbōgirin. Translated by Mark Tatz. Lanham, Md.: University Press of America, 1985.

Dhammapāla. *Paramatthadīpanī: Being the Commentary on the Vimāna-Vatthu*. Edited by E. Hardy. London: Henry Frowde, for Pali Text Society, 1901.

——. *Paramatthadīpanī: Theragāthā-Aṭṭhakathā, the Commentary of Dhammapālācariya*. 3 vols. Edited by F. Woodward. London: Luzac, for Pali Text Society, 1940–1959.

——. *Elucidation of the Intrinsic Meaning So Named: The Commentary on the Vimāna Stories* (*Paramattha-dīpanī nāma Vimānavatthu-aṭṭhakathā*). Translated by Peter Masefield and N. A. Jayawickrama. Oxford: Pali Text Society, 1989.

——. *Therīgāthā-Aṭṭhakathā* (*Paramatthadīpanī VI*). Edited by William Pruitt. Oxford: Pali Text Society, 1998.

Dhammaratana, H. *Buddhism in South India*. Wheel Publications, vols. 124–125. Kandy, Sri Lanka: Buddhist Publication Society, 1968.

Dharmadasa, K. N. O. "The People of the Lion: Ethnic Identity, Ideology, and Historical Revisionism in Contemporary Sri Lanka." *Ethnic Studies Report* 10/1 (1992):37–159.

——. "The Roots of Sinhala Ethnic Identity in Sri Lanka: The Debate on 'The People of the Lion' Continued." *Ethnic Studies Report* 14/2 (1996):137–170.

Dharwadker, Vinay. "Orientalism and the Study of Indian Literature." In *Orientalism and the Postcolonial Predicament*, edited by Carol A. Breckenridge and Peter van der Veer, 160–163. Delhi: Oxford University Press, 1994.

Eco, Umberto. *The Role of the Reader*. Bloomington: Indiana University Press, 1979.

——. *Six Walks in the Fictional Woods*. Charles Eliot Norton Lectures, 1993. Cambridge: Harvard University Press, 1994.

Eco, Umberto, with Richard Rorty et al. *Interpretation and Overinterpretation*. Edited by Stefan Collini. Cambridge: Cambridge University Press, 1992.

Elliot, Walter. "The Edifice Formerly Known as the Chinese or Jaina Pagoda at Negapatam." *Indian Antiquary* 7 (1878):224–227.

Encyclopedia of Religion. s.v., vol. 12, "Relics," by John S. Strong.

Encyclopedia of Tamil Literature. s.v., vol. 1, "Christianity and Tamil Literature," by G. John Samuel and L. R. John, 391–409.

Encyclopedia of Tamil Literature. s.v., vol. 1, "Contact of the Tamils with the Southeast Asian Countries," by K. D. Swaminathan, 65–71.

Encyclopedia of Tamil Literature. s.v., vol. 1, "History of Buddhism in Tamiḻnāṭu," by Shu Hikosaka, 187–197.

Encyclopedia of Tamil Literature. s.v., vol. 1, "Jainism and Tamil Literature," by R. Vijayalakshmy, 199–214.

Encyclopedia of Tamil Literature. s.v., vol. 1, "Literary Genres in Tamil: A Diachronic Study," by Annie Mrithulakumari Thomas, 339–357.

Ezhuthachan, K. N. *The History of Grammatical Theories in Malayalam*. Dravidian Linguistics Association, no. 17. Trivandrum, India: Department of Linguistics, University of Kerala, 1975.

Fausbøll, V., ed. *The Jātaka Together with its Commentary: Being Tales of the Anterior Births of Gotama Buddha*. 7 vols. London: Kegan Paul, Trench, Trubner, 1877–1897.

Faxian [Fa-hsien]. *The Travels of Fa-hsien (399–414 A.D.), or Record of the Buddhistic Kingdoms*. Translated by R. A. Giles. Cambridge: Cambridge University Press, 1923.

——. *A Record of the Buddhist Countries by Fa-hsien*. Peking: Chinese Buddhist Association, 1957.

——. *A Record of Buddhistic Kingdoms: Being an Account of the Chinese Monk Fa-Hsien of Travels in India and Ceylon (A.D. 399–414) in Search of Buddhist Books of Discipline*. Translated by James Legge. London: Dover, 1886. Reprint, New Delhi: Munshiram Manoharlal, 1991.

——. *Travels of Fah-Hian and Sung-Yun, Buddhist Pilgrims from China to India (400 A.D. and 418 A.D.)*. Translated by Samuel Beal. London: Trubner, 1869. Reprint, New Delhi: Asian Educational Services, 1993.

Fernando, C. M., trans. *The Nikāya-saṅgrahaya*. Colombo: H. C. Cottle, Government Printer, 1908.

Filliozat, Jean. "New Researches on the Relations Between Indian and Cambodia." *Indica* 3/1 (1966):95–106.

——. "The Oldest Sea-Routes of the Tamil Trade." *Bulletin of the Institute of Traditional Cultures, Madras* (July-December 1976):21–28.

Florida, Nancy K. *Writing the Past, Inscribing the Future: History as Prophecy in Colonial Java*. Durham, N.C.: Duke University Press, 1995.

Freeman, Rich. "Rubies and Coral: The Lapidary Crafting of Language in Kerala." *Journal of Asian Studies* 57/1 (1998):38–65.

Freund, Elizabeth. *The Return of the Reader: Reader-Response Criticism*. London: Methuen, 1987.

Fujita, Kotatsu. "The Doctrinal Characteristics of *Karman* in Early Buddhism." In *Indological and Buddhist Studies: Volume in Honour of Professor J. W. de Jong on His Sixtieth Birthday*, edited by L. A. Hercus, et al., 149–159. Canberra: Faculty of Asian Studies, 1982.

Geertz, Clifford. *Negara: The Theatre State in Nineteenth-Century Bali*. Princeton, N.J.: Princeton University Press, 1980.

Geiger, Wilhelm. *The Dīpavaṁsa and the Mahāvaṁsa and Their Historical Development in Ceylon*. Translated by E. M. Coomaraswamy. Colombo: Government Printer, 1908.

——, ed. *Cūlavaṁsa: Being the More Recent Part of the Mahāvaṁsa*. 2 vols. London: Humphrey Milford, for Pali Text Society, 1925.

Geiger, Wilhelm, and C. Mabel Rickmers, trans. *Cūlavaṁsa: Being the More Recent Part of the Mahāvaṁsa*. 2 vols. in 1. London: Oxford University Press, for Pali Text Society, 1929–1930. Reprint, New Delhi: Asian Educational Services, 1992.

Gerow, Edwin. *A Glossary of Indian Figures of Speech*. Paris: Mouton, 1971.

——. *Indian Poetics*. History of Indian Literature, vol. 5, fascicle 3. Edited by Jan Gonda. Wiesbaden: Otto Harrassowitz, 1977.

Gibson, Walker. "Authors, Speakers, Readers, and Mock Readers." In *Reader-Response Criticism: From Formalism to Post-Structuralism*, edited by Jane P. Tompkins, 1–6. Baltimore: Johns Hopkins University Press, 1980.

Gleason, Philip. "Identifying Identity: A Semantic History." *Journal of American History* 69/4 (1983):910–931.

Godakumbura, C. E. *Sinhalese Literature*. Colombo: Colombo Apothecaries, 1955.

Golobew, V. "Les legendes da la Nāgī et de l'Apsaras." *Bulletin de l'École Française d'Extrême-Orient* 24/3–4 (1924):501–510.

Gomèz, Luis O., and Hiram W. Woodward, Jr., eds. *Barabuḍur: History and Significance of a Buddhist Monument*. Berkeley Buddhist Studies Series, no. 2. Berkeley, Calif.: Asian Humanities Press, 1981.

Gonda, J. *The Indian Religions in Pre-Islamic Indonesia and Their Survival in Bali*. Handbuch der Orientalistik, Volume 2, Part 1: Religionen. Leiden: E. J. Brill, 1975.

——. *Old Javenese Literature*. Handbuch der Orientalistik, Dritte Abteilung, Dritte Band: Literaturen, no. 1. Leiden: E. J. Brill, 1976.

Gopalan, Subramania. "Dhammapada and Tirukkuṟaḷ: A Comparative Study." In *Pāli Buddhism*, edited by Frank J. Hoffman and Mahinda Deegalle, 57–77. Richmond, U.K.: Curzon, 1996.

Gopinatha Rao, T. A. "Bauddha Vestiges in Kanchipuram." *Indian Antiquary* 44 (June 1915):127–129.

Gray, James, ed. and trans. *Buddhaghosuppatti, or the Historical Romance of the Rise and Career of Buddhaghosa*. London: Luzac, 1892.

——. *The Kalyānī Inscriptions Erected by King Dhammaceti at Pegu in 1476 A.D.: Text and Translation*. Rangoon: Government Press, 1892.

Gunasegaram, S. J. "Early Tamil Cultural Influences in South East Asia." *Tamil Culture* 6/4 (1957):319–341.

Guṇasēkara, B., trans. *The Rājāvaliya, or a Historical Narrative of Siṅhalese Kings from Vijaya to Vimala Dharma Sūrya II*. Colombo: George J. A. Skeen, Government Printer, 1900.

Gunawardana, R. A. L. H. "The People of the Lion: The Sinhala Identity and Ideology in History and Historiography." *Sri Lanka Journal of the Humanities* 5/1 (1979):3–36.

——. *Robe and Plough: Monasticism and Economic Interest in Early Medieval Sri Lanka*. Association for Asian Studies: Monographs and Papers, no. 35. Tuscon: University of Arizona Press, for Association for Asian Studies, 1979.

——. *Historiography in a Time of Ethnic Conflict: Constructions of the Past in Contemporary Sri Lanka*. Colombo: Social Scientists' Association, 1995.

Gupta, Dharmendra Kumar. *A Critical Study of Daṇḍin and His Works*. Delhi: Meharchand Lachhmandas, 1970.

Haldar, J. R. *Early Buddhist Mythology*. New Delhi: Manohar, 1977.

Hall, Kenneth R. *Trade and Statescraft in the Age of the Cōḻas*. New Delhi: Abhinav, 1980.

Hallisey, Charles. "Recent Works on Buddhist Ethics." *Religious Studies Review* 18/4 (1992):276–285.

Hallisey, Charles, and Anne Hansen. "Narrative, Sub-Ethics, and the Moral Life: Some Evidence from Theravāda Buddhism." *Journal of Religious Ethics* 24/2 (1996):305–327.

Hardy, R. Spence. *A Manual of Buddhism, in its Modern Development*. Chowkhamba Sanskrit Studies, vol. 56. London: Patridge and Oakey, 1853. Reprint, Varanasi: Chowkhamba Sanskrit Series Office, 1967.

Harpham, Geoffrey Galt. "Ethics." In *Critical Terms for Literary Study*, edited by Frank Lentricchia and Thomas McLaughlin, 387–405. 2d ed. Chicago: University of Chicago Press, 1995.

Harṣa. *The Ratnāvalī of Śrīharshadeva*. Edited by Nārāyaṇa Bālakriṣṇa and Kāśināth Pāṇḍurang. 2d ed. Bombay: Nirṇaya-Sāgara, 1890.

——. *Nāgānanda of Śrīharṣa*. Edited and translated by Raghunath Damodar Karmarkar. Bombay: Visvanath, 1923.

——. *Priyadarśikā: A Sanskrit Drama by Harsha*. Columbia Indo-Iranian Series, no. 10. Translated by G. K. Nariman, et al. New York: Columbia University Press, 1923.

Hart, George L., III. *The Poems of Ancient Tamil: Their Milieu and Their Sanskrit Counterparts*. Berkeley: University of California Press, 1975.

——. *The Relation Between Tamil and Classical Sanskrit Literature*. A History of Indian Literature, vol. 10, fascicle 2. Edited by Jan Gonda. Wiesbaden: Otto Harrassowitz, 1976.

——. "Archetypes in Classical Indian Literature and Beyond." In *Syllables of Sky: Studies in South Indian Civilization in Honour of Velcheru Narayana Rao*, edited by David Shulman, 165–182. Delhi: Oxford University Press, 1995.

Hart, George L., III., and Hank Heifetz. *The Forest Book of the* Rāmāyaṇa *of Kampaṉ*. Berkeley: University of California Press, 1988.

Herath, Dharmaratna. *The Tooth Relic and the Crown*. Colombo: By the author, 1994.

Hicks, Nhung, trans. *Cambodian Folktales in Vietnamese*. Ho Chi Minh City, forthcoming.

Hikosaka, Shu. *Buddhism in Tamilnadu: A New Perspective*. Madras: Institute of Asian Studies, 1989.

Holland, Norman N. "Unity Identity Text Self." In *Reader-Response Criticism: From Formalism to Post-Structuralism*, edited by Jane P. Tompkins, 118–133. Baltimore: Johns Hopkins University Press, 1980.

Holt, John Clifford. *Buddha in the Crown: Avalokiteśvara in the Buddhist Traditions of Sri Lanka*. New York: Oxford University Press, 1991.

Hooykaas, C. *The Old-Javanese Rāmāyaṇa Kakawin, with Special Reference to the Problem of Interpolation in Kakawins*. Verhandelingen van het Koninklijk Instituut voor Taal-, Land- en Volkenkunde, deel 16. 's-Gravenhage, The Netherlands: Martinus Nijhoff, 1955.

——. *The Old-Javanese Rāmāyaṇa: An Exemplary Kakawin as to Form and Content*. Verhandelingen der Koninklijke Nederlandse Akademie van Wetenscappen, Afd. Leteerkunde, deel 65, no. 1. Amsterdam: N. V. Noor-Hollandsche Uitgevers Maatschappij, 1958.

Horner, I. B., trans. *The Minor Anthologies of the Pali Canon, Part III: Chronicle of the Buddhas* (*Buddhavaṁsa*) *and Basket of Conduct* (*Cariyāpiṭaka*). London: Pali Text Society, 1975.

Horton, H. Mack. "Japanese Spirit and Chinese Learning: Scribes and Storytellers in Pre-modern Japan." In *The Ethnography of Reading*, edited by Jonathan Boyarin, 156–179. Berkeley: University of California Press, 1993.

Hudson, Dennis. "The Courtesan and Her Bowl: An Esoteric Buddhist Reading of the *Maṇimēkalai*." In *A Buddhist Woman's Path to Enlightenment: Proceedings of a Workshop on the Tamiḻ Narrative* Maṇimēkalai, *Uppsala University, May 25–29, 1995*, 151–190. Acta Universitatis Upsaliensis: Historica Religionum, vol. 13, edited by Peter Schalk. Uppsala, Sweden: Uppsala University, 1997.

Huili [Hwui Li]. *The Life of Hiuen-Tsiang by the Shaman Hwui Li*. Translated by Samuel Beal. London: Kegan Paul, Trench, Trubner, 1911.

Humes, Cynthia Ann. "Vindhyavāsinī: Local Goddess Yet Great Goddess." In *Devī: Goddesses of India*, edited by John Stratton Hawley and Donna Marie Wulff, 49–76. Berkeley: University of California Press, 1996.

Ilakkuvanār, S., trans. *Tholkāppiyam* (*in English*) *with Critical Studies*. Madurai, India: 'Kuṛaḷ Veṛi' 1963.

Iḷaṅkō Aṭikaḷ. *Cilappatikāram mūlamum Arumpata uraiyum Aṭiyārkkunallār uraiyum*. Edited by U. V. Cāminātaiyar. Madras: Mahamahopadhyaya Dr. U. V. Swaminathaiyer Library, 1978.

——. *The Cilappatikāram of Iḷaṅkō Aṭikaḷ: An Epic of South India.* Translated by R. Parthasarathy. New York: Columbia University Press, 1993.

Iḷaṅkumaraṉ, I., ed. *Puṟattiraṭṭu.* Tinnevelly: South India Saiva Siddhanta Works Publishing Society, 1972.

Index des mots de la litterature tamoule ancienne. Publications de l'institut français d'indologie, no. 37. 3 vols. Pondichéry: Institut Français d'Indologie, 1967–1970.

Indian Archaeology: A Review. New Delhi: Archaeological Survey of India, 1961–1973.

Indrapala, K. "Buddhism Among the Tamils A.D. 1000–1500." In *Proceedings of the Fifth International Conference-Seminar of Tamil Studies,* vol. 2, edited by M. Arunchalam, 12/27–12/39. Madras: International Association of Tamil Studies, 1981.

Irākavaiyaṅkār, R. *Kuṟuntokai viḷakkam.* Aṇṇāmalai, India: Aṇṇāmalaip Palkalaik Kaḻakam, 1993.

Irschick, Eugene F. *Politics and Social Conflict in South India: The Non-Brahmin Movement and Tamil Separatism, 1916–1929.* Berkeley: University of California Press, 1969.

Irvine, Martin. *The Making of Textual Culture: 'Grammatica' and Literary Theory, 350–1100.* Cambridge Studies in Medieval Literature, no. 19. Cambridge: Cambridge University Press, 1994.

Iser, Wolfgang. *The Implied Reader: Patterns of Communication in Prose Fiction from Bunyan to Beckett.* Baltimore: Johns Hopkins University Press, 1974.

Iyer, T. V. Gopal, ed. *Tēvāram: Hymnes Śivaites du pays Tamoul.* Publications de l'institut français d'indologie, no. 68. 3 vols. Pondichéry: Institut Français d'Indologie, 1984.

Jacob, Judith M., trans. *Reamker (Rāmakerti): The Cambodian Version of the Rāmāyaṇa.* Oriental Translation Fund, New Series, vol. 45. London: Royal Asiatic Society, 1986.

Jacobi, Hermann. "Über das Alter der *Maṇimēkhalai.*" In *Kleine Schriften,* vol. 2, edited by Bernhard Kolver, 293–310. Wiesbaden: Franz Steiner Verlag GMBH, 1970.

Jaini, Padmanabh S., ed. *Paññāsa Jātaka or Zimme Paṇṇāsa (in the Burmese Recension).* Pali Text Society Text Series, no. 172. 2 vols. London: Pali Text Society, 1981.

——. "Stages in the Bodhisattva Career of the Tathāgata Maitreya." In *Maitreya, the Future Buddha,* edited by Alan Sponberg and Helen Hardacre, 54–90. Cambridge: Cambridge University Press, 1988.

——. "The Apocryphal Jātakas of Southeast Asian Buddhism." *Indian Journal of Buddhist Studies* 1/1 (1989):22–39.

Jauss, Hans Robert. *Toward an Aesthetic of Reception.* Theory and History of Literature, vol. 2. Translated by Timothy Bahti. Minneapolis: University of Minnesota Press, 1982.

Jayawickrama, N. A., ed. *Buddhavaṁsa and Cariyāpiṭaka.* Pali Text Society Text Series, no. 166. London: Pali Text Society, 1974.

Journal of Buddhist Ethics. Online. Available: http://jbe.la.psu.edu/.

Kachru, Braj B. *Kashmiri Literature.* History of Indian Literature, vol. 8, fascicle 4. Edited by Jan Gonda. Wiesbaden: Otto Harrassowitz, 1981.

Kālidāsa. *The Mālavikāgnimitra: A Sanskrit Play by Kālidāsa, with the Commentary of Kāṭayavema.* Bombay Sanskrit Series, no. 6. Edited by Shankar Pāṇḍurang. Bombay: Government Central Book Depot, 1889.

——. *The Abhijñānaśākuntalam of Kālidāsa, with the Commentary of Rāghavabhaṭṭa, Various Readings, Introduction, Literal Translation, Exhaustive Notes, and Appendices.* Edited by M. R. Kale. Bombay: Oriental, 1902. Reprint, Delhi: Motilal Banarsidass, 1994.

Kandaswany, S. N. *Buddhism as Expounded in* Maṇimēkalai. Annamalainagar, India: Annamamalai University, 1978.

Kāraikkālammaiyār. *Chants dévotionnels tamouls de Kāraikkāl-ammaiyār.* Publications de l'Institut Français d'Indologie, no. 1, edited by Kārāvēlane. 2d ed. Pondichéry: Institut Français d'Indologie, 1982.

Karunadasa, Y. "The Abhidharma Theory of *Paññatti*: The Category of the Nominal and the Conceptual." In *Buddhist Philosophy and Culture: Essays in Honour of N. A. Jayawickrema,* edited by David J. Kalupahana and W. G. Weeraratne, 71–92. Colombo: N. A. Jayawickrema Felicitation Volume Committee, 1987.

Kassapa. *Vimativinodani.* Edited by Beratuduwe Dhammadhara Tissa Thero. Colombo: Luxman, 1935.

——. *Mohavicchedanī Abhidhammamātikatthavaṇṇanā by Kassapatthera of Coḷa.* Edited by A. P. Buddhadatta and A. K. Warder. London: Luzac, for Pali Text Society, 1961.

Kaṭavuḷamāmuṉivar. *Tiruvātavūrarpurāṇam.* Edited by Kantacuvāmiyaiyar and Cuppāyamutaliyār. Kāñcīpuram: S. Kantacuvāmiyaiyar, 1888.

Kaviraj, Sudipta. "Writing, Speaking, Being: Language and the Historical Formation of Identities in India." In *Nationalstaat und Sprachkonflikte in Süd- und Südostasien* 25–68. Beiträge zur Südasienforschung, no. 149, edited by Dagmar Hellmann-Rajanayagam and Dietmar Rothermund. Stuttgart: Franz Steiner Verlag, 1992.

Kinsley, David. *Hindu Goddesses: Visions of the Divine Feminine in the Hindu Religious Tradition.* Berkeley: University of California Press, 1988.

Krishna Sastri, A. *Two Statues of Pallava Kings and Five Pallava Inscriptions in a Rock-Temple at Mahabalipuram.* Memoirs of the Archaeological Survey of India, no. 26. Calcutta: Government of India, Central Publication Branch, 1926.

Krishnaswami Aiyangar, S. *Manimekhalai in Its Historical Setting.* London: Luzac, 1928.

Kumaraswami Raja, N. "Sanskrit Influence on Vi:raco:ḻiyam (A Medieval Tamil Grammar)." *International Journal of Dravidian Linguistics,* 13/2 (1983):209–212.

Kuppuswami Sastri, S. "Problems of Identity in the Cultural History of Ancient India." *Journal of Oriental Research* 2 (1927):191–201.

——. "Aṟavaṇavaṭikaḷ (Ācārya-Dharmapāla?) Again." *Journal of Oriental Research* (1928):79–83.

LaCapra, Dominick. *Rethinking Intellectual History: Texts, Contexts, Language.* Ithaca, N.Y.: Cornell University Press, 1983.

Ledi Sayadaw. "Some Points in Buddhist Doctrine." Translated by Shwe Zan Aung. *Journal of the Pali Text Society* (1913–1914):115–169.

——. "On the Philosophy of Relations." *Journal of the Pali Text Society* (1915–1916):21–53.

——. "The Patthanuddesa Dipani, or The Buddhist Philosophy of Relations." In *The Manuals of Buddhism: The Expositions of the Buddha-dhamma,* edited by Union Buddha Sāsana Council, 61–120. Bangkok: Mahamakut, 1978.

Leeladevi, R. *History of Malayalam Literature.* Trivandrum, India: Educational Supplies Depot, 1977.

Le Goff, Jacques. *The Medieval Imagination.* Translated by Arthur Goldhammer. Chicago: University of Chicago Press, 1988.

Lévi, Sylvain. *Mémorial Sylvain Lévi.* Edited by Paul Hartmann. Paris: Rue Cujas, 1937.

Lilley, Mary E., ed., *Khuddaka Nikāya: Apadāna.* 2 vols. London: Oxford University Press, for Pali Text Society, 1927.

Liyanagamage, Amaradasa. "A Forgotten Aspect of the Relations Between the Sinhalese and the Tamils." *Ceylon Historical Journal* 25/1–4 (1978):95–142.

Lockwood, Michael. *Māmallapuram and the Pallavas.* Madras: Christian Literature Society, 1982.

Lockwood, Michael, and A. Vishnu Bhat, eds. and trans. *Metatheater and Sanskrit Drama.* Madras: Tambaram Research Associates, 1994.

Mahadevan, Iravatham. *Corpus of Tamil-Brāhmī Inscriptions.* Madras: Tamilnadu State Department of Archaeology, 1970.

Mahalingam, T. V. *Kāñcīpuram in Early South Indian History.* New Delhi: Asia Publishing House, 1969.

——. *Mackenzie Manuscripts: Summaries of the Historical Manuscripts in the Mackenzie Collection, Volume One (Tamil and Malayalam).* 2d ed. Madras: University of Madras, 1972.

Mahānāma. *The Mahāvaṁsa*. Edited by Wilhelm Geiger. London: Henry Frowde, for Pali Text Society, 1908.

——. *The Mahāvaṁsa, or the Great Chronicle of Ceylon*. Translated by Wilhelm Geiger and Mabel Haynes Bode. London: Henry Frowde, for Pali Text Society, 1912. Reprint, New Delhi: Asian Educational Services, 1993.

Majumdar, R. C. *Kambuja-Deśa or an Ancient Colony in Cambodia*. Philadelphia: Institute for the Study of Human Issues, 1980.

Malalasekera, G. P. *Dictionary of Pāli Proper Names*. 2 vols. London: John Murray, for Government of India, 1938.

Malathi Devi, K. K. *Prahasana in Sanskrit Literature and Kerala Stage*. Delhi: Nag, 1995.

Marr, David G., and A. C. Milner, eds. *Southeast Asia in the 9th to 14th Centuries*. Singapore and Canberra: Institute of Southeast Asian Studies, Singapore, and the Research School of Pacific Studies, Australian National University, 1990.

Marr, John Ralston. *The Eight Anthologies: A Study in Early Tamil Literature*. Madras: Institute of Asian Studies, 1985.

Martini, François, ed. and trans. "Dasa-Bodhisatta-Uddesa." *Bulletin de l'École Française d'Extrême Orient* 36/2 (1937):287–390.

Masson, J. L., and M. V. Patwardhan. *Śāntarasa and Abhinavagupta's Philosophy of Aesthetics*. Bhandarkar Oriental Series, no. 9. Poona: Bhandarkar Oriental Research Institute, 1969.

——. *Aesthetic Rapture: The Rasādhyāya of the Nāṭyaśāstra*. 2 vols. Poona: Deccan College, 1970.

McGregor, Ronald Stuart. *Hindi Literature of the Nineteenth and Early Twentieth Centuries*. History of Indian Literature, vol. 8, fascicle 2. Edited by Jan Gonda. Wiesbaden: Otto Harrassowitz, 1974.

Meenakshisundaran, T. P. *Foreign Models of Tamil Grammar*. Dravidian Linguistics Association, no. 15. Trivandrum, India: Department of Linguistics, University of Kerala, 1974.

Menon, A. G. "The Use of Sanskrit in South Indian Bilingual Royal Inscriptions: Social, Political and Religious Implications." In *Ideology and Status of Sanskrit: Contributions to the History of the Sanskrit Language*, 249–263. Brill's Indological Library, vol. 13, edited by Jan E. M. Houben. Leiden: E. J. Brill, 1996.

Miller, J. Hillis. "Narrative." In *Critical Terms for Literary Study*, 66–79. 2d ed., edited by Frank Lentricchia and Thomas McLaughlin. Chicago: University of Chicago Press, 1995.

Minayeff, J., ed. "The Cha-Kesa-Dhātu-Vaṁsa." *Journal of the Pali Text Society* (1885):5–16.

——. "Anāgata-vaṁsa." *Journal of the Pali Text Society* (1886):33–53.

——. "Gandha-vaṁsa." *Journal of the Pali Text Society* (1886):54–80.

Monier-Williams, Monier. *A Sanskrit-English Dictionary*. Oxford: Oxford University Press, 1899. Reprint, Delhi: Motilal Banarsidass, 1986.

Monius, Anne E. "Literary Theory and Moral Vision in Tamil Buddhist Literature." *Journal of Indian Philosophy* 28/2 (2000):195–223.

——. "The Many Lives of Daṇḍin: The *Kāvyādarśa* in Sanskrit and Tamil." *International Journal of Hindu Studies* 4/2 (2000):1–37.

——. "The *Maṇimēkalai*'s Buddhist Audience." In *Proceedings of the Eighth International Conference-Seminar of Tamil Studies*. Madras: International Institute of Tamil Research, forthcoming.

Monius, Anne E., and Rangarajan Vijayalakshmy. "*Ētunikalcci* in the *Maṇimēkalai*: The Manifestation of Beneficial Root 'Causes' and Renunciation." In *A Buddhist Woman's Path to Enlightenment: Proceedings of a Workshop on the Tamil̲ Narrative* Maṇimēkalai, *Uppsala University, May 25–29, 1995*, 261–275. Acta Universitatis Upsaliensis: Historica Religionum, vol. 13, edited by Peter Schalk. Uppsala, Sweden: Uppsala University, 1997.

Morris, Richard, ed. *Aṅguttara-nikāya*. 6 vols. London: Henry Frowde, for Pali Text Society, 1885–1910.

Mpu Prapañca. *Deśawarṇana (Nāgarakṛtāgama) by Mpu Prapañca*. Translated by Stuart Robson. Verhandelingen van het Koninklijk Instituut voor Taal-, Land- en Volkenkunde, vol. 169. Leiden, The Netherlands: Koninklijk Instituut voor Taal-, Land- en Volkenkunde, 1995.

Mudiyanse, Nandasena. "Buddhist Writings in Tamil and Relevant Sinhalese Adaptations." *Journal of Oriental Research, Madras* 38/3 (1969):17–21.

Murthy, R. S., and M. S. Nagarajan, eds. *Buddhism in Tamilnadu: Collected Papers*. Madras: Institute of Asian Studies, 1998.

Mutaliyār, Caṇmukacuntara, ed. *Civañāṉacittiyār parapakkam mūlamum Cattuvappirakācar uraiyum*. Madras: By the editor, 1894.

Nachimuthu, K. "A Critical Edition of Vīracōḻiyam." *KOLAM* 2 (July 1998). Online. Available: http://www.rrz.uni-koeln.de/phil-fak/indologie/kolam/kolam2/nacciol.html.

Nagaraju, S. "Emergence of Regional Identity and Beginnings of Vernacular Literature: A Case Study of Telugu." *Social Scientist* 23/10–12 (1995):8–23.

Nāgārjuna. *Mūlamadhyamakakārikā*. Translated by Kenneth K. Inada. Tokyo: Hokuseido, 1970.

Nagaswamy, R. *Kaveripoompattinam: A Guide*. Madras: State Department of Archaeology, Government of Tamilnadu, 1973.

——. *Roman Karūr: A Peep into Tamils' Past*. Madras: Brahad Prakashan, 1995.

Nakamura, Hajime. *Indian Buddhism: A Survey with Bibliographic Notes*. Intercultural Research Monograph, no. 9. Hikata, Japan: KUFS, 1980.

Narada, U., trans. *Conditional Relations (Paṭṭhāna)*. 2 vols. London: Pali Text Society, 1969–1981. Reprint, 1992.

Narayana Rao, Velcheru. "Coconut and Honey: Sanskrit and Telugu in Medieval Andhra." *Social Scientist* 23/10–12 (1995):41–55.

Narayana Rao, Velcheru, David Shulman, and Sanjay Subrahmanyam. *Symbols of Substance: Court and State in Nāyaka Period Tamilnadu*. Delhi: Oxford University Press, 1992.

Nattier, Jan. "The Meanings of the Maitreya Myth: A Typological Analysis." In *Maitreya, the Future Buddha*, edited by Alan Sponberg and Helen Hardacre, 23–47. Cambridge: Cambridge University Press, 1988.

Nicolas, René. "Le Ramayana Siamois (Analysé)." *Extrême-Asie: Revue Indochinoise Illustrée* 19 (Janvier 1928):297–308.

Niklas, Ulrike. "Introduction to Tamil Prosody." *Bulletin de l'École Française d'Extrême-Orient* 77 (1988):165–227.

Nilakanta Sastri, K. A. "Takua-Pa (Siam) Tamil Inscription." *Journal of Oriental Research, Madras* 6/4 (1933):299–310.

——. "Agastya." *Overgedrukt uit het Tijdschrift voor Ind. Taal-, Land-, en Volkenkunde* 76/4 (1936):471–545.

——. "An Episode in the History of Buddhism in South India." In *B. C. Law Volume*, edited by D. R. Bhandarkar et al., 35–49. Calcutta: Indian Research Institute, 1945.

——. *History of Sri Vijaya*. Sir William Meyer Lectures, 1946–1947. Madras: University of Madras, 1949.

——. *Development of Religion in South India*. Madras: Orient Longman, 1963.

——. *The Cōḻas*. 2d ed. Madras University Historical Series, no. 9. Madras: University of Madras, 1955. Reprint, 1984.

Noble, Sally A. "The Tamil Story of the Anklet: Classical and Contemporary Tellings of the *Cilappatikāram*." Ph.D. Diss., University of Chicago, 1990.

Norman, H. C., ed. *The Commentary on the Dhammapada*. 5 vols. London: Henry Frowde, for Pali Text Society, 1906–1915. Reprint, London: Luzac, for Pali Text Society, 1970.

Norman, K. R. "The Role of Pāli in Early Sinhalese Buddhism." In *Buddhism in Ceylon and Studies on Religious Syncretism in Buddhist Countries*, 28–47. Symposium zur Buddhismusforschung, no. 1, edited by Heinz Bechert. Gottingen: Vandenhoeck and Ruprecht, 1978.

——. *Pāli Literature: Including Canonical Literature in Prakrit and Sanskrit of All the Hīnayāna Schools of Buddhism.* History of Indian Literature, vol. 7, fascicle 2. Wiesbaden: Otto Harrassowitz, 1983.

Nussbaum, Martha C. *Love's Knowledge: Essays on Philosophy and Literature.* New York: Oxford University Press, 1992.

——. *Poetic Justice: The Literary Imagination and Public Life.* Boston: Beacon, 1995.

Nyanatiloka. *Buddhist Dictionary: Manual of Buddhist Terms and Doctrines.* Kandy, Sri Lanka: Buddhist Publication Society, 1988.

Obeyesekere, Gananath. *The Cult of the Goddess Pattini.* Chicago: University of Chicago Press, 1984. Reprint, Delhi: Motilal Banarsidass, 1987.

Oldenberg, Hermann, ed. *The Vinaya Piṭakam: One of the Principal Buddhist Holy Scriptures in the Pāli Language.* 5 vols. London: Williams and Norgate, 1879–1883.

Orr, Leslie C. "Jain and Hindu 'Religious Women' in Early Medieval Tamilnadu." In *Open Boundaries: Jain Communities and Cultures in Indian History*, edited by John E. Cort, 187–212. Albany: State University of New York Press, 1998.

——. *Donors, Devotees, and Daughters of God: Temple Women in Medieval Tamilnadu.* New York: Oxford University Press, 2000.

"At the Palace, Sacred Dances to Bring Rain (5th July)." *Kambuja: Monthly Illustrated Review* 3/29 (1967):20–23.

Pāṇini. *The Aṣṭādhyāyī of Pāṇini.* 2 vols. Edited and translated by Śrīśa Chandra Vasu. Allahabad: Panini Office, 1891–1897. Reprint, Delhi: Motilal Banarsidass, 1988.

Paranavitana, S., ed. and trans. *Epigraphia Zeylanica, Being Lithic and Other Inscriptions of Ceylon.* vol. 4. London: Humphrey Milford, for Government of Ceylon, 1943.

——. "Negapatam and Theravāda Buddhism in South India." *Journal of the Greater India Society* 11/1 (1944):23–31.

Patton, Laurie L. "Making the Canon Commonplace: Ṛg-Vidhāna as Commentarial Practice." *Journal of Religion* 77/1 (January 1997):1–19.

Pesala, Bhikkhu, trans. *The Debate of King Milinda: An Abridgment of the Milinda Pañha.* Buddhist Traditions, vol. 14. Delhi: Motilal Banarsidass, 1991.

Peterson, Indira Viswanathan. *Poems to Śiva: The Hymns of the Tamil Saints.* Princeton, N.J.: Princeton University Press, 1989.

——. "*Śramaṇas* Against the Tamil Way: Jains as Others in Tamil Śaiva Literature." In *Open Boundaries: Jain Communities and Cultures in Indian History*, edited by John E. Cort, 163–185. Albany: State University of New York Press, 1998.

Pigeaud, Theodore G. T. *Literature of Java, Volume I: Synopsis of Javanese Literature, 900–1900 A.D.* Koninklijk Instituut voor Taal-, Land- en Volkenkunde, no. 9. The Hague: Martinus Nijhoff, 1967.

Pischel, Richard. *Comparative Grammar of the Prākrit Languages.* Translated by Subhadra Jha. Delhi: Motilal Banarsidass, 1981.

Pollock, Sheldon. "Literary History, Indian History, World History." *Social Scientist* 23/10–12 (1995):112–142.

——. "Literary History, Region, and Nation in South Asia: Introductory Note." *Social Scientist* 23/10–12 (1995):1–7.

——. Review of *Genres litteraires en Inde*, edited by Nalini Balbir. *Journal of the American Oriental Society* 115/4 (1995):685–689.

——. "Philology, Literature, Translation." In *Translating, Translations, Translators: From India to the West*, 111–129. Harvard Oriental Series: Opera Minora, vol. 1, edited by Enrica Garzilli. Cambridge: Department of Sanskrit and Indian Studies, Harvard University, 1996.

——. "The Sanskrit Cosmopolis, 300–1300 C.E.: Transculturation, Vernacularization, and the

Question of Ideology." In *Ideology and Status of Sanskrit: Contributions to the History of the Sanskrit Language*, 197–247. Brill's Indological Library, vol. 13, edited by Jan E. M. Houben. Leiden: E. J. Brill, 1996.
——. "The Cosmopolitan Vernacular." *Journal of Asian Studies* 57/1 (1998):6–37.
Polo, Marco. *The Book of Ser Marco Polo the Venetian Concerning the Kingdoms and Marvels of the East*. Translated by Henry Yule. London: John Murray, 1926.
Pope, G. U., ed. and trans. *The Nāladiyār or Four Hundred Quatrains in Tamil*. Oxford: Clarendon, 1893. Reprint, New Delhi: Asian Educational Services, 1984.
——. *The Sacred Kurral of Tiruvalluva-Nayanar with Introduction, Grammar, Translation, Notes, Lexicon, and Concordance*. London: H. Frowde, 1886. Reprint, New Delhi: Asian Educational Services, 1990.
Poussain, L. De la Vallée, and E. J. Thomas, eds. *Niddesa, Volume One: Mahāniddesa*. 2 vols. London: Humphrey Milford, for Pali Text Society, 1916.
Prentiss, Karen Pechilis. "A Tamil Lineage for Śaiva Siddhānta Philosophy." *History of Religions* 35/3 (1996):231–257.
——. *The Embodiment of Bhakti*. New York: Oxford University Press, 1999.
Prince, Gerald. "Introduction to the Study of the Narratee." In *Reader-Response Criticism: From Formalism to Post-Structuralism*, edited by Jane P. Tompkins, 7–25. Baltimore: Johns Hopkins University Press, 1980.
Przyluski, Jean. "La princesse a l'odeur de poisson et la Nāgī dans les traditions de l'Asie Orientale." In *Études Asiatiques*, vol. 2, edited by G. Van Oest, 265–284. Paris: Publications de l'École Française d'Extrême-Orient, 1925.
Puttamittiraṉ. *Vīracōḻiyam*. Edited by C. V. Tāmōtaram Piḷḷai. Madras, 1881.
——. *Vīracōḻiyam mūlamum Peruntēvaṉār iyaṟṟiya uraiyum*. Edited by K. R. Kōvintarāja Mutaliyār. Madras: Pavāṉantar Kaḻakam, 1942. Reprint, Tinnevelly: South India Saiva Siddhanta Works Publishing Society, 1970.
Raffles, Thomas Stamford. *The History of Java*. 2 vols. London: John Murray, 1830.
Raghavan, V. *The Number of Rasas*. Adyar Library Series, vol. 21. Madras: Adyar Library and Research Center, 1975.
——. *The Ramayana in Greater India*. Rao Kamalashankar Pranshankar Trivedi Memorial Lectures, 1973. Surat, India: South Gujarat University, 1975.
Ramachandran, T. "The Nagapattinam and Other Buddhist Bronzes in the Madras Government Museum." *Bulletin of the Madras Government Museum* 7/1 (1954):1–150.
Ramamurti, Rajam. "What Happens When Foreign Grammatical Terms Are Used to Describe an Indigenous Language? A South Dravidian Situation." *International Journal of Dravidian Linguistics* 12/2 (1983):335–344.
Ramanujan, A. K. *Hymns for the Drowning: Poems for Viṣṇu by Nammāḻvār*. Princeton, N.J.: Princeton University Press, 1981.
——. *Poems of Love and War, from the Eight Anthologies and the Ten Long Poems of Classical Tamil*. New York: Columbia University Press, 1984.
——. *The Interior Landscape: Love Poems from a Classical Tamil Anthology*. Bloomington: Indiana University Press, 1967. Reprint, New Delhi: Oxford University Press, 1994.
Ramaratnam, S. *Prahasana in Sanskrit Literature*. Mysore: Kavyalaya, 1987.
Ramaswamy, Sumathi. *Passions of the Tongue: Language Devotion in Tamil India, 1891–1970*. Berkeley: University of California Press, 1997.
Ramayana: Masterpiece of Thai Literature Retold from the Original Version Written by King Rama I of Siam. 2d ed. Bangkok: Mrs. Chalermkwan Jumsai Publisher, 1967.
Ray, Himanshu P. *The Winds of Change: Buddhism and the Maritime Links of Early South Asia*. Delhi: Oxford University Press, 1994.
Reat, N. Ross, ed. and trans. *The Śālistamba Sūtra*. Delhi: Motilal Banarsidass, 1993.

Reynolds, Frank E. "Buddhist Ethics: A Bibliographic Essay." *Religious Studies Review* 5/1 (1979):40–48.

——. "*Rāmāyaṇa*, *Rāma Jātaka*, and *Ramkien*: A Comparative Study of Hindu and Buddhist Traditions." In *Many Rāmāyaṇas: The Diversity of a Narrative Tradition in South Asia*, edited by Paula Richman, 50–63. Berkeley: University of California Press, 1991.

Rhys Davids, T. W., and William Stede. *The Pali Text Society's Pali-English Dictionary*. London: Pali Text Society, 1921–1925. Reprint, 1992.

Richman, Paula. "Religious Rhetoric in the *Maṇimēkalai*." Ph.D. Diss., University of Chicago, 1983.

——. "The Portrayal of a Female Renouncer in a Tamil Buddhist Text." In *Gender and Religion: On the Complexity of Symbols*, edited by Caroline Walker Bynum et al., 143–165. Boston: Beacon, 1986.

——. *Women, Branch Stories, and Religious Rhetoric in a Tamil Buddhist Text*. Foreign and Comparative Studies/South Asia Series, no. 12. Syracuse, N.Y.: Maxwell School of Citizenship and Public Affairs, Syracuse University, 1988.

—, ed. *Many Rāmāyaṇas: The Diversity of a Narrative Tradition in South Asia*. Berkeley: University of California Press, 1991.

——. "Gender and Persuasion: The Portrayal of Beauty, Anguish, and Nurturance in an Account of a Tamil Nun." In *Buddhism, Sexuality, and Gender*, edited by José Ignacio Cabezón, 111–136. Albany: State Univesity of New York Press, 1992.

Ricoeur, Paul. *Oneself as Another*. Translated by Kathleen Blamey. Chicago: University of Chicago Press, 1992.

Rogers, Captain T., trans. *Buddhaghosha's Parables*. London: Trubner, 1870.

Ryan, James. "The 'Civakacintamani' in Historical Perspective." Ph.D. Diss., University of California, Berkeley, 1985.

——. "Erotic Excess and Sexual Danger in the *Cīvakacintāmaṇi*." In *Open Boundaries: Jain Communities and Cultures in Indian History*, edited by John E. Cort, 67–83. Albany: State University of New York Press, 1998.

Saddhātissa, H., ed. and trans. *The Birth Stories of the Ten Bodhisattas and the* Dasabodhisattuppattikathā. London: Pali Text Society, 1975.

——. "The Six Root-Conditions." *One Vehicle* (1984):135–138.

Sam, Chan Moly. "Muni Mekhala: The Magic Moment in Khmer Court Dance." In *Text, Context, and Performance in Cambodia, Laos, and Vietnam*, 93–113. Selected Reports in Ethnomusicology, vol. 9, edited by Amy Catlin et al. Los Angeles: Department of Ethnomusicology, University of California, Los Angeles, 1992.

Samuel, Geoffrey. "The Gesar Epic of East Tibet." In *Tibetan Literature: Studies in Genre*, edited by José Ignacio Cabezón and Roger R. Jackson, 358–367. Ithaca, N.Y.: Snow Lion, 1996.

Sanjeevi, N. "Vaṭamoḻi: Sanskrit? in Ancient Tamil Literature." *Annals of Oriental Research, University of Madras* 24/1 (1972):1–11.

Sarkar, Himansu Bhusan. *Corpus of the Inscriptions of Java* (*Corpus Inscriptionum Javanicarum*) (*up to 928* A.D.). 2 vols. Calcutta: Firma K. L. Mukhopadhyay, 1971.

Schaffner, Christina. "Editorial." In *Cultural Functions of Translation*, edited by Christina Schaffner and Helen Kelly-Holmes, 1–8. Clevedon, U.K.: Multilingual Matters, 1995.

Schalk, Peter. "On the Beginning of Buddhism in Tamiḻakam." In *Studies in South Indian History and Culture: Professor V. R. Ramachandra Dikshitar Centenary Volume*, edited by R. Nagaswamy, 249–254. Madras: V. R. Ramachandra Dikshitar Centenary Committee, 1977.

——. "On the Beginning of Buddhism in Tamiḻakam." *Temenos* 29 (1993):157–163.

——. "The Controversy about the Arrival of Buddhism in Tamiḻakam." *Temenos* 30 (1994):197–232.

——. "The Oldest Buddhist Artefacts Discovered in Tamiḻakam." In *Being Religious and Living Through the Eyes: Studies in Religious Iconography and Iconology: A Celebratory Publication in Honour of Professor Jan Bergman*, edited by Peter Schalk and Michael Strausberg, 307–327. Acta Universitatis Upsaliensis: Historia Religionum, no. 14. Uppsala, Sweden: Faculty of Theology, Uppsala University, 1998.

Schalk, Peter, et al. *Pauttamum Tamiḻum: Inventory, Investigation and Interpretation of Sources Pertaining to Buddhism Among Tamiḻar in Pre-Colonial Tamiḻakam and Īḻam (Ilaṅkai)*. Acta Universitatis Upsaliensis: Historia Religionum, vol. 15. Uppsala, Sweden: Uppsala University, 2001.

Selby, Martha Ann. "Desire for Meaning: Providing Contexts for Prākrit *Gāthās*." *Journal of Asian Studies* 55/1 (1996):81–93.

Sesha Aiyar, K. G. "The Date of Maṇimēkalai." *Journal of Oriental Research* 1/4 (1927):321–329.

Sewell, Robert. *The Historical Inscriptions of Southern India*. Edited by S. Krishnaswami Aiyangar. Madras University Historical Series, no. 5. Madras: University of Madras, 1932.

Shanmugam Pillai, M. "*Vīracōḻiyam*: The Earliest Contrastive-Transfer Grammar in Tamil." In *Buddhism in Tamilnadu: Collected Papers*, edited by R. S. Murthy and M. S. Nagarajan, 339–344. Madras: Institute of Asian Studies, 1998.

Shih Pao-ch'ang. *Lives of the Nuns: Biographies of Chinese Buddhist Nuns from the Fourth to Sixth Centuries*. Translated by Kathryn Ann Tsai. Honolulu: University of Hawaii Press, 1994.

Shinohara, Koichi. "The Story of the Buddha's Begging Bowl: Imagining a Biography and Sacred Places." In *Sacred Biography and Sacred Place: Explorations in the Formation of Religious and Social Identity in Asia*, edited by Neil McMullin. Toronto: University of Toronto Press, forthcoming.

Shulman, David. *Tamil Temple Myths: Sacrifice and Divine Marriage in the South Indian Śaiva Tradition*. Princeton, N.J.: Princeton University Press, 1980.

——. *The King and the Clown in South Indian Myth and Poetry*. Princeton, N.J.: Princeton University Press, 1985.

——. "Poets and Patrons in Tamil Literature and Literary Legend." In *The Powers of Art: Patronage in Indian Culture*, edited by Barbara Stoler Miller, 89–119. Delhi: Oxford University Press, 1992.

——. "Cāttaṉār's Dream Book." In *A Buddhist Woman's Path to Enlightenment: Proceedings of a Workshop on the Tamiḻ Narrative* Maṇimēkalai, *Uppsala University, May 25–29, 1995*, 241–260. Acta Universitatis Upsaliensis: Historica Religionum, vol. 13, edited by Peter Schalk. Uppsala, Sweden: Uppsala University, 1997.

Sibley, David. *Geographies of Exclusion: Society and Difference in the West*. London: Routledge, 1995.

Singaravelu, S. "A Comparative Study of the Sanskrit, Tamil, Thai, and Malay Versions of the Story of Rāma with Special Reference to the Process of Acculturation in the Southeast Asian Versions." *Journal of the Siam Society* 56/2 (1968):137–185.

——. "The Episode of Maiyarāb in the Thai Rāmakien and Its Possible Relationship to Tamil Folklore." *Indologica Taurinensia* 13 (1985–1986):297–312.

Sivaraja Pillai, K. N. *Agastya in the Tamil Land*. Madras: University of Madras, 1930. Reprint., New Delhi: Asian Educational Services, 1985.

Sivaramalingam, K. *Archaeological Atlas of the Antique Remains of Buddhism in Tamilnadu*. Madras: Institute of Asian Studies, 1997.

Sivaramamurti, C. "Amaravati Sculptures in the Madras Government Museum." *Bulletin of the Madras Government Museum,* New Series 4 (1942): 1–376.

Soekmono. *Chandi Borobudur: A Monument of Mankind*. Amsterdam: UNESCO, 1976.

Somadasa, K. D. *Catalogue of the Hugh Nevill Collection of Sinhalese Manuscripts in the British Library*. vol. 4. London: British Library, 1990.

Sponberg, Alan. "Introduction." In *Maitreya, the Future Buddha*, edited by Alan Sponberg and Helen Hardacre, 1–4. Cambridge: Cambridge University Press, 1988.

Srinivasalu, Suram. *Hāsya and Prahasana: A Critical Study*. Guntur, India: Navodaya, 1989.

Stein, Burton. *Peasant, State and Society in Medieval South India*. New Delhi: Oxford University Press, 1980.

Stock, Brian. *The Implications of Literacy*. Princeton, N.J.: Princeton University Press, 1983.

Strickmann, Michel. *Mantras et mandarins: le bouddhisme tantrique en Chine*. Paris: Gallimard, 1996.

Strong, John S. "*Gandhakuṭī*: The Perfumed Chamber of the Buddha." *History of Religions* 16/4 (1977):390–406.

——. *The Experience of Buddhism: Sources and Interpretations*. Belmont, Calif.: Wadsworth, 1995.

Subrahmanya Aiyer, K. V. "The Larger Leiden Plates (of Rājarāja I)." *Epigraphia Indica* 22/6 (1934):213–266.

Subrahmanya Sastri, P. S. *History of Grammatical Theories in Tamil and Their Relation to the Grammatical Literature in Sanskrit*. Madras: *Journal of Oriental Research*, 1934.

——. *Tolkāppiyam, the Earliest Extant Tamil Grammar: Poruḷ-Atikāram–Tamil Poetics*. Madras: Kuppuswami Sastri Research Institute, 1956.

Subrahmanyam, R. "Kāñchīpuram Excavations." *Journal of the Andhra Historical Research Society* 34/1–4 (1974–1975):23–31.

Subramaniam, T. N. *The Pallavas of Kanchi in South-East Asia*. Suvarnabhumi and Tamilnadu, no. 1. Madras: Swadeshimitram, 1967.

Subramanian, Nellai K. "Sankhya Philosophy in Manimekalai and Neelakeci." In *Proceedings of the Fifth International Conference-Seminar of Tamil Studies*, vol. 2, edited by M. Arunachalam, 12/2–12/26. Madras: International Association of Tamil Research, 1982.

Suleiman, Susan, and Inge Crosman, eds. *The Reader in the Text: Essays on Audience and Interpretation*. Princeton, N.J.: Princeton University Press, 1980.

Sundaram, P. S., trans. *The Kural*. New York: Penguin, 1990.

Sundaramoorthy, G. *Early Literary Theories in Tamil, in Comparison with Sanskrit Theories*. Madurai, India: Sarvodaya Ilakkiya Pannai, 1974.

Suryanarayanasastri, S. S. "The Manimekalai Account of the Sankhya." *Journal of Indian History* 8/3 (1929):322–327.

Takahashi, Takanobu. *Tamil Love Poetry and Poetics*. Brill's Indological Library, vol. 9, edited by Johannes Bronkhorst. Leiden: E. J. Brill, 1995.

Tamil Lexicon. 7 vols. Madras: University of Madras, 1982.

Taṇṭi. *Taṇṭiyalaṅkāram Cuppiramaṇiyatēcikar uraiyuṭaṉ*. Edited by K. Irāmaliṅkat Tampirāṉavarkaḷ. Tinnevelly: South India Saiva Siddhanta Works Publishing Society, 1938. Reprint, 1997.

Tāranātha. *Tāranātha's History of Buddhism in India*. Edited by Debiprasad Chattopadhyaya. Translated by Lama Chimpa and Alaka Chattopadhyaya. Delhi: Motilal Banarsidass, 1990.

Tarling, Nicholas, ed. *The Cambridge History of Southeast Asia, Volume One: From Early Times to c. 1800*. Cambridge: Cambridge University Press, 1992. Reprint, 1999.

Thirugnanasambandhan, P. *The Concept of Alamkara Sastra in Tamil*. Madras: Samskrita Academy, 1977.

Tirukkuṟaḷ mūlamum Parimēlaḻakar uraiyum. Tinnevelly: South India Saiva Siddhanta Works Publishing Society, 1991.

Tolkāppiyam: Eḻuttatikāram, Iḷampūraṇar uraiyuṭaṉ. Tinnevelly: South India Saiva Siddhanta Works Publishing Society, 1955. Reprint, 1996.

Tolkāppiyam: Iḷampūraṇar uraiyuṭaṉ: Poruḷatikāram. Tinnevelly: South India Saiva Siddhanta Works Publishing Society, 1977.

Tolkāppiyam: Pērāciriyar uraiyuṭaṉ: Poruḷatikāram. Tinnevelly: South India Saiva Siddhanta Works Publishing Society, 1966.

Tompkins, Jane P. "The Reader in History: The Changing Shape of Literary Response." In *Reader-Response Criticism: From Formalism to Post-Structuralism*, edited by Jane P. Tompkins, 201–232. Baltimore: Johns Hopkins University Press, 1980.

——, ed. *Reader-Response Criticism: From Formalism to Post-Structuralism*. Baltimore: Johns Hopkins University Press, 1980.

Trenckner, V., ed. *Milindapañho: Being Dialogues Between King Milinda and the Buddhist Sage Nāgasena*. James G. Forlong Series, vol. 5. London: Royal Asiatic Society, 1928.

Tubb, Gary A. "Hemacandra and Sanskrit Poetics." In *Open Boundaries: Jain Communities and Cultures in Indian History*, edited by John E. Cort, 53–66. Albany: State University of New York Press, 1998.

Upasak, C. S., ed. *The Sāsanavaṁsa*. Patna, India: Nava Nālandā Mahāvihāra, 1961.

Valantasis, Richard. "Constructions of Power in Asceticism." *Journal of the American Academy of Religion* 63/4 (1995):775–821.

Vamadeva, Chandralekha. *The Concept of* Vaṉṉaṉpu *'Violent Love' in Tamil Śaivism, with Special Reference to* Periyapurāṉam. Uppsala Studies in the History of Religions, no. 1. Uppsala, Sweden: Uppsala University, 1995.

van Buitenen, J. A. B., trans. *The Mahābhārata*. 3 vols. Chicago: University of Chicago Press, 1973–1978.

Varatarāja Ayyar, E. S. *Tamiḻ ilakkiya varalāṟu*. Madras: Aṇṇāmalaip Palkalaik Kaḻakam, 1957.

Vedachala Iyer, P. S. "The Sources of Tolkāppiyam." *Journal of Oriental Research, Madras* 7/1 (1933):53–58.

Vēluppiḷḷai, A. "*Viiracoozhiyam* as a Grammar for Inscriptional Tamil." In *Proceedings of the Second International Conference Seminar of Tamil Studies*, vol. 1, edited by R. E. Asher, 345-348. Madras: International Association of Tamil Research, 1971.

——. "Historical Background of the *Maṇimēkalai* and Indigenization of Buddhism." In *A Buddhist Woman's Path to Enlightenment: Proceedings of a Workshop on the Tamiḻ Narrative* Maṇimēkalai, *Uppsala University, May 25–29, 1995*, 53–94. Acta Universitatis Upsaliensis: Historica Religionum, vol. 13, edited by Peter Schalk. Uppsala, Sweden: Uppsala University, 1997.

Venkatachari, K. K. A. *The Manipravala Literature of the Śrī Vaiṣṇava Ācāryas*. Bombay: Ananthacarya Research Institute, 1978.

Veṅkaṭarāmaṉ, H., ed. *Naṟṟiṇai mūlamum uraiyum*. Madras: Mahamahopadhyaya Dr. U. V. Swaminathaiyer Library, 1989.

Venuti, Lawrence. "Translation and the Formation of Cultural Identities." In *Cultural Functions of Translation*, edited by Christina Schaffner and Helen Kelly-Holmes, 9–25. Clevedon, U.K.: Multilingual Matters, 1995.

Verdonk, Peter, and Jean Jacques Weber, eds. *Twentieth-Century Fiction: From Text to Context*. London: Routledge, 1995.

Vijayalakshmy, R. *A Study of the Peruṅkatai: An Authentic Version of the Story of Udayana*. Madras: International Institute of Tamil Studies, 1981.

——. *Tamiḻakattil Ācīvakarkaḷ*. Madras: International Insitute of Tamil Studies, 1988.

Vijayavenugopal, G. "Some Buddhist Poems in Tamil." *Journal of the International Association of Buddhist Studies* 2/2 (1979):93–97.

Vijayawardhana, G. "Siya-Bas-Lakara and a Theory of Suggestion." *University of Ceylon Review* 22/1-2 (1964):21-27.

——. *Outlines of Sanskrit Poetics*. Chowkhamba Sanskrit Studies, no. 76. Varanasi: Chowkhamba Sanskrit Series Office, 1970.

Vimalakīrti. *The Holy Teachings of Vimalakīrti* (*Vimalakīrtinirdeśa*). Translated by Étienne Lamotte (French) and Sara Boin (English). London: Pali Text Society, 1976.

Vinson, Julien. *Légendes Bouddhistes et Djainas: Traduites du Tamoul*. 2 vols. Paris: Maisonneuve, 1900.

Wallдèn, Ruth. "The Presentation of Sāṁkhya in the *Maṇimēkalai.*" In *Kalyāṇamitrārāgaṇam: Essays in Honour of Nils Simonsson*, edited by Eivind Kahrs, 303–312. Oslo: Norwegian University Press, 1986.

——. "Materialism as Expounded in the *Maṇimēkalai*, the *Nīlakēci*, and the *Civañāṉacittiyār.*" In *Orientalia Suecana*, edited by Trygrove Kronholm, 246–251. Stockholm: Almovist and Wiksell International, 1991.

——. "Notes on Some Dates of the Buddha in the *Maṇimēkalai.*" In *Die Datierung des historischen Buddha* [*The Dating of the Historical Buddha*], 200–207. Symposium zur Buddhismusforschung, vol. 4, no. 2, edited by Heinz Bechert. Gottingen: Vandenhoeck and Ruprecht, 1992.

Wang-Toutain, Françoise. "Le bol du Buddha: Propagation du bouddhisme et legitimité politique." *Bulletin de l'École Française d'Extrême-Orient* 81 (1994):59–82.

Warder, A. K. *The Science of Criticism in India.* Adyar Library General Series, no. 7. Madras: Adyar Library and Research Centre, 1978.

——. *Indian Buddhism.* Delhi: Motilal Banarsidass, 1970. Reprint, 1991.

Wheatley, Paul. *The Golden Khersonese.* Kuala Lumpur: University of Malaya Press, 1961.

——. "The Mount of the Immortals: A Note on Tamil Cultural Influence in Fifth-Century Indochina." *Oriens Extremus* 21/1 (1974):97–109.

Winternitz, M. *History of Indian Literature.* vol. 3. Translated by Subhadra Jhā. Delhi: Motilal Banarsidass, 1967.

Wolters, O. W. *History, Culture, and Region in Southeast Asian Perspective.* Singapore: Institute for Southeast Asian Studies, 1982.

Woodward, F. L., trans. *The Book of Gradual Sayings.* 5 vols. London: Pali Text Society, 1932–1936.

Wray, Elizabeth, et al. *Ten Lives of the Buddha: Siamese Temple Paintings and Jataka Tales.* New York: Weatherhill, 1979.

Xuanzang [Hsuan-tsang]. *Si-Yu-Ki: Buddhist Records of the Western World.* 2 vols. in 1. Translated by Samuel Beal. London: Kegan Paul, Trench, Trubner, 1884. Reprint, Delhi: Motilal Banarsidass, 1981.

Yijing [I-tsing]. *A Record of the Buddhist Religion as Practiced in India and the Malay Archipelago* (*A.D. 671–695*) *by I-Tsing.* Translated by J. Takakusu. Delhi: Munshiram Manoharlal, 1966.

Yi-Liang, Chou. "Tantrism in China." *Harvard Journal of Asiatic Studies* 8/3–4 (1945):241–332.

Yocum, Glenn E. "Buddhism Through Hindu Eyes: Śaivas and Buddhists in Medieval Tamilnad." In *Traditions of Contact and Change: Selected Proceedings of the XIVth Congress of the International Association for the History of Religions*, edited by Peter Slater and Donald Wiebe, 143–162. Waterloo, Ontario: Wilfrid Laurier University Press, 1983.

Zbavitel, Dusan. *Bengali Literature.* History of Indian Literature, vol. 9, fascicle 3. Edited by Jan Gonda. Wiesbaden: Otto Harrassowitz, 1976.

Zürcher, E. "'Prince Moonlight': Messianism and Eschatology in Early Medieval Chinese Buddhism." *T'oung Pao* 68/1–3 (1982):1–75.

Zvelebil, Kamil V. *The Smile of Murugan on Tamil Literature of South India.* Leiden: E. J. Brill, 1973.

——. *Tamil Literature.* Handbuch der Orientalistik, Zweite Abteilung: Indien, vol. 2, no. 1. Edited by Jan Gonda. Leiden: E. J. Brill, 1975.

——. *Classical Tamil Prosody: An Introduction.* Madras: New Era, 1989.

——. *Companion Studies to the History of Tamil Literature.* Handbuch der Orientalistik, Zweite Abteilung: Indien, no. 5. Edited by Jan Gonda. Leiden: E. J. Brill, 1992.

——. *Lexicon of Tamil Literature.* Handbuch der Orientalistik, Zweite Abteilung: Indien, vol. 9. Edited by J. Bronkhorst. Leiden: E. J. Brill, 1995.

Zydenbos, Robert J. "The Jaina Nun Kavunti." *Bulletin d'études indiennes* 5 (1987):387–417.

Index